ALAN JUDD

Ford Madox Ford

First published in Great Britain in 1990 by Collins

This revised edition, with new postscript,
first issued in 1991 by Flamingo,
an imprint of HarperCollins Publishers,
77–85 Fulham Palace Road,
Hammersmith, London W6 8JB

9 8 7 6 5 4 3 2 1

Printed and bound in Great Britain by
HarperCollins Book Manufacturing, Glasgow

TO JUDY

Illustrations

Except where otherwise stated, all photographs are courtesy of Janice Biala/Cornell University Library

Acknowledgments

I should particularly like to thank Stuart Proffitt for his sustaining enthusiasm, Richard Holmes for his selfless encouragement, Dr Max Saunders for his kindly scholarship and Janice Biala for her untiring help and hospitality (also, Alain and Ebony for their forbearance). Among the many others I should like to thank at greater length than I can are Mr and Mrs Cook, Mrs Clare Crankshaw, Dr Margaret DeJong, Anthony Goff, Tony Gould, Graham Greene, Mrs A. E. T. Hills, Mr R. W. Hunt, Canon Eric James, Peter Jay, John Keegan, Mr and Mrs Francis Pagan, Rachel Scott, Miranda Seymour and Francis Wyndham.

I am pleased to acknowledge the generosity of the Authors' Foundation and the K. Blundell Trust, both administered by the Society of Authors, in awarding me grants. Similarly, I am indebted to Princeton University Library for permission to make use of Ford's letters, to Cornell University Library for permission to draw on the Violet Hunt and other papers, to Harper and Row, Inc. for permission to quote from Arthur Mizener's *The Saddest Story*, the chronology of which I have generally followed, to Roland Loewe for permission to quote from Stella Bowen's published writing and unpublished letters, to Mrs Sheila Garson and Mrs Caroline White for permission to quote from Olive Garnett's diary; and, again, to Janice Biala for granting me full use of all the Ford papers and photographs in her ownership.

I have generally tried to follow the spelling and accenting (sometimes inconsistent) of the originals. To scholars who may regret the lack of more detailed references and footnotes, I can say only that I regret any inconvenience; since the lack is deliberate, to say more would be insincere. I wanted to write a book in which the spirit of its subject could be at ease and to have annotated it as scholarship necessarily demands would have meant sacrificing something of the impression of how Ford's life was lived; he was never a man to be detained by a footnote or checked by a reference. I should add that the responsibility for this is wholly mine, not my publisher's. Finally, my thanks to the staff of that excellent institution, the London Library.

ONE

There are also the rich in spirit. It overflows and is seen in everything they do. They are never mean, not even with money. In the 1930s, when Ford was hard up in Paris, a Georgian prince – every Georgian in Paris was a prince in those days – came to him and asked for some. Ford had never met the man before but let him have a cheque. The prince was outraged by the smallness of the sum and never visited Ford again, though he kept the cheque. It was for one half of the money Ford owned.

He neither begrudged the money nor resented the prince's anger; by then he probably expected it. He had become ironic, as when, following one of the occasions when he was attacked in print, he responded by protesting that he had never done anything to help his attacker, had never given him money, had not arranged for his first book to be published – so why was he thus attacked? People were quite often rude about him, often the people he had helped. Hemingway was perhaps the most notorious and ungrateful example. He caricatured Ford cruelly and said he smelt. Others said he didn't. Whether he did or not, it's a curious way to criticise a writer. Ford was almost never rude about anyone.

As a kind of Catholic, or agnostic, or Catholic-agnostic – what he would have said would have depended upon his audience and when he was speaking – Ford would almost certainly have known Ignatius Loyola's 'Teach us to give and not to count the cost.' He never made the mistake of preaching it, but that was how he lived. He said of his immediate ancestors and the Victorian figures of his childhood: 'They had their passions, their extravagances, their imprudencies, their follies. They were sometimes unjust, violent, unthinking. But they were never cold, they were never mean.

They went to shipwreck with high spirits.'[1] He was like that himself, only never unthinking and never violent.

Richness of spirit is not, of course, an inoculation against other sins. Ford's failings are well known and have been re-heated and served up many times. Aspects of his personality and his private life became better known, in his lifetime and after, than his books. Yet he did nothing sensationally – or even unusually – bad. He had a chequered married life, told some lies, a greater number of tall stories and sometimes just embroidered the truth, often after saying that that was what he was doing. He had for facts, he said, a profound contempt, but he guaranteed his accuracy as to impressions; and his impressions were frequently more vivid and revealing than most people's facts. His point was that it was impressions that counted in human affairs, that they were what influenced people's responses and were what remained afterwards. The task of a writer was to render that impression and his duty was to find the best way of doing it accurately. The facts could be re-arranged so as better to convey the impression. Stella Bowen, one of his wives, said that he used facts as an artist used paints, selecting, mixing, changing in order to get the all-important effect.

He was a bit like that with wives, too. There were four – Elsie Martindale, Violet Hunt, Stella Bowen and Janice Biala – plus a number of affairs. Yet he wasn't a philanderer. He liked women, unlike many philanderers, and they liked him. But what in others was tolerated or even admired was regarded in Ford as disgraceful, though some were amused by it. His friend James Joyce sent the following lines to Harriet Weaver after the ageing Ford had taken up with the youthful Janice:

> O Father O Ford, you've a masterful way with you,
> Maid, wife and widow are wild to make hay with you,
> Blonde and brunette turn-about run away with you,
> You've such a way with you, Father O'Ford.

In law, of course, he had only one wife – Elsie, who wouldn't divorce him – but he treated her successors as if they were married,

[1] *Ancient Lights*

always presented them as his wives, and had a daughter by one.

Proclaiming Ford the most underrated English novelist of the century is a tradition that began, like the denigration of his personality, in his own lifetime. As early as 1915 Rebecca West was calling him the Scholar Gipsy of English letters. He was, she said, 'the author who is recognised only as he disappears round the corner'.[1]

Also, from early days, even his most earnest detractors have acknowledged the help he gave to younger writers such as Lawrence, Jean Rhys, Ezra Pound, Wyndham Lewis, Hemingway, Graham Greene; most now would acknowledge the genius of some of his novels, particularly *The Good Soldier* and the *Parade's End* tetralogy. What is generally overlooked, though, is the way he worked. He wrote almost daily from adolescence onwards, publishing eighty-one books in his lifetime and over four hundred articles. It was too much, he admitted, and if he'd written less he might have written more that was first-rate. But it is daunting to contemplate that drive, that compulsion that took him daily to his desk – any desk, anywhere, upturned boxes, suitcases, anything. Part of it was money, of course. His books never sold well and so he could never ease off, could never get off the treadmill (except when he joined the Army during the First World War and found Army life a great deal easier and more congenial than the making of books). He used to boast that every member of his family had left the world a poorer man than he had come into it. It was certainly true of him; he owned almost nothing when he died, no house, practically no furniture, not many clothes, hardly any cash. He thought of possessions as 'simply things that have floated into my kitchen'. But he was one of the rich.

He never wanted a biography and asked that there shouldn't be one. He hated academic biographies, feeling that they put in everything but what was important, and was probably fed up with the concentration on his life at the expense of his works, which generally sold poorly (in Britain more so than in America). Also, he might have felt that he had written his own biography. It is there in his reminiscences and memoirs, a great rich unreliable tapestry which gives an impression of his life that no biographer

[1] *Daily News*, 2nd April 1915

could hope to equal. Even a biography as thorough as Arthur Mizener's is no more than a detailed map. We need the man himself, the 'great grey behemoth in tweeds', to take us by the arm and lead us on a ramble, haphazard, discursive, repetitive, way off all the maps and ending without apparently arriving anywhere; until we realise that the ramble was the point, that his soft tones, his stories, his contradictions, his unqualified assertions and his many qualifications are an architectonic creation. We need that voice, soft, like his blue eyes, to help us see in that far country. 'A writer holds a reader by his temperament,' he wrote. 'That is his true gift.' What we get from Ford is a genuinely liberal education, the impress of a mind large and generous, a way of seeing. Like his friend Conrad, he wanted to make you see.

But, being Ford, he also provided an excuse for biographers. In his last book, *The March of Literature*, he wrote: '. . . once you are really saturated in the work of a writer it is legitimate to enquire into the circumstances of his life. It is human nature – and not only that, for details of an author's life may cast light on passages of his work and on the nature of Literature itself.' That should be sufficient reason but it is not the whole story. After all the analysis, after all the achievements and all the failures, there's still something else, something left over that needs accounting for. This was apparent to those who knew him. Violet Hunt wrote about him, as did Stella Bowen, Jean Rhys, Douglas Goldring, Wells, Edward Crankshaw, Hemingway, Robert Lowell and various others. Many people these days may be blessed with several spouses but few provoke books by those spouses as well as by secretaries, assistants, enemies and friends. Yet he wasn't widely known – was never really famous – and no one could have hoped to make money out of him. When all the stories were told and the only end had come, people still felt they wanted to account for him. They still do.

It wasn't enough to read him and to read about him. The confident feeling of having understood was too easily gained; it felt fraudulent, as if real insight had to be earned. Not that complete understanding is possible; the point is to get as near to it as we can, to know all that can be known in order to stand, if only for a moment, at the edge of what cannot.

TWO

He was always tall and in later life put on much weight. His fingers were long, his hair blond, his skin pink or ruddy and his movements slow. He had a receding chin and a prominent nose; his eyebrows and mouth sloped downwards, so that he sometimes looked like a big solemn spaniel. ('You are a patient but extremely stupid donkey,' his father used to tell him.) He often spoke in the rounded paragraphs and periods of his written work, so that his conversation could sound like his books (in fact, he dictated many of them, especially as his fingers stiffened and writing and typing became more difficult). His voice was light and soft, a calm drawl, unassertive but compelling. He used words precisely and the rhythm of his speech was a comforting undulation. In a surviving radio recording, made in America in the 1930s, his sentences have the dying fall that used to be associated with the sermons of the older clergy. He never signposted his irony, not even by a flicker of tone or a shade of emphasis, and so it was often missed. The more upset he was, the more quietly he spoke, not in menace but in the effort to maintain a balance which he often felt was slipping from him. Many women liked him, partly because he liked them but also because he was attentive, sensitive and warm. He created memorable women characters.

His eyes were very blue and quiet. Whatever persona he adopted, they remained watchful and intelligent. 'Ford', D. H. Lawrence wrote in a letter to Violet Hunt, 'daubs his dove-grey kindliness with a villainous selfish tar, and hops forth a very rook among rooks, but his eyes, after all, remain like the Shulamite's, dove's eyes.' He had a kind smile.

As a young man he is thought to have been Henry James's model for Morton Densher in *The Wings of the Dove*. He recognised himself in the description:

> He was a longish, leanish, fairish young Englishman, not unamenable on certain sides to classification – as for instance being a gentleman, by being rather specifically one of the educated, one of the generally sound and generally civil; yet, though to that degree neither extraordinary nor abnormal, he would have failed to play straight into the observer's hands. He was young for the House of Commons; he was loose for the Army. He was refined, as might have been said, for the City and quite apart from the cut of his cloth, sceptical, it might have been felt, for the Church. On the other hand, he was credulous for diplomacy, or perhaps even for science, while at the same time he was perhaps too much in his mere senses for poetry and yet too little in them for art . . . The difficulty with Densher was that he looked vague without looking weak – idle without looking empty.

James was right to see in the physical symptoms of a deeper uncertainty. Ford had not then found himself. Some, like Wells,[1] would say he never did: 'Ford is a long blond with a drawling manner . . . What he is really or if he is really, nobody knows now and he least of all; he has become a great system of assumed personas and dramatised selves.'

This idea that whatever Ford did was act or contrivance pursued him throughout his life. It touched even those most sympathetic to him. Olive Garnett, with whom he grew up, noted the youthful Ford putting on a certain manner or assuming a certain role, while Stella Bowen, in her excellent autobiography, *Drawn From Life*, described how the tendency had developed in his fifties: 'He presented a wonderful appearance of a bland, successful gentleman, whose shabbiness was mere eccentricity and who regarded a preoccupation with the relative merits of Foyot and Larve, Vionnet and Poiret, the Ritz and the Hotel George V, as very natural and necessary.'

[1] *Experiment in Autobiography*

It is interesting that his capacity for assuming personae should have attracted as much adverse criticism as it has, particularly from his chief biographer, Mizener. It is as if Ford were failing in his duty to be something else or were behaving improperly. The point, surely, is that he was a writer. It doesn't matter what else he was or pretended to be – pig farmer, country gentleman, cook, man-about-town, editor, man of letters, soldier, cricket enthusiast – because everything was subservient to that. In fact, for him it was a 'very natural and necessary' part of it. He was each of the above at different times but he was never not a writer. Katherine Anne Porter made this point[1]: '. . . he led an existence of marvellous discomfort, of insecurity, of deep and pressing anxiety as to his daily bread; but no matter where he was, what his sufferings were, he sat down daily and wrote, in his fine crabbed hand, with pen, the book he was working on at the moment; and I never knew him when he was not working on a book.'

It is understandable that Ford's assumed personae may have irritated some of those who knew him, but it is curious that they should also have irritated some of those who did not. After all, the game-playing didn't actually matter; it was not as if he were sent into the world to be one thing and somehow cheated by pretending to be several. In fact, if anyone was ever sent into the world to be something, Ford was; and he achieved it.

It may be that in his youth he lacked confidence in himself and that this sometimes resulted in an assumed arrogance of manner. The lack could have dated from his childhood days as a 'patient but extremely stupid donkey', pressured from above by a demanding father, from below by a popular and assertive younger brother and from the sides by clever Rossetti and Garnett children. Stella Bowen noticed the result: 'Poor Ford! There was something about the sight of his large patient fingers tapping at the keys, that I always found infinitely touching. He was a writer – a complete writer – and nothing but a writer. And he never even felt sure of his gift. He needed more reassurance than anyone I have ever met.'

His lack may have led him to dramatise himself, just as it may also have contributed to his almost uncanny ability to identify with

[1] *New Directions* No. 7, 1942

others. He couldn't help seeing all sides of an argument but, hating all arguments and scenes, he nearly always fled from them. He couldn't help feeling how others would feel but at the same time was not prepared to give up anything he really wanted. The result was that effective action was often paralysed until someone else sorted things out. Yet his sensitivity, almost as much a problem as a gift, never left him. Towards the end of their affair, Violet Hunt told him she had spent time at her cottage in Selsey with another man. Ford listened and then quietly re-created the conversation Violet had had with her admirer – according to her, almost word for word – on the basis of his knowledge of them both.

A valuable gift for a novelist, of course, and hardly surprising if, while trying to pull himself together in Sussex after the First World War, he should present himself to some people as Captain Ford, smallholder and genial old buffer, to others as the forgotten poet and novelist who had turned his back on literature, to yet others as the great writer dragging himself out of the abyss, each day an inch forward.

This tendency has been regarded as signifying a split personality or as evidence of a gulf between Ford's idea of himself and the supposed reality, the gulf being by implication condemned. But it could equally well be regarded as consistent and coherent: given the writer that Ford was, his whole life took on the nature of imaginative experiment and sympathetic identification. He knew well enough what he was and when he played games he probably expected others to see them as such and to understand the need for them. Janice Biala, in her interview with Sondra Stang[1], recalled a conversation in which it was mentioned that Shakespeare was supposed to have had an ancestor called Hill; Ford remarked that he, too, had an ancestor called Hill and that it was therefore possible that he was descended from Shakespeare, adding, '*Someone* has to be.' Part of the problem is that he was often dogged by the literal-minded who either disregarded or didn't hear such additions. It may also be that what has been interpreted as his sense of inadequacy was – at least when he was older – part of another game. Although he frequently praised books written by other

[1] *The Presence of Ford Madox Ford*

people, he was often reticent about or dismissive of his own. When taxed with this by Janice Biala, he smiled and said, 'Have you never heard of the pride that apes humility?' Unlike Stella, Janice did not find him constantly in need of reassurance.

In the autumn of 1928 he was walking in a Parisian park with Allen Tate when he suddenly spoke, as if to himself: 'One might be a peer of the realm or a member of the Académie Française – there is nothing else.' Tate continued in puzzled silence and later quoted the remark as evidence of eccentricity, if not worse. But surely what it shows, apart from its good sense, is how Ford's mind was running: always trying on new clothes. It is the same with many imaginative people, only he, in this respect as in others, was writ larger than most.

No doubt it would be possible to debate at length as to whether he ever 'found himself' in the normal sense of the term, whether he ever achieved the integrated personality which we are all supposed to evolve. But would it matter? He was a man who did the sorts of things other men did, liked what they generally liked, was warm, was good company – in fact, a good club man – inspired great affection among diverse people and apparently lacked malice to a dangerous degree. Split or integrated, that ought to be enough, even without his achievements. Also, the last fifteen years or so of his life – which ended in 1939 – do seem to show us a man who had arrived somewhere, who knew what he was and what he wanted, and who had pretty strong ideas about what the world ought to be. Graham Greene, who met him in the 1930s, put it well in *The Lost Childhood*:

> I don't suppose failure disturbed him much: he never really believed in human happiness, his middle life had been made miserable by passion, and he had come through – with his humour intact, his stock of unreliable anecdotes, the kind of enemies a man ought to have, and a half-belief in a posterity with would care for good writing.

In 1925 Ford was fifty-one and Stella Bowen thirty. They had been together for about six years and had a daughter, Julia (often called Julie). They were travelling back to Paris from their beloved

Provence, having left Julie with their maid, the awesome widow, Madame Annie. They decided to detour to Castelnaudary and took a ramshackle hired car. (Ford never drove but in his youth he liked cars, the bigger, redder and swifter the better.) They went, wrote Stella

> to eat the cassoulet. I remember that day well; it was at Easter, and the first heat of the year lay upon the white roads and white houses of the little town. The Hotel de la Reine Jeanne, where the cassoulet had sat on the fire without a break for the last three hundred years, was one of those unpretentious but excellent establishments where the commercial travellers sit round a big table in the middle of the room, and private clients at small tables round the walls. The sun blazed outside the screened windows, the flies buzzed, and we partook of one of the most stupendous meals of our whole gastronomic experience. After finishing our second bottle of admirable wine, and sampling the *fine maison*, Ford said that we really ought to send p.c.'s to all our friends to commemorate the menu. He was very unwilling, however, to stir from the depths of his chair, so I said I would go in search of picture postcards. The distinctly vague feeling from which I was suffering was enhanced by the blazing emptiness of the provincial noon-day. But when I observed a shop full of antique furniture plainly marked in very low figures, I remembered that we were on our way to Paris where an empty studio awaited us. A notice on the door of the shop said the proprietor, *en cas d'absence*, was to be found at the café, so there I sought him, and announced that I would buy the *armoire rustique*, the grandfather clock (it was a pot-bellied thing that did not work but looked nice), the walnut knee-holed writing table, and the antique flap-desk. These came to 800fr altogether, and I then sought Ford to obtain the cheque book from his pocket. He was extremely sceptical about the whole transaction, and was convinced that the goods would never reach Paris – but I carried the day. Later, I discovered that I had been given no receipt, and Ford almost persuaded me that (a) the purchase had never taken place, and (b) that the shopkeeper would pocket the money and keep the goods, or that (c) they would take six

months to arrive and there would be hundreds of francs to pay for the carriage. But I had faith, and when all the things turned up in Paris safe and sound, with almost nothing to pay and looking lovely in the studio, he generously admitted that I had had good judgement, even in my cups![1]

Eight hundred francs represented a substantial portion of their capital. That they were prepared to go to those lengths to sample the cassoulet, that they wanted to let their friends know about it, that Ford was so typically unwilling to leave his table, that Stella did what she did and he didn't mind, says much about them both – and about a marriage which can yield such pleasures after six years. Whether or not Ford was 'a system of assumed personas', Stella clearly felt she was having lunch with something rather more substantial; indeed, although generally he was more a discriminating than a voracious eater, in the matter of lunches English letters would be hard put to show his equal.

[1] *Drawn from Life*, Virago, p. 148

THREE

He was born, then, on 17th December 1873 at Number 5, Fair Lawn Villas, Merton, Surrey. Now Number 245 Kingston Road, it is a large square Victorian building, originally two semi-detached houses with steps going up to their front doors; substantial and respectable but by no means grand. Some of the neighbouring houses are still as they were but the former Number 5 has been converted into shoddy flats. The steps are gone, the doors have been moved to the sides, the garden is littered with cats, bicycles and dustbins and the Kingston Road – perhaps a lime-shaded lane in 1873 – is a running sore of traffic.

He was christened Ford Hermann Hueffer (usually pronounced Hoofer, sometimes Huffer) and was the first of three children, Oliver following four years later and Juliet eight. His mother, Catherine, was the daughter of the Pre-Raphaelite painter Ford Madox Brown, while his father, Franz Hüffer (anglicised to Francis Hueffer) had emigrated from Germany four years before. The Hüffers were a prosperous publishing and business family originating in Münster and spreading their tentacles wide. Francis was a musicologist, a proponent of Schopenhauer and Wagner, a composer of librettos, editor of a magazine, writer of philosophy and history and music critic of *The Times*. His family was Roman Catholic but he was atheist. He was energetic and erudite, described by William Rossetti (brother of Christina and Dante Gabriel, man of letters, Secretary of the Inland Revenue and benign avuncular influence on Ford and his family) as 'a rather bulky but not a tall man, of very Teutonic physiognomy: brilliant, ruddy complexion, brilliant yellow hair, blue eyes radiant with quickness and penetration . . . though not a melancholy person in his ordinary demeanour, he had a certain tinge of hypochondria in his outlook on life.'[1] Ford was named Hermann after one of Francis's three half brothers.

Energy, physical appearance, wide-ranging cultural interests, Catholicism, scepticism and the hypochondriacal tinge were all passed on to the first-born. Crucial to the francophilia of Ford's later life was Francis's enthusiasm for Provence and its romantic traditions. Francis wrote a book about it called *The Troubadours, A History of Provençal Life and Literature in the Middle Ages*.

Family influences passed on by Ford's mother, Catherine, were equally pronounced and in some cases complementary. The name Ford came into the family because Ford Madox Brown's grandfather, an eighteenth-century doctor who was etched by Blake and driven from England by the medical establishment because of his advanced views, gave it to his own son in honour of a favourite pupil. He also bequeathed a love of France – Madox Brown was born there and had, according to Ford, 'a strong French twinge to his English'. Another inheritance from both sides of the family was a tradition of love for and hard work at the arts. Catherine was herself a talented painter but she was considerate and self-denying, willing to sit up with the sick and to look after anyone who needed it, and she never fully developed her talent. She was an attractive woman, devoted particularly to her younger son, Oliver.

Another joint inheritance was the tradition of being multilingual and cosmopolitan. Ford learned to breathe in an atmosphere of truly European civilisation which may be less common now, for all the political structures, than then. Education was based on the classics and included as a matter of course more than one contemporary tongue. It was also assumed that children would learn to read, play (and often write) music, sing, paint, or at least be familiar with painting, and be very literate. The three families of Hueffer, Rossetti and Garnett children (the Garnetts were close friends) were all reared in an educational hothouse. They grew up conscious of themselves as heirs to a culture that transcended national boundaries.

For part of his life Ford appeared to suffer from a sense of inadequacy. It would be rash to ascribe final causes but it is clear

[1] *Some Reminiscences*, pp. 232–3

that family influences again combined. His father, like most people, seems to have thought better of younger brother Oliver. But the maternal pressures towards inadequacy were more complicated and perhaps even more telling. Like his Garnett friends and Rossetti cousins, Ford adored Madox Brown, the white-maned, kindly, fierce old man. (After Madox Brown's death Ford, then aged twenty-two, wrote a biography of him.) Madox Brown had a son, Oliver, who had died aged nineteen, the year after Ford was born. This boy was regarded as brilliant, had already published a novel and was held up ever more as the true heir to the family genius. Wherever he subsequently lived, Madox Brown kept a spare room full of Oliver's possessions (he also did a drawing of the corpse, moving and chilling in its detail). Ford's brother was named after Oliver and was thought to take after him far more than Ford did. Brother Oliver became the apple of everyone's eye and Ford, in his own words, grew up 'feeling like the ugly duckling'.

Oppression by genius was, he thought, the most significant feature of his childhood, which he described as a time of 'moral torture'. He grew to dislike '. . . the middle Victorian, tumultuously bearded Great . . . a childish nightmare to me; . . . by sheer reaction of inheritance I had even then[1] an absolute hatred for the "toll-loll" Great Figure, the Quarterly Reviewer, the Bibliographer and the ceaselessly-mouthing Great Poet, who had overshadowed my childhood.' He was brought up to believe that artists were the only serious people, that everyone else was simply 'stuff to fill graveyards', and when he spoke of going to university or joining the Army or the India Office he caused outrage, particularly on the part of his beloved grandfather. The children of the three families were intended by their parents for artistic or literary genius and were not supposed to be content with anything less.

As with many parental pressures, though, reproduction was often partial and sometimes produced its opposite. On the one hand, Ford did regard literary and artistic endeavour as the only proper occupation for the properly adult and he inherited the family tendency to look upon publishers as tradesmen whose task was simply to serve authors (with one or two exceptions such as

[1] 1900

René Byles and Stanley Unwin); on the other hand, he idealised people with practical and executive skills in a way that ran quite counter to the family view on material for graveyards. Many of his favoured fictional characters demonstrate practical knowledge of the world and an ability to cope; for example, Tietjens in *Parade's End*, Colonel Blood in *Mr Fleight*, Throckmorton in the *Fifth Queen* trilogy. He liked to talk to people who were engaged in the world – Masterman, the Liberal politician, was one of his close friends – and he liked cricket and golf and the people who played them.

It is, of course, tempting to assume that romanticising the practical is a sign of impracticality in the romanticiser. This may be partly true and it was certainly commonplace among those who knew Ford that he was quite impractical in any normal business sense, and hopeless with money. If that was how he appeared, it was probably how he was; his financial dealings were certainly not starred with success. But it is worth setting such charges in context: firstly, many genuine business people fail, the ability to cope with manifold affairs not being a common one; secondly, many people, practical in other ways, are less so with money, sometimes because it causes anxiety, sometimes because they don't like having to deal with it, sometimes because they are too easily tempted; thirdly, judging by the posts he was given, Ford seems to have been a capable administrator in the Army and was commended for his skills by one of his commanding officers; fourthly, though he lost money heavily on the two literary magazines he edited (like most people who get involved with literary magazines), what he produced in them was outstanding.

These are not arguments for saying that he was practical after all; merely that success in practical matters is not as widespread as is often assumed and that Ford was not necessarily worse than many. In some ways he might have been better – Janice Biala pointed out that to have written what he did was a sign of organisation, not its lack. Like many imaginative people, he could not be bothered with nuts and bolts, and he had been brought up to believe he shouldn't have to. His reaction was to admire those who did.

Childhood holidays with the Rossetti cousins increased the

pressure of expectation. They were organised by William's wife, Lucy, an experience which Ford described as being 'delivered over to the educational fury of our aunt'. A tireless worker at everything she did, she could not forgive a moment's idleness in herself or others. She would listen to lessons given by the governess and would quite often take over herself, with rather more strictness. Both Ford and Oliver felt they were intellectually out-gunned by the Rossetti children, though they had ways of getting their own back: 'I bagged my cousin Arthur with one collar-bone, broken on a boat-slide in my company, while . . . Olive Rossetti, I also remember, cut her head open . . . because she wanted to follow me down some dangerous steps and fell onto a flower pot . . . My cousins, in the full glory of their genius, were never really all of them together quite out of the bonesetter's hands.'[1] This rivalry between the Hueffer children and the Rossettis grew with their ages and their paths diverged, politically as well as in other ways. At one point, using a printing press in the basement of the eminently respectable William's house, the youthful Rossettis started an anarchist magazine called *The Torch*. Partly as a result of mixing in this milieu, Ford met a number of the anarchistically-inclined as well as, later, some Russian dissidents. Later still he was able to advise Joseph Conrad on anarchist themes and characters. At the time, though, Olive Garnett recorded an early example of his attitude towards political enthusiasms: his reaction to *The Torch* was to talk of founding a rival, a journal of universal pessimism called *The Extinguisher*. In the event there was no need because *The Torch* extinguished itself when William, alarmed by police surveillance and the anarchist explosion at the Greenwich Observatory, threw out the printing press.

Ford was a nervous child – 'I can still see the shadows of the wolves if I lie in bed with a fire in the room'[2], and his unwonted capacity for imagining horrors pursued him in later life. In *No Enemy*, a novel based on his war experience, he says of the hero: 'Ever since he had been a tiny child, he had . . . been so much a creature of dreads that the war was, in a sense, much less than

[1] *Memories and Impressions*
[2] *Return to Yesterday*

dreads to which he had been well accustomed. The dreads of original sin, of poverty, of bankruptcy, of incredible shyness, of insults, misunderstandings, of disease, of death, of succumbing to blackmailers, forgers, brain-troubles, punishments, undeserved ingratitudes, betrayals.'

Whatever its horrors, though, Ford's education was a good one. He went to the Praetorius School at Folkestone and to University College School, London. Except in scientific matters, which he disdained, he was a widely and well educated man. He had fluent French and German, some Italian, some Flemish and considerable Greek and Latin (in his middle age, in the trenches, he and another officer competed in the writing and translating of sonnets in English and Latin). He could quote large chunks of his favourite contemporary reading, sing, compose, play the piano and criticise music and painting as a specialist. *The March of Literature* – a massive and idiosyncratic survey from Confucius to Conrad – betrays a highly personal but bewildering and daunting erudition. Nor was erudition his sole inheritance. The Victorian Great he so disliked had bequeathed other characteristics. He became an exponent of the Grand Manner, perhaps adopted partly in imitation and partly to hide his lack of confidence. He learned it in childhood and by late adolescence it was well entrenched. His friend Olive Garnett, who was devoted to him (though she, like most others, found brother Oliver more attractive), wrote of the nineteen-year-old Ford in her diary: 'I must say that his lordly air is caviar to me, it delights me hugely, it is so absolutely unblushingly put on. I said that he might repent sitting up so late (writing till four) one day, that health was the most precious possession and so forth – the usual platitudes. "We were speaking of Goethe, I think," he said when I paused.'

This manner was commented on throughout his life, nearly always in terms of his putting it on. It was one of the aspects some people most disliked about him and was particularly marked in moments of stress or when he felt the need to impress. However it started, it seems likely that by the time he reached maturity it was ingrained and had become a habit. He was a witty man but by his own confession hopeless at repartee or any form of confrontation. The Grand Manner, with its remote oracular pronouncements, its withdrawal from emotional engagement, its disdain for the fray; was a form of defence rather than attack and was no less real for probably having started as a device.

Nevertheless, at nineteen much can be forgiven, and Ford had in any case some excuse for smugness. By that year (1892) he had published two fairy stories, *The Brown Owl* and *The Feather*, and a novel, *The Shifting of the Fire*. The following year he would publish a volume of poetry, *The Questions at the Well*, the year after that another fairy tale, *The Queen Who Flew*, and two years after that – when he was still only twenty-three – his biography of his grandfather.

In those few years Olive Garnett was also to write the drafts of two novels and several stories, as well as find time to keep her diary. Apart from the Grand Manner, she noted other Fordian characteristics that were to develop into life-long themes. One was that he already had a reputation within the family for telling tall stories, albeit stories designed to please rather than deceive. Probably many of his later tall stories were similarly intended. They certainly give more pleasure than most factual accounts and yet often still contain, he would say, the essence of truth.

There have been other explanations. Douglas Goldring, who was to be his editorial assistant and who knew him well, quotes him as saying in later life that he had been to Eton, when he hadn't. Goldring excuses this on the grounds that Ford was mixing with many Americans at the time, that Eton was the only English public school they knew, that it was where they expected every well-known Englishman to have been and that it was simply Ford's way of saying that he'd been to an English public school.

One problem with this kindly explanation is that Ford said at other times that he'd been to Winchester. Goldring's error was to assume that such lies stand in need of individual excuse or explanation, whereas their interest is really as symptoms of a tendency. Perhaps Ford wished to act out, for his own benefit and for that of his audience, a series of visions of the world as he thought it ought to have been. Or he may have assumed a shared conspiracy, as if everyone knew it wasn't really true just as they knew that that wasn't really the point. If someone had nudged him after he'd mentioned Eton and said, 'Surely, Praetorius, Folkestone?' he would probably have nodded and said, 'Of course, yes, but you know what I mean. That sort of thing.'

More significantly, Olive also recorded Ford's early interest in Roman Catholicism and noted the ambivalence of its origin. He had recently returned from a long walk in the region of Rye and Appledore, in Kent, where he would subsequently live and about which he would write. He was eighteen. Olive noted on Friday, 25th March, 1892:

> . . . We went into the dining room, where we had a long and uninterrupted argument, just for the pleasure of thinking & talking, & exchanging impressions, with never the possibility of agreeing or convincing. But still delightful enough besides, a voyage of discovery into an intelligent being's mind, seasoned with laughter, is intoxicating always. I was however very much shocked when Ford admitted that as a relief from the gospel of perfect indifference to everything, he sought refuge in bigoted pietism in the Brompton Oratory, not that he thought that Catholicism was rational, outside its circle, but that it satisfied his sensual religious needs, he found poetry in it, etc.
>
> In fact, he started the paradox theory saying that in the mean lies torpor, in extremes madness, he balanced the two parts of his nature one against the other. Atheistic indifference on the one hand, bigoted pietism on the other. To my well ordered & I think carefully trained little rational mind, such confessions seemed to reveal an abyss at my feet . . . His conscience does not reproach him for conceit or selfishness, nor would it for any crime; what is crime? But this way lies madness.

Enjoyable undergraduate knockabout, self-dramatising, self-engrossed and fun; but it contain the seeds of the ambivalence that characterised Ford's religious belief and practice. He was received into the Roman Catholic Church later that same year in Paris and remained nominally a Catholic for the rest of his life, though his practice was irregular and his belief at best ambiguous. On the one hand, he liked ceremony and respected tradition and faith. He had his two daughters enter the church (in Germany this time) because he felt it would be good for them to have something to hold on to when trouble came. He prayed for them both the last time he saw them, just before he went to the Front. In his portrait of Katharine Howard in *The Fifth Queen* trilogy he portrayed the Old Faith sympathetically, though not uncritically, and he introduced a martyr priest with an untainted moral role into *Parade's End*. He allied Catholicism with his favoured political attitude (an imagined feudal Toryism that was really socialism without the state) and was often scornful of Protestantism which he lumped together with dour and stodgy 'Anglo-Saxondom'.

On the other hand, in letters to Elsie Martindale before their marriage, he referred to God as stupid, as a 'plaguing beast', and to all religion as 'humbuggery'. The variety of Catholicism he preferred was the Albigensian, according to which Christ was an angel with a phantom body who thus did not suffer or rise again and whose redemptive work consisted only in His teaching. The adherents of this twelfth- and thirteenth- century heresy were brutally dealt with by successive popes until the Inquisition finished them off completely in the fourteenth century. Perhaps part of the attraction for Ford was that the Albigenses flourished in the south of France, though he may also have found the doctrine a convenient answer to awkward questions about the historicity of Christ.

Although he wanted his children to become Catholics, he was reluctant to allow his elder daughter Christina to board at a convent in Rye because 'You never know what nuns get up to . . . she's such a loyal little thing.' He allowed himself to be won over only to find that his fears were indeed prophetic: the nuns got to work on her and Christina became one and cut herself off from her family. Ford last saw her when she was nineteen. He tried to persuade her to delay her decision until he returned from the war – if he did – but she would not.

His own church attendance was intermittent and seems to have coincided mainly with visits to France and Germany, as if religion were part of his Continental heritage and had nothing to do with his British life (though he did attend services in the Army). When he took up permanent residence on the Continent, however, he seemed to revert to his British habits. Janice Biala, who lived with him during the last decade of his life, told Sondra Stang:

I don't remember any talk about religion. It didn't play any role in our life. I am an unreconstructed Jew. Ford was certainly no practising Catholic. He brought his children up as Catholics because he thought all children should be brought up in some religion, and he preferred Catholicism because he said if you wanted to break away from it you could make a clean break. Apparently, Catholics have to believe the whole works or nothing. He did say he admired the organisation of the church . . . When we entered a church Ford would make a half-hearted bow in the direction of the Virgin – but perhaps more because she was a woman than because she was the Virgin. And I imagine he believed in Catholicism philosophically.

As so often with comments about or by Ford, there is that qualifying last sentence. The penultimate one echoes a passage in Jean Rhys's *Quartet* (first published as *Postures*), the novel she wrote after her affair with Ford. Novels, even those based most closely on events, should not be regarded as reportage, but the glimpse Jean Rhys gives us of Heidler in church is revealing (Heidler is the lover of her heroine and was based on Ford):

> The church was very cool and dark-shadowed, when they came in out of the sun. It smelled of candles and incense and ancient prayers. Marya stood for a long time staring at the tall Virgin and wondered why she suggested not holiness but rather a large and peaceful tolerance of sin. We are all miserable sinners, the dust of the earth. A little more or a little less, a dirty glass or a very dirty glass, as Heidler would say . . .
>
> 'And you don't suppose it matters to me,' said the tall Virgin smiling so calmly above her candles and her flowers.
>
> Marya turned to watch Heidler go down on one knee and cross himself as he passed the altar. He glanced quickly sideways at her as he did it, and she thought: 'I'll never be able to pray again now that I've seen him do that. Never! However sad I am.'

This is the kind of incident that might well have been based on the actual or, if not, it might reflect a truth in the Fordian sense:

that is, it is not that he did it but it was the sort of thing he did and it shows what he was like. Certainly, it has the ring of truth, though Marya's reaction is a little too histrionic to be entirely convincing.

Of course, Ford – if he did do it – was neither the first nor the last to want to be seen praying, but the incident illustrates what seems to have been the character of his religious life, in so far as he had one. It was the practice of religion, the observance of tradition, the ceremony of worship and the embodiment of faith that attracted him – as he said to Olive, the sensual and poetic. He probably appreciated the sense of belonging and felt that, whether historically true or not, religious beliefs were beneficial. But his practice was very occasional and there is no indication of any other level of religious life, no reference to the way in which beliefs might have shaped his actions; no sign, in fact, that he actually believed at all. His religion seems to have taken its place alongside his agricultural endeavours, his fallible enchanting memoirs, his enthusiasms and his women: it was a part of the rich tapestry he made of his life but it was not the determinant. Nothing ever competed with that.

FOUR

Whether school was a success because of or despite Madox Brown's dictum that teachers didn't know anything and therefore what they said need not be heeded, though they themselves should be treated with respect since they were teachers, is hard to say. It was a co-educational school at Folkestone run by Dr Alfred and Mrs Elizabeth Praetorius and named after them. They were disciples of Froebel, admirers of English middle-class social graces and of the cult of the gentleman. They were friends of Madox Brown.

Ford was sent to them in 1881, following a period of poor health (he had his throat scraped). He liked the school. He was much influenced by Elizabeth Praetorius and by David Watson, the Scots usher with whom he construed Latin. He wrote of it later: 'There can scarcely have been at any stage of the world's history a happiness greater than that, say, of an English schoolboy during the decades of the eighties and nineties. There you were, vicariously ruling the waves of the world, building up the empire on which the sun never sets . . . You were furnished, without effort on your part, with traditions of valour and of physical perfection.'

He became captain of cricket and was one of the school's best tennis players. Later in life he would sometimes say that watching Kent win at Canterbury was one of his ideal ways of spending a day. Such remarks were held to be evidence of yet another Ford persona, that of the gentleman cricketer, but the fact remains that he played it, enjoyed it and was captain. As for tennis, there is little evidence that he played very much beyond his later games in Holland Park with Ezra Pound, zany and enthusiastic affairs in which the scoring was likely to be haphazard and hotly disputed.

He read widely and was famed for it at school. By fourteen he had encompassed Plutarch, Gibbon, Marryat, Scott and Defoe, along with *Westward Ho!*, *Sweeney Todd* and *Lorna Doone*. Uncle William Rossetti encouraged his reading and a poetess friend of Madox Brown's, Mathilde Blind, read to him her book on Shelley. Neither he nor Shelley ever recovered from this. Half a century later he wrote in *The March of Literature*:

> As against Keats, Shelley is diffuse. It is impossible to disassociate these two whose careers on earth seemed indissolubly intertwined. The splendours, the almost supernatural beauty of the active mind of Shelley will obviously forever gild his poems and blind one to the mediocrity of thousands of his inferior lines. But the gold is an exterior gold; we bring it ourselves to his shrine, and his shining soul only very seldom illuminates his poems from within. He is almost never natural; he is almost never not intent on showing himself the champion of freedom, the Satan of a Hanoverian Heaven. And even when he is natural his sheer carelessness will spoil – for the impatient prose writer – his most satisfactory poems. Take
>
> I awake from dreams of thee
> In the first sweet sleep of night,
> And the winds are breathing low
> And the stars are burning bright:
>
> I awake from dreams of thee
> And a spirit in my feet
> Has led me, who knows how,
> To thy chamber window, sweet . . .
>
> The poem is beautiful, but imagine the meanest short-story writer introducing into it that 'who knows how?' It gives the effect of a large piece of red hot iron suddenly put into water. A writer should precisely 'know how' things happen in his prose or verse. If he does not he should not write.

This is typical Fordian criticism: generous, biased, to the point (that 'almost never natural' is striking) and practical; his concern is with how writing works. The beginning of his next paragraph is also typical: 'So, skipping Tennyson because we have had quite enough of him . . .'

Oliver, too, was happy at Praetorius. There seems not to have been any serious jealousy between the brothers, although Oliver's manifold activities included novel-writing, but it may nevertheless have been a relief to Ford to be free for the first year or two of the upward pressure of this rampant cuckoo who was always in trouble, always beloved, baled out, forgiven and fired anew for the next venture. They never seem to have been close and saw little of each other in later life but remained friendly enough. Ford described Oliver as an exaggerated version of himself and, judging by Oliver's financial and social escapades, this could well have been true. Physically, they were thought to be very alike but their photographs, even though they had more or less the same build and colouring, do not look very like. It may be unfair, but it is tempting to think that Oliver had everything except originality.

Apart from the educational, Praetorius had two enduring influences on Ford's life. One was his love for Kent and Sussex, the counties where he spent the early years of his married life and where his friendship and collaboration with Conrad developed. He was to write vividly about the Romney Marsh and its people, 'those brown, battered men and women of an obscure Kentish countryside' – Meary Walker, Meary Spratt, Ragged Arse Wilson and Shakin' Ben 'who had been ruined by the bad gels of Rye'. He also wrote *The Cinque Ports*, a large, impressive, expensive book, illustrated by Henry Hyde.

The other enduring influence was the girl who became his wife, Elsie. Her father, Dr Martindale, was a well-known chemist from Carlisle who had settled in London, where he and his wife knew Madox Brown. Most of the pupils at Praetorius were from professional families and Elsie and her elder sister, Mary, had attended the previous Praetorius school, a kindergarten in London.

Elsie was three years younger than Ford. They became friends and went around together so much that she was known to schoolfellows as 'The Captain's Wife'. Ford's courtship thus began early and with it, mutedly, another theme that was to accompany them for a good part of their lives together. While still at school, he went on holiday to Germany, a visit that 'represented my first absolute freedom from parental control'. He wrote about it in *Harper's* many years later (April 1933):

> It was in that last village [Geisenheim] many years ago that I bought my first cigarettes from my – in true Rhine fashion – first love. She wore her hair in pleats over her ears and represented for me a blonde Flemish Madonna in an altarpiece. I do not think I ever saw her move, so still she sat, and I am sure I never addressed to her two words beyond the mere request for cigarettes.

It was neither his last love nor his last cigarette.

While Ford was still a young child the Hueffer family had moved to 90 Brook Green, Hammersmith. His sister Juliet described it in her book, *Chapters from Childhood*, as small and pretty, with 'not many stairs'. There was Chippendale furniture, many paintings and plenty of flowers: 'My mother made any room pretty that she went into . . . She always chose books with the brightest and prettiest covers to put in the front of the shelves in the bookcases and put the ugly ones behind, even if they were learned. She said it was quite easy to get them out if you wanted to, and the bookcases glowed and gleamed like great big jewels.' She was equally determined that her children should read. She introduced Ford to *Silas Marner*, *The Mill on the Floss*, *Wuthering Heights*, *Sidonia the Sorceress*, *The Woman in White*, *The Moonstone*, Diana of the Crossways and *Far From the Madding Crowd*. Francis Hueffer thought Dickens vulgar and Stevenson meretricious, except for *The Inland Voyage*, but Ford managed to read them anyway. His grandfather recommended *Madame Bovary*, *Tartaria de Tarascon*, *Tartarin sur les Alpes*, *Roderick Random*, *Humphrey Clinker*, *Snarleyyew*, *Mr Midshipman Easy* and Waterton's *Wanderings in South America*. Uncle William Rossetti gave him *The Castle of Otranto*, *Caleb Williams*, *Frankenstein* and Meinhold's *The Amber Witch*. Trollope, Ford remarks in *The English Novel*, 'I had to find out for myself, oddly enough.'

The house is still there. Tall and terraced, it faces the green and the tennis courts, as respectable now as it was then. There are blue plaques on the walls of two of its neighbours – Number 84 commemorates Arthur and Rex Silver, designers; Number 56, Sir Frank Short, engraver and printer – but none to Ford.

It all changed in January 1889 when Francis Hueffer died of a heart attack, aged forty-three. He had been a vigorous and energetic rather than tender father, sometimes a bully to his children, but nonetheless it was a blow. The family fortunes changed abruptly: Ford and Oliver had to leave school and move with their mother into Madox Brown's house at 1 St Edmund's Terrace near the British Museum, while Juliet had to live two doors away with the Rossettis. Their loss brought the family closer and, though the children didn't see much of each other in adulthood, they were on good terms for the rest of their lives. Mrs Hueffer in particular was always unquestioningly loyal: she stuck with Ford during the later troubles of his courtship, was always prepared to go to Germany with him when he was ill (it was where he usually went to escape) and she publicly associated herself with him and Violet Hunt when many ostracised them. Ford's letters to her are fond and confiding.

He and Oliver started at University College School in Gower Street. It wasn't very good, though Plutarch and Latin were taken seriously, and Ford played truant to go to afternoon concerts, thinking at that time that music might be his career. He left after less than a year, on publication of his first book, and it appears that satisfaction at the parting may have been mutual. He was eighteen. But that final school year and the two following it were valuable. He drifted about London, was rejected by the Royal College of Music, saw a lot of Madox Brown, argued in cafés – London had them then – where artists and the intelligentsia gathered, had the run of the hospitable Garnett household, disagreed with the Rossettis, went to Fabian meetings, listened to anarchists and took tea with Russian dissidents (Juliet recalled his taking her to see Prince Kropotkin). He also knew Vaillant, who subsequently exploded a bomb in the French Chamber of Deputies, and remembered walking the streets with Stepniak and Volkholsky 'dogged by the Russian spy allocated to each of these distinguished lecturers'. (This is not as far-fetched as it sounds: the Ohkrana, the Tsarist secret police, surveilled and penetrated dissident groups in the same manner as their communist successors, albeit on nothing like so grand a scale.)

He went to lectures at the British Museum, courted Elsie (and according to Olive Garnett, an un-named lady in Hampstead), invented fairy stories for Juliet (which became his first book, *The Brown Owl*), and later took to wearing D. G. Rossetti's black Inverness cape and Madox Brown's fifteen-year-old blue linen shirt and red satin tie. He wrote poetry and some music. Juliet described him at that time as 'a fair, clever young man, rather scornful, with smooth pink cheeks and a medium-sized hook nose like my grandfather's, a high, intellectual forehead, and quiet, absent looking blue eyes that seemed as if they were always pondering over something. I was nervous with him, because he was very critical and thought that nearly everyone else was stupid and not worth disagreeing with. But he was very kind. . .' Juliet herself seems to have inherited her mother's equable temperament and was as blonde as her brothers, but considerably more beautiful.

Those years were for Ford the equivalent of time spent at university, something he probably would have done had his grandfather not opposed it, a general trying out of things amidst apparent idleness or aimlessness. But Ford was not idle and he was rarely without an aim; he was simply, at that time of his life, undecided. Family lore had it that, like all the children, he was supposed to be a genius though he didn't yet know at what. Music claimed as much, if not more, of his attention as literature.[1] In some writers the springs of creativity flow better unforced and Ford was at just that stage.

Nor was he insensitive to other aspects of London: 'I fancy the physical gloom of London adds to the heaviness of my memory of those days. A city whose streets are illuminated by the flicker of rare street-lamps seems almost darker than one not lit at all . . . Above the darkness brooded the Hard Times (I am talking now of the early nineties). It is difficult to think how people lived then.

[1] Cornell University has about 80 pages of unpublished music by Ford, demonstrating that he was a more serious musician than is generally appreciated. For a discussion of his compositions and the effect of music on his verse and his novels, see the article by Sondra Stang and Carl Smith in the University of Wisconsin Press's *Contemporary Literature*, Vol. 30, No. 2 (summer 1989).

In cold, in darkness, lacking sufficient clothes or sufficient food . . . You lived in slums in Seven Dials, Whitechapel, Notting Hill. You burned the stair rails and banisters, the door jambs, the window frames for fuel . . . The natural corollary of these pressures was . . . Anarchism, Fabianism, dynamitings, Nihilism. I saw a good deal of the inner workings of these.'[1]

It is not always easy to place his politics because they varied with the issue or occasion. He described his grandfather as a Tory by instinct and a Liberal by reason and he seems to have shown something of the same ambivalence himself, although perhaps as a result of his attendance at gatherings of the Left in the 1890s he later maintained that the socialist tail wags the liberal dog. He was a life-long feminist, believed that the passion for impersonal property (i.e., possessions such as furniture and clothes but excluding tools, agricultural produce and books) was the source of all evil, sympathised with Irish republicanism (particularly after the execution of Casement) and was in later life a pacifist believer in the ideal of the small producer. He was also patriotic, volunteered for war, disliked all state compulsion – in fact, disliked the state as a political entity – believed passionately in the freedom of the individual, supported Zionism and foresaw the terror inherent in the Soviet system at a time when most of his kind saw only an ideal. Whatever the labels or issues, he remained temperamentally liberal and individualistic but supportive of authority provided it stayed within fairly narrow limits.

The fledgling Oliver, meanwhile, was also out of school. He put himself about town with precocious enthusiasm, acquiring friends, fiancées, career plans and debts. The family continued to indulge him, even tolerating his occasional unauthorised pawning of Madox Brown's possessions in order to pay for his gambling, though he later became a serious financial drain on both his grandfather and his mother. Later still in *It was the Nightingale* Ford was to describe how Oliver, 'with the swiftness of the seasons at St Agrève, ran through the careers of Man About Town, Army Officer, Actor, Stockbroker, Painter, Author and under the auspices of the father of one of his fiancées, that of Valise Manufacturer.'

[1] *Return to Yesterday*

Madox Brown remained the major family influence, an irascible, loveable, belligerent, kindly god. Juliet described him as:

> One of the kindest, gentlest, handsomest old gentlemen that ever lived. Everybody loved him. He wore a blue cloth tam-o'-shanter when he was at work, and in the winter sat with his legs in a big bag made of fur inside, like those worn at the North Pole. His cheeks were pink, and he had blue eyes, and his hair fell straight down on both sides of his face nearly to the bottom of his ears, and my grandmother cut it straight and even all the way round behind. It was wonderfully thick and pure snow white, and so was his beard. He wasn't very tall but his shoulders were broad and he looked somehow grand and important. He nearly always smiled when you looked at him, not an empty smile, but a kind, understanding one, though his eyes looked quite sad all the while . . . he used to take my grandmother's little dog out for a walk on Primrose Hill. He couldn't walk very fast, because he had the gout, but the little dog was very old and couldn't go very fast either, so it didn't mind. He would stop from time to time and look behind to see if it was coming, and then it used to stop too, and sit down and look at him and hang its tongue out and wag its tail, and they went on again.

He enthusiastically encouraged younger artists, telling Ford that he should always be prepared to sacrifice his own work to that of someone else whose genius was greater (thinking perhaps of his own patronage of D. G. Rossetti). He was also unbusinesslike, occasionally melancholy, hard-working, devoted to his art, good company and the only real friend that D. G. Rossetti ever had. In all respects save the last, Ford resembled him. It would be hard to exaggerate the influence he had on his grandson – hard, perhaps, even for Ford himself, to whom exaggeration came so naturally. Olive Garnett describes an incident in which she suggested that interfering altruism might sometimes have motives other than the pure and straightforward and was surprised and upset by the brutality and bitterness with which Ford attacked her. Moser[1]

[1] *The Life in the Fiction of Ford Madox Ford*

suggests that Ford may have had unconscious worries about the psychological sources of altruism and it seems likely that behind his over-reaction was the threatened image of his adored grandfather. Janice Biala believes that Madox Brown was *the* major personal influence on his life, an impression she gained even though she did not know Ford until he was in his mid fifties.

Madox Brown's death in the summer of 1893 hit them all. Juliet touchingly describes it in *Chapters from Childhood* but Ford, who had just returned from Germany with his mother, says little about it. In fact, he never wrote or said very much about death. Characters die in his novels, of course, and he mentions the ends of some of the Kentish people he wrote about, but he never dwells on the subject. Wisely, perhaps, since there is nothing new to be said and anyway there is no reason why we should expect literature to encompass the whole of experience. Nonetheless, death is present in his work, like sex, in a subliminal sense; indeed, much of his work can be seen as elegiac, as if elicited by death. But the lack of direct dealing might also have been another manifestation of his fear of confrontations and of his dislike of finality. He would probably not have agreed that the best way of dealing with things was always to face them or write about them or 'talk them through'. For some the best way of coping with disaster is not to confront it directly but simply to try to carry on. That does not mean that they are not aware but rather that they are aware also of their own limits. For Ford those limits were often not very far away.

Nor was it only death he avoided. Several of the women who loved him have recorded with varying degrees of exasperation his unwillingness to face unyielding facts about their relationships. 'He had a genius for creating confusion', wrote Stella Bowen, 'and a nervous horror of having to deal with the results.' It may have been cowardice, or a mute acknowledgement of his own incapacities, or selfishness, or even a chosen way of coping with the immutable. Whatever it was, he was far too perceptive for there to have been any question about his awareness. It was, in any case, a characteristic that had its beneficial aspect. Edward Crankshaw was twenty-four when he met the sixty-year-old Ford and they knew each other for the rest of Ford's life. Crankshaw describes him at that time:

> This heavy, rather lumpy figure in shapeless, battered tweeds, panting, gaping, often gasping like a fish, would sit upright, legs apart, on a hard chair in a bare attic room like a king on his throne – and talk like an angel about everything under the sun – without the faintest suggestion that he had no idea where next week's rent was coming from – showering on his listeners pure gold.[1]

In seeking to render through his writing what he thought important in life, he made no attempt to be comprehensive. He did not describe sex and usually avoided scenes of action, preferring instead to describe the before and after, the effects or mental fall-out of events not directly depicted. There was, of course, no reason why he or any writer should attempt to be comprehensive but it is nonetheless worth noting what he chooses not to write about since a writer's limitations are partly the limits of his personality. Avoidance of scenes of action, for instance, or presentation of them as a series of mental impressions, may be symptomatic of Ford's own horror of 'scenes'. He may not have wanted to grapple with the actual.

It was probably the same with sex. He was deeply involved with a number of women and a main theme in several of his novels – most evidently in *The Good Soldier* – is passion, but he does not deal directly with sex. Certainly, the pressure of sex is pervasive, along with the assumption that the reader is sophisticated enough not to need it described, but the motive spring is passion – a gaseous mixture of dream and desire, of deceit, of self-sacrifice fuelled by ego, of guilt, fear and affection. Similarly, the atmosphere of *The Fifth Queen*, the Tudor trilogy, is imbued with sex, as heavy, still and ominous as the tapestries, but the thing itself is hardly mentioned. In many of his novels we see the results of sexual passion, jealousy, fidelity and infidelity subtly and intelligently worked out. He was too good a novelist to anaesthetise or cheaply to seduce his reader. He offers and demands thought and sensitivity. The proof of this is that after reading him we understand more about people; or know there is more to be understood.

[1] Sondra Stang, *The Presence of Ford Madox Ford*

FIVE

Publication and marriage both came early, neither entirely by his own efforts. Madox Brown read his grandson's first fairy story, *The Brown Owl*, liked it, illustrated it himself and persuaded Edward Garnett to get Fisher Unwin to publish it. The book was a success. Ford later wrote that 'the publisher paid me ten pounds for it and . . . it sold many thousands more copies than any other book I ever wrote.'[1] It came out when he was eighteen and was followed later that same year by another fairy story, *The Feather*. The third, *The Queen Who Flew*, was published in 1894. He also wrote about a dozen shorter fairy stories, some of which were published much later (1906) in *Christina's Fairy Book*, and a volume of poetry.

Though Ford was to describe the stories as being 'about Princes and Princesses and magicians and such twaddle', they are better than that implies. He liked children and was always good with them (he was later to nurse Conrad's son, Borys, with such devotion that even Conrad's wife, who disliked him, praised him for it). He could enter into their imaginative worlds, believing almost as they did. Though the books are rather cluttered with adverbs and adjectives – like the early work of many writers – they read easily. *The Queen Who Flew* is said by Alison Lurie to 'deserve a place among the classics of English children's literature'. Lurie's discussion of the three books is in Sondra Stang's *The Presence of Ford Madox Ford* (University of Pennsylvania Press) and is worth reading not only for its analysis but also for the parallels between events in Ford's own life and his imagined narratives. She concludes

[1] *Portraits from Life*

by quoting the final paragraph of *Christina's Fairy Book* (Christina was one of Ford's daughters):

> I think that this is the last fairy tale that this Pumpums (the children's name for Ford) will tell his kiddies. For now when at nightfall he goes to them they say no longer: 'Tell us a fairy tale', but 'Tell us some history'. For, you see, they have grown out of believing in the untruths that are most real of all, and they are beginning to believe in those truths that are so false. And I do not know that that does not make this Pumpums a little sad. Still, it is the way of all flesh.

Untruths more real than truths that are false: an early example of the tendency for which he was later to become famous, or notorious. What is behind it is a belief in imaginative truth – that is, the imaginative apprehension of enduring truths which are rendered more visible via the unreal than the real. Conscious believers in this power of imagination have probably always been a minority though the unconscious assumption of it may be more widespread. On the stage, for instance, we are accustomed to see truths about ourselves, about guilt, about power, alienation, love or whatever presented through a carefully arranged unreality. We accept the convention that what we see is make-believe and that what is signified is real. Whether Ford would have argued like this it's hard to say; he would probably have thought it so obvious as to be not worth arguing about.

In 1892, however, he had more than fairy stories and the status of truth on his mind. Youthful marriage on elopement is an exciting proposition and they were exciting days for all involved. Quite a few people were, which is one of several typically Fordian features. There were others: a loyal party, an outraged party, a party unwittingly injured, a female confidante who was not the bride, press reports, legal complications, frantic journeyings, seeds of later drama unknowingly sown, general exhaustion, particular exhaustion of Ford and reflections of events in his works. Most of these features were repeated during his later involvement with Violet Hunt.

He began his courtship of Elsie Martindale (as opposed to his friendship which, as we have seen, was already of long standing) in the summer of 1892. Her family lived in London but had a house in Winchelsea, Sussex, where he visited them for a weekend in August. Dr Martindale was an able and respected man, for some years Mayor of Winchelsea, but his wife was something of an alcoholic and their elder daughter, Mary, seems to have given cause for concern fairly early on. They worried about her stability and felt that for much of the time she was verging on hysteria. Mary was tall and vivacious with red-gold hair, an attractive girl, but it was the younger daughter, then only fifteen, who had all along claimed Ford's attention. Olive Garnett thought Elsie the more attractive: 'She is a charming girl, exceedingly pretty and not merely so, but she has a soul in her face. I recognised the gold thread in her brown hair, the oval sweep from ear to chin, and the light deep down in her hazel eyes, especially the light in her eyes . . . I like best the "unconsciousness" in her, but perhaps that is because she is in love.' H. G. Wells, in his *Experiment in Autobiography*, was later to describe her as, 'Tall, high-breasted and dark with a bold eye and a rich, high colour like a ripe nectarine.' There were worries about her health. Olive Rossetti said she had 'an iron knee-cap and a hole in her breast. Diseased bones show consumption . . .' In fact, she had tuberculosis in her knee which was to trouble her for the rest of her life, but though she developed other ailments the tuberculosis does not seem to have spread to her lungs.

Nor was the eighteen-year-old Ford entirely healthy. His family worried about his heart but it is not clear whether on sound medical grounds or whether they were observing early symptoms of stress. That summer his mother sent him to Germany to see the wealthy Hueffer relatives and to become, like them, Roman Catholic. He stayed with his Uncle Hermann in Bonn but was influenced against Catholicism by an atheistic Lutheran clergyman, by students with Marxist views and by a female cousin who 'wore a Russian, almost Nihilist, fur toque, smoked cigarettes and when bicycling appeared in knickerbockers'. He returned to England still not formally a Catholic. Mrs Hueffer was worried about both her sons, neither of whom seemed destined for security of any sort.

On 3rd October 1892 he sent Elsie a ring for her sixteenth

birthday and a letter to her mother which was at once a proposal, an acknowledgement that a proposal would not be acceptable and an offer to renounce all future proposals: 'If however, you should consider the matter entirely out of the question I beseech you to say as much and I will resign myself not to trouble you or her again . . .' He then went off to his Uncle Leopold in Paris and this time, on 7th November, was received into the Roman Catholic Church. By early 1893 he was back at Brook Green with his mother, again pursuing his courtship. Both he and Elsie were very keen and the relationship gathered a momentum from which it was clear that something would have to give; her parents, though reluctant openly to oppose the match at this stage, were at best lukewarm, in fact increasingly unhappy.

Meanwhile, Olive Garnett was faithfully chronicling the affair and wondering to herself what would now become of the previously admired but un-named Hampstead lady. It is clear that Ford was confiding in Olive and that she fulfilled – or shared in the fulfilment – of the need he had throughout his adult life for intimate female friendship. Her tone sometimes suggests that the relationship might well have gone farther though there is no evidence that it did. Ford was in an over-excited state for much of the time, which affected her, but not so much as to get out of control. At one point he was advised by Madox Brown to go walking in the area of Salisbury and – curiously – Oliver was sent along to look after him. It was an area to which he subsequently sent a number of his fictional heroes.

By this time he had started writing his first adult novel, *The Shifting of the Fire.* An improbable tale about a chemist in love, in which the hero is an idealised version of Ford, it is strongly influenced by the cult of destructive passion associated with D. G. Rossetti. Despite the clutter of adverbs and adjectives, however, something of spirit comes through. Conrad was later to find the book 'delightfully young' – stressing his delight – and even Ford subsequently thought better of it than in the first few years after it was written. The book indicated some of what was to come and shows that concern with the destructiveness of passion that was more than simply the fell shadow of Rossetti but a major theme of Ford's personal and artistic life. Olive records that she was 'much surprised when Ford also declared that the only thing really interesting and unfathomable was love, not the higher kind, but the lower kind.' When the book's hero is in love he quotes Berlioz, which is what Ford did to Elsie. He was particularly fond of Berlioz's alleged last words: 'When I see the way in which certain people look on love and what they seek in artistic creation I am involuntarily reminded of hogs rooting and grunting under the grandest tree.' There are also recognisable equivalents not only of Ford but of his father, his grandfather, Elsie and Dr Martindale.

In its depiction of man as wolf to man – something he was fond of quoting – the book foreshadows both *The Young Lovell* and its successor, *The Good Soldier*. The major themes of his artistic maturity – passion and renunciation, altruism and selfishness, integrity and deceit – may all be seen in his first four books. It may also be fairly depressing for a novelist to consider that his youthful apprehensions of certain truths, or perhaps of one big truth, are all he's going to get; that the rest of his career will consist in striving to find better ways of illustrating these truths and that the best of all will be that in which the message is so welded into the structure of the vehicle that it functions both for itself and for the message; that at no time is he likely to apprehend a new truth. Perhaps the very greatest writers do apprehend more truths – would we guess the mature Shakespeare from the early plays? – but most are more strictly rationed.

He was impatient to get married. Throughout the rest of 1893 he saw much of Elsie and wrote many letters. He stressed the importance of being able to talk to her, a theme that featured largely in all his relations with women and which no doubt was a substantial part of his own attractiveness. Nor was it simply that he had a quiet, reassuring voice and manner and was sensitive: talk was to him the final communion of souls. It was what it was all about. In *Parade's End* he has Christopher Tietjens say:

> You seduced a woman in order to be able to finish your talks with her. You could not do that without living with her. You could not live with her without seducing her; but that was the by-product. The point is that you can't otherwise talk. You can't finish talks at street corners; in museums; even in drawing-

rooms. You mayn't be in the mood when she is in the mood – for the intimate conversation that means the final communion of your souls.

For Elsie he had the most urgent and normal desire as well as a yearning for communal and romantic fulfilment. Their eagerness was intensified by parental opposition which became more evident the more Ford pressed his case. Neither of the lovers knew the real reason for it and much later Elsie said that had she done so she would probably have yielded to her parents and renounced him. She was an ardent, determined and single-minded young woman but she had a strong sense of responsibility and duty and it is quite possible that she would have made so hard a choice. As it was, she was as dissatisfied as Ford with the plausible but seemingly insufficient subsidiary reasons for her parents' opposition: Dr Martindale was alarmed by the Hueffer connection with the youthful Rossetti anarchists; Oliver's notoriety was widely trumpeted and Ford was thought to resemble him; Ford was not rich and the fact that he was a published author and even at that age always working on a book was not thought to be any sort of security (rightly); he was suspected of being after Elsie's money (wrongly) and his appearances at socialist meetings at William Morris's Kelmscott House were thought to indicate undesirable tendencies. This last point was ironic since Ford was already an unbeliever as far as the socialists were concerned. 'I did my best and decried any kind of force physical or moral but it weren't no good,' he wrote to Elsie after one meeting. 'I got howled down by the entire audience inclusive of the four Anarchists.'

In fact, the Martindales' reason was much closer to home; vivacious, unstable Mary with the red-gold hair had long harboured a passion for Ford and her parents feared for her stability in the event of his marrying their younger daughter. It is not known when this passion developed nor how it manifested itself. Did it, for instance, date from schooldays at Praetorius when Elsie was already called 'The Captain's Wife'? Or did it originate with Ford's courtship proper? How was it that both parents were aware of it but apparently neither Elsie nor Ford? Most people are aware if they are the object of passion, especially over a period, and Ford was more sensitive than most. Could it have been that he and Elsie were aware, at least vestigially, but that Mary simply wasn't taken seriously? Some people are not. Their concerns and passions are regarded as more lightweight than other people's and they are dismissed as having been 'always a bit like that', or with some such formula. But Mary's parents took her seriously. If they'd been more open about it there might have been less trouble later.

Another unanswered question is whether Ford himself encouraged her. If hers was a susceptible nature, unsettled by a successful younger sister and close at times to hysteria, it might not have taken much attention from him to provoke a response. He was always attentive to women and would not necessarily have intended the effects that sheer attentiveness can have. When he and Elsie did eventually marry Mary got engaged to a Frenchman, though she later broke it off. In May 1893 matters came to such a pass that Madox Brown went to call on the Martindales. Still they said nothing about Mary. It was a chance missed and it is tempting to wonder whether there wasn't something else about her which they were trying to keep secret.

In August of that year Ford's mother took him off to Germany again and it was on their return that Madox Brown died. Ford subsequently spent some time travelling in England but was back in London by January 1894. He resumed his courtship and the pace of events quickened beyond anyone's contriving. In February he had a silly row with Dr Martindale about which cloak Elsie should wear and in March Dr Martindale forbade them to meet any more. Ford responded extravagantly in a letter to Elsie: . . . 'we can always cut our throats and have it over . . . at worst there's a garter – or a second storey window – or your hair – your soft hair, that too would be like kisses.' This is all right so long as no one feels obliged to do anything about it, and no one did. Instead, he loitered outside Elsie's house and took her off to Madox Brown's old house, returning her only after Dr Martindale had promised not to lock her up again.

On the 16th March 1894 Elsie and Mary travelled by train to the Martindales' house at Winchelsea. They had to change at Ashford and while doing so Elsie gave Mary the slip and boarded a London train. Her daughter, Katharine Hueffer Lamb, was later to say that her mother had not planned to elope but simply to flee from her parents, intending to stay with aunts in Carlisle until her parents agreed she could go on seeing Ford. She seems to have been met in London by Olive Garnett's lawyer brother, Robert, who got her across London and on a train to Bath. She subsequently stayed in Clifton with some Garnett cousins, then in Gloucester with Mrs Garnett's retired maid.

It is very likely that Elsie's flight was planned because the Garnetts were much more Ford's friends than hers and it would have been through him that their assistance was arranged. It is also significant that although she and Ford were apparently happy to confide in the Garnetts they apparently did not confide in Mary. If they did, Mary's reactions – alarm and mystification – and her subsequent telegraphing to her father were a very convincing act.

What might have changed Elsie's plans was her father's response once he believed she really had gone. He did not take Mary's alarms fully seriously and only believed them when he received a telegram from a family friend, the composer Elgar, who was then living in Kent and who confirmed that one daughter was missing. Dr Martindale promptly had Elsie made a ward of court and took proceedings against Ford to prevent their seeing each other. He also hired private detectives to trace her, without result. Ford heard about the proceedings and sought Robert Garnett's help; they both travelled down to see Elsie. When at Easter the time came to move her to Gloucester, Garnett went alone to help since everyone seems to have been at pains to see that there should be no question of impropriety. It was Garnett's firm that notified Dr Martindale that his daughter had not been kidnapped by Ford but was staying with a respectable lady.

Ten days before Elsie's flight Ford's fairy tale, *The Queen Who Flew*, had been published. Everyone involved in the drama was excited and novelistic comparisons were made. Indeed, they all felt they were taking part in a novel. They were all young: Robert Garnett was twenty-eight, Olive twenty-two, Ford twenty and Elsie seventeen. The heady days continued up to and beyond Ford and Elsie's marriage in a registry office in Gloucester on 7th May, 1894, where they lied about their ages. The honeymoon was in the Doone Valley in Exmoor and at nearby Lynton. They returned to London to face Dr Martindale's proceedings and the sale of Madox Brown's effects.

Dr Martindale failed to get Elsie made a ward of court but he did get a court order forbidding further intercourse, which meant that Elsie and Ford had to live separately until the order was suspended in June. That was not quite the end of the legal story because Ford had contempt charges outstanding against him, a result of his conniving with a journalist friend to publicise the link between the elopement and *The Queen Who Flew*. A number of papers carried the story and the court proceedings were reported in *The Times*. The judge was irritated but in the end lenient, and Ford was let off with having to pay costs.

There were thus nearly two months – 16th March to 7th May – between Elsie's flight and her marriage, which lends weight to her daughter's assertion that elopement was not at first the aim. Additionally, Olive Garnett's reaction to the decision to marry was: 'I myself do not see what else was to be done, considering their position, Elsie will at any rate be happier'. This seems fairly conclusive since, whatever the plan was, the Garnetts had been privy to it from the start.

Olive and Elsie were to become lifelong friends but at that time they did not know each other at all well. Olive was still eagerly gathering information, such as this from Robert: 'He says she is most attractive. Sketches, sings beautifully when she has any voice, is full of fun, walks well and looks so lovely that people in the street turn around to look at her. But he also thinks her hard, extravagant, very youthful, changeable, loving only Ford and him to distraction.'

The last sentence is the earliest of several descriptions of Elsie which emphasise a certain hardness. Douglas Goldring compared her with Mary Tudor and Ford himself is sometimes said to have drawn on her for some of his severer female characters. Also, she was early described as 'serious' in comparison with her vivacious sister. But it would be easy to be unjust: Elsie was a devoted and loyal wife who tried very hard and had a great deal to put up with, not only from her husband but also from ill-health. In her youth she dressed with some flamboyance and during those early court appearances she wore a feather in her hat – a tribute, it was assumed, to Ford's fairy tale of that name. She was to be a published author and translator. In the early years of their marriage they made music together, he on the piano and she singing a fine mezzo-soprano.

Another feature of this affair was that touch of the absurd which seemed so often to follow him and of which he was ruefully and humorously aware. When he was in the Army he was about to defend a soldier at court-martial but the soldier went violently mad the night before, tried to strangle his father and bit Ford. Ford commented in a letter that if there was any trouble around, it usually seemed to find him. When he died a drunken gravedigger buried him in the wrong place, of which Janice Biala remarked, 'That was Ford all over.' It is tempting to think that getting married and being forbidden intercourse was also Ford all over. When he was trying to get divorced, he was virtually ordered to resume it.

Also typical was the ambiguity about his role in the events leading to his marriage. Indeed, in the first stages of the drama there is curiously little evidence of his reactions. It seems likely that he was taken by surprise by Dr Martindale's legal action – he broke the news to Robert Garnett on top of a bus – and, as often when he was under stress, he may simply have absented himself for some of the time. Certainly he did not see much of Elsie though this could have been so as not to reveal her whereabouts to the private detectives and not to compromise her more than she had been already. Although there is no doubt that he wanted to marry her, he probably would not have chosen to do it in the way it happened. Like many deeply unconventional people, Ford was a respecter of proprieties and liked to see things done properly. At that time of his life he might well have wanted a grand church wedding, though whether Roman Catholic or Anglican (Elsie's tradition) is a moot point. It is significant that Olive, his confidante throughout, did 'not see what else was to be done'. The implication is that they married because they felt they had to, Elsie's position being otherwise intolerable.

Once things were under way, however, he seems to have thrown himself into them and to have become very excitable. Whereas in court Elsie was outwardly composed, Ford was 'pink and white and limp – he had been obliged to take brandy beforehand'. Olive added that at times he hardly seemed to know what was going on. This was one of the effects on him of confrontations: they so appalled him that his overheated imagination would seize up and he would participate as in a daze. When he was at his quietest and most apparently detached and haughty, he was usually making a great effort not to go to pieces.

His ruse to publicise his novel by getting it linked with the court proceedings was a success, despite the contempt charges. For most of his life he had a horror of publicising his private concerns and it was torture for him to hear them debated in the public way they often were (his divorce attempt, as well as his marriage, featured in *The Times*). On the other hand, he was very happy to see his books publicised in any way he could, though he didn't usually manage to do it so successfully as to make national news.[1]

Olive wrote an account of a dinner she had with him in the month of Elsie's flight: 'It seemed to be tacitly agreed that we were real friends, & meant to take and enjoy just for the moment what we found good in one another. Trouble behind, trouble ahead, & that lent a zest to the present, just this little oasis of time – a dinner – in which we might rest, & which we were wise enough to make the most of . . . I had never found Ford so delightful, so good, the ideal so near and conversation so enthralling. I shall never forget that dinner.' This gives a powerful impression of the effect that his conversational intimacy could have. It is almost possible to hear his own words behind Olive's – 'this little oasis of time . . . in which we might rest.' His chameleon sensitivity meant that he was always able to identify with those with whom he talked, and he could often excite them to sympathy with him.

Thus, at the age of twenty, he was the author of four published books and a volume of poetry, and was married.

[1] On only one other occasion – after he had left Elsie – did he lower his guard enough to permit publicity about his marital affairs. The effect then was disastrous, not only for himself.

SIX

The Romney Marsh was more remote then than now. Stretching along the southern coast of Kent, it was known for its smuggling, its sheep, its Martello towers and the closeness (in the sense of hostility to outsiders) of its people. Since then the elms have died, the hamlets, hump-backed farms and squat churches are more visible and the four-wheel-drive tractors and the motor car have ensured that nothing is undisturbed and nowhere distant. In later life Ford wrote nostalgically about the clouds crossing from the west to fill the huge sky, the driving rain and the glimpse of ships' sails beyond the sea wall at Lydd. The skies are still as big and the sea wall is still there but the horizon is broken now by pylons leading from the power station at Dungeness. There are caravan parks and holiday camps at Camber, the pubs have music and fruit machines, the old rectories are sold off. But you can still find rookeries, dykes and ditches, lonely churches, sheep's wool on the hawthorns, places of haunting stillness, Armageddon sunsets, frosts that bite in mist and silence. It was there that Ford and Elsie went in the summer of 1894. They were to spend the next decade on or near the Marsh.

After a short holiday in Germany they had walked from Hythe on the eastern edge of the Marsh inland to the village of Aldington and its neighbour Bonnington. Both villages are on low hills that look out towards the sea. In Bonnington they took Bloomfield Villa (now Fir Trees Villa), a bare house in a hollow, damp and cold. They were there for a year and a half. When Olive Garnett visited she found them cheerfully playing at being bohemian Pre-Raphaelites, with Ford wearing D. G. Rossetti's cape and Elsie a costume 'that looks as if it had come from an old street scene at the Lyceum'. They were known locally as 'the Frenchies'. There was no drainage and drinking water had allegedly to be fetched from about a mile away. Ford cleaned their boots by dropping them into a well. They lay in bed hiding from the sweep when he came for his money, and Elsie – no doubt a distressing and unaccustomed experience – had to hide from the butcher. At a time when Lloyd George estimated that £3 per week was an adequate minimum wage for a man with a family, the Hueffers were living on £2. One half of this was subsidy from Ford's mother, who had promised £4 a week but had had to reduce it in order to cope with Oliver's already daunting financial indiscretions. Elsie, at seventeen, ran an orderly house – Ford observed that she would have made an excellent hospital matron – but he was neither an orderly nor a cheap husband. He ate and drank heartily and looked on domestic arrangements with a certain detached nonchalance. 'I love luxury', he was later to remark, 'but I hate comfort.' It was true. Throughout his life he was never much troubled by the lack of flushing lavatories, hot water, electric light, furniture or heating, but the lack of decent claret, a good dinner and a view was an altogether more serious matter. He had, additionally, a positive talent for domestic disorganisation: 'I once told Fordie,' Ezra Pound was to say[1] 'that if he were placed naked and alone in a room without furniture, I would come back in an hour and find total confusion.'

Ford was hard up for most of the rest of his life and he got poorer as he got older. What seems odd now is that neither he nor any of his associates, who were often just as hard up, ever considered getting a job. In fairness, he had thought about careers while still in his teens but had been discouraged. Perhaps it was assumed that artists ought not to have to work at anything except their art. It is unlikely to have been simply because they regarded themselves as gentlemen who were above work, since Uncle William Rossetti and a number of the Garnetts had jobs (and even brother Oliver did, after his fashion). It does appear, though, that Ford and many of his contemporaries regarded themselves as professional artists in a sense that might not have been recognised a century or so before, in that the serious business of rendering

[1] V. S. Pritchett, *The Working Novelist*

reality was a vocation beyond the fashioning of entertainment or engendering of social reform. Even if they could not make a reasonable living it was still their duty to persevere, like a priesthood.

It is difficult to say at which point Ford came to think of himself wholeheartedly as a writer. By the end of the first year of marriage the process had clearly started but whether he saw it as his sole future or whether it was still something he was doing, like his musical interest and his early poems, while waiting for the serious business of life to start, is hard to say. But write he did. During 1895 he wrote both an unpublished novel and most of his biography of Ford Madox Brown.

This latter came to him unsought. It had been suggested by Longman's to William Morris, who had refused it, then to William Rossetti, who refused it and suggested his wife, who died. For Ford it was a labour of love. It is long, painstaking, illustrated, indexed, formal and self-effacing (so self-effacing as to refer to his own *The Brown Owl* as a 'book by one of his grandsons'). He ends on a sentimental and affectionate note that, like much of what he wrote, was prophetic of his own life:

> During a long life he received little honour, and few honours, and was in some ways a singularly unlucky man. But he managed to work on, to do good work, and, as he quaintly phrased it, 'to go to bed with both ears on'. Moreover, he remained to the end of his life young in his mind and, that being so, perhaps the gods loved him after all.

Despite having helped with the book, Edward Garnett didn't like it. Olive recorded his reaction: 'German – cumberous – slovenly – vague – will generalise about things of which he knows nothing etc.' He didn't really like Ford, either, though in youth and early manhood they saw quite a lot of each other and Garnett had discerned Ford's talent in *The Shifting of the Fire*. They both had a genius for discovering unknown talent and, as a publisher's reader, Garnett must have been one of the best ever. They respected without ever really liking each other. Garnett later confessed to a physical distaste for Ford and there does seem to have been something visceral about their mutual unease. 'A friend to me mine enemy is,' Ford said of Garnett in a letter to Stanley Unwin in 1937. 'He was a pretty vindictive foe to me – or rather of what I stand for, but I had a certain affection for him.' Garnett was a bespectacled, thoughtful-looking man, with his own equivalent of Ford's domestic nonchalance. According to his son, David (*The Golden Echo*), he frequently walked naked about the house, greeted guests with his flies unbuttoned and never shared a bedroom with his wife.

There was, Olive Garnett thought, much love and contentment in Bloomfield Villa despite poverty, privation, damp and, later, Elsie suffering a miscarriage. She perhaps thought that Ford had found in Elsie the rest and peace he longed for in one of his early poems, 'Du Bist die Ruh' ('You are Rest and Peace', Ford's translation of Rückert). She noted, however, what she called Elsie's 'masculine powers' and her 'treating Ford like a well-meaning baby', something for which Elsie was mocked by Edward. She noted also that Elsie had had a dream that she rather than Mary had been left at the station; and, what is more, left by Ford and Olive.

But twenty-six years later, when writing his biography of Joseph Conrad, Ford referred to these first few years on the Marsh as 'the most depressing period' of his life. Despite his tendency towards superlatives and exaggeration, it is not difficult to imagine that, appearances apart, it might have been true. This is not to say that his love for Elsie had diminished, though it might have, so much as that there were sufficient other reasons for unhappiness. One might have been the corrosive worry about money which so often spreads like mildew through a marriage; another might have been the attitude of his parents-in-law (he and Elsie attempted a reconciliation with them at Christmas 1894, which failed); another was perhaps his own aspirations as a writer (Was that what he really was? Would he be any good at it? Would he *sell*?); yet another, his sudden assumption of responsibility for a life or lives other than his own; finally, the sheer hard work. On this last point, apart from his unpublished novel and the biography, there is evidence that he had also begun the unpublished *Seraphina* by 1896. This was a story about smugglers and pirates which Edward

Garnett was rightly to tell him was unpublishable but on which Ford's and Conrad's subsequent collaboration, *Romance*, was to be based.

It could be that he was disillusioned with marriage, although there is no early hard evidence. They were both very young and may have found rural confinement, even though friends visited, an unexciting end to a forbidden courtship. He suffered from eye trouble and was to develop a history of such ailments during periods of stress. It may also have been the case that being young simply didn't suit him, that he found it more or less permanently unsettling. In many of the books he wrote before his mid-forties there are longings for rest and peace which become less common later as fulfilment of one sort or another takes their place. There are people who appear to have an ideal age at which they are most fully themselves, confidently and attractively engaged with the world while firing evenly is, as it were, on all cylinders within; Ford's time was still a long way off.

Whatever his state of mind, he didn't stop noticing what went on around him. The observations of the country and its people which so vividly inform such books as *Return to Yesterday*, *Women and Men*, *The Spirit of the People* and *The Heart of the Country*, were begun during this period; so too, perhaps, was his detailed interest in the area which resulted in *The Cinque Ports*. Despite his youth and despite his playing at the bohemian Pre-Raphaelite 'Frenchie' – which probably aroused local suspicion and hostility – he could always get people to talk to him. He became adept at conveying the atmosphere of place and personality in a few sentences. Much of the village of Bonnington, he wrote in *Return to Yesterday*, had been built on common land:

> But this common land had long since been squatted on so that it was a maze of little hawthorn hedges surrounding little closes. Each close had a few old apple or cherry trees, a patch of potato ground, a cabbage patch, a few rows of scarlet runners, a few plants of monthly roses, a few plants of marjoram, fennel, borage or thyme. And in each little patch there stood a small dwelling. Mostly these were original squatters' huts built of mud, whitewashed outside and crowned with old thatched roofs

> on which there grew grasses, house leeks or even irises. There were a great many of these little homes beneath the September sunshine, and it was all a maze of the small green hedges.

Despite the spoliation, most English villages are probably in a better state of repair now than they ever were and the few thatches that remain would not be permitted to sprout grasses. His mention of this is reminiscent of the description by John Clare nearly a century earlier of green thatched villages. We would never nowadays think of roofs as green nor of cottages as squatters' huts.

In more than one of his books, most notably in *Return to Yesterday*, he describes Meary Walker, a countrywoman he got to know. He writes about her with a quite unsentimental understanding, sympathy and respect. The result, over a few pages, is a vivid impression of personality:

> Her face was as large, as round and much the same colour as a copper warming pan. Her mouth was immense and quite toothless except for one large fang and, as she smiled cheerfully all the time, her great gums were always to be seen. Her shoulders were immense and moved with the heave and roll of a great bullock. This was the wisest and on the whole the most estimable human being that I ever knew at all well . . . she also told me that we can't have everything and that the only thing to do is to 'keep all on gooing'.

At about the time of the First World War Ezra Pound remarked that much of the best of Ford's writing was to be found in forgotten paragraphs here and there, buried deep in books that had never been widely read. This is particularly true of his writing about rural scenes where, though his perspective is that of a gentlemanly sub-species of squire (an assumed perspective because he was, of course, a Londoner with a cosmopolitan background and education), his observations have the insight born of sympathy. In a poem of that period, 'The Peasant's Apology', he excuses the bitterness of peasant humour:

Down near the earth
On the steaming furrows
Things are harsh and black enough
Dearth there is and lack enough,
And immemorial sorrows
Stultify sweet mirth
Till she borrows
Bitterness and blackness from the earth.

After a few more years of it he was to write 'The Soliloquy of the Small Farmer' ('From the Soil'):

I wonder why we toiled upon the earth
From sunrise until sunset, dug and delved,
Crook-backed, cramp-fingered, making little marks,
On the unmoving bosoms of the hills,
And nothing came of it. And other men
In the same places dug and delved and ended,
As we have done; and other men just there
Shall do the self-same things until the end.
I wonder why we did it . . . Underneath
The grass that fed my sheep, I often thought
Something lay hidden, some sinister thing
Lay looking up at us as if it looked
Upwards thro' quiet waters; that it saw
Us futile toilers scratching little lines
And doing nothing. And maybe it smiled
Because it knew that we must come to this . . .
I lay and heard the rain upon the roof
All night when rain spelt ruin, lay and heard
The east wind shake the windows when that wind
Meant parched up land, dried herbage, blighted wheat,
And ruin, always ruin creeping near
In the long droughts and bitter frosts and floods.
And when at dawning I went out-o-doors
I used to see the top of the tall shaft
O' the work house here, peep just above the downs,
It was as if the thing were spying, waiting,

Watching my movements, saying, 'You will come,
Will come at last to me.' And I am here . . .
And down below the Thing lay there and smiled;
Or no, it did not smile; it was as if,
One might have caught it smiling, but one saw
The earth immoveable, the unmoved sheep
And senseless hedges run like little strings
All over hill and dale . . .

Whether writing prose or verse on such subjects he did so with a naturalness and simplicity often lacking in his more contrived lesser fiction, where he was being more consciously artistic and where his concern with form could lead to a merely formal effect – technically admirable, sometimes, but lacking substance. When he sets out simply to describe a person or a place he does it very well; but when he sets out to 'render' that person the result sometimes draws attention away from the subject and towards the method. Fortunately, this was not always the case.

There were escapes from Bonnington. He had the use of a London flat which he shared with Harrison Cowlishaw, an architect who was brother-in-law to Edward Garnett. Also, relations with the Martindales were re-established. They visited Bonnington with Mary, and Ford and Elsie were entertained at Winchelsea. Ford also wrote to and called on Henry James at Rye, possibly because he hoped James would give a favourable notice of his biography of Ford Madox Brown but no doubt also in genuine admiration. His friendship with James, which was to blossom and to wither, did not begin until 1901 when he and Elsie moved to Winchelsea but good relations were established before then. Ford was one of the first to be told in December 1897 of James's move from the Vicarage to Lamb House, and he was invited to call.

In October 1896 he and Elsie found a much more satisfactory house at Pent Farm, Postling, only a few miles from Bonnington. They had found it while cycling. Dr Martindale, now a concerned and perhaps even fond father-in-law, was relieved because he had been worried about the damp at Bloomfield Villa (particularly, no doubt, because of Elsie's history of tuberculosis). The position of the Pent – according to Ford 'under the most magnificent sheep downs near Canterbury' (*sic*), and according to Elsie 'at the foot of those bleak downs we used to see from Aldington Corner' – was and is a good one. It is on the Pilgrims' Way about half a mile west of Postling, has a stream, a pond, a farmyard near but separate and a view across the fields to the railway in the middle distance (in those days steam, of course). The front door, which is at the side, used to look on to a great thatched tithe barn, one of the largest in southern England, which later burned down and has now been replaced by a modern version. The thatch was a haven for rats which could be seen running along and through it all day. Later, when Conrad was living at the Pent – Ford having sub-let it to him at a small rent – they used to stand in the garden together and take pot-shots at the rats. Ford didn't recall that either of them ever hit one though he did say that he once fired at a repulsively large grandfather rat as it dragged itself across the lane, and that the creature simultaneously died. He thought it probably suffered a heart attack at the sound of the shot but it was logged as a kill and referred to ever after as 'Ford's rat'.

Elsie was pleased with the new house. There was plenty of room for their furniture, it wasn't damp and the rooms were large: '. . . a huge kitchen,' she wrote to Olive, 'quite twenty feet I should think and a large pantry. Five good-sized bedrooms.' Ford liked it, too. The kitchen had a brick floor and was homely, there were beams and ingles to be exposed and, with help, he set about 'restoring it on the most approved lines to its original antique condition of great rafters and huge ingles with ratchets and crocks.' Both he and Conrad found it a good place in which to live and write: there was room enough inside, a lawn to pace upon, a stream to ponder and a view. The steep slope of the North Downs immediately behind it is now tree-covered but would then have been more plainly visible. The tops are still for grazing, the climb is brisk and the views good. The railway line might also have made a difference about how they felt about being in the country, a daily reminder that although they had peace and quietness London and the world were reachable. The popular image of writers burying themselves in the country in order to write and see no one is only occasionally accurate. Most writers seek routine and freedom from bother but few seek real isolation for anything but short periods. Writing is a lonely business and they usually like to come from it towards people. Ford was certainly no exception; he was gregarious, interesting and interested. His self-discipline was already such that he could get on with the work in hand regardless of what was happening around him. Though sympathetic, intuitive and, like his mother, everlastingly helpful, he had the necessary selfishness.

The help he had in exposing beams and so on was another of his rural discoveries, Ragged Arse Wilson, whose nickname was given him 'because of the frailty of his nether garments'. He was 'singularly handsome, dark, with a little beard like Shakespeare's and that poet's eyes. He was slow, soft-spoken, and very gentle. In years I never knew him run or lose his temper and, for sure, he kept on going . . . I never knew that man not working. Even after supper in his great stuffed chair, between the fire and lamp, with his pipe going he would be netting onion-bags, making rabbit snares, fashioning axe-helves . . . there was nothing he could not do, patiently and to perfection. He was a wonderful gardener; he could make a stake-and-hedge better than any other man; he could get out of the underwood more of the fourteen kinds of woodcraft than any other man in the Weald of Kent . . . He was an admirable thatcher, a careful waggoner, a wonderfully good shepherd. He could lay bricks, cut out rafters, plaster, hang paper, paint, make chains, corner-cupboards, fish, poach, snare, brew, gather simples, care for poultry, stop foxes' earths . . . There was nothing he could not do but write, and later in life he taught himself to read – after he had discovered that with the aid of a pair of old spectacles he could tell a great A from a bull's foot . . . he had his meals with me; where he slept I never knew . . . I think he was happy.'

It sounds more likely that Ford was assistant to Wilson than the other way round.

His interest in these characters, his eye for the detail, for the comic, the exaggerated and the pathetic prompts the question as to why he didn't write novels about them. He had the eye and the ear, the sympathy and the imagination and he had the raw material – we have only to think what Dickens would have made of Ragged Arse or of Shakin' Ben, the village idiot who was fed by the cottagers and of whose intriguing ruination by 'the bad gels of Rye' we have, alas, no detail. They would have been household names – though Ragged Arse's would have had to change – and the subjects of musicals, the epitomes of established 'types'. Or consider what Hardy might have done with Meary Walker, who crawled seven miles from hospital with a broken leg to tend her dying man and to see to her hens: 'She told me also that her husband had died fifteen years before of the sting of a viper, that his poor old leg went all like green jelly up to the thigh before he died and that he had been the best basket-maker in all Kent.' Ford wrote or co-wrote thirty-two novels; there should have been room for these characters.

He would have argued that this whole approach was wrong. Good novelists, he would have said, do not choose their subjects in the way in which they might choose their next pair of shoes or their holiday; rather, their subjects choose them and novelists must write 'with the extreme of simplicity that is granted to you, and you must write of subjects that spring at your throat'.[1]

Secondly, he might have argued that novels set in rural poverty would indulge in special pleading and would therefore be less effective: 'That great genius, Dickens, thrashed oppression and shams with the resplendent fury of an Isaiah . . . But those words of propaganda had either no literary value at all or when, as in the case of Dickens, they did have the literary value that genius can infuse in work however faulty, their work itself suffered by the very intensity of their reforming passions.'[1] He does not deny that novels can bring about social improvement but does assert that the social impact, which derives from artistic effect, is less the more overtly propagandist the novel. Issues and people were not simply black and white, as propaganda always demanded, and a good novelist would, in Ford's view, remain aloof, even cold, so that what was important could be *shown* but never *told*. He might have said that the best way to write about these rural characters was the very way he did, in his readable and memorable non-fiction.

Thirdly, and perhaps most importantly in his eyes, he would have argued that the best novels were not a matter of creating 'characters' in the Dickensian sense, nor of pleading causes. He didn't like what he saw as the English tradition of the interven-

[1] *The English Novel*

tionist, moralising author who uses characters to put over a view or makes a sentimental or humorous appeal to the reader which detracts from the main progression of the novel. Properly adult novels were not about the idiosyncrasies of character nor about causes, social, moral or political; they were a rendering of life, above and beyond all characters and causes, including them but not about them. 'Life' was what occurred in the interaction between the individual and the world; it was what happened to people as a result of their relations and of their beliefs and conventions. That was what the novel was supremely suited to render and the novelist could best show it if he kept himself, his comments and prejudices, out of his books.

For these reasons he found *Tess of the D'Urbervilles* as irritating as it was admirable because Hardy was not content mercilessly to render but intervened and pleaded. Hardy would presumably have written similarly in a novel about Meary Walker but if Ford had done so he would have depicted the evolution of an Affair, a part of life symptomatic of the essence but not of the whole, involving Meary, her ailing man, her friend Meary Spratt, a well-meaning but agonised squire and an outbreak of fowl-pest. There would have been no tragic heroine but all would have been victims of the intricate, delicate, destructive processes of life, the quintessence of which would be not dust, but anguish.

Of course, these were the principles and practices of Ford's maturity, which, as a very young man renting a house in the country with his even younger wife and lacking any intellectual society but that that he had always known, he had yet to evolve.

SEVEN

1897 brought to Pent Farm the benefits of a death and a birth. The death occurred in February when Ford's German Uncle Leopold, who had encouraged him in his entry into the Roman Catholic Church, left the three young Hueffers three thousand pounds each. Until not long before the First World War, Ford always had expectations of his German relatives. He had probably been encouraged in this since childhood and though the expectations were not, as this bequest demonstrated, by any means unrealistic, they never provided him with the financial independence for which he hoped.

Nevertheless, three thousand was a very useful sum and Ford began to spread his wings. He took up golf at Hythe, made friends with the politicians Macnamara and Masterman and entertained on a larger scale. One guest was Jayme Batalha-Reis, the Portuguese Consul General on whom Tomas Castro of *Romance* was modelled. Ford still kept up the 'Frenchie' image but by now had added his more or less life-long agricultural ambitions. Not that these were great – 'I was at that time in a severely Small Producer frame of mind' – but towards the end of his life he preached the gospel that the world would be a better place if everyone else did the same: 'I am not, you understand, a pessimist: I don't want our civilization to pull through. I want a civilization of small men each labouring two small plots – his own ground and his own soul. Nothing else will serve my turn.'[1] In September he grew a beard.

Meanwhile, on the 3rd July 1897, Elsie was delivered of Christina Margaret Madox Hueffer. It had not been an easy pregnancy and she had been ill for much of the time. At one point their servant-girl, Annie, was also pregnant and ill, and Ford found himself

[1] *Provence*.

running the house and acting as sick-nurse. He probably did it quite well. It wouldn't have bothered him that the wash-house was outside or that Ragged Arse Wilson may have been chiselling away at another fireplace; he was already a good cook and he was good with the sick. In fact, his culinary interests proved to be life-long and he later told Janice Biala that an uncle had employed a man who had been a cook in the Vatican and that he had learned to cook from him. In Paris he became famed for a punch he could make and he had a favourite chicken recipe involving two pounds of garlic. However, he did have some help during this period of the two pregnancies: Mary, Elsie's sister, came and stayed.

But still he worked. Some of the material that went into *The Cinque Ports* was probably being prepared at this time (Olive Garnett helped him with sources) and not long after Christina's birth he cycled across Kent to Guildford to see Henry Hyde, who was to illustrate the book. He may also have been researching a planned biography of Henry VIII since many state papers had recently become available and he was intrigued by both the king and the period. He regarded it as the start of the modern world and Henry and some of those around him as essentially the first modern men. He may also have sensed parallels with his own times – the break-up of the old order, the collapse (as he saw it) of a belief, the beginnings of new ways. His father had looked like Henry and during the mid-nineties he often went to sleep thinking or dreaming of the king. He abandoned his plans for a biography on discovering that A. F. Pollard was already at work on one but the yeast continued to ferment. The result was *The Fifth Queen* trilogy, still a decade ahead. There is some evidence that at this period he saw himself more as an historian than a novelist; what is more, he never forsook his historical interest and it was one of his greatest disappointments that his *A History of Our Own Times* was never published in his lifetime.[1]

It may be that learning about Henry led Ford to certain conclusions as to how little we can know other people, conclusions crucial to his later fiction. He said he thought he knew practically everything there was to know about Henry, that he dreamt of

[1] It is now, thanks to Carcanet, nearly half a century after his death.

him, had almost lived with him for years, yet felt that for all the information and all the detail he really knew no more than that Henry was a stout man with a red beard who always went first through the door. Thus the surface impression that, in a gleam, reveals the truth within.

He and Elsie kept in regular touch with Edward Garnett and his wife, Constance, who had moved to High Chart near Limpsfield, Surrey, and in March 1898 they sub-let the Pent to Walter Crane and moved to Gracie's Cottage, Limpsfield. The cottage was named after Constance Garnett's sister, who had gone abroad, and it had been built by Harry Cowlishaw. The Garnetts had also had a house built for themselves – in a wood and with a view – and the settlement became a rural intellectual outpost comprising Fabians, Russian dissidents, translators of Russian (most notably Constance, of course, but also Ford's sister, Juliet), writers and literati.

On the face of it, this might seem an odd move for Ford and Elsie. Edward Garnett's son, David, described in *The Golden Echo* the deep temperamental differences that had existed since childhood between the Garnetts and the Hueffers. The young Garnetts, he said, were 'sceptical, unworldly and over-critical', while the two Hueffer boys were 'credulous, worldly (without being worldly-wise) and over-confident'. The Garnetts thought the Hueffers were 'half egregious asses and half charlatans'; the Hueffers were increasingly exasperated by the Garnetts' 'sceptical attitude and their straight-laced almost puritanical contempt for success and notoriety which constituted the breath of romance for Ford and Oliver'. There was also the personal unease that developed between Ford and Edward.

But they had more in common than might be thought. They probably all seemed like 'Frenchies' to the locals, playing at romantic medievalism – Ford wore smock and gaiters at Limpsfield – and they came from the same background, had the same literary and cultural interests and the same assumption that the pursuit of those interests was the only life worth living. Their differences were like those within a family: deep enough on occasion but not so deep as to prevent the family from forming a united front in the face of adversity. It is possible, too, that they saw themselves as being in a more or less permanent state of opposition, or at least as torch-bearers in the van of a reluctant and often wilfully ignorant world. It was an arrogant assumption but not wholly unjustified.

It is also likely that Ford and Elsie missed the social and intellectual stimulus that had been an everyday part of life until marriage. Although they entertained at the Pent and were meeting and visiting more people, they were still not living amongst their own kind with the day-to-day contact that they had taken for granted before. They were probably in need of refreshment.

Edward Garnett called the place Dostoievsky Corner because of the number of Russians who visited, causing turmoil in the hearts of the ladies, including his wife's. One who came and stayed was the exile David Soskice, who eventually married Juliet Hueffer after he and his wife had divorced. People thought them ill-matched but it was a good marriage. Soskice was a lawyer, a factual man with a reputation for painstaking accuracy. David Garnett described how Soskice set out to learn about England from Ford, a process that was later to cause D. H. Lawrence much amusement. Apparently, Soskice would sit on the doorstep and take notes while Ford paced up and down, telling him that Britain's largest grain crop was rye, all of which was exported to the Continent, and that 'the most profitable crop in England was a very tall cabbage, the stalks of which supplied the walking out canes for soldiers in the British Army.' Such leg-pulling doesn't seem to have caused any lasting damage. Juliet and David prospered and one of their children achieved senior positions under both Attlee and Wilson.

It is also clear from David Garnett that Ford, though very much part of the scene, had nevertheless one foot outside it. He usually did. He kept ducks and made for them a pond out of a hip-bath, before which they used to queue to bathe. He named each after ladies of the Garnett family, which didn't entirely please: 'When Ford dug in the garden at Gracie's Cottage, the ducks stood round in a semi-circle, waiting to gobble up earthworms. "Lucy is so very greedy," Ford would pronounce in a sorrowful drawl, "she always manages to eat some of Gracie's share." "Katie was such a clumsy thing, she broke one of my tomato frames. Really, I could *not* feel fond of her so we had her roast on Sunday, rather tough." It was a simple way of teasing, but effective: 'My aunts would repeat such remarks to each other, but their laughter was not without a trace of indignation.'

Ford's appearance at that time struck David Garnett as 'tall and Germanic . . . with a pink and white complexion, pale, rather prominent blue eyes and a beard which I referred to when we first met as "hay on his face" . . . he was a most charming entertainer of my youth. He would suddenly squat and then bound after me like a gigantic frog. He could twitch one ear without moving the other – a dreadful but fascinating accomplishment.'

Seraphina, the pirate novel on which Ford was then working, had been suggested to him by Edward's father, Richard. As we have seen, Edward advised that it was unpublishable and Ford abandoned it. That and the collapse of his Henry VIII plan could not have made this an easy choice but he respected Edward's advice. An indication of how like members of the same family they were, in terms of not having much to hide, is provided by David in an account of a lunch his father had with Ford. It was probably at a later date than the Gracie's Cottage period and David must have had the account from his father:

> Ford was not necessarily lying, but his statistical principles were peculiar. On one occasion my father and he were having lunch in London when a successful journalist came up to them and Ford began to talk about the wonderful success of his last novel. The journalist enquired as to sales. 'It has sold twelve thousand copies in three weeks,' drawled Ford, 'and is still heading the list of best-sellers.' After the journalist had gone away, Edward asked Ford: 'How can you tell him such awful lies? You know we have sold only just over a thousand copies.' 'My dear Edward,' said Ford in his very slow drawl and his most dégagé manner, 'truth is relative. You and I knew that my book has done extraordinarily well to have sold over a thousand copies, but that fellow would never have understood that. When I told him it had sold twelve thousand copies, it astonished him to just the same degree that you and I are astonished by its having sold twelve hundred. Truth is relative.'

*

In this as in others of his tales, Ford's eye is on the right effect, not the right fact. It is as if he were writing a novel. It is not that he did not see the difference between the truth and what he said but that he chose on the basis of effect, as a novelist would. He was almost too much a novelist for his own good and carried his novelistic approach into history, being always prepared to create in order to get the right effect. Whether in talk or in writing, he was impressionistic, re-arranging the surface facts so as to give the effect that he thought important and most real. In the matter of the twelve thousand, however, there was no doubt another motive at work: a book could be 'talked up' then as now and few were immune to the custom. Ford actually believed in 'talking up' books, not only his own but any he admired; it was not to his eye a weakness or an unfortunate professional necessity but a positive duty, owed by all readers and writers to all good books.

Gracie's Cottage and The Cearne – the nearby house in which Edward Garnett lived – had, however, a more lasting effect on him than intellectual and social stimulation. He met there the American writer Stephen Crane, subsequently to be one of the group of the best known writers who lived on or near the Romney Marsh (James, Ford, Conrad and Wells were of the others). 'There are few men that I have liked – nay, indeed revered – more than Crane. He was so frail and so courageous, so preyed upon and so generous, so weighted down by misfortunes and so erect in his carriage. And he was such a beautiful genius.'

Crane was a lively, febrile iconoclast, author of a very successful war novel, *The Red Badge of Courage*. He was married to Dora, who had formerly run a bar in America and whom Ford liked, describing her as 'large, fair and placid'. (In fact, he usually mentions her in terms reminiscent of his description of Mark Tietjens's French wife in *Parade's End*, although Janice Biala believes that the painter Juan Gris's wife was the more likely inspiration.) Crane and Dora were already in debt, which deepened when they moved to Brede Place near Rye and Crane died there of tuberculosis in 1900. Ford afterwards said that it was being infected with the medieval romanticism of the Limpsfield community that led them to damp, debt and death in the ancient pile, where 'Mrs Crane wore hanging sleeves, hennings and pointed shoes. Beneath the refectory table were rushes where the dogs lay and fought for the bones that were dropped to them.'

But at Limpsfield Crane was still energetic and hopeful of repeating his early success. After a stuttering start he and Ford seemed to have got on well and when Ford was later accused of being patronising, Crane defended him: 'You must not mind Hueffer, that is his way. He patronises me; he patronises Mr Conrad; he patronises Mr James. When he goes to Heaven he will patronise God Almighty, but God Almighty will get used to it for Hueffer is all right!'[1]

More significant, though, was Ford's meeting with Conrad at Gracie's Cottage in the first week of September 1898. The introduction was performed by Edward Garnett and it changed their lives. The friendship lasted, with intermissions, until Conrad's death in 1924 and it had for them both aspects of a love-affair. Not in any sexual sense – something they would probably have found deeply distasteful – but in terms of affection, sympathy and intellectual endeavour. Whatever personal differences they may have had, dedication to their calling united them. They worshipped the same gods. It may be futile to try to say which was the more influenced or which benefited more, though it is the case that Ford was the more loving. Conrad at times depended on Ford and owed a great deal to him, some of which he acknowledged, and he certainly expressed affection on many occasions. But there was something equivocal about him, a reserve, a coldness, a selfishness. He was two-faced. He would write an affectionate letter and in the same week write coldly and dismissively of his correspondent in a letter to someone else. He could bestow and inspire affection but it is a matter of conjecture whether he really opened his heart – whether, in fact, there was much to be opened. Like Ford, perhaps like all writers, he had his own version of the necessary selfishness. Nevertheless, he gave enough of himself for Ford to love. Ford did so wholeheartedly and without reserve, in a way that brooks no question. He loved other people in his life and loved his art above all, but after his grandfather his deepest and

[1] quoted by Ford in *Return to Yesterday*

most lasting personal passions was probably his friendship with Joseph Conrad.

If it is futile to attempt a profit and loss account of the relationship, it is worthwhile looking at it in terms of areas of influence. For instance, in the three books on which they collaborated – *The Inheritors*, *Romance* and *The Nature of a Crime* – we have a fairly detailed record of who did what and how they wrote. Not surprisingly, the collaborations are by no means the best work of either, though each must have achieved a pretty good understanding of how the other worked. This was particularly the case with the more impressionable Ford. They constantly discussed style, books, paragraphs, sentences, words. Ford was on several occasions responsible for keeping Conrad going, not simply in terms of literary inspiration or technique but in terms of moral and physical support. He also helped him with his use of English (Conrad's reason for proposing their collaboration) and with certain of his books. Most of Conrad's best work was written during periods of their intimacy.

It is less easy to say what Conrad did for Ford. Despite Ford's throwaway statement to Herbert Read - 'I learned all I know of Literature from Conrad - and England has learned all it knows of Literature from me' – it is not clear what he actually learned, apart from how to write like Conrad when the need arose. They discovered a mutual enthusiasm for Flaubert (each had chunks by heart), and for such themes as The Invisible Author, The Importance of Style and The Necessity for High Art in the Novel. But these were not ideas Ford learned from Conrad though discussion no doubt heightened and elaborated them. Conrad did not help Ford with his books – he probably could not have even if wanted, since he was not a natural imitator – and he never helped Ford keep going in the way that Ford helped him. Conrad was no nurse of others, even at a distance. Some years later, when Ford was in Germany recovering from nervous collapse, Conrad wrote a letter which began: 'I am awfully grieved to hear of your state. Mine though not identical is just as bad.'

What he did, perhaps, was to help Ford find himself. Ford's literary career up to then was impressive in terms of productivity but unfocused and unsettled, as he was himself. He was still only twenty-four when he met the forty-one-year-old Conrad. He had yet to find his themes and his voice. He didn't find them immediately on meeting Conrad but in their friendship he found an intellectual seriousness that matched his own yearnings, as well as a dedication and companionship he had not found elsewhere. He also found someone who took him seriously yet with whom he could laugh and, more importantly, someone who needed him. It might not be going too far to say that until then Ford had felt un-needed; he had throughout his life an urge to help people, especially in the matter of intellectual or literary encouragement, and until then there had been no one who much needed that. Elsie needed him of course, but differently, and she could not anyway offer the intellectual stimulation of the mature Conrad. It may have been because he felt he owed so much of himself and of the direction of his life to that friendship, because Conrad helped solidify something in him which until then had been gaseous, that Ford was forever afterwards unstinting and generous in a way that Conrad, though fond, never was.

Conrad's dissenting note was sounded from the early years of their intimacy. They had been collaborating on *The Inheritors* and Conrad, within a few days of writing an affectionate letter to Ford, wrote to Edward Garnett: 'I set myself to look upon the thing [*The Inheritors*] as a sort of skit upon the sort of political (?!) novel, fools of the Morley Roberts sort do write. This is in my heart of hearts. And poor H was dead in earnest! O Lord. How he worked! There is not a chapter I haven't made him write twice – most of them three times over . . . and in the course of that agony I have been ready to weep more than once. Yet not for him. Not for him.'

When Garnett published this letter after Conrad's death, despite having been asked by Conrad to burn it, Ford was deeply hurt. He wrote: 'My affection for Conrad was so great and remained so unchanged that I have never been able really to believe in his death . . . he could not really get on without me any more than I could or can get on without him, and I do not shrink from saying that at this moment I cannot see for tears.'

Conrad's letters were designed to please his readers; what he really felt is hard to get at. It may even be that his heart came to life only in proximity to an audience. On the other hand, there is no doubt what Ford felt. His love for Conrad was a love that did not seek its own and Conrad, so good at making others see, himself saw only in part.

EIGHT

Garnett had introduced them during the first week of September 1898. Ford described it in *Return to Yesterday*:

> Conrad came round the corner of the house. I was doing something at the open fireplace in the house-end. He was in advance of Mr Garnett, who had gone inside, I suppose, to find me. Conrad stood looking at the view. His hands were in the pockets of his reefer-coat, the thumbs sticking out. His black torpedo beard pointed at the horizon. He placed a monocle in his eye. Then he caught sight of me.
>
> I was very untidy in my working clothes. He started back a little. I said, 'I'm Hueffer.' He had taken me for the gardener.
>
> His whole being melted together in enormous politeness, his spine inclined forward; he extended both hands to take mine. He said: 'My dear faller . . . Delighted . . . Ench . . . ante.' He added: '*What* conditions to work in. Your admirable cottage . . . Your adorable view.'
>
> It was symbolic that the first remark he should make to me should be about conditions in which to work.

Ford and Elsie left Limpsfield very shortly after this. He didn't like being reformed. The evangelising Fabian atmosphere 'disgusted me with the life of the Intelligentsia as lived in the London suburbs . . . meetings sanctioning the marriages of members – in the case of the Committee usually with wealthy American women – were held. Mr Shaw's marriage was there sanctioned.'

A week later, back at The Pent, he received Conrad's letter proposing collaboration. This seems to have been suggested to Conrad by Edward Garnett and W. E. Henley. Conrad had told them of the difficulty he had in writing English and of 'the particular devil that spoils my work for me'. Garnett, knowing Ford's unpublishable *Seraphina*, thought there was in it material to be worked up into something publishable by the pair of them. Henley had also said, according to Conrad: 'Why don't you ask H to collaborate with you? He is the finest stylist in the English language of today.'

Ford makes clear in his autobiographical writings that he was sure Henley had never said this, nor anything like it.[1] It was in fact an early example of Conradian oriental politeness. Ford's description of the arrival of Conrad's letter is worth quoting, not simply because it marks the beginning of the collaboration but because it illustrates his novelistic approach to his own history. This is not to say that it didn't happen as he described so much as that, whether it happened or not, he makes you hope it did:

> In the Pent Farm beneath the North Downs, there was a great kitchen with a wavy brick floor. On this floor sat a great many cats: they were needed to keep down the rats and they got some milk of a morning. Each morning a wild robin with a red breast and a greenish-khaki body would hop, not fly, across the floor of the kitchen between the waiting cats. The cats would avert their glances, pulsing their sheathed claws in and out. The robin would hop to the inner doorway of the kitchen, across an angle of the low dining-room and so up to the bed-room stairs. When the maid with the morning letters and the tea-tray opened the bed-room door the robin would fly through the low, dark room and perch on a comb stuck into a brush on the dressing-table, against the long, low leaded window. It awaited crumbs of bread and tiny morsels of lump-sugar from the tea-tray. It had never been taught to go on these adventures. This robin attended the opening of the first letter that . . . the writer received from Joseph Conrad. The robin watched with its beady eyes the sheet of blue-grey paper with the large rather ornamental handwriting . . . it was afterwards drowned in a cream-jug which took away from its aspect of a supernatural visitant.

[1] though it is still quoted as an example of Fordian vanity

Everything about that passage – the detail, the build-up, the fate of the robin and the effect it had – is aimed at an effect. Whether it is accurate as a matter of record seems a not-quite-appropriate question, a little off the point. This can be said of much of Ford's autobiographical writing; factual truth becomes less important because of the sheer persuasiveness of the account, because of the preservation of the essential truth (Conrad did write that letter, The Pent was that kind of place, there were many rats) and because of the partial suspension of disbelief that vivid writing encourages. The unstated assumption is that the reader should attend to the creation, not to that which gave it rise.

The two men met and agreed to collaborate. Probably both were flattered, Ford because Conrad was a highly regarded novelist (though not yet very well known) and nearly old enough to be his father, Conrad because Ford was a young man with good literary connections, some success and an apparent authority on all things pertaining to England and Englishness. They talked, dined and talked, late into the night. They felt each other's minds and sympathies, probing, quoting, exchanging enthusiasms. They agreed on their three gods, Turgenev, Flaubert, Maupassant, agreed on how novels should be written and what poetry was. Conrad was

> small, rather than large in height; very broad in the shoulder and long in the arm; dark in complexion with black hair and a clipped black beard. He had the gestures of a Frenchman who shrugs his shoulders frequently. When you had really secured his attention he would insert a monocle into his right eye and scrutinise your face from very near as a watch-maker looks into the works of a watch. He entered a room with his head held high, rather stiffly and with a haughty manner, moving his head once semi-circularly. In this one movement he had expressed to himself the room and the contents; his haughtiness was due to his determination to master that room, not to dominate its occupants, his chief passion being the realisation of aspects of himself . . .

He might almost have been a character out of Conrad. They got on.

The arrangements for collaboration were completed by the beginning of October 1898. They included Ford's sub-letting The Pent to Conrad and his family so that they could leave their depressing house in Stratford-le-Hope, Essex. This was Fordian generosity: Conrad was not happy writing in Essex, Ford thought he would be able to write at The Pent, therefore he should have The Pent. It worked. Conrad turned out over a hundred thousand words in the next fourteen months, a considerable number for him since he normally wrote with difficulty, often in despair. The agreed rent was twenty pounds a quarter but – another typical feature of their relationship – it was not always paid.

Ford's eye infection recurred, preventing the Conrads moving in until the end of October. After that he and Elsie went on a cycling holiday in the South of France. On their return they stayed for a while with the Conrads although The Pent, as Jessie Conrad noted, was not large enough to house two families and two writers, each of whom wanted both privacy and communion apart from their families. Eventually, after a brief reversion to Gracie's Cottage, the Hueffers took another Aldington cottage called Stocks Hill. It was in a field and very damp but was near to Aldington Knoll with its recompensing view across the Marsh. Views were always important to Ford.

At this period money was not as scarce as it was to become. Ford and Elsie were still benefiting from Uncle Leopold's inheritance, her parents – now concerned and generous – were not too far away and Ford still had hopes of making money from literature. He was optimistic that the collaboration would produce a best-seller. Also, although he and Conrad started very quickly on re-writing *Seraphina* into *Romance* and then got into *The Inheritors*, which was mainly Ford's work, each was carrying on his own books at the same time. Conrad was under way with *Lord Jim* and Ford, with Edward Garnett's help (despite their mutual unease, they maintained for some years what appears to have been a friendly professional relationship), had found a publisher to commission *The Cinque Ports*. He was also planning a novel based on Oliver Cromwell and had interested a publisher, but the book was never written. It did, however, make an imaginary appearance in *The Inheritors*, where it was the result of collaboration between

Churchill and Grainger. The latter refers to it in terms which probably reflect how Ford had seen it: '. . . one of those glorious novels that one plans – a splendid thing with Old Noll as the hero or the heavy father'.

A number of those who knew them both disliked the collaboration from the start. Edward Garnett disapproved of their living and working in such proximity and after they had called on H. G. Wells at nearby Sandgate to tell him, Wells was provoked to cycle to Aldington in the spring of 1899 to express to Ford his disapproval. He feared that Ford would destroy Conrad's 'delicate oriental style'. Wells was already a successful and influential author, a voice to be reckoned with, and he had written very favourably of Conrad's *Almayer's Folly*. He had built Spade House at Sandgate and his book *The Invisible Man* had appeared in 1897. When Ford and Conrad had called on him

> . . . There was a curious incident. As we stood on the door-step of Mr Wells' villa, in the hesitant mind of those paying a state call, behold the electric bell-push, all of itself, went in and the bell sounded . . . Conrad exclaimed '*Tiens*! . . . The Invisible Man' and burst into incredible and incredulous laughter. In the midst of this the door opened before grave faces . . . the incident of the bell-push was of a nature that had a peculiar appeal to Conrad's humour. For years after, a translation of Mr Wells' book having appeared in Italian, you could never mention that author's name without Conrad saying, '*Tiens*!, . . . *L'Uomo Invisibile*' . . .

This has been quoted as an example of Ford's unreliability because what apparently happened was that Conrad pushed the bell and, as he recorded, 'an invisible finger kept the button down'. Also, Wells denied the story in a letter to the *Manchester Guardian* of 27th November, 1924; but it remains another good example of the partial relevance of fact.

Henry James was another who disapproved. When Olive Garnett and Elsie went to tea with him at Rye his verdict on the collaboration was: 'To me this is like a bad dream which one relates at breakfast. Their traditions and their gifts are so dissimilar.

Collaboration between them is to me inconceivable.' Following this pronouncement, 'The two ladies sipped their tea and ate their bread and butter, and no more was said upon the subject.'[1] There is evidence that these and similar judgements hurt Ford but they didn't stop the collaboration. He and Conrad thus began nearly a decade of intimacy.

The three books that resulted were not what was most important about the collaboration. They are readable, certainly, but they are likely to interest only readers who have a prior and detailed interest in their authors. Ford was primarily responsible for *The Inheritors* and *The Nature of a Crime*, whereas *Romance* is more truly a joint effort. The main interest of *The Inheritors* is that some of the major themes of Ford's personal and literary life become evident, as well as his political views on such events as the Boer War and the Belgian atrocities in the Congo. Central to the story is a hard, attractive woman and a man whose self-doubts focus on the likelihood that a writer or artist may devote his life to his work yet die without the recognition that is his due. Ford worried that the better his work, the less likely he was to be famous. He thought that Madox Brown was an example of this. Also, like his fictional hero, he was constantly distracted by journalism. In fact, he was very good at it; his articles are lively and fresh and often have the immediate appeal of good conversation. Being also something of a performer, it is likely that had he lived now television would have got him.

The Nature of a Crime was written considerably later, in 1906, but was not published until serialisation in *The English Review* in 1908–9, and not as a book until 1924. Like the other collaboration, it is in the first person. It is very short and is really a novel about Ford's life at the time of writing, taking the form of a love letter to a married woman whose situation resembled that of Elsie, who was in Rome at that time. His and Elsie's marriage was by then disintegrating. The first line is: 'You are, I suppose, by now in Rome.' The tone and language of the book are Fordian, the chronology – according to Moser – Conradian. Certainly, that first line is distinctively Fordian in its assumption of a quiet

[1] David Garnett, *The Golden Echo*

voice, its suggestion of weariness, perhaps even exhaustion, its detachment, and in its removal of the narrator from the time and place of the action. But though distinctively Fordian it is not Ford at his best. That 'I suppose' is unconvincing; it is a too obvious contrivance. Although it gets in the quietness, detachment and action-recollected-in-exhaustion feel that Ford wants, it does so in a manner that is too button-holing and lapel-clinging. The author is making the narrator speak with his own assumed drawl; it is not natural. Had he, for instance, written, 'You must be in Rome by now,' and then let the tone and detachment develop it would have been more convincing, as if he really had been writing to the lady rather than trying to draw attention to himself. That said, it is a striking first line and in so far as that is important – which it is – it succeeds.

There are other reasons why the book is worth looking at. Firstly, Ford wrote a poem called 'Views' on the same theme and the first few lines of the novel and first few of the poem stand comparison as a good illustration of how close his prose and poetry often were. The novel reads:

> You are, I suppose, by now in Rome. It is very curious how present to me are both Rome and yourself. There is a certain hill – you, and that is the curious part of it, will never go there – yet, yesterday, late in the evening, I stood upon its summit and you came walking from a place below. It is always midday here: the seven pillars of the forum stand on high, their capitals linked together, and form one angle of a square. At their bases lie some detritus, a broken marble line . . . your dress brushed the herbs . . .

The poem begins:

> Being in Rome I wonder will you go
> Up to the Hill. But I forget the name . . .
> Avantine? Pincio? No: I do not know.
> I was there yesterday and watched. You came.

The seven Pillars of the Forum stand
High, stained and pale 'neath the Italian heavens,
Their capitals linked up form half a square;
. . . Your dress just brushed the herbs . . .

He is a very underrated poet and he wrote too many, of course, this being certainly not one of his best. The tone is the same as in the novel but it works better in the poem because the more obvious contrivance of verse makes it more acceptable. More than that, the poem is an illustration of the quiet, informal, conversational, technically deft but seemingly seamless verse that Ford more or less pioneered in English.

He introduced the poetry of the everyday and anticipated the notion of the objective correlative some years before Eliot. He thought there should be nothing artificial about poetry but that it should be of its day and in the language of its day, while aiming at an absolute precision of observation and rendering. In a memorable passage in the introduction to the first edition of his *Collected Poems* he wrote that better as a subject than the comfrey under the hedge

> . . . the ash-bucket at dawn is a symbol of poor humanity, of its aspirations, its romance, its ageing and its death. The ashes represent the social fibres, the god of the hearth, of the slumbering, dawn populations; the orange peels with their bright colours represent all that is left of the little party of the night before, when an alliance between families may have failed to be cemented, or being accomplished may have proved a disillusionment or a temporary paradise. The empty tin of infant's food stands for birth; the torn up scrap of a doctor's prescription for death. Yes, even if you wish to sentimentalise, the dustbin is a much safer card to play than the comfrey plant.

That style of poetry we have come to take for granted but when he started writing it he was virtually alone. Pound acknowledged the poetic debt as, later, did Robert Lowell, Allen Tate, William

Carlos Williams and Basil Bunting, but few others have.[1]

He wrote poetry very casually and quickly. We have not only Janice Biala's testimony for this (his last group of poems, which includes some of his finest, was written for her) but also Robert Lowell's: 'He himself wrote poetry with his left hand – casually and even contemptuously.' The originals of the last group, called 'Buckshee', are hand written and have very few if any corrections. As with his prose, he would often sit and play patience, working it out, word for word, and then simply do it. He revised very little and disliked even proof-reading.

Another reason for lingering over *The Nature of a Crime* is that when the book finally came to be published in 1924 each author wrote a preface. Conrad was obviously wary; he thought the book too fantastic and referred to it as a 'fragment', but for him as for Ford what was important was the process of collaboration, not its results. His final paragraph reads:

> After signing these few preparatory words, I will pass the pen to him in the hope that he may be moved to contradict me on every point of fact, impression and appreciation. I said 'the hope'. Yes. Eager hope. For it would be delightful to catch the echo of those desperate, earnest, eloquent and funny quarrels which enlivened those old days. The pity of it is that there comes a time when all the fun of one's life must be looked for in the past!

Ford was inclined to be kinder to the book but felt nonetheless that he had to apologise for its rhetorical strain:

[1] The problem with the poetry as with so much of Ford's writing, is that no one knows it. It is typical of his publishing history that there are two editions of his collected verse, one published in 1913 and the other in 1936. The first was published in Britain and cannot be found outside the major libraries. The second, much more important, edition was published only in America and cannot be found in Britain at all. It was to have been published by OUP but became a casualty of war and publishing incompetence. In 1971 Basil Bunting edited a volume of selected Ford poems, published in America by the Pym-Randall Press, Cambridge, Massachusetts, but never in Britain. It is a useful book because Ford wrote far too many slack poems and without selection they tend to swamp his good ones.

And I should like to make the note that our collaboration was almost purely oral. We wrote and read aloud the one to the other. Possibly in the end we even wrote *to* read aloud the one to the other: for it strikes me very forcibly that 'The Nature Of A Crime' is for the most part prose meant for recitation, or of that type.

But for him, too, it was the collaboration that mattered:

> . . . I would read on and on. One begins with a fine propulsion. Sometimes that would last to the end but, as often as not, by a real telepathy, with my eyes on the page and my voice going on, I would grow aware of an exaggerated stillness on the part of my Collaborator in the shadows. It was an extraordinary kind of stillness: not of death: not of an ice age. Yes, it was the stillness of a prisoner on the rack, determined to conceal an agony. I would read on, my voice gradually sticking to my jaws. When it became unbearable I would glance up. On the other side of the hearth I would have a glimpse of a terribly sick man, of a convulsed face, of fingers contorted. Guido Fawkes beneath the *peine forte et dure* looked like that. You are to remember that we were very serious about writing. I would read on. After a long time it would come: 'Oh, . . . Oh, Oh, . . . Oh, my God, . . . My dear Ford . . . My dear faller . . .' (that in those days was the fashionable pronunciation of 'fellow'.)

A book is different if written to be read aloud. It is of a piece with the tones and inflexions that will accompany it, is partly a performance and will tend to be less concentrated, more diffuse, discursive and declamatory. If then read in silence by someone who does not know the writer great slabs are likely to remain flat on the page, lacking a voice to lift them, and the impression of the whole will be of something less pregnant and pointed, something altogether lighter and looser and easier. Dialogue is different, of course, but in narrative the effect is often obvious because the attention of the reader is then being directed not only to what happens but also to what sounds. It becomes less exact, sentence structure changes, there will be more deliberate repetition, more onomatopoeia, more atmosphere and usually less action. Some of the same effects may often be seen in books that are dictated.

In much of his work Ford consciously sought a speaking voice – 'A limpidity of expression that should make prose seem like the sound of someone talking in rather a low voice into the ear of the person that he liked.' Perhaps the best example of this is *The Good Soldier* (much of which was dictated) where the quiet, intimate voice informs a book that is at the same time so subtly and meticulously crafted that, whether read a sentence or a chapter at a time, the effect is mesmeric. In 1906 that balance and control was still some way off.

Nearly all serious novels draw on an author's personal experience, directly and indirectly. It is that investment of the personal that charges the novel with whatever energy it has but the mistake that is often made – by great novelists in their lesser work, by lesser novelists most of the time – is the assumption that the closer the book is to the author's experience, the more powerful it will be. To carry the ore of personal experience rough-hewn from the mine is not enough. The author needs distance from experience in order to render it in such a way that it means something to others; that distance is achieved partly through form.

When Ford got Conrad to help him write *The Nature of a Crime* – in effect a disguised letter to his own wife – there was behind it a heavy investment of the personal but he had not yet the artistic maturity to achieve a form that would, independently of himself, embody all that he wanted to say about intimate relations, about fidelity and deceit, and about the sexual guilt which by then he might have been feeling.

NINE

In 1898 all that was still some years ahead, but by the end of that year the great collaboration was under way. It provided a focus of intellectual excitement although producing the books – particularly *Romance* – was a long process, often arduous and un-rewarding. It was discussions and ideas and the books they were writing independently that excited them; the collaborations were something they kept going. It is indeed hard to imagine that the prolonged spark that turns a competent novel into a very good or great one can be sustained between two individuals. Comedies may be turned out, perhaps good thrillers – anything where plot is paramount – but what informs great novels is an almost pre-conscious apprehension, a mixture of feeling and idea, something immanent of which the book is one expression, one working-out, but not the conclusion. Such works are born only of an individual consciousness.

To be fair to Ford and Conrad, they were not attempting great literature, though they were trying out some of the techniques which they meant individually to employ. They wanted to write an exotic thriller that would be as successful as R. L. Stevenson's books. They set *Romance* among pirates and intriguers in the Caribbean, put the hero, Kemp, on trial (criminal cases, guilt and the problem of innocent suffering always interested Ford) and, on and off, worked hard at it. It came out at near five hundred pages, earned a moderate critical reception and a modest sum for the two authors, rather less than they had hoped. One critic thought it nearly merited comparison with Stevenson.

It is too static to be a good thriller, with too many deliberate scenes and too much atmosphere. Neither author in his own writing was very strong on narrative and they wrote *Romance* as the book they would have liked to read rather than in the manner best suited to the genre. It is an interesting mistake because in later life Ford was keen on thrillers and thought that much of the best of British writing was then to be found in detective stories, which were generally beneath contemporary literary notice. Perhaps it is always a mistake for a writer to try to write other than as he does naturally, as if any other writer's clothes would always fit. Most people write the way they do because they find it the only way that will get them through a book to the end. It may be that in order to write a good thriller a writer needs to be capable of being thrilled, or at least of imaginatively participating in the chase, and neither Ford nor Conrad really wanted that. What they wanted was exotic flavouring and intense experience. The note is struck in the first few lines of the book:

> To yesterday and to today I say my polite *vaya usted con dios*. What are these days to me? But that far-off day was my romance, when from between the blue and white bales in Dom Ramon's darkened storeroom in Kingston . . .

As Ford wrote later in his book on Conrad, this was obviously 'an opening for a long novel in which the dominant interest lies far back in the story.'

In April 1901 Ford and Elsie moved across the Marsh to Winchelsea but meetings with Conrad continued to be frequent. There was much talking late into the night, much pacing the lawn at The Pent (as well as, presumably, some ineffectual rat-shooting) and long summer nights on the verandah at Winchelsea, cigars glowing and drinks to hand. Not everyone enjoyed it, though. Jessie Conrad complained of being kept awake by Ford thumping the beams in The Pent kitchen as he made his points while Elsie must often have felt that he made full use of the opportunities to get away from the family that the great collaboration provided. It couldn't have helped that Conrad usually gave the impression of being irritated by the presence of his family (Borys recalled that when they went on rail journeys his father would insist on travelling as if alone, forbidding his family to address him once they were in the carriage and he was hiding behind whatever he was reading).

Although as we have seen Conrad would write to others in terms suggesting that the collaboration was all rather a nuisance, that his heart wasn't in it (as it surely wasn't), that he kept it going partly for Ford's sake, he was nevertheless aware of how much he depended on Ford simply to keep him going. It wasn't only what he called his 'particular devil' that might have stopped him; he had more trouble with his English than might be guessed from his books. According to H. G. Wells, he 'spoke English strangely . . . He had for example acquired an incurable tendency to pronounce the last "e" in these and those. He would say, "What shall we do with thesa things?"' A Winchelsea resident who was a little girl at the time[1], recalled that he 'spoke in a rather guttural way'. He often doubted his understanding of his audience. Ford believed that one reason for the eloquence of his prose, however, was that he used the Latin words of English as the French use theirs, and that he thought in French and translated into English. The hours they spent discussing individual words and phrases and the nuances of translation and interpretation probably gave him confidence as well as competence. One phrase in particular – 'Excellency, a few goats . . .' – which they coined in *Romance* became a private joke and remained a touchstone for them both ever after. But is Conrad's prose eloquent? It could be argued that its effectiveness is due at least sometimes to the sheer weight of adjectival bombardment rather than to any internal tightness or rhythm.

In the early years in Kent and later in London Ford managed some of Conrad's affairs and got him through periods of despair and fatigue. He was adept at a kind of amateur shorthand and took *The Mirror of the Sea* at Conrad's dictation as well as parts of *Some Reminiscences.* Even Jessie Conrad acknowledged that the former would never have come into being without Ford. He could also do perfect imitations of Conrad's style and when Conrad was in a state of collapse in London he actually wrote some sections of *Nostromo*. It is very likely that he wrote parts of Conrad's venture into drama, the unsuccessful play *One Day More*. He described some of their dictating sessions:

[1] K. Forbes-Dunlop, *Winchelsea Memories*, published by Anthony Neville, Rye.

> I would . . . walk up and down in front of Conrad who would groan, extended in a steamer chair. I would say: 'Well now, what about the *Tremolino*?' or 'What about the diamond mine you owned in the Transvaal?' and after explaining a dozen times: 'Nonsense, no one will want to hear about that,' he would begin to talk about the Ukraine of his uncle's day and Palmerston's emissary with a sledgeful of gold or about Venice when he was a boy or about his exile in Siberia or, of course, if I suggested that he should talk about the Ukraine or Venice or Siberia, he would insist on telling anecdotes about the *Tremolino* or his Transvaal mine. In any case, once he was started, he would go for a long time and as I wrote shorthand very fast, I could take them down without much trouble.

Ford's appreciation of Conrad had been great and immediate and, perhaps remembering his grandfather's dictum about helping artists he thought may be greater than himself, he was prepared to do virtually anything for him. There was no professional jealousy. They worked with 'absolute one-ness of purpose and an absolute absence of rivalry'. Ford's own estimation of his own use was, if anything, an underestimate:

> I was useful to Conrad as a writer and as man in a great many subordinate ways during his early days of struggle and deep poverty . . . I did, at such times as he was not himself equal to them, absolutely all of his literary dustings and sweepings, correcting his proofs, writing from his dictation, suggesting words when he was at a loss, or bringing to his memory incidents that he had forgotten. It was still more, perhaps, that I was large, blond, phlegmatic on the surface . . . Conrad passionately needed some moral support of the type that such an individual could afford him.

Nor was Conrad unappreciative – at least to Ford, if not more publicly. During an interlude in their sessions he wrote that he missed them terribly, in tones almost suggestive of a lover who feared being left. Also, at the very start, in November 1899, he had written: 'Whether I am worth anything to you or not, it is for you to determine. The proposal certainly came from me under a false impression of my power for work. I am much weaker than I thought I was . . .'

Ford became a life-long promoter of Conrad's work and never lost an opportunity to 'boom' him. He wrote articles for various magazines more or less from the time they met, sometimes pseudonymously, and after *Romance* was published he 'boomed' Conrad at the expense of himself in *TP's Weekly*: 'all through *Romance* one catches what, for want of a more precise word, one may call the glamour of Mr Conrad.' Also, inevitably, he lent Conrad money. Whether he noticed that Conrad never did as much for him is hard to say. He doesn't seem to have expected it. Conrad never 'boomed' Ford, never dedicated a book to him and was tardy in repayments. Ford gave without counting the cost, and Conrad accepted. It was the way they were with each other.

Apart from the books they were working on jointly, they would also discuss and read aloud to each other from their own individual works. Those beam-thumping sessions in The Pent kitchen would be about anything from single words to the concept of the novel. They felt they were among very few in England who thought the novel should be more than a narration, more than a story, that it should render an affair, a bit of life, bringing out what was important – such as the inevitability of character – rather than rounding things off to present a settled but false view. Ultimately a novel should identify what was real – which was not to be confused with being realistic – and hold it up so that all were made to see. They thought Flaubert best demonstrated how this was to be done, invisible behind his work, the almost perfect, merciless creator, who insisted on the exact word and said the thing once and for ever.

Yet, for all their admiration and theory, neither actually wrote like that. Both were more diffuse, more suggestive and often deliberately imprecise. They did not seek to nail the thing once and for all; they wished rather to leave a space around it which could be filled with suggestion, imprecision and nuance so as to convey the feeling that the real meaning, the real thing, was over and above the meanings of the words used.

But what they did have in common with Flaubert and the French tradition was what they called the *progression d'effet*. Ford defined it thus: 'In writing a novel we agreed that every word set on paper – *every* word set on paper – must carry the story forward, and that, as the story progressed, it must be carried forward faster and faster and with more and more intensity. That is called *progression d'effet*, words for which there is no English equivalent.'

In other words, progression, momentum or build-up. Like other points of technique which they discussed and practised, or did not practise, this has generated many yards of critical commentary, much of which seems either obvious or not particularly important. To be fair to Ford, he added to that paragraph three sentences in italics: 'But these two writers were not unaware – were *not unaware* – that there are other methods of writing novels. They were not rigid even in their own methods. They were sensible to the fact that compromise is at all times necessary to the execution of the work of art.' Similarly, he did himself point out that his much-discussed use of the time-shift in rendering an affair – for example, describing an incident from different times and perspectives – is commonplace in detective stories.

It may be that these matters seem unexceptional to us because their espousal by Ford and Conrad did in fact help to bring about changes in the ways the novel in English was written. In any case, few of us has any idea of what they are protesting against because we do not often read the bad literature of the past. Ford tells us what he did not like about Thackeray and Fielding but he does not say much about his unknown contemporaries, the novels he picked up, read quickly and discarded, despairing of their botched meanings, trite characters, complacent conclusions and otiose authorial comments. It was the same with his verse; most of us know only the poets of that period who have survived and we are not familiar with the poetical background that prompted Ford later to remark to Pound that poetry 'should be at least as well written as prose'. We would normally take that for granted; indeed, because it is more concentrated, we might assume that poetry needs to be more carefully written than prose. For this reason it is hard, too, to appreciate the originality of the informal, colloquial style of verse that Ford developed after about 1912. We take it for granted now.

On the other hand, were Conrad and Ford part of the cause of change in the novel in English or were they symptoms of a wider intellectual development? This is a matter for literary historians but it is worth touching on briefly. Consider the following:

> For in truth all art does not consist in the removal of surplusage . . . the one word for the one thing, the one thought . . . In the highest as in the lowliest literature, then, the one indispensable beauty is, after all, truth: – truth to bare fact in the latter, as to some personal sense of fact, diverted somewhat from men's ordinary sense of it, in the former; truth there as accuracy, truth here as expansion, that finest and most intimate form of truth, the vrai verité . . . Parallel, illusion, the illusive way generally, the flowers in the garden;- He (the true artist) knows the narcotic force of these upon the negligent intelligence to which *any* diversion, literally, is welcome, any vagrant intruder, because one can go wandering away with it from the immediate subject.

Not Ford – not his style – but in tune with a lot of what he wrote. The author is Walter Pater and the extracts are from his essay called 'Style'; longer extracts, similar to what Ford wrote about Impressionism, could be taken from Pater's *The Renaissance*. Pater was a well-known intellectual figure and his books were widely read. Although there is no direct evidence that Ford read him, it is very likely that he did; if not, that he was at least aware of such ideas as part of the intellectual currency of the time. There is some evidence that Conrad admired Pater and he very probably featured in their discussions. It is also likely that Ford would have been ambivalent in view of Pater's Victorian Great figure status. Dr Max Saunders has highlighted the double-edged phrase in *The Good Soldier* in which Ford refers to Pater. Dowell, the narrator, has to try to keep his wife's conversation on 'safe' topics such as 'the finds at Knossos and the mental spirituality of Walter Pater'. Dr Saunders comments:[1] '*Mental* spirituality? – an odd phrase which sounds as if it's avoiding the paradoxical idea of *physical* spirituality. It might suggest something effete about Pater – or about Dowell, who is avoiding Pater's hedonism, as he is avoiding the sexual implications of possible Minoan bull-worship.'

[1] Letter to the author

Whether Ford is speaking for himself or for Dowell in this, it does suggest that he was familiar with Pater and the likelihood is that the ideas he and Conrad enthused about were more current than is often assumed. What was unusual was the extent to which Ford wrote about such ideas and the way they both adapted them to their own practice. Later in life, when writing *The March of Literature*, it was the practical aspects of formal construction that Ford identified as his and Conrad's distinctive contribution:

> That we did succeed eventually in finding *a* new form I think I may permit myself to claim, Conrad first evolving the convention of a Marlowe who should narrate, in presentation, the whole story of a novel, just as, without much sequence or pursued chronology, the story will come up into the mind of a narrator, and I eventually dispensing with the narrator but making the story come up in the mind of the unseen author with a similar want of chronological sequence.

Books have been written about what Ford and Conrad said and did about technique, and there will no doubt be more, but the best summary of what they tried to put into their writing can be found in those sections of Ford's *Joseph Conrad* which deal with the supposed neighbour, Mr Slack: These are entertaining and useful passages, too long to quote in full, but a couple of examples may give a sufficient idea:

> GENERAL EFFECT
> We agreed that the general effect of a novel must be the general effect that life makes on mankind. A novel must therefore not be a narration, a report. Life does not say to you: in 1914 my next door neighbour, Mr Slack, erected a greenhouse and painted it with Cox's green aluminium paint . . . if you think about the matter, you will remember, in various un-ordered pictures, how one day Mr Slack appeared in his garden and contemplated the wall of his house. You will then try to remember the year of that occurrence and you will fix it as August, 1914, because having had the foresight to bear the municipal stock of the City of Liège you were able to afford a first-class season ticket for

the first time in your life. You will remember Mr Slack – then much thinner because it was before he found out where to buy that cheap Burgundy of which he has since drunk an inordinate quantity, though whisky you think would be much better for him – Mr Slack again came into his garden, this time with a pale, weasely-faced fellow, who touched his cap from time to time. Mr Slack will point to his house several times at different points, the weasely fellow touching his cap at each pointing. Some days after, coming back from business, you will have observed against Mr Slack's wall . . . At this point you will remember that you were then the manager of the fresh-fish branch of Messrs Catlin and Clovi in Fenchurch Street . . . What a change since then . . . Millicent had not yet put her hair up . . . You will remember how Millicent's hair looked, rather pale and burnished in plaits. You will remember how it now looks, henna'd; and you will see in one corner of your mind's eye a little picture of Mr Mills the vicar talking – O, very kindly – to Millicent after she had come back from Brighton . . . But you had better not risk that. You remember some of the things said by means of which Millicent made you cringe – and her expression . . . Cox's Aluminium paint . . . you remember the half-empty tin that Mr Slack showed you – he had a most undignified cold – with the name in the horseshoe and a blue circle that contained a red lion asleep in front of a real-gold sun.

And, if that is how the building of your neighbour's greenhouse comes back to you, just imagine how it will be with your love affairs that are so much more complicated . . .

SELECTION (SPEECHES)

. . . The rendering in fact of speeches gave Conrad and the writer more trouble than any other department of the novel whatever. It introduced at once the whole immense subject of under what convention the novel is to be written. For whether you tell it direct and as author – which is the more difficult way – or whether you put it into the mouth of a character – which is easier by far but much more cumbersome – the question of reporting or rendering speeches has to be faced . . .

. . . Yet the object of the novelist is to keep the reader entirely oblivious of the fact that the author exists – even of the fact that he is reading a book. This is, of course, not possible to the bitter end, but a reader *can* be rendered very engrossed, and the nearer you can come to making him entirely insensitive to his surroundings the more you will have succeeded.

CONVERSATIONS

One unalterable rule that we had for the rendering of conversations – for genuine conversations that are an exchange of thought, not interrogations or statements of fact – was that no speech of one character should ever answer the speech that goes before it. This is almost invariably the case in real life where few people listen, because they are always preparing their own next speeches. When, of a Saturday evening, you are conversing over the fence with your friend, Mr Slack, you hardly notice that he tells you he has seen an incredibly coloured petunia at a market gardener's because you are dying to tell him that you have determined to turn author to the extent of writing a letter on local politics to the newspaper of which, against his advice, you have become a large shareholder.

> He says 'Right down extraordinary that petunia was . . .'
> You say, 'What would you think now of my . . .'
> He says, 'Diamond-shaped stripes it had, blue-black and salmon . . .'
> You say, 'I've always thought I have a bit of a gift . . .'
> Your daughter Millicent interrupts. 'Julia Gower has got a pair of snake-skin shoes. She bought them at Winston and Willcocks's.'

You missed Mr Slack's next two speeches in wondering where Millicent got that bangle on her wrist. You will have to tell her more carefully than ever that she must *not* accept presents from Tom, Dick and Harry. By the time you have come out of that reverie Mr Slack is remarking:

> I said to him, 'Use turpentine and linseed oil, three parts to two, what do you think?'

★

What Ford said and what he did were not, of course, always the same. He intervened very considerably in most of his own books, not crudely, as author commenting on his characters, but penetratingly and universally, like a soft rain. His voice, attitudes and views saturate his stories, sometimes reducing them to little more than contrivances, at others achieving that unity of subject and expression and that investment of the particular with the general that makes for great art.

Again, his playful use of Mr Slack tempts regret that he did not write a novel of lower middle-class urban life. He might well have produced a Mr Polly or a Mr Pooter or something Dickensian; but though some of his talents and sympathies lay in that direction, his passions and aspirations pointed elsewhere. Even in fulfilling these he was not satisfied to be impersonal and simply to record; he could not be impersonal – it was one of his charms – and, like most artists, he imposed more than he recorded.

When he wrote that Conrad's was one of those deaths he could not believe in, it was of the nights and days of heady talk about these matters that he was probably thinking. Those days had become a part of him and he could no more exorcise the presence of Conrad from his consciousness than he could alter the past. Nor did he wish to. That presence and the love it called forth never left him, as neither did his solicitude, his affection and his passion for good writing.

TEN

The turn of the century found him busy, not only with the collaboration but with *The Cinque Ports*, poetry and articles. Elsie was pregnant again. But in the midst of being a fond father and probably a still-fond husband, in the midst of his observations of Meary Walker et al, his gardening, his widening social life, his friendship with Conrad, his own writing – at the start, indeed, of the long process of becoming the writer he really was – there was another level, not apparent to all. Olive Garnett noticed it. In June 1899 she noted that he looked ill and in August he told her, 'I haven't got any friends but you and the Cowlishaws.'

He was subject to periodic depressions and was sometimes more worried about what he was and what he could do with his life than is apparent from this distance. Wells, in his *Experiment in Autobiography*, wrote that Ford at this time was 'a little undecided between music, poetry, criticism, the Novel, Thoreau-istic horticulture and the simple appreciation of life'. His eventual decision may have been more painful and protracted than is generally realised; in fact, it may not have been a decision at all so much as an irresistible but still uncertain process. He had a strong sense of family responsibility – duty plays a large part in his novels – and he may have worried that he would not be able to provide for his family as he thought a husband and father should. It is also possible that he was worried by a growing awareness that a part of his nature would remain outside the confines laid down for good husbands. There is no evidence that he had at this stage been unfaithful to Elsie but it is likely that he wanted to and knew he couldn't help wanting; this would probably have worried him. He was still only twenty-six and had to choose between a lifetime of suppressed desire and a lifetime of guilt. The desire, he knew, would not go away. As he had Pauline Leicester say in *A Call* (published in 1910): 'It's saddening that a man can't be quite true, even when he adores you; but he can't. That's all.' When any of his characters comments on the difficulties of monogamy or the consequences of infidelity, it seems to be his own voice coming through clearly.

At the same time, he maintained a friendly though not intimate correspondence with Edward Garnett and was cheerfully sympathetic when criticising the writings that Olive sent to him. David, Edward's young son, was sent to stay at Aldington Knoll and to his child's eye there was nothing wrong:

> Ford was at his most lovable and genial. There was a stream running through the garden, and Ford had installed a little water-wheel with two brightly painted wooden puppets who seemed to be working very hard as they bent down and straightened up incessantly. Really, the water turned the wheel and the wheel made them move up and down, bending their backs.

He was seeing a doctor in Hythe about indigestion and sleeplessness. Perhaps he was working too much, writing being a neurotic and sedentary business from which it benefits everyone to get up and walk away. He liked walking on the Marsh but *The Cinque Ports* became a big book, the collaboration with Conrad was always harder and went on longer than intended, articles and poetry continued to be spawned. He may also have been worrying about money and perhaps even felt trapped.

On 16 April 1900 Elsie gave birth in hospital in Hythe to another daughter, Katharine Mary Madox Hueffer. Jessie Conrad said that both parents were disappointed that Katharine was not a boy and Ford's biographers generally emphasise his disappointment, but there is not actually very much evidence of it. Janice Biala is quite sure that he was not for ever after – as has been alleged – hankering after a son. If there was any disappointment it was probably temporary; he was very fond of Katharine.

The Boer War was by then in progress and it was perhaps the first time that public affairs had impinged upon him in a personal way. He had always followed affairs, albeit rather detachedly, but this affected his daily life. The Garnetts and the Limpsfield crowd were openly pro-Boer and were the subject of local hostility. Ford did not go quite that far but he was against the war and thought, rather unusually for that time, that neither British nor Boer had any business in South Africa and that Africa should be left to the Africans. He was disgusted by the jingoism that the war provoked, with its assumption that all who did not join were against. There is no evidence, but it is also possible that the war might have made him more self-conscious about his foreign surname (as happened, not surprisingly, in the First World War).

Not long after Katharine's birth it was agreed that the Hueffers and the Conrads would go to Bruges, where the two authors would do a burst on *Romance* and escape the oppressive jingoism. Ford, Elsie and the children went in July and the Conrads were to join them when *Lord Jim* was finished.

It was a fiasco. Ford found Belgian jingoism worse than British – 'abroad, where I passed for an Englishman, I witnessed and suffered from more ferocity . . . than I did in England, where I passed for a pro-Boer.' Predictably, the finishing of *Lord Jim* took longer than planned and the Hueffers had to wait in the English pension in the rue Anglaise, which was, according to Conrad, 'distinguished chiefly by brown linoleum, bent wood chairs in long perspectives, long teeth in withered faces, dimness and placards forbidding you to take water between certain hours from certain taps.'

Conrad eventually finished *Lord Jim* in an all-night stint and, 'exhausted but volcanic', arrived with his family. They all moved to a better hotel in Knocke-sur-mer where the two authors planned to work on *Romance* while Conrad wrote *Typhoon* in the mornings. Little work was done because Conrad had an attack of gout and his son went down with dysentery. Ford writes about the comings and goings that Borys's illness occasioned, the doctors 'who had to be fetched at midnight in the teeth of westerly gales', but does not mention his own nursing of the sick child which prompted complimentary words from Jessie Conrad: 'I have nothing but praise for FMH. He earned my gratitude and appreciation by the manner he showed his practical sympathies. He was always at hand to shift my small invalid, fetch the doctor, or help with the nursing.' When his own children were ill he would lie on the bed and tell them stories and he probably did so this time. It was not the only time he was to help the young Conrad. They all returned to England in August and Ford stayed at The Pent for two weeks in September, working at *Romance*. Conrad wrote dismissively of it to Galsworthy.

The Cinque Ports was published in the autumn of 1900. It is an impressive work and a handsome book, well produced and illustrated, the result of considerable research and written with a detail and accuracy (qualities not often associated with Ford but proof that he could display them when he wanted) that speak for his love for and knowledge of the subject. It describes the history and the then present condition of the original Cinque Ports, Hastings, Romney, Hythe, Dover and Sandwich, and of the two Ancient Towns of Winchelsea and Rye. Only five hundred and twenty-four copies were printed and they sold at three guineas each, which was very expensive (a little over, remember, what Lloyd George some years later reckoned to be the adequate weekly wage for a family man). He sent one to Henry James.

Although *The Cinque Ports* is an informative and painstaking book, it is clear from the dedication (to Robert Garnett) that Ford had started with other ideas: 'It was to be a piece of literature pure and simple, an attempt, by means of suggestion, to interpret to the passing years the inward message of the Five Ports. You, you will remember, very safely advised me to limit myself to a desire for accuracy . . . I then and there determined that I would print assertively no single statement for which I had not found chapter and verse . . .' It is clear from this that his later ideas, expressed in both fiction and non-fiction, about facts and reality, about suggestion and impression, were a development of his early- to mid-twenties.

The book also shows other themes that were to become more evident: his francophilia ('. . . the nation to whom all the world should cherish a tender feeling . . .'), his own cherishing of the old traditions ('. . . one is so aridly rational that the little dying flames of whimsical lights should be sedulously guarded . . .') and his detestation of bad or ugly architecture, which caused people to become 'mere inmates of excrescences like those on Seaford shore.' There are further indications of his youthful yearning for rest and peace, such as when he says of Camber Castle that 'one can lie in the slopes of earth in the shelter of the outer walls, and one can read a lazy book and be beguiled into thinking that, after all, life is good.' He praises Winchelsea for its restfulness and says – rightly – of walking through the Marsh along the nearby canal: 'But linger and saunter through it, and you are caught by the heels in a moment. You will catch a malady of tranquillity – a kind of idle fever that will fall on you in distant places for years after and one must needs be the better, in times of storm and stress, for that restful remembrance.'

It is an always amiable and at once wistful and sceptical ramble along the coast and across the Romney Marsh. He indulges his own preferences while taking more care of detail than he would later. Of Romney Marsh itself he writes evocatively and with a loving eye, recommending that no attention be paid to maps and statistics because they mislead by failing to convey the sense of vastness that the small area gives. That impression of vastness can be conveyed to a reader 'only by wholesale lying' since if one 'looks at a stupid map, untrue acre-measurements of surveys, one loses the sense of magic . . . It would be like reading a statistical account of one's lady-love.' There is good description:

> Little by little, as one follows the winding roads, the highlands sink out of sight. They disappear very slowly; but, suddenly, as one looks back from a turn in the road they have disappeared, have vanished. One goes on, as little by little the conviction forces itself upon one that the hills were a hallucination, that they do not exist, that they never did exist, that they never could have reached up towards Heaven. One realises that there is nothing in the world but flat, rushy land. A little nearer the sea one has seen great ships, great towers of gleaming canvas rise up above the farm roofs. In the depths of the Marsh one does not see even that; nothing rises, nothing aspires; the sky presses on down. One is so low, so near the earth, that even a small thorn-bush shuts out a great part of the world. One sees tiny cowering houses, stunted thorn-trees, sheep that never raise

their heads – an infinite number of sheep. Sometimes a heron stands silently in a shallow pool, not offering itself to the sight, but so silent, so primeval in its motionlessness, that the eye must search for it a long time.

Silence is the characteristic of the place, a brooding silence, an inconceivably self-centred abstraction. Impossible to disturb the calm to draw attention to oneself. One counts for so little. Sometimes the reeds that line the dykes whisper something – but so low that it is impossible to catch what they say, to understand them. The roads themselves are wayward, and wind about in an anciently arbitrary manner, suggestive of the tyrannies of the old time before us. One is forced to follow them; no modern, hurrying, democratic suffrage can frighten these kings into concessions . . .

On a moonlight night, however, the Marsh has a charm of its own. The mists rise up and lie perfectly level round one. There is not a swirl, not a single isolated wreath. The moon drives a broadening path along the silver of it, and one seems to be walking neck-deep through an intangible sea. The black thorn-bushes rise out of it, like sea-rocks, gleaming a little with the dew in their branches.

He was twenty-six when it was published. At about this time he and Elsie were seeing a lot of Wells and his wife. There were mutual visits, including a stay at the Wellses' Spade House where they played charades. Wells recalled one game in which Ford 'was the sole croupier at a green table in a marvellous Monte Carlo scene, and Jane [Mrs Wells] was a gambling duchess of entirely reckless habits.' But they were soon to move again, as we have seen. Dr Martindale worried about the damp at Stocks Hill, perhaps particularly now that there were two young children. In January 1901 he bought a property in Winchelsea called 'The Bungalow', which he made over to Elsie, and in April she and Ford moved in. Winchelsea was and is a small, quiet hill town within sight of Rye, allegedly the only example of town planning in Britain between the end of the Roman occupation and the eighteenth century. It was ravaged by French raiders in medieval times and garrisoned during the Napoleonic. It has few streets, mostly cobbled, all at right angles and mostly lined with white weather boarded houses. Dr Martindale had been mayor and his thankless efforts to improve the town's drainage were drawn on by Ford in his novel *The Benefactor*. Dr Martindale's own house, Glebe Cottage, is a substantial place within a hundred yards of the one he bought for his daughter. Mary was living there with her parents. It was the first time in Ford's marriage that he and Mary had lived within easy proximity. At about the time of the move Olive Garnett dreamt that he was dead. He was very upset about it.

The Bungalow was in fact a small house, built for his retirement by the first governor-general of Canada – 'in exact imitation', Ford said, 'of a Canadian (clap board) framed house.' It had a verandah, across the front, now gone, over which hops grew and on which Ford and Conrad sat talking in the warm summer nights. It was later enlarged by Elsie and later still was bought by an old school friend of Ford's, Charles Kinross, who in 1955 had a plaque commemorating Ford put on the front. Now called The Little House, it is, despite alterations, more or less as when Ford and Elsie lived there.

With interruptions, Ford's Winchelsea years spanned most of the first decade of this century. Much of what happened then was to echo throughout the rest of his life. Not only was there the flowering and fruition of his friendship with Conrad but it was also the period of his relationship with Henry James, of the forming of his friendship with Arthur Marwood, of the break-up of his marriage, of his own nervous collapse and possibly of his affair with Mary, Elsie's sister. Nor was this all: between 1901 and 1908 he published seventeen books, including two of the collaborations.

Little is known about the affair with Mary although its ramifications followed him to the end of his days. He remained silent, as about all his intimacies, unless forced. He kept no diaries or letters, was not indiscreet with friends and seems to have mistrusted any impulse towards introspective analysis. Whether this is unusual in one to whom insights came so easily – indicative, perhaps, of a refusal to face things – or whether it is itself an insight into the futility of much introspection, is hard to say. In fact, there is no direct evidence from Ford that the affair ever happened, though his novels frequently reflect entanglements with two or more women.

The only evidence we have comes from his second daughter, Katharine, who on marriage became Katharine Hueffer Lamb. She had the story from her mother and told it to Arthur Mizener. She believed, but wasn't certain, that the affair began in 1903. It could well have been earlier. Her mother told her how surprised she was to come in one day and find Mary sitting on Ford's lap, though this was not how the affair came to light. That apparently occurred because of the mistaken delivery to Elsie of a telegram from Ford to Mary. Nor did Elsie's discovery finish the affair, though it was supposed to have, for it continued intermittently until Ford became almost wholly London-based and involved with Violet Hunt and *The English Review* in 1908–9.

It must have been an affair of snatched moments, telegrams, hotel rooms and secret signals. No doubt it was exciting. Mary, always more vivacious than her more serious-minded younger sister, was probably an ardent though unstable mistress. The closeness of Glebe Cottage to the bungalow, with daily opportunities for meetings, would have fostered desire, but the smallness of Winchelsea – still a town in which it is hard not to be noticed – would have made privacy very difficult. K. Forbes-Dunlop remembers Ford at that time as 'solemn, quick-moving, giving a grey appearance', a man who 'usually failed to notice our childish, polite "Good morning" and we were a little afraid of him.' Elsie seems to have been equally preoccupied, often wearing 'long, floating, yellow garments so we called her "The Mustard Pot". She usually swept past us unnoticing and we didn't really like her.' There is no mention of Mary.

Looking at the place now, it is easy to see how the affair came about but difficult to see how they managed it. Perhaps they met in nearby Rye but that is another small town where neither was a stranger. More likely it was on visits to London where Mary lived for most of the time after 1902. It may also be that what we are calling an affair, implying continuity, was in fact no more than a few incidents.

It is also possible that it did not happen at all. Katharine's is the only evidence and such a business might have been expected to cause some talk within the family, perhaps rumours amongst friends, perhaps even oblique references from Ford later on. Douglas Goldring knew Ford for the last twenty or so years of his life and Violet Hunt for the last thirty or so of hers, which includes the period when she and Mary were close friends with Ford as ex-lover in common, and he apparently knew nothing. He wrote biographies of Ford and Violet, noting in one that 'The Bungalow was constantly filled with visitors, Ford's devoted sister-in-law, Mary Martindale, being for a time almost one of the household . . .' Either his tongue was very far in his cheek or he was quite unsuspecting. We might also have expected Mary to have told Violet about it during the period when they were united in resentment of Ford, and we might then have expected Violet, who was usually indiscreet and whose mind anyway wandered in old age, to say something to Goldring. He was one of the few friends of her last years and one of the only people to whom she could talk about Ford (still, sadly, her obsession). The only clue is one of Violet's diary entries in April 1917, which suggests something but it is not specific: 'And Ford writes – coldly – a letter that he wd not have written even to Mary Martindale in the old days.'

But to assume that it did not happen we should have to posit that either Elsie or Katharine was making it up and we should have to leave out of account Mary's history of enthusiasm for Ford. It could, of course, have been invented: it is not hard to imagine that someone in Elsie's position might have had her own motives and there are question marks over one or two of Katharine's later statements. For instance, after Ford's death she told Janice Biala that she had written many letters to Ford over many years and never had a reply. Janice is certain that Ford received no letter from Katharine during the nine years that she was with him and is confident that, had any arrived during the previous decade when he was with Stella Bowen, they would not have been kept from him. There is less room for doubt about Mary's early enthusiasm. She was also a believer in what used to be called free love and later carried her resentment of Ford, once she had teamed up with Violet, to the extent of following him up to Campden Hill Road cursing him aloud. (This was at the end of the First World War.)

In after years she and Elsie shared a house but it was said not to be a happy arrangement because Mary kept wanting to talk about the past, which Elsie wanted to forget.

It seems possible, too, that guilt played a part in Ford's nervous breakdown in 1904. The trigger incident in *A Call*, one of his novels which is most obviously a working through of his own concerns, is slightly reminiscent of the telegram which is said to have given him and Mary away. Dudley Leicester, one half of the two central male figures who make up the *Doppelgänger*, answers the telephone at night in the house of an old flame who is not his wife, and hears the caller recognise his voice. He is virtually paralysed by guilt for the rest of the novel. Ford, in his breakdowns, suffered a similar paralysis of his capacity for normal effective action.

What is frustrating is not the possibility that the affair may not have happened, nor the slightly greater likelihood that there may not have been very much to it (Ford's supposed guilt should not be taken as evidence that it happened more frequently rather than less, since the more habitual it was, the less guilty he might have felt); rather, the frustration comes of not knowing what kind of relationship it might have been. Was there any love in it or was it sex and excitement? Did the excitement fade? Did Ford consider leaving Elsie? Did Mary want him to? Did either try to break it off and find themselves more or less blackmailed into continuing? Lacking some undiscovered box of letters, we shall have to wait for the novel about Ford – which would be his true biography, revealing by Fordian truth – to tell us.

One relationship of the Winchelsea years that proceeded less mysteriously, though there is still some room for doubt, was Ford's friendship with Henry James. The doubts come from James's principal biographer, Leon Edel, who has a low opinion of Ford. He thought of him as a writer who had 'borrowed a high seriousness about the art of fiction' from Conrad and James and as a persistent and unwelcome visitor whom James avoided whenever he could, even to the extent of leaping ditches and hiding behind trees. This is half true but of the latter – post-1906 or 1907 – period of their acquaintance rather than the earlier. Letter evidence from the eight or nine years following 1897 bears out the impression Ford gave in his reminiscences, minus his exaggerations and made-up incidents, of frequent entertainments at Lamb House in Rye and at The Bungalow, of their mutual enjoyment of the Rye-Winchelsea walk, of talks and of teas. K. Forbes-Dunlop remembers James as a 'fairly frequent' visitor to Winchelsea, recalling particularly his habit of letting his bicycle fall to the ground after he had dismounted. Edel's evidence is drawn from Theodora Bosanquet, who worked for James but not until 1907, by which time the friendship had cooled.

Ford was always prepared to love anyone who loved good writing and if they also wrote well he was prepared to worship them. He believed James to be the greatest living writer and usually referred to him as the Master or the Old Man. He was not jealous and, indeed, records rather disarmingly James's aloof disregard for his abilities: 'I do not think that Mr James ever had the least idea what I was, and I do not think that to the end of his days, he regarded me as a serious writer . . . My relation with James was in no sense literary – and I never knew what it *was* . . . Constantly, and with every appearance of according weight to my opinions, though he seldom waited for an answer, he would consult me about practical matters – investment now and then, agreements once or twice – and, finally, unceasingly as to his fantastic domestic arrangements . . .' Ford sent James copies of his books as they came out and James would reply with elaborate courtesy or forbidding gravity – 'Curious and interesting', he said of a book of poems. Of *Romance*, he wrote to Ford that 'it was an immense English plum-cake which he kept at his bedside for a fortnight and of which he ate a nightly slice.'

When in 1914 James wrote an essay on the younger generation of novelists he did not include Ford nor did he read the book on him that Ford wrote at that time. Indeed, forsaking his usual elaborate courtesy, he wrote (not to Ford) that he would not touch it with a barge-pole. With the exception of *The Fifth Queen* trilogy Ford's best work was still to come, of course, but there is no reason to doubt his self-deprecating description of how James viewed him. Nor is there any good reason to doubt his description of their lively social intercourse during the early years. As for his stories about James, whether or not they happened is unimportant now. The point is that they give us Henry James more surely than a catalogue of corroborated facts. Consider, for instance, the one about Kipling's motor car:

> When I was admitted into his [James's] presence by the astonishingly ornate man-servant, he said: 'A writer who unites – if I may use the phrase – in his own person an enviable popularity to – as I am told – considerable literary gifts and whom I may say I like because he treats me –' and here Mr James laid his hand over his ear, made the slightest of bows and, rather cruelly rolling his dark and liquid eyes and moving his lower jaw as if he were revolving in his mouth a piquant tit-bit, Mr James continued, 'because he treats me – if again I may say any such thing – with proper respect' – and there would be an immense humorous gasp before the word 'respect' – '. . . I refer of course to Mr Kipling . . . [who] has just been to see me. And – such are the rewards of an enviable popularity! – a popularity such as I – or indeed you, my young friend, if you have any ambitions, which I sometimes doubt – could never dream of, far less imagine to ourselves – such are the rewards of an enviable popularity that Mr Kipling is in the possession of a magnificent one-thousand-two-hundred-guinea motor car. And, in the course of conversation as to characteristics of motor cars in general and those of the particular one-thousand-two-hundred-guinea motor car in the possession of our friend . . . But what do I say? . . . Of our cynosure! Mr Kipling uttered words which have for himself no doubt a particular significance but which to me at least convey almost literally nothing beyond their immediate sound . . . Mr Kipling said that the motor car was calculated to make the Englishman . . .' and again came the humorous gasp and the roll of the eyes . . . 'was calculated to make the Englishman . . . think.' And Mr James abandoned himself for part of a second to low chuckling. 'And', he continued, 'the conversation dissolved itself, after digression on the advantages attendant on the possession of such a vehicle, into what I believe are styled golden dreams – such as how the magnificent one-thousand-two-hundred-guinea motor car after having this evening conveyed its master and mistress to Bate-

mans, Burwash, of which the proper pronunciation is Burridge, would tomorrow devotedly return here and reaching here at twelve would convey me and my nephew William to Burridge in time to lunch, and having partaken of that repast, to return here in time to give tea to my friend Lady Maud Warrender who is honouring that humble meal with her presence tomorrow under my roof . . . And we were all indulging in – what is it? – delightful anticipations and dilating on the agreeableness of rapid – but not, for fear of the police and consideration for one's personal safety, *too* rapid – speed over country roads and all, if I may use the expression, was gas and gingerbread when . . . There is a loud knocking at the door and – *avec des yeux effarés* . . .' and here Mr James really did make his prominent and noticeable eyes almost stick out of his head . . . 'in rushes the chauffeur . . . And in short the chauffeur has omitted to lubricate the wheels of the magnificent one-thousand-two-hundred-guinea motor car with the result that its axles have become one piece of molten metal . . . The consequence is that its master and mistress will return to Burwash, which should be pronounced Burridge, by train and the magnificent one-thousand-two-hundred-guinea motor car will *not* devotedly return here at noon and will *not* in time for lunch convey me and my nephew William to Burwash and will *not* return here in time for me to give tea to my friend Lady Maud Warrender who is honouring that humble meal with her presence tomorrow beneath my roof or if the weather is fine in the garden . . .'

'Which,' concluded the Master, after subdued ho, hos of merriment, 'is calculated to make Mr Kipling think.'

Even where he worshipped, Ford remained clear-sighted. He did not expect goodness and badness to be demarcated any more clearly in life than they were in the novels he admired. He was usually silent about the faults of his acquaintances – despite 'Man is wolf to man' being a favourite quotation – but the picture he left of James is as convincing for its reticence as for its perception:

At that date Henry James was clean-shaven. As clean-shaven was then comparatively rare, he had in his relatively quiet

> moments the air of a divine; when he was animated, he was nearly always humorous and screwed his sensitive lips into amused or sardonic lines. Then he was like a comedian. His skin was dark, his face very clear-cut, his brow domed and bare. His eyes were singularly penetrating, dark and a little prominent . . . His vitality was amazing. You might put it that he was very seldom still and almost never silent. Occasionally when he desired information and you were giving him what he wanted he would sit gazing at you with his head leaning back against his grandfather's chair. But almost immediately he would be off with comment and elucidation – always more questions accompanied by gestures, raising of the eyebrows and the humorous twisting of his lips. His peculiarities were carefully thought out by himself. A distinguished man in his fifties must have peculiarities if he has a strong personality . . . At times he was unreasonably cruel – and that to the point of vindictiveness when his nerves were set on edge . . . a cold fury in voice and eyes . . . I will not say that lovableness was the predominating feature of the Old Man; he was too intent on his own particular aims to be lavishly sentimental over surrounding humanity . . . below that protective mask was undoubtedly a plane of nervous cruelty. I have heard him be to simple and quite unpretentious people, more diabolically blighting than it was quite decent for a man to be, for he was always an artist in expression . . . And yet there was a third depth – a depth of religious, of mystical, benevolence . . . To do a kindness when a sick cat or dog of the human race *had* 'got through' to his mind as needing assistance, he would exhibit all the extraordinary ingenuities that are displayed in his most involved sentences.

The trouble with Ford's unreliable anecdotes about other writers is that their sheer vividness has obscured many of his real insights and observations. Many people know the stories, not many people have read the other bits. Consider, for example, his account of the evolution of those famous Jamesian sentences:

> I fancy that his mannerisms, his involutions, whether in speech or in writing, were due to a settled conviction that, neither in

his public nor in his acquaintance, would he ever find anyone who would not need talking down to . . . He was aiming at explicitness, never at obscurities – as if he were talking to children.

Because of that he could never let his phrases alone . . . How often when waiting for him to go for a walk haven't I heard him say whilst dictating the finish of a phrase: 'No, No, Miss Dash . . . that is not clear . . . Insert before "we all are" . . . Let me see . . . Yes, insert "not so much locally, though to be sure we're here; but temperamentally, in a manner of speaking."' So that the phrase, blindingly clear to him by that time, when completed would run: 'So that here, not so much locally, though to be sure we're here, but at least temperamentally in a manner of speaking, we all are.'

No doubt the habit of dictating has something to do with these convolutions, and the truth of the matter is that during these later years he wrote far more for the ear of his amanuensis than for the eye of the eventual reader. So that, if you will try the experiment of reading him aloud and with expression, you will find his even latest pages relatively plain to understand. But, far more than that, the underlying factor in his later work was the endless determination to add more and more detail, so that the exact illusions and exact facts of life may appeal, and so that everything may be blindingly clear even to a little child . . . For I have heard him explain with the same profusion of detail to Conrad's son of five why he wore a particular hat whose unusual shape had attracted the child's attention. He was determined to present to the world the real, right thing!

There in a few paragraphs is what some people take books to say. Ford could do it about most of the writers he was interested in, particularly those he had known. A minor literary puzzle is why there was no E. M. Forster in his gallery. Forster was publishing from 1905 and had early achieved a good reputation. Ford knew of his writing and later was to publish *The English Novel* partly because of his dislike of Forster's *Aspects of the Novel*, but there does not appear to have been any significant contact between them.

He could imitate in speech or writing most of those he admired.

Robert Lowell attended a lecture he gave in America in the 1930s. Ford was old and breathless, his health was poor and his speech in public was not always easy to follow: 'I watched an audience of three thousand walk out on him as he exquisitely, ludicrously and inaudibly imitated the elaborate periphrastic style of Henry James. They could neither hear nor sympathise.' It is a sad picture, the voice of another era preaching a fading tradition to an indifferent generation. But not wholly sad because Ford was laughing. He was being funny, though they didn't see it. A lot of people haven't.

Those he regarded as leading lights in that tradition were all, in the early years of the century, living within easy reach of Winchelsea. James was at Rye, Conrad across the Marsh at The Pent and Stephen Crane at Brede House, inland of Rye. There was also Wells near Hythe and Kipling in Sussex. In discussing Crane, whom he greatly admired, Ford summed up what it was about the first three that he thought was so important:

> He [Crane] gave you the pattern in . . . physical life, in wars, in slums, in western saloons, in a world where the 'gun' was the final argument. The life that Conrad gives you is somewhere half-way between the two; it is dominated – but less dominated – by the revolver than that of Stephen Crane, and dominated, but less dominated by the moral scruple than that of James. But the approach to life is the same with all three; they show you that disillusionment is to be found alike at the tea table, in the slums and on the tented field. That is of great service to our Republic.

Wells, from the other side of the Marsh, jokingly referred to those three plus the half-German Ford and the American W. H. Hudson (who was also in the area) as a ring of foreign conspirators plotting against British letters. For a time it was nearly true. They were conscious literary artists who felt isolated by their devotion to their art, though they nevertheless envied Kipling his enormous sales. An elegant study of their relationships is Miranda Seymour's *A Ring of Conspirators*; she posits that the reason for James's later distance from Ford might have been that he knew of Ford's adultery with Mary. There is no evidence that he did though it remains hypothetically possible. James would certainly not have approved of anyone touched by scandal, as Violet Hunt was later to discover, and the dates do roughly coincide in that Elsie was said to have discovered the affair in 1905 and James's change of attitude is evident from about the same time. Also, there is a suggestion of something along those lines in Ford's reminiscences: 'But once he [James] had got it well fixed into his head that I was a journalist, he conceived the idea that all my friends must be illegally united with members of the opposite sex.'

It is possible that this is Ford saying that he became disreputable in James's eye without coming clean about why; but it still seems unlikely that James knew, no matter how much or little there was to know. If he had, others surely would have, but no one mentions it. What is more likely, though there is still no hard evidence, is that relations between Ford and Elsie might have become publicly strained and Ford's general behaviour less acceptable as a result of his going to pieces for most of 1904. His personality and life at that time might well have struck a jarring note to the Jamesian ear. Nor is it unusual for friendships to run their course. We often speak as though it is natural for them to last until death; that may be ideal or desirable but more often than not they last a few years. This is particularly true of gregarious people such as James and Ford who packed many other people into their lives and seemed often to meet new ones.

It is also very easy to make a lot out of a little, particularly when seeking to justify a view. For instance, during the period 1906–9, when relations between them had cooled, James's letters to Ford and Elsie remain friendly enough, though not effusive, and he was sympathetic during Ford's nervous breakdown. It may be that our desire to see patterns in carpets leads us both to exaggerate and to over-simplify. We can be sure that much of whatever we say would be disclaimed by the actors whose unseen drama we describe: 'But it wasn't,' they would say, 'like that.' It almost never is – quite – even in contemporary accounts of contemporary affairs. This was one reason why Ford disliked biography. Biographers, Janice Biala has come to think, are like blind men with their sticks.

The other important friendship of those Winchelsea years was, as already noted, that with Arthur Pierson Marwood. Women were essential to Ford, they inspired and supported him, he wrote better when in love, he could not manage without them; but it may be that it was womankind he needed rather than particular women. The three greatest influences on his artistic imagination were male: Madox Brown, Joseph Conrad and Arthur Marwood.

Marwood was born in 1868 at Busby Hall, Stokesley, near Middlesbrough, where his family descended from Edward III, had been landowners for centuries. He had four brothers and seven sisters. The eldest brother died, the second was a senior civil servant and the third was with the Army in India. It would have been for Arthur to run the estate but his ill-health prevented it. He had tuberculosis. A promising mathematician, illness had forced him to leave Trinity College, Cambridge, without taking his degree. He married his nurse, Caroline, in Leeds in 1903 (herself one of ten daughters and seven sons) and for the sake of his health moved to Winchelsea where one of his sisters lived at The Old Forge. Winchelsea was a good choice as it is on a hill, has a southern aspect, sea breezes and more sun than most of Britain. Ford reckoned that there was 'practically no day throughout the year on which a proper man cannot eat his meal under a south wall out of doors'. This was an exaggeration but a pardonable one. (He also said that you can see the French cliffs on 'most days', which is not true now. He probably had good eyesight or perhaps the atmosphere was clearer then, or perhaps 'most' should be taken to mean 'occasionally'.) Marwood later moved to Walter Farm, near Aldington (possibly that which is now named Marwood Farm). Caroline ran it.

It is generally thought that he and Ford met in 1905 although it could have been earlier. He is mentioned in a letter from Ford to Olive Garnett which Sondra Stang in her *Ford Madox Ford Reader* dates as *circa* 1901, but this would mean that Marwood had moved to Winchelsea before marrying in Leeds and there is no evidence that he did. Further, he does not appear on the electoral roll until 1st January 1905, which would imply that he moved there sometime in 1904. Had it been much earlier we should have expected the two to have met before that date since Winchelsea is a small town and the gentry in those days would all have known each other. (At the risk of falling into Fordian exaggeration, it could be claimed that even now there is no house in Winchelsea from which a proper man might not walk to his farthest neighbour within ten minutes.) What we do know is that by Christmas 1905 Ford knew Marwood well enough to present him with an inscribed copy of his book on Rossetti.

He described Marwood as 'a powerfully-built, leisurely man . . . the heavy Yorkshire squire with his dark hair startlingly silver in places, his keen blue eyes, his florid complexion, his immense, expressive hands and his great shapelessness.' He always stressed Marwood's intelligence, common-sense and knowledge of the world; having been brought up amongst writers and artists, it might, as we have seen, have appealed to him to have an intimate who was not a practitioner of the arts and not a Fabian. It would have chimed with his self-admitted cussedness (he confessed he did not read Henry James until quite late because of the way all the other members of his circle raved about him) and with his admiration for practical people.

Nearly all commentaries on Ford have described in detail the effect of Marwood on his fiction, particularly in relation to the hero of the *Parade's End* tetralogy, Tietjens. Critics have stressed the degree to which Ford invested himself in his Marwood-types. Marwoodian shapelessness and ability is usually combined with Fordian sensitivity and Ford's feudal Toryism with Marwood's practical paternalism. These composite characters are devoted to pre-industrial ways and values yet see more clearly than most the essence of the vulgar present; they love good letters, despise ambition, are always decent, always honourable and usually suffer for it; they are misunderstood and condemned by many, loved and worshipped by some; they are nearly always anguished, often paralysed into inaction by their own perceptions, yet somehow they stumble through. Such a character is, of course, part Marwood and part Ford but he is also Ford's reconstructions of Marwood and of himself, part an author's delineated dramatic foil, part device, part expression of the author's beliefs and aspirations, part criticism of them, part English and part German romantic.

There is legitimate scholarly and biographical interest in sorting out these strands. For instance, there is a train scene in *The Good Soldier* in which Edward Ashburnham sets out to comfort an unhappy servant girl and ends up in court, his sympathy having carried him a little too far. That, according to Janice Biala, was exactly how Ford was with women; his sympathies would be engaged and then everything else would follow. There are examples in his own life: the German girl whom he picked up and looked after in London during his affair with Violet Hunt, or Jean Rhys, at the beginning.

But we should beware of looking upon every element of a fictional character as relating to elements in the author or his friends, as if we were pinning string from the author's heart to his character's. It is a form of autopsy which tells us something of what the author was like but not always as much as we think. The most important point about fictional characters is whether they work within the contexts of their fictions. Convincing fictional characters are present to our minds in a way similar to the image of someone whom we used to know but who is not at that moment before us. No description can ever be quite complete, no account final, and in the space that is left dwells the mystery that makes man. We talk about convincing fictional characters in the same way in which we talk about people we knew and what makes both alive to us is not the known facts but the suggested life, the felt, unseen quiver of being. The important questions about such characters as Tietjens is not so much how far they resemble their creator or their creator's friends, but do they live? If they live in their books, they live beyond them, and if they do that, so does their author. Ford lives partly because Tietjens lives; he imparted some of his unknown to Tietjens's unknown and it is in that that we sense reality.

In presenting us with the English gentleman who clings to a chivalrous ethic long after his peers have abandoned it – supposing they ever had it – Ford writes not as one born into the gentry would have written. He was neither fully English nor of the landed gentry and, though close enough to both, he always viewed them as if from without. If the English gentry were characterised by anything it was by intelligent pragmatism and it is tempting to say that only a German romantic would have attempted to infuse the concept of the gentleman with such ethical rigour as Ford displays. The Marwood–Ford creations provided their author with a way of pointing out the dilemma of the moral individual in a morally decadent and changing world; like most serious novels, Ford's were novels of conscience and the fact that he chose to dramatise the conflict by having his leading characters hark back to a notional earlier age is both a strength and a limitation. It is a strength because of the edge it gave him for dissecting the moral features of his own time and because he was able to invest his characters with a great degree of conviction and imaginative sympathy. It is a limitation because it was idiosyncratic and remote from the way that moral concerns actually impinged on most people, gentry or not. His triumph was to overcome this self-sought limitation by striking in all his major work the keynote that finds a general response: the note not of passion, not of despair not of hopelessness – though all are present – but of anguish. He is the novelist of anguish.

Marwood was, like Conrad, another whose eventual death Ford could never quite believe in. He absorbed each to such an extent that they lived on within himself. Meanwhile, the busy, fraught and productive Winchelsea years continued. They were to become the London years but it was a gradual process. The great love for Conrad spanned them all. 'I miss you more and more,' Conrad wrote after an interval in their collaborations. 'I am certain that with no other man could I share my rapture.' Also, 'I miss our collaboration in a most ridiculous manner, I hope you don't intend dropping me altogether . . .' It was not all one-sided.

ELEVEN

In February 1902 Dr Martindale was found dead in his laboratory in London. Ford, who had lately got on much better with his father-in-law, produced a wreath and verses for the funeral. It is almost certain that Dr Martindale killed himself but this was hushed up. Olive Garnett noted in her diary for 5 February: 'Dr M took prussic acid on Sunday morning. Melancholia.' He left a letter and two days later Olive noted: 'Ford hopes to take Elsie to Paris directly. Mr M wrote "thank Ford" at the end of his letter.' In fact, Ford and Elsie went to Germany.

There has been speculation about this 'thank Ford'. Was it meant at face-value – Ford had been helpful to Dr Martindale and had been a sympathetic observer of his attempts to get Winchelsea to improve its drainage – or was it sarcastic? Was Dr Martindale saying that in some measure Ford was responsible for his suicide, and, if so, could it have been that the affair with Mary had already started and Dr Martindale knew about it? This is teasing speculation which, in the absence of evidence, should not be allowed to become more. Apart from his concern for Elsie, Ford's feelings about the incident are not known. His actions, however, were those of a sympathetic son-in-law rather than someone under a cloud. He quoted from 'Adonais' for the wreath:

> And that unrest which men mis-call delight
> Can touch him not and torture not again.

There is no good time for family death but this must have been a particularly bad one for Ford and Elsie. Like many couples with young children, they seem to have been permanently tired and from about this period Olive begins to show as much concern for Elsie's health as she had previously for Ford's. Over a year later Elsie was still wearing mourning and Olive thought her 'thinner and less active than formerly', concluding one entry with a cryptic, 'Elsie lonely'.

Money was becoming more of a problem as Ford was getting busier without getting richer. He was in the throes of the *Romance* collaboration which necessitated visits to The Pent and was taking longer than either author wanted; he was working on his novel, *The Benefactor*, as well as on his book on Rossetti; his brother Oliver was losing their mother's money in various business misadventures and had married Zoë Pyne (with whom Ford did not get on); the servants at The Bungalow – they had at least two – were causing trouble; the children were unbearably noisy; Elsie was trying to write a novel which was not going well and they seemed to be surrounded by the sick or dying. Ford wrote to his mother about Ellen Terry, long time resident of Winchelsea and a family friend: 'Ellen Terry was in the other day; she asked to be remembered to you. She's, poor thing, getting rather groggy and old. Rheumatic, troubled with failing memory & eyesight &, I'm afraid, with failing purse too. James too has been very ill & isn't anymore his charming self.' As usual, Conrad was also spasmodically ill – gout, toothache, and 'My mind is becoming bone, my hand heavy, my tongue thick' – while Ford was still being ineffectually treated for indigestion and sleeplessness. Elsie's tubercular knee caused her to fall and break her arm badly in one of the Winchelsea town gates; at home she was depressed and unhappy, then Christina fell ill. The novel Elsie was working on could have been *Ellen Slingsby*, which was never published, or *Margaret Hever*, which was published in 1909. It is possible that by writing at such a time may have been her attempt to overcome the feeling of being left out of Ford's literary (i.e. real) life. There are a number of indications that she felt left out despite his and Conrad's later encouragement of her literary activity.

With family life in full spate, there were nevertheless some times of quiet domesticity. Ford's poem, 'To Christina at Nightfall', is tender:

Little thing, ah, little mouse,
Creeping through the twilit house,
To watch within the shadow of my chair
With large blue eyes; the firelight on your hair
Doth glimmer gold and faint . . .

The Martindales, Hueffers, Garnetts and Conrads all seem at this time to have been leading harassed lives. It is easy to imagine those late Victorian and early Edwardian days as having been as spacious as their houses, their books written by gentlemen in fire-lit studies, already certain of their secure places in literature. The picture that emerges of Ford and Conrad, though, is of haste and harassment, of debilitating pecuniary anxiety, of domestic strife, of personal and family ill-health, of publishers who were unenthusiastic or unreliable, of books that disappointed. It is true that nobody had to go and do the washing up or get a job but that itself may have made room for everything else. What seems to us to have been enviably leisured, felt otherwise.

Ford, more helpful than wise, got involved in Conrad's money-raising schemes. These usually comprised trying to raise money on the strength of insurance policies in ways that, if not actually illegal, nevertheless involved the deception of someone at some point. They also involved Ford's trying to sell some of his Pre-Raphaelite heirlooms. Robert Garnett, Olive's solicitor brother who had facilitated Elsie's elopement and to whom *The Cinque Ports* was dedicated, fortunately acted as a restraining influence; although as each ploy failed Conrad would go away and think up another. He was safest when borrowing money from Ford and subsequently from his literary agent, Pinker, whom he nonetheless tried frequently to fiddle.

J. B. Pinker was a man who deserves a biography to himself. He was not the first literary agent in London, being preceded by A. P. Watt and Curtis Brown, but he was the archetype of all good agents. A small, shrewd, fox-hunting Scotsman with an eye for a good horse – 'unusual for Scotsmen', Ford thought – as well as for the writers of good rather than simply profitable books, he represented Wells, James, Bennett, Conrad, Crane, Ford and many others. Ford almost certainly came to him through Conrad. Both had an ambivalent attitude towards him, often convincing each other that he was making unreasonable profits out of them while they were getting less than their books deserved. This alternated with periods of gratitude and affection – 'The Pinker of literary agents', Conrad once called him. They – particularly Conrad – borrowed from him on the strength of anticipated advances on books unwritten and on the strength of royalties as yet unearned. He got them money, publishers, syndication in magazines and newspapers, saw through their often silly attempts to con more money out of him but stayed with them and gave support – to Conrad in particular – when probably no one else would have. Ford, who once tried to repay him in pigs, was never really convinced that agents were a good thing. Like Shaw, he thought that their relations with publishers were such that it was not always in their interest to get the most they could for any given book. But, writing after Pinker's death, he was characteristically generous:

> . . . without him you could never have had Conrad, and poor Crane could hardly have lived. He smoothed out, too, furrows in the later paths of Henry James. I had mysterious and obscure rows with him myself. I never understood what they were about. I suppose he was sensitive and I was patronising . . . to his favourite clients – and they were not all the most prosperous – Pinker was all gold . . . you could have little real idea of what the literary world I am portraying for you was like unless you imagine that Scotsman as looming always somewhere in the background of lettered thoughts . . . [he] would take quite long odds in backing you. Conrad must have been many thousand of pounds in debt to him before *Chance* really brought him before the public eye. On the other hand, the little man could softly and inexorably turn down anyone in whom he did not believe.

They stayed with Pinker until his unexpected death from pneumonia in New York in 1922 when he was on the point of arranging a contract with Macmillan that Ford hoped would keep him in clover for the rest of his life. That was unfortunately typical of Ford's publishing history, not only because the contract was never signed but also because Ford very likely had a too optimistic idea of what it might do for him. He lived off advances, nearly always refusing to publish without one – a practice by no means as common then as now – but the advances were never enough. Pinker handled much of Ford's and Conrad's work from 1902 onwards, Conrad's *Typhoon* being the first. He not only found them markets and commissions, but acted for some of the time as editor; the chore of *Romance* was prolonged because he rightly insisted that they cut it. He also got them to be more realistic about the advance they could expect for it.

The way Pinker encouraged and tolerated his authors, some of whom were childishly feckless, envious and deceitful, while recognising and encouraging talent, is greatly to his credit. He played a back-stage but significant part in English letters and perhaps one day someone will give him his due.

Though living at Winchelsea, Ford was still the legal tenant of The Pent and was still paying rent for it. He couldn't afford to do so, particularly as Conrad was not keeping up with his contributions, so he tried to give up the tenancy. Conrad, however, would not contemplate moving and Ford quickly gave in. Whatever happened, work went on. Ford's most vivid description refers to the period when he was at Aldington:

> We would write for whole days, for half nights, for the half the day, or all the night. We would jot down passages on scraps of paper or in the margins of books, handing them one to the other or exchanging them. We would roar with laughter over passages that would have struck no other soul as humorous; Conrad would howl with rage and I would almost sigh over others that no other soul perhaps would have found as bad as we considered them. We would recoil one from the other and go each to our own cottage – our cottages of that period never being farther the one from the other than an old mare could take us in an afternoon. In those cottages we would prepare other drafts and so drive backwards and forwards with packages of manuscripts under the dog-cart seat. We drove in the heat of summer, through the deluges of autumn, with the winter snows blinding our eyes – always, always with manuscripts. Heavens, don't my fingers still tingle with the feeling of undoing the stiff buckles long past midnight of a horse steaming with rain – and the rubbing down in the stable and the backing the cart into the coach-house. And with always

at the back of the mind, the consideration of some unfinished passage, the puzzledom to avoid some too-used phrase that yet seemed hypnotically inevitable.

Jessie, meanwhile, would be confined to another part of the house or kept awake in her bedroom. Early on, she seems to have liked Ford. Conrad's letters include messages from her, remembrances of love and affection and so on, and at Ford's suggestion she was to write a cookery book. But her attitude changed. No doubt, like Elsie, she felt excluded and perhaps also felt that Ford tolerated her only because she was the wife of Joseph Conrad; she might also have felt insecure with regard to Joseph himself, feeling she had no part in the principal concern of her husband's life. It was also the case that Ford was not a man to endear himself to all housewives. He was big and sprawling, took up a lot of room, talked a great deal, disdained domestic conventions, could make himself at home anywhere but wasn't interested in organised comfort (loving luxury but despising comfort, remember), could cook well, wasn't above interfering in the kitchen, didn't notice what he was doing to the furniture and usually did notice what he wasn't meant to see. At that stage of his life he was probably what people used to call a know-all; also, he monopolised Jessie's husband.

The domestic background of Jessie's dislike is neatly summarised in Miranda Seymour's *A Ring of Conspirators*. It was 1906, both Ford and Elsie were away from Winchelsea for much of the time and Ford had lent The Bungalow to the Conrads for a couple of weeks, himself coming down at weekends in order to collaborate on *The Nature of a Crime*. Conrad was working on *The Secret Agent*:

> . . . Ford came over for weekends which seemed to Jessie interminably long, 'the longest I have ever known, and a fit punishment for any sins I might have committed, or ever contemplated.' The recitation of her sufferings could be tediously petty but it is, to a heartless reader, perversely enjoyable if regarded as material for the Grossmiths' chronicles of Mr Pooter's misfortunes, 'The Diary of a Nobody.' Jessie has much in common with Mr Pooter.
>
> There was, first of all, the incident of the greasy Panama hat

which Ford dared to put into the oven to dry over Jessie's Sunday joint. 'I removed it to a chair as close to the fire as possible, and resolutely closed the oven, voicing my displeasure in as few words as possible.' The few words did not discourage Ford from making the 'fantastic request' that she should sew a new ribbon into the hat, since she had been kind enough to point out the greasiness of the old one. Jessie did so, 'dutifully'. Next morning, accused by Ford of making a hole in Elsie's tablecloth, Jessie took her revenge. She did not think that mattered, she sweetly said, since Elsie would not be seeing the tablecloth. To which Ford responded, why not? 'I rose quickly to my feet and hastily turned another corner of the cloth towards him, saying slowly and distinctly: "I said she would most probably not see it. You see my name is on the corner, I brought my own linen, and I shall take it home with me. Are you satisfied?" Forgivably, Ford walked out without answering. She simmered with rage when Henry James – 'so essentially a gentleman' – came to tea and Ford shut her in the kitchen. Her temper reached boiling point when she found that Ford had hung his bed covers up as a curtain and wrapped himself for the night in Conrad's 'carefully pressed and ironed' morning coat and striped grey trousers.

It must have been like having an ageing undergraduate hanging about the house; worse, one who probably made her conscious of her relatively humble origins (a number of Conrad's acquaintances felt he had married beneath himself). Ford must have been well aware of her dislike and in later years she published damaging allegations about him, the chief of which was untrue but it nevertheless caused lasting damage to his sales and reputation, damage which still reverberates. Typically, he never attacked her, though his silence may be eloquent testimony.

But he was never not helpful. In 1902 Conrad was working at The Pent on the second instalment, for Blackwood's, of *The End of the Tether*. (It had originally been called *The End of the Song* but Ford got him to change that; it was also Ford who suggested he write the story.) It was the 23rd June and the manuscript was due in Edinburgh the following day; Conrad's oil lamp exploded and started a fire. The table, which was one of Ford's valued heirlooms

– designed by William Morris for Madox Brown – was badly burned and Conrad's manuscript destroyed. 'The fire', Conrad wrote to Ford from The Pent, 'ran in streams and Jess and I threw blankets and danced around on them; the blaze in the window was remarked in Postling. Then it was all over but the horrid stink . . . This morning looking at the pile of charred paper – MS and typed copy – my head swam; it seemed to me the earth was turning backwards.'

Conrad was in despair, The Pent in a mess, and Elsie, at The Bungalow, was not well. Ford metaphorically harnessed the mare and galloped to the rescue: he rented a small cottage opposite The Bungalow, installed the Conrads in it and laid on his full range of moral, literary, material and gastronomic support. His account is dramatic but is not contradicted by any other references:

> Conrad wrote: I corrected the manuscript behind him or wrote in a sentence – I in my study on the street, Conrad in a two-roomed cottage that we had hired immediately opposite. The household sat up all night keeping soups warm. In the middle of the night Conrad would open his window and shout, 'For heaven's sake give me something for *sale pochard*; it's been holding me up for an hour.' I called back, 'Confounded swilling pig' across the dead-still, grass-grown street . . .
>
> Our telegrams would ask what was the latest day, the latest hour, the latest half-minute that would do if *The End of the Tether* was to catch the presses. Blackwood's answered at first, Wednesday morning, then Thursday. Then Friday night would be just possible . . . at two in the morning, the mare – another mare by then – was saddled by the writer and the stable boy. Stable boy was to ride to the junction with the manuscript and catch the six-in-the-morning mail-train. The soup kept hot; the writers wrote.

The new instalment was finished about three weeks after the fire.

Following this Ford went walking in the New Forest for a few days. He was tired and unwell; it was an area to which he would return, under worse circumstances, but this time it was loneliness that got to him more than anything. He was a gregarious man and was not good on his own. In a letter to Elsie he describes writing as 'an endless business, of course, but then, so is life – and if occupation fills up life – passes it away – that's always so much to the good.' He congratulated her on finishing her novel, adding that she had done so 'just as I am never going to write again', and, 'I expect you are tired of my letters as of me'. But life and occupation soon picked up. A short while later he was persuading Conrad to write *Nostromo* and Elsie had set about translating de Maupassant. Conrad helped her and she in turn gave him her criticism of *The Heart of Darkness*, saying that Kurtz was too symbolic. He agreed:

> What I distinctly admit is the fault of having made Kurtz too symbolic or rather symbolic at all. But the story being merely a vehicle for conveying a batch of personal impressions I gave rein to my mental laziness . . .

The two families spent Christmas together and early in 1903 held an elaborate joint birthday party for Borys and Christina, for which Ford wrote verses for the children. He was considering another book along the lines of *The Cinque Ports* but about London and then spent some time there, trying and failing to get a publisher to commission it. He eventually started writing without one. The book was to become *The Soul of London*. He enjoyed being busy in the capital, breakfasting with Galsworthy who lived in a house that 'backed on to the marvellous coppices in Holland Park and the pheasants used to fly from the garden'. Galsworthy's breakfasts were enticing although Ford, not at that stage an early riser, probably didn't go very often. The impression he leaves, however, is memorable: 'I would breakfast with Jack at his sun-lit converted stable . . . At any rate that is how it comes back to me – the doors and windows always open, the sun-light streaming in on the hissing silver tea kettle, the bubbling silver entree dishes, the red tiles of the floor, the bright rugs, the bright screens . . .'

The year 1903 – his thirtieth – was discouraging and harbinger of a worse. His insomnia did not abate, Elsie's health was mysteriously uncertain, the anticipated profits of *Romance* diminished with each assessment. At the end of 1902 he estimated in a letter to his mother that he had earned that year barely one hundred pounds. By the end of the year he had had to get Robert Garnett to arrange a loan of £150; Elsie's broken arm, which occurred in November, proved an expensive business. He argued with Olive, though not too seriously, about Conrad's lack of understanding of women, had to revise *The Benefactor* two or three times, saw it rejected by various publishers, continued making notes on Henry VIII without any definite aim beyond vague thoughts of a novel about Katharine Howard and wrote short stories which were not always easy to place. The one promising step was that he started to research for a short book on Holbein – suggested, interestingly, by Edward Garnett – and visited Berlin and Basle. He did actually write the book and his researches influenced the way in which the Katharine Howard trilogy was subsequently written, some of the scenes being his own imaginative recreations of Holbein. A 1903 letter to Wells shows that he was already considering how to use Tudor words and rhythms in modern English: 'I lament to see you fall into the error of upholding "Elizabethanism". – That sort of thing is the curse of modern English. – What we want is to use our vernacular so skilfully that words, precious or obsolete, will not stick out and impede a reader . . . If you will consider the matter you will see that slang is an excellent thing (Elizabethan writing is mostly slang) and, as soon as practicable we sh'd get into our pages every slang word that doesn't (in our selective ears) ring too horribly . . . We must do that or we shall die, we & our language.'

The proofs of *Romance* were corrected at The Pent in April of that year and the much-cut, much-worked-on, much-sweated-over, never-much-liked book was published in October to, as we have seen, a not very enthusiastic critical response. As he approached his thirtieth birthday, an age at which he might have expected to feel a certain firmness of purpose, maturity and sense of direction, Ford was probably more sure about what he wanted to do than he had been a decade earlier but less optimistic of being able to do it. Lack of money was no longer a problem to be overcome by energy and enthusiasm but an enduring, debilitating fact of life, as unavoidable as grey weather. Romance had turned into marriage and love-making into responsibility; he had found the great friendship of his life and the worm in his own bud; he must have sensed that rest and peace, for which he often said he longed, would not be his, at least not for a long time.

A partial picture of most lives might easily appear dire and if Ford's tended to lurch at times towards the extremes of depression or fraughtness, it veered also the other way. It seems likely that, at least in the earlier years, he and Elsie were reasonably happy; he loved his children; his relations with his own family were, as always, affectionate; he had discovered, partly through Conrad, the great direction of his life and he had achieved a literary reputation which meant that he was at least known. He had also had a pretty good social time, partly in London but mostly in Kent and Sussex. He was on terms with the leading writers of the day. There were boisterous parties at Stephen Crane's damp and rambling Brede Place, while the doomed host looked on, pale and quiet, and H. G. Wells played games with broomsticks. There were walks, dinners, teas and charades. Like most novelists, Ford's best work was written after his twenties but it was during that decade that the strata from which they were mined were laid down. The basic themes – passion, anguish, loyalty, infidelity, conscience and duty – were during those years embedded in his soul. What was wanted now was that he should live enough and write enough to bring them out.

TWELVE

Towards the end of 1903 the family decamped to London. They stayed at 10 Airlie Gardens, Campden Hill, a 'very large, absurd house' which was also very expensive and belonged to Oliver and his wife Zoë, who had moved to Manchester. Ford called it 'a monstrous sepulchre, grey with the greyness of withered bones'. It was triangular – 'the façade was thus monstrous, the tail, ignoble' – and had seven flights of stairs. There were no lifts. He was truly back in the tradition of uncomfortable dwellings. (The house is still there, an imposing, cheerless building of six storeys now divided into at least fourteen flats.) Shortly after this the Conrads, staying first with Galsworthy, took rooms at nearby 17 Gordon Place. Perhaps they were all fleeing before another rural winter in which the long nights discouraged company.

When writing his biography of Conrad Ford referred to the first quarter of 1904 as 'the most terrible period' in his and Conrad's lives. Jessie Conrad fell in the street and permanently injured her knees, both families got the 'flu and Conrad's writing, difficult enough for him in the easy times, ground to a halt. *Nostromo* was being serialised in *TP's Weekly* and it was at this point that Ford not only kept him going but wrote passages himself. Parts of the manuscript are in Ford's hand. This was also when he took sections of *The Mirror of the Sea* by dictation:

> No one was left on his feet except the hospital nurse I got in – she was an added flail! – the cook and myself. The cook, the nurse and I ran the family meals. There was fortunately a sort of dumb-waiter hoisted by ropes that ran up several storeys of the house. It made a rumbling like intoxicated thunder but

> would carry several trays of food at a time. Conrad came into lunch everyday because he was trying to work very hard in his lodgings round the corner. He used to come in in the mornings, and, having climbed the many stairs to my small, dreadful study, would sit for hours motionless and numb with a completely expressionless face. Every now and then he would say: 'I can't do it. It can't be done. Je suis foutu.'

Fortunately, the cockney nurse, whom no one else could tolerate, was soothing to Conrad and Ford credits her as much as himself with getting Conrad to write. When the cook succumbed to the 'flu Ford did the lunches, imitating her cooking, so that Conrad should not know that there had been a further disturbance of routine.

Olive recorded in her diary on 6 March 1904 a visit made by her brother Robert to the Ford household after Christina's hair had caught fire: 'Robert went to Airlie Gardens yesterday and found a scene of desolation. Elsie in bed with something internal, a trained nurse with her. Christina's hair and skin burned, nurse burned. All talking of returning to the country, & leaving Winchelsea, Mrs Conrad returned homesick to The Pent. Ford & Elsie got into such a state of depression & "nerves" that they attributed their misfortunes to the possession of an opal ring Ford gave Elsie; Ford tried to lose it down drains & at last, meeting a Little Sister of the Poor, asking her to sell it for charity. Elsie now says it should have been put under running water to break the charm. Very sad!' It would be easy to see this gesture as a mutual acknowledgement that their marriage was fading, something that Ford might have had better reason to suspect than Elsie, but the explanation may simply be that opal has long been regarded as an unlucky stone.

Despite all this, he continued writing *The Soul of London* and also managed to entertain at an impressive rate, seeing quite a bit of James, Pinker and Galsworthy. There were periods of his life when he entertained little, usually because of geographical remoteness or lack of money, but even then there would be a trickle of people to stay. When he was in a metropolis, such as London, Paris or New York, there was a daily torrent. Presumably he was able to stay head and shoulders above it because he floated on a growing raft of his own books. He worked come what may, often in the mornings so that the rest of the day would be free. He must have eaten and drunk rather more than the great majority of mankind but he was never dissipated, thanks to that solid daily basis of work done. The routine, however grinding, was sustaining.

He wrote *The Soul of London* in about three months, finishing some time in March, then pestered Pinker to find a magazine to serialise it. He heard with alarm that James was to do a similar book and wrote deferentially to him. The following month he received a friendly reply from on high: 'Lord bless you, it is all right about your book, of which I am delighted to hear.'

The Soul of London should be read, as should its successors, *The Heart of the Country* and *The Spirit of the People*; not only because of its subject but, fittingly for a book about a great city, because it is in the end a book about life. It is wise, understanding, sympathetic, observant, curious and, naturally, out of print. It leaves an impression of leisured thoughtfulness with no sign of haste in the writing nor of the fraught life which its thirty-one-year-old author was then living. There are good descriptions of street scenes, of the wooden pavements, of the trouble caused when a horse goes down between the shafts, of the hawkers and of the wagons that even then blocked the City. There is awareness of the effects, for good and ill, of modern urban life: 'If in its tolerance it finds a place for all eccentricities of physiognomy, of costume, of cult, it does so because it crushes out and floods over the significance of those eccentricities . . . And, in externals, that is the high watermark of achievement of the Modern Spirit.'

Many of London's inhabitants now would agree that 'it is a place in which one exists in order to gain the means of living out of it', though some would recognise themselves in the description of those held to it not by their present activities but by imagined possibilities. Ford cites the case of an unemployed labourer, formerly a countryman, who turned down Ford's offer to get him another job in the country because of the hold of those imagined possibilities: 'London for those who have once, for however short a space, been Londoners, is always on the cards, is always just beyond the horizon.' He sympathises with the unemployed because they 'suffer for no apparent principle, for no faith, for no fame, for no nation, for no glory; they suffer the shame of poverty, without the compensating glory of defeat. They have not ever seen their Napoleon ride slowly along their cheering lines.' Noting 'the crowds of philanthropists who make swallow flights into slums . . . socialist prophets who read in the skies signs of an approaching Armageddon after which all men shall be alike in taste as in habitation', he vividly describes his own visit to the house of a poor family sustained by the making of matchboxes. He comments, shrewdly and unfashionably, that aid to the poor woman might be no real help at all. It is a passage worth quoting at length:

> She was married – or perhaps she was not married – to a waterside labourer, who when he could work, made fair money. As a rule he suffered from chronic rheumatism, and was next door to a cripple. She had four children under nine. She was a dark, untidy-haired woman with a face much pitted by smallpox and she had a horribly foul tongue. The room looked out on a boxlike square of livid brick yards, a table was under a window, a sugar box held coal. Another, nailed above the mantle, held bits of bread, a screw of tea in white paper, a screw of sugar in blue, and a gobbet of margarine in a saucer. When her man was in work or bad enough to be in hospital, when, at any rate, he was out of the house, there would be no coal in the one box because he was not crouching over the fire, and a bit of bacon in the other because there was no fuel to pay for. What he made went for the rent. There was nothing else in the room except a mattress and, on a damp and discoloured wall, a coloured mezzo tint of Perdita, the mistress of George IV. I do not know how she came to be pasted up there.
>
> Till the school bell rang the children worked at her side. I don't think they were ever either dressed for school or given breakfasts by her. She made matchboxes for 2¾d. the hundred and forty-four. It was wonderful to watch her working – engrossed, expressionless, without a word, her fingers moving deftly and unerringly, the light very dim, the air full of the faint sickly smell of paste and of the slight crackling of thin wood, and the slight slop-slopping of the paste brush. Sometimes she

would sigh, not sorrowfully, but to draw a deeper breath. It was the only sound that was not all arbitrary, the only variation in the monotony of her life, the only thing that distinguished her from a wonderfully perfect machine. Now and then a piece of the thin wood cracked along the line of a knot, but she showed no sign of exasperation.

Her husband, as a rule, sat in front of the fire; his right hand had lost two fingers, his others were too swollen to be able to catch hold of a paste brush; he sucked silently at the end of an empty pipe. To me, however – I used to stand in the doorway and watch her – what was appalling was not the poverty. It was not the wretchedness because, on the whole, neither the man nor the woman were anything other than contented. But it was the dire speed at which she worked. It was like watching all the time some feat of desperate and breathless skill. It made one hold one's own breath.

In the face of it any idea of 'problems', of solutions, of raising the submerged, or of the glorious destinies of humanity, vanished. The mode of life became, as it were, august and settled. You could not pity her because she was so obviously and wonderfully equipped for her particular struggle: you could not wish to 'raise' her, for what could she do in any other life, in any other air? Here at least she was strong, heroic, settled and beyond any condemnation.

As for ideals . . . she had not even ideas. She was an expressed and admirable machine, but if you gave her 2¾d. the price of a gross of boxes – if you gave her time literally – she would utter long bursts of language that was a mixture of meaningless obscenities and of an old fashioned and formal English. She did not see why the Irish were allowed in Southwark, and she would shoot forth a monologue of grievances against her husband's mates, shouldering the poor chap out of a job, and stealing his 'bacca, and him next door to a cripple; she had stuck the carving knife through the arm of a drunken man because he had tried to come into her room one night when her man was in hospital. She laughed hoarsely at the idea, and made feints with her hands.

These topics seemed to come out of her as words came out of machines, unnatural and disturbing. She had not much desire to talk, her hands and eyes were continually going back to her paste brush. But as for ideals! She wanted to keep off the rates; she wanted the Charity Organisation people, 'them enquiry blokes', to keep away. She wanted her children to get their schooling done and easy things up a bit, helping her with the pasting. Above all she wanted the two lads to keep out of bad ways, and the two gals not be bad gals with these here shiny top boots. She wanted them to stop indoors and paste matchboxes. Sooner than see them on the streets she would use the carving knife to them; she had a sister, a flower hand, making artificial flowers, who had 'fallen'.

These were her ideals. If you translate them into terms of greater material prosperity you find them identical with anyone else's. One desires for the later years of one's life a little ease. She would have it when the law permitted her children to aid her. One desires privacy when one suffers, she would have it if the enquiry blokes could keep away. One desires that one's children should grow in virtue.

I should say that she was as contented and as cheerful as myself: she probably knew better than people more enlightened and with higher ambitions the truth of the saying that was constantly on her lips, 'We can't b . . . well have everything' and, as I have said, to be in her presence was to find all 'problems', police court missionaries, societies, and sisters of the poor, grow dim and childish along with their Modern Spirit itself. It was like interviewing the bedrock of human existence in a cavern deep in the earth . . .

It had once been a model dwelling: the stairs were of stone, but the railings, the banisters, the panels of nearly all the doors, and sometimes the very doorposts, every cupboard and every shelf, had been chopped down for firewood . . . That problem that is no problem – the matter of the very poor workers – becomes the only question of London . . . Their whole nerve force, and nearly all their thoughts are given to their work. They are the dust filtered down from all the succeeding dominant types . . . they are forming, and have been forming for years, an hereditary class. Education hardly touches their children . . .

★

He always left people with their dignity, particularly the poor. Though a compulsive generaliser himself, he mistrusted people who generalised others into groups and sought to organise them. He sensed the coercion latent in reform, the overriding of the individual, and he didn't like it.

Geographically, he defined London as starting where the tree-trunks were blackened by soot: '. . . a line drawn from Leigh, in Essex half-way through the Epping Forest, to the north of Hendon, to the west of Brentford, the south-west of Barnes, well to the south of Sydenham, well to the east of Bromley and so up to Leigh again.' The most noticeable tree on the roads leading to London was then the elm. Like many people now, he believed that the great emporia were doing away with local tradesmen.

The leisured classes, he thought, resembled a deer-park within London, or a zoological garden within Regent's Park. London was different from most European capitals in that access to high society depended less on blood and more on people making themselves acceptable, which meant suppressing individuality in the interest of not offending others – which, in turn, meant not discussing anything serious. Thus: 'There is not, in fact, any etiquette in London, there is only a general rule against obtruding your personality . . .' Leisure without work was a laborious business but leisure within work was important – 'the pause in the beat of the clock that comes now and then to make life seem worth going on with.' His novels reflect this definition of the malaise of the leisured classes, particularly with regard to the conventions of conversation.

He regretted the passing of Georgian squares, alleyways and slums but saw it as inevitable. Of contemporary Edwardian building he wrote: 'We see terra-cotta ornamental excrescencies, meaning nothing to us; heavy masses that, to those of us who care about architectural proportion, are repulsive, because, for us, they have no associations. The Memoirists have not yet written them up but to our great-grandchildren these excrescencies will have meanings and associations, these heavinesses will be suggestive, because we, their ancestors, lived amongst these things our pathetic, petty and futile lives.'

There was in Ford no distinction between the novelist and the man. The qualities he listed as necessary to an observer of London are very close to those he would have listed for a novelist: 'to see London steadily and see it whole, a man must have certain qualities of temperament so exhaustive as to preclude, on the face of it, the faculties which go to the making – or the marring – of great Fortunes . . . an impressionability and an impersonality, a single-mindedness to see, and a power of arranging his illustrations cold-bloodedly, an unemotional mind and a great sympathy . . . an avidity and a sobriety of intellect, an untireable physique and a delicately-tempered mind. These things are antitheses.'

His curiosity is constant – 'if one stayed to think, one would like to know what kind of poor wretch set out the fifth stone in the third tier of the pyramid of Cheops' – and leads him to comment on sights which were commonplace then but are no longer, such as the evening promenading of the young that could be seen from Westbourne Grove to Whitechapel, from Shepherd's Bush to Mile End Road. It was part of the mating ritual and was how they met.

His curiosity also led him to the observation of individuals, such as the plasterer's mate who was an enthusiast of home-brewed treacle-beer (he put it in a pail by his bed and would lie in all Sunday morning, imbibing through a tube) and of chaffinches. Ford reckoned that 'the companionship of animals . . . gives them [people] a chance to get rid of some of the stores of tenderness towards all living things, which for lack of words, they cannot so well lavish on their wives and children.'

He thought that de-humanising work in which the person is only part of a process cut people off from each other, just as ease of travel made for less actual communication rather than more: 'The days of most rapid travelling are the days of most frequent misunderstandings between the races of mankind.' His point was that modern travel made it possible for the traveller to take his world and his prejudices with him, whereas if he had to cross continents on foot or horseback he would have undergone an education – the edges would have been rounded, he would have had to adapt, learn, compromise, tolerate, understand.

The book ends on a poetical note: London is 'A cloud as it

were of the dust of men's lives.' Aside from his observation and perception, it is his generosity of temperament and his love of generalisations – which, whether you think them true or not, are always stimulating – that make the book so lively and warm. It is an early example of his true voice.

After finishing *The Soul of London* he had what appears to have been a nervous breakdown. It is difficult to be more precise because terms relating to mental illness are still not always easy to apply with precision and in those days the study of such conditions was in its infancy. He was variously described, then and later, as suffering from agoraphobia, neurasthenia, depression, shell shock and 'nerves'. He displayed symptoms of each but not in so full a range as to justify a confident diagnosis, except possibly depression. Agoraphobia is apparently more commonly found in women and applies as much or more to busy city streets as to open spaces; neurasthenia usually involves listless withdrawal from all activity and engagement; shell-shock and 'nerves' were loosely applied to a variety of conditions, at the root of which was often depression consequent upon exhaustion.

It is important not to underestimate the role that exhaustion might have played. He lived and worked hard, lived a lot on his nerves and was a worrier. His pushing things away from him and refusing to discuss them – money, for instance, and later the question of divorce – were not the reactions of a confident cavalier but of a man tried beyond his capacity by confrontation. An illustration of the sometimes mercurial nature of his moods can be found in David Garnett's later account of a walk with him from The Cearne (the Garnett house) to Westerham Station:

> He had been cheerful at tea, but in Squerries Park a mood of melancholy stole over him, and he sang me one melancholy song after another, some French, some German, ending with the Westmorland 'Poor Old Horse'. Ford's voice was not bad, his ear was good, and expression he put into the words of the horse's cruel master was pathetic in the extreme . . . then in the most unhappy voice Ford broke in to say something like this: 'I am that poor old horse, David . . . The world is cruel to the old, David. It is very cruel to me . . . Once I was a brilliant

> young poet, a famous writer . . . now I am no more use to anyone and they kick me, now they have got me down . . . Poor old horse . . .' I was in tears and, seeing this, Ford wept also. Then brushed his tears aside for a moment to look at his watch and make sure that he was not late for his train.

He began referring to himself as old whilst still in his thirties and, as we have seen, in his late teens and early twenties he often acted older than he was. It is possible that a part of him actually *wanted* to be old. He was certainly more fully, more roundedly (in every sense) and more confidently himself in later than earlier life. He may have sensed it before he got there.

His way back from depression or breakdown was never through easing off and resting; it was through the very work that helped bring him down. Successful work, especially if it were paid for and had a prospect of good sales, was the best restorative. Work that went badly and which no one seemed to want brought on depression and a sense of hopelessness. He might well have had these depressions anyway but there is little doubt that unsuccessful work made them worse. By the spring of 1904 he had on his hands two completed books, *The Benefactor* and *The Soul of London*, which no one wanted to publish. He left London for Winterbourne Stoke, near Salisbury, and spent time there and in the New Forest. In April his third volume of poetry, *The Face of the Night*, was published to a depressing lack of critical notice, though Wells admired it. Conrad was also having a bad time and they both considered joining George Gissing in Spain.

In May Elsie and the children came down to join him. There were further domestic dramas. Elsie burned her face with carbolic acid and had to ask Olive to come down. Olive stayed for ten days. Her diary entries are not very detailed, but, inspired nearly half a century later by David Garnett's *The Golden Echo*, she added to her recollections:

> Ford met me with a trap and seemed pleased to see me. I think I had never then heard of neurasthenia: & for a few days all went well; but it was a hot July & on leaving Lake House (to which a college friend had given me a general invitation) to walk over

the Plain to Amesbury, Ford had an attack of agoraphobia & said if I didn't take his arm he would fall down. I held on in all the blaze for miles, it seemed to me, but the town reached he walked off briskly to get tobacco and a shave; and when I pointed this out to Elsie she said 'nerves'. He can't cross wide open spaces. She said he had already consulted a local doctor. We explored further & went to Stone Henge, but he got worse. He was unusually silent while I argued and philosophised on our walks but at last he burst out in a vitriolic attack on 'respectable' Garnetts & said '*I* would rather be notorious & hanged,' and was tearful: and next day on the Plain as we lay about in the heat, we all wept. It seemed so hopeless. I was put up in a cottage across the road, and next morning Elsie came over and woke me & said I could catch the six o'clock bus with the market-women to Salisbury. Ford was asleep and wouldn't be up till mid-day. He had gone downstairs at 2 am & afraid that he might commit suicide, she had crept after him, and found he was only putting the kettle on. Evidently I could do no good by staying longer and had better go.

Vitriolic attacks were uncharacteristic. Perhaps his sudden dislike of the Garnetts' 'respectability' might have been due to the fact that he felt, because of Mary, that he wasn't respectable. Whatever the reason, it seems that the purpose of Olive's visit shifted rather from helping Elsie after her burn to her helping her with Ford – unless it had really been that all along.

Following the visit, Olive made a diary entry quoting Ecclesiastes and Matthew: 'The bowl is broken . . . the axe is laid to the root.' Did she mean the marriage? Possibly; it is hard to see what else she may have meant. In late July Ford visited a specialist in London. Olive remarked that 'the verdict was "nervous breakdown" recovery *might* be in two years: sea voyage & no work for 6 months. I walked over to West Hill, & Ford walked over to sleep there, sitting down on every seat & putting a lozenge in his mouth against agoraphobia.'

He could bear neither isolation (he never could) nor his family (the doctor had specified that the voyage be taken without Elsie). Nor was he working. He continued to plan other books and continued his reading and note-taking on Henry VIII and Katharine Howard, but when he was not engaged in imaginative work he was like a bird with a broken wing, able neither to walk properly nor fly. If the doctors had arranged immediate publication to critical acclaim and the mass buying of the two unpublished books, recovery would have been quicker.

His letters of the period refer to his research and do not make heavy weather of his condition. His correspondents – Galsworthy, W. H. Hudson, Richard Garnett (Olive's father) – were helpful and sympathetic. In September Conrad wrote to reassure him of Pinker's continued belief in him – 'you are for him the man who can write anything at any time – and write it well – he means not in an ordinary way. His belief in you is by no means shaken. He admits in effect that he has failed both with the London and with the novel. But does not admit that he has failed finally. The things are not topical. They exist. They are not lost.' In October Uncle William Rossetti wrote to tell him not to worry about a loan – 'that tin' – but to treat it as a gift, while in August James had written to Elsie: 'What you tell me of your husband's condition, past and actual, excites my liveliest sympathy . . . though I don't know the details of your worriments the sense of them in the air was not at any moment far from me . . . I rejoice that Hueffer has meanwhile found a thorough asylum.'

The asylum was Germany. He could not afford the recommended sea voyage and so had decided to go up the Rhine. In order to pay for it he tried unsuccessfully to get back some of the hundred pounds that Conrad owed him and seemed, Olive notes, 'decidedly better' at the prospect of travel. He lunched cheerfully with Galsworthy and Edward Garnett before leaving, despite which he was unable to get up the ship's gangway unaided.

Elsie was in not much better condition. She wrote sadly and selflessly to Mrs Hueffer to the effect that Ford 'has really in the last year had more worries & anxieties than any mortal can bear . . . he cannot get about at all or else he would come to see you. I wonder if you could go to see him off. He will start on Saturday . . . He thinks it better for me not to go up again for many reasons. This letter I'm afraid is very incoherent but I am tired and worn out to distraction with all this misery . . .

Tunnycliffe [the doctor] thinks it better that he should go without me – but it is hard to bear since we have never once been separated for so long since our marriage.'

She signed the letter, 'Yours affectly Elsie M. Hueffer'. She got on well with Mrs Hueffer and this formality no doubt reflects the conventions of the time but it may also be something more; Elsie was very proud of her full married name, how proud was still to be seen. Conrad's sympathy was, as quoted earlier, more evenly divided between himself and Ford.

Ford's time in Germany was peripatetic, confusing and a failure, though with apparently successful interludes. He went to Boppard, a small town on the Rhine where two of the Hueffer aunts lived. They treated him as a 'sort of demi-God' and he was later to dedicate a book to each of them. Things appeared to go well at first and he wrote to Elsie that he could 'now walk anywhere, particularly when I have someone with me'. But then he was depressed by the thought that he might be a hypochondriac – 'I am a pretty miserable skunk' – and soon came to think that he was either mad or dying. He passed from one nerve specialist to another, one hydropathic establishment to another, feeling worse all the time. He was even homesick – 'I fancy homesickness does as much to pull me down as anything else' – which was unusual for him since he normally relished his continental stays. It was at this time that he wrote 'Romney Wall', a poem which drew on scenes he always found evocative:

God, to be in Romney Marsh
And see the ships come above the wall –
I'd give these lakes and Alps and all
For just an hour of storm and shower,
And just a glimpse of Lydd Church Tower,
And just to hear the wind in the thorns –
Just not to hear the cow bells' din,
Just not to hear the cowman's horns –
But just to mark the tide come in –
Dear God by Romney Wall.

*

The aunts, Tante Laura and Tante Emma, were alarmed when he began working again. His project was the Holbein book and his reason for doing it was to help pay for his trip. Elsie was having difficulty raising the money and he must have felt responsible. It may not have been the whole reason, though: he was not happy without work in progress and it could be that he felt his way to recovery was more likely to be through successful work than through hydrotherapy.

The aunts, however, did not think so. Tante Emma took away his candles, which didn't stop him, and then Tante Laura offered to pay him the amount he would expect to make on the book so long as he did not write it – an unusual offer for an author and one that, if generally taken up, might benefit writers and readers alike. Ford was the most inveterate and natural of writers, a man through whom ink flowed as plentifully as blood and whose pen stopped only with his breath, but he agreed – for the time being. He went to Münster where the Hueffer family came from and was there kept busy by 'half a hundred Hueffers'. He was entertained and taken shooting and met the Schücking family, with whom he exchanged poetry readings. His condition improved for a while but he suffered a relapse before returning to Boppard.

At about this time Robert Garnett, the solicitor, drew up a memorandum of Ford's financial position. It showed that he owned two properties in London which had been bought in 1896 for £779 17/6d (the house of the lady who made matchboxes was one he visited because someone had suggested it to him as an investment) and Hurst Cottage in Aldington which he had bought for £150 in 1901 ('a sort of final asylum', he called it.) It was tiny but had wide views across the Marsh to the sea – always important to him. He also had £500 invested at 3%. The annual income from all these was £75 17/10d out of which he had to pay interest of £27 per annum on debts of £425. He was owed nearly £200 by Conrad (the loan plus rent arrears).

Personal debts among family and friends seem to have been more common then than now. People did not borrow from banks in the way that has since become acceptable and there were not the credit institutions that we have. It was normal to pay interest on money borrowed from friends and relatives, though the practice was not invariable. There were therefore many whose financial circumstances were based on a complicated network of loans amongst people they knew, more as in Shakespeare's and Marlowe's time than in our own. William Rossetti's telling Ford not to repay the money he had borrowed for the trip (£50) was not only typical of that generous man but not unusual within families, yet Ford did repay it two years later. Meanwhile, he urged Elsie not to spend her own money on him nor to mortgage Hurst Cottage. She disobeyed and raised a mortgage of £250 to add a studio to The Bungalow for Ford to work in. Designed by Cowlishaw, it is a large extension at the back that takes up nearly all the garden, and is a touching testimony to Elsie's attempt to help her husband and to save her marriage. It did neither but the fact that she tried suggests that at that period she was neither resentful nor despairing.

Tante Laura's tactics did not work for long; Ford was soon back at work on the Holbein book. He still suffered from his agoraphobia but for the first time for months he was able to sleep without bromides. A heavy smoker for most of his adult life, he stopped for this period. Conrad offered to try to get his letters from Germany published through Pinker but nothing came of it. It was also at this time that he reluctantly agreed to Christina's being sent to the Roman Catholic convent in Rye. He wrote regularly to her.

At one point he suggested that Elsie and the children settle with him in Germany but when she resisted he agreed, describing his own suggestion as 'mostly part of the disease'. He told Elsie that he thought his troubles would disappear if he were back with her, then that they wouldn't because they were too 'deep within my nature.' In Bonn his Uncle Hermann was dying; in Basle he stayed with a bereaved professor who wept most of the time amidst the ticking, striking, chiming and cuckoo-ing of Swiss clocks. He didn't like the Basle doctor and hated the baths but he did a lot of work before breaking down again in mid-October 1904. It was, he said, worse when he was in the New Forest, and he specifically asked Elsie not to join him. She wanted to come but the English doctors also advised that she shouldn't. His mother, however, did come.

In the meantime he was looked after by cousins who moved

him, sometimes with difficulty, from place to place. He estimated that during thirty days of treatment he had ninety cold baths and thirty tepid soda water douches – 'even if the so-called agoraphobia had not interfered with my walking I should hardly have been able to get about'. That 'so-called' is presumably indicative of his public attitude towards his own illness but it is hard to know if that was how he really viewed it. There is less doubt of his attitude to his various treatments but how he saw himself at this period is not so easy to come at. What indications there are point to his regarding the illness as originating within himself rather than being imposed from without. He disliked introspection, as we have seen, and would probably have argued that his condition would not improve by being talked about. He might have been right. He was sceptical about much of the treatment he received, whether counselling, dietary, or surgical. (The latter involved his having a number of teeth out. He had trouble with teeth from then on.)

He cheered up after his mother arrived but then had another relapse as a result of which he was put on a diet of pork and ice-cream and bad salads. There were few things he was less forgiving of than a bad salad. In another place he was fed dried peas and grapes, one grape every quarter of an hour for sixteen hours a day. There were farcical attempts to prove that his condition had a sexual origin – '[the doctor] would suddenly produce from his desk and flash before my eyes indecent photographs of a singular banality. He expected me to throw fits or faint. I didn't.' This has been cited as an example of his alleged unwillingness to come to terms with sexual matters but that is to ignore the fact that his reaction was to the 'singular banality'. When he wrote about his illness in *Return to Yesterday*, he was inclined to play down psychological and nervous aspects and to ascribe it to his heart (from adolescence onwards his family had been worried about his heart): 'I was suffering from a slight fluttering of the heart which, after periods of intense overwork and fatigue, caused – and indeed still does cause – me to feel slightly faint for a second or two. This will naturally sometimes happen in the street. The result therefore a little resembles agoraphobia . . .' He said that in the three years 1903 to 1906 he saw nineteen specialists, sixteen or seventeen of whom attributed his illness to sexual abnormalities.

It was by one of these that the bad salads were introduced. They were made with lemon juice and the white of an egg instead of oil and vinegar, which were held to be sexually exciting. At one period he was given three times a day a boiling shampoo and a foot-bath of iced water. The only result of all this, in his opinion, was to reduce his weight to nine stone and two pounds (he was six feet tall).

Whatever the causes of his troubles, it is likely that stress and fatigue played a major part. It happened time and again during his life, usually less dramatically but to a similar pattern. Nor was it simply a case of his not being good at taking strain or of his tiring easily; he demanded a great deal of himself, more than he demanded of others. An enthusiast, he never went half-way in anything and quite often went the whole way in several directions: 'I have all my life been incapable of inaction . . . If I had to advise, I should say: "Work yourself all out, to the limit of your passion for activities. Then take what you get for it."' He believed his 1904 breakdown toughened him and made him better able to endure subsequent trials.

He and his mother decided to return to London and by Christmas 1904 he was staying alone at 3, St Edmund's Terrace, lent to him by William Rossetti, who was away, so that he could avoid Christmas with the family. From this distance, there is no fully satisfactory way of describing exactly what had been happening to him. He simply broke down for a while, as an engine does, so that he was unable to function normally. Not only was his work affected but he was unable to maintain the normal relationships of life without exhaustion, sometimes unable to walk and for much of the time unable to cope alone. No doubt daily routines which when well we all perform without thinking required constant, enervating effort. Sometimes he would stagger in the streets, at others lose his belongings; at yet others, be apparently all right.

Recovery began in St Edmund's Terrace where he lay in bed and read and slowly and easily did just what he liked. There were caged birds in his bedroom, which soothed and engaged him. There was also the admirable Dr Albert Tebb. He, like Pinker, is another of the unsung heroes of literature but is even less likely to be blessed by a biographer. Though they had briefly met before, it was at Conrad's urging that Ford consulted him. Tebb had been an admirer of Madox Brown, was a friend of William Rossetti's and became doctor to the Conrads and the Hueffers and, later, to Violet Hunt. She described him as a 'queer, clever, weedy man who stooped so for despair, not laziness. Himself he could not save. But you called him and he came, hasting, his baggy umbrella in front of him, the flaps of his greatcoat nearly catching the ground, looking like Santa Claus or the Ol' Clo' Man bringing the babies . . . He was a magician, a wonder-doctor as one would have expected from his quack-like appearance, white-complexion, blue-eyed, bewildered . . . He was always poor – and likely to remain so.'

Ford's story of how Tebb cured him is normally regarded as unlikely but the touch of eccentricity noted by Violet lends it some credence. Ford said that Tebb, 'with a hollow and mournful vindictiveness', told him he would be dead in a month. 'As soon as he was gone I jumped up, dressed myself and . . . took a hansom to Piccadilly Circus . . . I walked backwards and forwards across the Circus for an hour and a half. I kept on saying: "Damn that brute. I will not be dead in a month."' At the end of the month he saw Tebb again. 'Tebb said, "If I hadn't told you you would be dead you would have been dead."'

What happened may not have been as cut and dried as that but there may have been an element of truth as regard the tactics Tebb used. He understood his patients well and subsequently had Ford to live with him. They kept in occasional touch for the rest of their lives. Ford held him in affectionate regard – not his habit with doctors – and Tebb's last letters were written in the 1930s from the Royal Hospital for the Incurables where the poor man was so impoverished he had to sell everything, including his autographed Conrad first editions.

In time, Ford became convinced that his illness was 'purely imaginary: . . . that made it none the better . . . I had nothing specific to be depressed about but the memory of those years is one of uninterrupted mental agonies. Nothing marks them off one from the other. They were lost years.' He published no journalism between March 1904 and February 1906.

After some to-ing and fro-ing, Elsie and the children moved

back to London to her mother's house at 93, Broadhurst Gardens, off the Finchley Road. It was not a relaxed household, despite Olive Garnett's recording in January 1905 that Elsie and Ford seemed happy together, and Ford established a pattern of commuting between Winchelsea and Dr Tebb's house. It was now Elsie's turn to be ill and her ailment, though clearly physiological, seemed at the time to be as mysterious in origin as Ford's. He spent a lot of time with her, read to her and was sympathetic, but perhaps because of what he came to think about his own condition he began to think that she, too, had an 'imaginary' illness. In fact, she had tuberculosis of the kidney, but diagnosis was still some three years off.

He continued working on the Holbein book; recovery was gradual but it was noticeable that his condition improved as Pinker began to place his unsold books (he did not think that he was fully recovered, though, until after he and Elsie had visited America in the autumn of 1906). Pinker placed *The Benefactor*, still without an advance, with Brown Langham, and *The Soul of London* with a new firm, Alston Rivers. Life began to pick up: Ford started work on *The Fifth Queen* trilogy and on the successors to *The Soul of London*. (All three in that series were published in America as *England and the English*.) *The Soul of London* was well received and he began to put himself about again. He joined the National Liberal Club – Masterman, Wells, Jerrold, and Byles, the enthusiastic entrepreneur behind Alston Rivers – were there, and he went to Tuesday lunches in the Mont Blanc restaurant in Gerrard Street at which there were more familiar faces – Conrad, Marwood, Edward Garnett, W. H. Hudson, and others. He also put in an occasional appearance at G. K. Chesterton's lunch club. London was all right: 'In my day in London, one – if you will pardon the expression – bloody well knew that London was the bloody world and if anything went wrong anywhere one said that something must be done about it . . . and something was done about it. That at least was the frame of mind.' That last sentence is important, both because it is probably accurate and because it qualifies what came before it. It is another of Ford's generally unnoticed qualifying sentences.

1905 and 1906 were great improvements on the two years that

preceded them. Collaboration with Conrad was renewed, on *The Nature of a Crime*, and Ford's friendship with Marwood developed. Alston Rivers was a boon. They published *The Soul of London*, *The Heart of the Country* and two volumes of *The Fifth Queen* trilogy, as well as a volume of poetry called *From Inland*, *Christina's Fairy Book* and, subsequently, *The Spirit of the People*. They did Ford well, selling him reasonably – but not, because of their lavish advertising, making much for themselves – and giving him the confidence and recognition he needed. He was made editor of their poetry series and appeared daily in their office with suggestions, recommendations and manuscripts from all and sundry. It was what he loved – being involved in publishing, in discovering new talent and in 'booming' reputations. Unfortunately, the firm lasted only a couple of years. It comprised L. J. Bathurst, the novelist Archibald Marshall and René Byles (of Huguenot descent, according to Ford, with the original family name of Boileaux). Everyone liked Byles except Pinker, who had more or less set up the firm, and Ford once wrote that without him 'it is almost certain I should have given up writing.' After the failure of the firm, Byles went to Japan to run a mineral water business though he returned later when Ford was running the *English Review*. Ford got on less well with Bathurst and Marshall, the latter of whom was still abusing him as late as 1933.

Only one volume was produced during his time as editor of the poetry series. It was Norah Chesson's *Dirge for Aione*, which he put together after her death to help provide for her children. He was subsequently abused for this by her widower.

He was also at this period re-writing his Holbein, revising articles for the *Encyclopaedia Britannica*, doing more journalism, and probably starting on *Lady Whose Bright Eyes*. *The Fifth Queen* trilogy (*The Fifth Queen*, *Privy Seal*, *The Fifth Queen Crowned*) appeared in 1906, 1907 and 1908. *The Soul of London* appeared in 1905, *The Heart of the Country* in 1906 and *The Spirit of the People* in 1907. *The Benefactor* and the Holbein book came out in 1905, *An English Girl* – another novel – and *The Pre-Raphaelite Brotherhood* in 1907. It is a daunting rate of productivity but he was happier being busy. His blue eyes, David Garnett wrote, 'twinkled gaily when he was amused . . . his too mobile lips were sensitive and in some of his moods would open into an engaging smile.'

It was in June 1905 that Conrad's unsuccessful play, *One Day More*, ran for three nights at the Royal Theatre. Conrad was always ambiguous or defensive as to how much of it was written for him by Ford, but there are forty-three manuscript pages in Ford's hand.

Of this formidable list, the successors to *The Soul of London* – *The Heart of the Country* and *The Spirit of the People* – and *The Fifth Queen* trilogy are most likely to interest the general reader. *The Heart of the Country* has the same generous thoughtful voice, the same movement from the particular to the general, the same good observations as its predecessor. As often in Ford's writings, it is also prescient: 'If it be the fate of the country to be turned into one vast territory of pleasure parks eventually, we shall accept the pleasure park as standard, just as now, upon the whole, we accept the small farm.' In this book we meet Meary Walker and other characters such as the tramp Carew who gives prisons the names of countries, workhouses the names of cities. It is clear that Ford spent time talking to representatives of 'the brown flotsam' of the road and, though interested in them, he is unsentimental, not taken in. He writes of the beauty of the country, bemoaning the way that even then the ugly London accent was spreading out into Kent, admiring the independence of sturdy unlettered people like Meary, but never romanticising the widespread ignorance. It was, he thought, worsened by the drift to the towns: 'There are whole stretches of England where a really full-witted or alert youth of between sixteen and thirty will absolutely not be found.' Nor does he have any illusions about harsh working conditions or the bleakness of much of life. Of the field labourer he says: 'His diet is atrocious; it is atrociously cooked; his cottage, as a rule, is insanitary, damp and too small. His work is too hard, his opportunities for mental relaxation pitifully too restricted . . . such virtues as he has, he has in spite of his environment; his vices are nearly all the product of his hard life. You cannot expect much more than a decent friendliness, sobriety and openness of mind from a man whose function in life is no more than to keep on going; and the wonder is how he does it.'

He speculates repeatedly as to why the country people have never combined to improve their lot and he writes of farmers large and small, of the sadness of farm sales and the hardship of the life with insight and concern. He details what he would do if he had fifty thousand acres, which would be to divide it into plots and farms on which it was possible for tenants to improve themselves. It is an imaginative and, for the conditions of the time, plausible scheme: 'Utopian in a sense, but in a sense, too, founded on the eternal necessity of mankind to struggle upwards . . . not one of those bright, cast-iron schemes in which all provision for development, for flux and reflux, all chances of change, are left out.'

Again, his subject is not only the book's title but also modern life, both in general and in particular relation to his own. He draws an early parallel between a man's feeling for the heart of the country and for the heart of a woman, in which man 'will carry always these two small fardels, regret for neglected loves, longing for the unattainable'. The country is a place where you seek rest and consolation but which sometimes reacts like a jealous wife, saying, 'No, you bring yourself to me only in your worst moods, find yourself another consoler.' That sounds like a personal note, as does his nocturnal contemplation of his razor in the quiet moonlit village, when he had to leave the house to avoid suicide. So also does the observation: 'He did not find in that solitude any alleviation but, perhaps because his particular cross drew him away from the real contemplation of material objects, that spot remains to him something glamorous, something mysterious.' On the one hand the sounds of children's voices in the woods, the blue floors of coppices in May, the feel of the wind on the forehead are 'the things that keep us going'; on the other, 'the very sunlight lies like a blight'.

As an example of the way things become real for people he quotes some directions he was once given: 'You go down the lane till you come to the place where Farmer Banks's old barn used to stand when he kept his six cows in it.' This sort of incident has clear reference to the presentation of truth and reality in his mature fiction. The same could be said of his view that no scenery would hold us 'without at least a fictitious crop of historical facts'. Though many of us may love solitude or even hate the sight of living man, few can dispense with 'the invisible presence of the dead'. He talks of the 'detritus of the dead', 'the dust' and 'the patina': 'We see our countrysides through veils, and the trees, the hillocks, and the smithies seem to speak to us with human voices.' The summoning of invisible presences was an essential part of his way of writing. While playing patience and planning he would imagine every detail of the scene he was about to do, right down to the positions of door handles and chairs, then, feeling he had them fixed, he was free of them and could write the scene without mentioning them.

The perspective from which he writes is neither that of countryman nor quite of gentry. For all his knowledge of the locals, he doesn't pretend to be anything other than an outsider. He recalls an occasion when provisions hadn't arrived and, 'One is forced to ask all sorts of favours, and to stand cap in hand before peasants whose rigidity of soul one discovers, enhanced by one's own physical emptiness.' This probably dates from his days as a 'Frenchie'. Later he writes of the ideal as being a country living or estate which is supported by investments and not by country-earned income. He writes also about 'good people', indicating by the use of inverted commas that he means 'good' in the sense of social position, about the social cachet of old acres and county positions, about coming into the great house after a day's hunting with, at dinner, 'the show of candles on women's shoulders'. (Women's shoulders must have been on his mind at this time; in *The Benefactor* they appear as 'solid, dazzling'.)

The countryside he describes is a mixture of Wiltshire and Kent, mainly the latter, but with a touch of East Sussex. He makes frequent references to the country as state of mind and existence, to longings, to emptiness, to the search for the Herb Oblivion; also, to the possibility then of walking along thirty-seven miles of woodland footpaths from Aldington Knoll. He also refers, once, to digging potatoes and feeling the 'flesh-warm' earth after dark. This reference was linked by Moser to an incident in Ford's childhood when he put his hand amongst nesting doves, disturbing them and provoking a telling-off from his grandmother. Moser builds a Freudian structure on these two references, from which he conducts an analysis of Ford's attitude to women, guilt and sex.

However, the simpler and more convincing explanation is surely that which is closer to hand: 'to me,' Ford writes of feeling for the potatoes, 'it has always seemed like finding the breast of a woman.'

The Spirit of the People is not surprisingly more diffuse than the two earlier books; lacking a geographical location to describe, it attempts a cultural geography of Englishness. It is generalising and interpretive and its generalisations tend to linger in the mind, either as truths or provocative part-truths, long after their context has been forgotten. It is likely that Ford experienced the same problem, himself, which is why reading him is a little like reading the Bible: there is so much of him that repetitions and contradictions can always be found. Nonetheless, *The Spirit of the People* is as good a description of the moral and intellectual background to his art as can be found. It is almost a coda to the major themes of his novels and to much of his verse.

He begins by saying that he had intended in all three books to write about only what interested him and he goes on to give his views as to what a work of art ought to do: 'Primarily it should give enjoyment. Secondly – and that is its social value – it should awaken thought.' The artist, he thinks, 'should be an exact scientist. (This is not a paradox.) His province is to render things exactly as he sees them in such a way that his rendering will attract the imagination of the reader, and induce him to continue an awakened train of thought . . . It is all one as to whether the artist be right or wrong as to the facts; his business is to render rightly the appearance of things. It is all one whether he can convince his reader or cause to arise a violent opposition. For the artist's views are of no importance whatever. Who cares whether Dante believed the Guelfs to be villains or saviours?'

This is surely at least half right. What it ignores is that the artist's views might well have been an essential ingredient of his inspiration; they might be why he created and shaped something as he did, so they are important. But they are also irrelevant in that whether the work stands for centuries or fades with the majority owes nothing to the political or other views of the artist. Opinions do not make art.

Not, of course, that Ford did what he recommends. No writer does. They may go half way towards it, rendering the appearance of things in such a way as to strike the imagination, awaken thought or open eyes as to what is real, but no writer renders things exactly as he sees them. He shapes and arranges them according to what he wants to show up, like the artist mixing colours. He leaves a lot out. The usual analogy with Impressionist painters is misleading not because the two are not analogous but because it ignores the fact that Impressionist paintings are equally the result not only of observations of appearance but of a shaping and selecting intelligence. An Impressionist work can be as didactic in its way as a sermon. Ford's nearly always were, in that he was trying to put over views which were aligned with a desired impression of life. His books succeed not because of what his views were but because his dramatisation of them was artistically effective.

Considering English society of his day, he makes observations on street violence, hooliganism (then a new word) and on allegations of police brutality. Little, it seems, might have changed. He thinks the most valuable gift that England has bequeathed humanity is not the arts, the sciences or the Empire but 'its evolution of a rule of thumb system by which men may live together in large masses'. Rubbing along, in other words, making space for people, standing back, not forcing anyone but somehow getting everyone through is an art-form: 'In the great sense, the supreme art is the supreme expression of commonsense.' Thus Nelson was not only the greatest Englishman but the one artist that England has ever produced, whereas 'There have certainly been writers as great as Shakespeare.' This view of art as the supreme expression of commonsense may perhaps be a sophistication of his early admiration of the practical and of the ability to cope.

The converse of this native genius for tolerance is that the Englishman 'is singularly apt to be lacking in that imagination which is insight'. There are few worse countries in which to suffer mental distress, as opposed to material or financial, since '. . . for mental distress he has only "Therein the patient must minister to himself"; or that most soul-wounding of all maxims "There are hundreds worse off than you, my friend."' (It is easy to know what he means but it is a pity that someone didn't jog his elbow at this point and put in a word for Dr Tebb.)

He does not use the word 'English' to describe a racial group – the peoples of England are too mixed for that to make any sense – but to describe commonality of spirit and self-perception. This consciousness absorbed foreigners, in evidence of which he cites the case of a fast-bowling West African prince at his school (in this, one of his infrequent references to his own cricketing, it becomes apparent that he was wicket-keeper). He also cites a school fight arising from disagreement about English history. He lost, and spent a week sulking in bed 'not because of my injuries, but because of my passionate rebellion against fate'.

Of direct relevance to his *Fifth Queen* trilogy, and a point made also in his Holbein book, is as we have seen his reckoning of modern England as beginning with the Tudors. He also thought Thomas Cromwell, whom he depicts as a tyrant, as the great man of his age. Comparison between Dürer and Holbein illustrates, he says, the change in the governance of England: 'Dürer's lord rode hunting in full steel from small castles in rugged rocks; the flesh of his fingers is hardened, dried and tanned by exposure to the air. But Holbein's lords no longer rode hunting . . . The change had set in fully by 1530 or so, when Holbein chronicled the English Court. His lords were precisely indoor statesmen; they dealt in intrigues, they inhabited palaces, not castles; their flesh was rounded, their limbs at rest, their eyes sceptical.' This Holbein type is 'a heavy, dark, bearded, bull necked animal, sagacious, smiling, but with devious and twinkling eyes'. It reminds him, he says, of W. G. Grace.

He had some unusual and imaginative ideas about the Tudors and Stuarts, as that it was the Puritan and Cromwellian cause that was romantic, not the Stuart: 'For in essentials, the Stuarts' cause was picturesque; the Cromwellian cause was a matter of principle. Now a picturesque cause may make a very strong and spirited appeal, but it is, after all, a principle that sweeps people away. For poetry is the sublime of commonsense; principle is wrong-headedness brought up to the sublime pitch – and that, in essentials, is romance.' The tendency of this emphasis on commonsense is to suggest that art is not, after all, simply a matter of impressions, but a recognition of the real.

He considers that the puritan revolution has a lot to answer for, in that it 'did away with the artistic spirit as a factor in life . . .' and '. . . began that divorce of principle from life which . . . has earned for the English the title of a nation of hypocrites . . . very broadly, we may say that Catholicism, which is a religion of action and of frames of mind, is a religion that men can live up to. Protestantism no man can live up to, since it is a religion of ideals and of reason . . . Before that date a man could live without his finger on his moral pulse; since then it has grown gradually more and more impossible.'

He portrays this feeling of the moral pulse in his novels, but the effect of the Puritan revolution did not stop at that. It 'did away with true Toryism which is Socialism . . . and it gave us two centuries of enmity to France and of growing subjection to German ideals.' It also tended to produce the blond sentimentalist as dominant type (Tietjens). The future, he thinks, will bring war with Germany and the need for a strong popular leader (this was written, remember, in 1906–7).

Elements of Englishness are also, of course, to be found in the Anglican Church. He admires the beauty and peace of Anglican services as they then were, particularly the silence at the end which emphasises the peace which passeth all understanding. He is struck by the difference between this and the horror-stories that may be read aloud in the lesson and thinks it demonstrates an English ability to ignore the most terrible facts. There is no belief in hell or purgatory, therefore no recognition that you cannot have your cake and eat it, therefore a weakened perception of the relation between cause and effect – loss of which is disastrous for all, individuals or societies. Some of what he says would fit easily into contemporary comment on the Church of England: 'I should say that what distinguishes the worshippers belonging to the Established Church is a frame of mind and not a religion – a frame of mind of which, though the ethical basis of Christianity is more or less excellently preserved, the theological conditions remain in a very fragmentary condition.' He makes a good simile of the sun of belief sinking unnoticed, leaving the land visible but with 'the last tinge of red gone from the shadows'. A capacity for faith remains but 'of a vague and humanitarian nature' because 'the influence of the world upon the Churches is eminently destructive of the letter of laws.'

Even if we lived forever, we should still need religion. 'We may, that is to say, become of many days: we have still to face sorrow. It is there that God comes in. For the function of God, after all, is to teach us to live that our strength may be as our days.' This is probably as good a statement as there is about what Ford thought religion should do. It does not shed much light on his faith but it does indicate why he thought it was important.

He sees England as a country of Christism in which, for the Englishman at worship, there is little of the supernatural: 'His problem, much more than the saying of "Holy, holy, holy" is that of how we shall do as we would be done by.' This is partly why the English live tolerantly and partly what leads them not to 'Examine the other man's nature and see how he would be done by.'

Perhaps women will found the churches of the future. He describes a feminist gathering and concludes that women have more time to think and feel as the men become more specialised, harried and ineffectual. It is women that keep the Catholic Church going. Protestantism is of 'nobler intellectual growth' while Catholicism is 'almost entirely of the sentiments and weaknesses of humanity.' The future may be a reversion to early Teutonic states of matriarchy. 'Monogamy', he says, 'is the one powerful, the one universal law that woman has given us.'

By way of illustration of these national tendencies, there are excursions into – sadly – still familiar areas such as the nonchalance and want of enterprise amongst officials who run the railways, the passivity of the ill-treated commuters and the impotence and inaction of the Foreign Office (in the matter of Leopold II, King of the Belgians and cannibalism in the Congo). There are also some surprisingly shrewd observations on the questions of legal practice.

But he is soon back to his main theme. The English feel deeply and reason little, he thinks. The problem is not too little feeling but too much and they hide it, or from it. He recalls being forbidden in childhood to talk about 'things' – religion, relations between the sexes, the Boer War – in fact, 'every subject from which one can digress into anything moving . . . And that is what makes English conversation so profoundly, so portentously troublesome to maintain . . . It is as if one were set on making oneself interesting with the left hand tied behind one's back.' He describes an incident of a wounded, half-crippled young soldier returning from the Boer War to be met by his father. 'Their greeting was, "Hello, Bob!" and "Hello, Governor!"' and he comments: 'that a race should have trained itself to such a spartan repression is none the less worthy of wonder.'

He then recounts an incident in which his friend P asked him to accompany himself and a Miss W to the station, from which Miss W was to begin a long voyage. It appears that P and Miss W were illicitly in love. They talked of trivia or of nothing. Ford realised that he was there to ensure that passion should not erupt through a polite normality. The couple parted as if for a day or two and P drove off in the dog cart without a word, forgetting he had left Ford at the station. It was a fine achievement, Ford thought, playing the game to the bitter end – but Miss W died at Brindisi and P spent three years attempting rest cures on the continent. Ford commented: '. . . it seems to me that at that moment of separation a word or two might have saved the girl's life and the man's misery without infringing eternal verities . . . a silence so utter, a so demonstrative lack of tenderness, seems to be a manifestation of a national characteristic that is almost appalling.' He used this incident to good effect in *The Good Soldier*, which he wrote nearly a decade later, saying then that the idea had been in his mind for some years and that he had 'had it from Edward himself'. There is no indication as to the identity of the unfortunate couple. The location was probably rural which makes the Aldington/Pent or Winchelsea areas the most likely. Both had small stations within an easy ride. It could have also have been part of the goings-on at Dostoievsky Corner.

He believed this repression of emotions to be the secret to harmonious social existence but it has the added disadvantage that it sacrifices the arts, which are concerned with expression of emotion: '. . . every street and every office would be uninhabitable to a people could they see the tragedies that underlie life and voice the full of their emotions.' The Englishman is always a poet, almost never a critic; he 'loses the critic in the sympathiser'. Also – perhaps a more personal note – 'he knows very well that the truth is an impractical thing, the thing to make life a weariness, since, hard-pressed, he will acknowledge that life itself – unless we can console ourselves with illusions – is an illusion.' The great defect is still 'the want of sympathetic imagination' rather than hypocrisy. The Englishman is not a hypocrite really, more an idealist. Finally, the main factor in shaping national character remains climate. It is the one unalterable.

Near the end he refers to his own time in Germany and again describes the longing for home that prompted the Romney Wall poem, quoted earlier. He was, he says, 'obsessed always with an intense longing to see once more the sails of ships above the sea wall, the wide stretch of land, that church spire of Lydd breaking the distant horizon.' He never mentions that landscape without making it clear that it meant a lot to him; but the full story of what happened there, of what moved him to see life as an illusion just – but only just – worth preserving, is not known. He often revisited the Marsh and retained his connections with it for years but he never inhabited it again. He went on to other climes.

THIRTEEN

It is usually only in retrospect that people's lives seem to fall into periods. Living through them feels to the fortunate like a seamless progression, to others a seamless repetition or downward spiral. It is therefore hard to know whether changes that began in Ford's life in 1906 felt at the time like changes. He reckoned 1906 to have been the year of his recovery, but that was in retrospect.

Existing themes continued, some with greater intensity, others with less. Among the latter was his marriage. He and Elsie had already established a peripatetic and separate pattern, she living in Hurst Cottage or with her mother or travelling on the continent, while he was living with Dr Tebb or with his own mother or in Winchelsea. They continued to meet, of course, and sometimes they shared a roof, but those times became less frequent. It is usually thought that this was consequent on Ford's supposed affair with Mary and possibly it was, but he and Elsie still wrote affectionately to each other and there are no obvious signs of bitterness. Like many parents, they worried about money and about the children, who had by this time both been received into the Roman Catholic Church. Elsie, an Anglican, had reservations about this; it was to cause her lasting regret.

One change that was apparent was that Olive Garnett's friendship with Ford cooled as she became closer to Elsie. She became more worried about Elsie's health than Ford's. She didn't like their leading such separate lives, either knowing or sensing that it suited Elsie less than Ford, and she recorded instances of the change in relations between herself and him: 'We had a Free Trade discourse; & a moment of hate? distrust? some thing peeped out.' It is also at this period that Elsie went to Rome for a while. Ford's letter to her describes his busy social life and says he misses her; it is not like the manuscript of *The Nature of a Crime*, which he was then writing.

He was busy not only with books but with journalism, friendships and incidental projects and enthusiasms which throughout his life he fell into with a frequency and good-nature as endearing as his ill-luck. For instance, Wells got him to join the Fabian Society as part of his own campaign to oust the old guard such as the Webbs, the Blands and Shaw. Ford, of course, was not a socialist in any sense that most socialists would accept though they seemed to find him a tempting prospect for conversion, and he probably did it out of friendship for Wells and dislike of reformers. He read papers at the Society and in March 1906 took part in an ultimately unavailing attack on the old guard. It was an enjoyable period of plotting and dashing about between London, Rye, Sandgate and Winchelsea – once in a hired car, a luxury that greatly pleased him. He thought Fabianism 'a curious thing, made up of socialism, free thought, the profession of free love going hand in hand with an intense sexual continence that to all intents and purposes ended in emasculation, and going along, also, hand in hand with lime-washed bedroom walls and other aesthetic paraphernalia.' He thought the speech he had made in the failed coup attempt had probably done more harm than good: 'I must have imagined statistics or something.'

It was during this time that his friendship with Arthur Marwood put down its roots. He believed Marwood to be possessed of a great and original mind and took delight in introducing him to all his friends. He listened with pleasure while Marwood and Wells argued, sincerely but not bitterly, and was pleased to see him become a part of the Jamesian scene. Later, he observed that Marwood usurped him in his own role as confidant to Conrad but he showed no bitterness. It is very likely that he enthused about him to Elsie, as no doubt he had about Conrad. Moser points to an exchange in *A Call* in which Katya says to Robert of his friend, Dudley: 'No wonder you can't give in to me if you've got to be thinking of him all the time . . . All my life you've tortured me . . . you always had someone like that, that you took an interest in, that you were always trying to get *me* to take an interest in.'

Like much else in the book, this has the ring of the personal. It is easy to imagine that Ford had been so accused, that Elsie might have felt neglected and patronised in just that way. He was never a man to keep his enthusiasms to himself, always wanting others to share. It was the same when he was disappointed or frustrated; Stella Bowen later wrote that when he wanted something he was like a child, filling the sky with a huge ache.

Marwood was a saint in his wife's eyes and a snob so far as the rest of his family was concerned. He apparently insisted on all the proprieties – dinner to be dressed for, doors to be knocked on, servants not to be fraternised with, the domestic chores not to be done by Mrs Marwood – and came to be regarded in Kent, Moser says, as a 'proud, cultured, gentleman farmer'. The younger generation of the family had the impression from Mrs Marwood that she thought Ford a nuisance and scrounger and Conrad a sponge. The three men certainly were close friends over a number of years and although, of the three wives, Elsie is the only one of whom there is no actual record that she resented her husband's friendships, she probably did.

Ford and Conrad saw less of each at this time because there was less collaboration in progress and because both travelled more than they had a few years before. They were starting to go their separate ways but the friendship, which never died on Ford's side, was also still there on Conrad's. He wrote from Montpelier: '. . . every day I go about entranced, I miss you more and more . . . I am certain that with no other man could I share my rapture.' In January 1907 he sent Ford a cookery book that Jessie had written at Ford's suggestion, in which Ford is acknowledged as the 'onlie Begetter'. This was after the hat-in-the-oven series of incidents, so Jessie must either have swallowed her dislike or it was less strong at the time than she later recollected. He tried unsuccessfully to place the book with Alston Rivers but it was eventually published by Heinemann.

He continued leading the life of a too-busy London man. He still visited James, wrote articles, tried to get Pinker to pay for him to go on a trip to Russia in order to write a book about it, nearly bought the *Academy* magazine on money put up by Sir Alfred Harmsworth but was 'swayed by prudence' (a rare thing for him in literary ventures), wrote 'Literary Portraits' for the *Daily Mail*, on which he thought he was assistant literary editor (there was a dispute about that), took the girls on holiday to Germany, tried to reassure Elsie that he wasn't neglecting her, went everywhere and saw everyone. He was pretty well recovered.

It wasn't only that it was his nature to be busy. He needed money. He had to borrow to pay rent, school bills, medical expenses for Elsie and finally income tax, which he much resented, so that by the end of 1907 he owed about £800. Of this, £600 was owed to Pinker for various advances and small loans. During the previous year he had travelled to America with Elsie, a trip that was intended as a sales promotion but probably cost more than it earned him. The problem was simply that his books did not sell well enough. As anyone who has tried it knows, an author's reaction to a book that has not sold well is often to write another quickly, and then another and so on. Pecuniary pressure does produce ideas and words but profits may nonetheless remain elusive. They are at best only loosely related to hard work or merit. *The Fifth Queen*, the first of the trilogy, was a relative success but it still sold only 2,850 copies and earned him £128 5/–.It did not sell at all in America.

He and Elsie were in America during August and September 1906, visiting a large number of places but particularly New York, Boston and Philadelphia. He sold the *England and the English* series to McClure, met William Bradley, who has to become his agent and friend in Paris in the 1920s, managed to get to Boston when everyone else was away, visited the Hurlbird sisters – spinsters he had met in Germany in 1904 and who appear in *The Good Soldier* – nursed Elsie when she became ill again, borrowed more from Pinker and came home in a cattle-boat. America took hold of his imagination and he generalised confidently and inaccurately on the basis of this visit, though he later got to know the country better. He was always interested in anything new and America was not only a new experience but a big market. He began to have high hopes.

And, of course, he wrote. They sailed for the United States on 3 August and by 1 September he had written twelve thousand words of *Privy Seal*, the second volume of the trilogy. He did another ten thousand in America and finished the book in November. It was published in February 1907. In May of the same year he published *An English Girl*, a superficial novel based on his trip, and by June he had finished *The Half Moon*, another ignorable novel set in seventeenth-century Rye and in America. That he should follow a book like *Privy Seal* with two lightweight works is not really surprising given his own fecundity and the financial necessity that drove him. He would probably have written too much anyway, since it came as naturally to him as talking, but fewer of his books might have been novels if he had had more money. He strained after effect in those lesser novels; the themes are there, the artistry too, but the matter does not bear the weight that is put upon it. It is not difficult to have good ideas – many people do – but it is difficult to breathe independent life into a book while at the same time making sure that it bodies forth the driving idea. In tired books the driving idea shows too nakedly, like the ribs of an old ship.

When he returned from America he found himself assailed by 'a whole flight of cheques' he had written, probably hoping they would not be presented for many months. 'God damn the day I went there,' he wrote, not entirely seriously, to Pinker. There was worse to come. In September 1907 Elsie's doctor brother, Harri, did a urine test on her and wrongly diagnosed ulcer of the bladder and kidney stones. She was operated on. Ford had to borrow yet more money from Pinker, having not enough to get Elsie to London let alone pay for the surgery. She convalesced with Tebb, who himself may already have been in debt to Ford, and afterwards in rooms Ford took at 84 Holland Park Avenue. These rooms were in the great tradition of Fordian residences, cramped, inconvenient and noisome because of the poulterer and fishmonger below. But – and this was equally part of the tradition – Mr and Mrs Chandler, who kept the shop, liked him and provided him with daily ice for his small ice-box. Douglas Goldring, who was later often there, recalled 'an impression of almost pushing my way through the suspended carcasses of rabbits, fowls and game-birds to get to the door, and of standing in a mixture of blood and sawdust as I rang the bell.' Ford had his favourite pieces of furniture there, he liked the street and shop-lights, the busy-ness and the urban variety. It suited him. (The building is still just identifiable despite restoration and the intrusion of a car-hire firm.)

It did not suit Elsie. He looked after her, reading aloud to her James's *American Scene*, but the hectic quality of his London life, the comings and goings which he so relished, exhausted her. She went back to Winchelsea and he visited at weekends. Not only did his life tire her but she felt that it left her out, that it was pulling him away from his family, that his associations with 'giddy' and 'fast' women – as Mary seemed to have become and as Violet Hunt was – were not good for his writing. She thought such women demented. She worried too, that the strain of this life would be too much for him and she was not alone in this. Conrad, at last leaving The Pent for Bedfordshire, said the following year that he thought anyone who lived as Ford lived could not be a serious writer.

What his new life did was bring to light changes that really had already happened. His country period had ended and he was back to being a city man. Though he could still write appreciatively of the 'winter calm' of Winchelsea, he felt it was a place to which 'genteel families came . . . in search of health and quiet which they find in abundance. It was not a place for intellectual society.' But the end of the country period also marked the end in essence of what had begun in 1894 – his marriage. It continued on a part-time basis for some time and in name for much longer, but the cohesion had gone.

Left to herself, Elsie did not stay long in Winchelsea but moved back across the Marsh to Hurst Cottage, which she preferred. They still kept up the appearance of marriage, not only to the outside world but to each other, perhaps also to themselves. Ford would spend weekends in Aldington and she and the girls came to London for Christmas, when his entertaining continued unabated (Violet Hunt noted in her diary that he and Elsie quarrelled at a tea-party they gave). It was during this period that he came to believe that her illness was what we would call psychosomatic, no doubt largely because nothing was found during the operation.

Treatment of one sort of another nonetheless continued and he told Pinker that the £330 he had borrowed had gone into the pockets of 'nurses, doctors, chemists and specialists'. The worry was getting to him. He fell out briefly with Pinker and with Alston Rivers. He even paid a doctor to pretend he had found something wrong with Elsie and then pretend to cure it, and for a while it seemed the ruse had worked. This sounds a heartless thing to do, with the benefit of hindsight, but he actually believed that she only thought she was ill. He had come to think the same of his own illness and he was in desperate financial straits. It was a ploy not unknown to modern medicine. It did not work.

It was May 1908 before tuberculosis of the kidney was correctly diagnosed. Elsie returned to Winchelsea and was operated on there by a surgeon called Fenwick, who was assisted by two nurses and the children's nanny. The operation was performed on the kitchen table at The Bungalow. It was successful and Elsie went back to Aldington for a lengthy convalescence, much of which she spent in the garden under a thatched shanty with sail-cloth sides, similar to that under which Ford has Mark Tietjens end his days in *Parade's End*. He had to borrow 400 guineas from Marwood to pay for the operation.

When she came round one of the first questions Elsie asked Dr Fenwick was whether she would be able to resume sexual relations with her husband. It was a sad question. There is some evidence that things between them had worsened sufficiently by the time of the operation for them to discuss separation but in what terms we can only guess. Similarly, we can only guess at Elsie's state of mind. She left no account of her marriage, probably believing that it was not something one should talk about. Many people of her generation would have felt the same and Ford, as we have seen, certainly did. He never wrote or spoke against his wife, never drew attention to anything in his novels as depicting his own marriage nor discussed it in any way accessible to us. We do not know to what extent she was, within marriage, the 'dark, tall, "formidable" woman, stern, implacable, of rigid principles' whom Goldring had described. Ford's version of Mary in *The Fifth Queen* trilogy is like that and he generally does a pretty good line in implacable women, but Elsie's sad question does not suggest such a person. Nor does her continuing to want her husband after his supposed affair with her sister, nor her agreeing against her wishes to have the children brought up as Catholics. It is important to remember that she was ill for some years. Ford would have been the first to agree that there is no knowing what goes on in a marriage; his own, for all the assumptions that have been made about it, remains largely a mystery. What does seem fairly clear, though, is that Elsie did not want to lose it. She probably still loved her husband. Many years later, when he was with Janice Biala, Ford got drunk one night (a rare occurrence, for all his drinking) and Janice asked him about Elsie. He replied to the following effect: 'I used to have her weeping on my breast night after night because she was in love with some other man.' This could be said to cast into doubt the usual view of Ford's marriage but its prime use is, perhaps, to serve as a warning against drawing any firm conclusions about what went on within it.

The achievement of those years was *The Fifth Queen* trilogy. Whatever else was happening and whatever else he was writing, behind it all, in quick succession, he turned out these three volumes of what must be one of the greatest historical novels of our language. 'The swan song of historical romance,' Conrad called it at the time, adding ambiguously, 'and frankly, I am glad to have heard it.'

It takes courage to go on writing as he did then. These books were neither pot-boilers nor obvious big sellers; they were the distillation of years of thought and reading about Henry VIII and Thomas Cromwell, both of whom are dominating presences in the books. Even those books that *have* to be written require sustained determination; the courage is in the sustaining. His book on Holbein is almost a companion volume to the trilogy, a kind of coda of what he thought important about the Tudor period and what he thought different about those people.

The difficulty with the historical novel is that the genre itself is usually regarded as a kind of literary sub-species. It is neither history nor quite 'pure' novel, presumably because the possibilities of imaginative development are not as open as in a 'pure' novel, being closed by our prior knowledge of what has to happen. It is curious that this attitude persists and that it is so selectively applied; it is not, for instance, applied to classical drama or to William Shakespeare. Perhaps it is that not enough novelists of the first rank have written historical novels.

The Fifth Queen trilogy has been the subject of reasonable critical attention and is available as an Oxford University Press paperback with a good introduction by A. S. Byatt. Argument about the book centres upon such themes as whether Katharine Howard is too good a character to be plausible (Ford said in a 1904 letter to Richard Garnett that he was 'white-washing' her) or whether she is in fact a fanatic who would kill anyone in the name of God's love. There are three general aspects, though, that are particularly striking. One is Ford's eye for power, both in depiction of those who have it and in his sense of how it is used and how it affects. Given that he had no more experience of the exercise of power than most British novelists, his King Henry, Thomas Cromwell and Throckmorton are masterly portraits. They are glimpsed mainly in corners and by spluttering candlelight, but when he chooses to get inside them he does so with a sureness born of real imaginative sympathy. In personality, aspiration and imagination he must have had very little in common with Thomas Cromwell's genius, but the insight he shows into the visionary mind of that man of power is convincing and remarkable:

> Cromwell was meditating above a fragment of flaming wood that the fire had spat out far into the tiled fore-hearth. He pressed it with his foot gently towards the blaze of wood in the chimney.
>
> His plump hands were behind his back, his long upper lip ceaselessly caressed its fellow, moving as one line of a snake's coil glides above another. The January wind crept round the shadowy room behind the tapestry, and as it quivered stags seemed to leap over bushes, hounds to spring in pursuit, and a crowned Diana to move her arms, taking an arrow from a quiver behind her shoulder. The tall candles guarded the bag of the Privy Seal, they fluttered and made the gilded heads on the rafters have sudden grins on their faces that represented kings with flowered crowns, queens with their hair combed back on to pillows, and pages with scalloped hats. Cromwell stepped into an aumby, where there was a glass of wine, a manchet of bread, and a little salt. He began to eat, dipping pieces of bread

into the golden salt-cellar. The face of a queen looked down just above his head with her eyes wide open as if she were amazed, thrusting her head from a cloud.

'Why, I have outlived three queens,' he said to himself, and his round face resignedly despised his world and his times. He had forgotten what anxiety felt like because the world was so peopled with blunderers and timid fools full of hatred . . .

. . . He sipped his wine slowly. It was a little cold, so he set it down beside the fire. He wanted to go to bed, but the Archbishop was coming to hear how Henry had received his Queen, and to pour out his fears. Fears! Because the King had been sick at sight of the Cleves woman! He had this King very absolutely in his power; the grey, failing but vindictive and obstinate man known as Henry, was afraid of his contempt, afraid really of a shrug of the shoulder or a small sniff.

With the generosity of his wine and the warmth of his fire, his thoughts went many years ahead. He imagined the King either married to or having repudiated the lady from Cleves, and then dead. Edward, the Seymour child, was his creature, and would be King or dead. Cleves children would be his creature creations too. Or if he married the Lady Mary he would still be next to the throne.

His mind rested luxuriously and tranquilly on that prospect. He would be perpetually beside the throne. There would be no distraction to retain a foothold. He would be there by right; he would be able to give all his mind to the directing of this world that he despised for its baseness, its jealousies, its insane brawls, its aimless selfishness, and its blind furies. Then there should be no more war, as there should be no more revolts. There should be no more jealousies; for king craft, solid, austere, practical and inspired, should keep down all the peoples, all the priests, and all the nobles of the world. 'Ah,' he thought, 'there would in France be no power to shelter traitors like Brancetor.' His eyes became softer in the contemplation of this Utopia, and he moved his upper lip more slowly.

Truncated though it is, this passage is also a good example of a second general aspect, which is Ford's use of surface detail to convey atmosphere, mood and latent meaning. It is often referred to as his impressionism but it is in fact a very common technique, though not usually so well done. Edging the piece of wood back to the fire is something most of us have done and we know immediately the musing mood in which we would do it – as Cromwell does – gently. Like much of *The Fifth Queen*, the scene is static and deliberately reminiscent of Holbein. The picture of the queen is as pregnant with reference to Cromwell's rise and fall, as the frugality of his meal is to the man himself. His lips are suggestive of his mind. His musings, which a lesser writer would have made gloomy and tyrannical (and his appetites lascivious), are in essence those of a man who would see things well done, not ill. This last, a by no means universal desire, is probably the feature that Ford had in common with Cromwell and on to which he battened in order, as it were, to board his character. The practical, the ability to cope and the wisdom that accompanies it were probably what he found sympathetic. Any writer has to have some such point of entry into any convincing character.

It might be argued that the literary techniques Ford and Conrad discussed during their friendship were more successfully exemplified in *The Fifth Queen* trilogy than in any of their collaborations. There we can see the lack of authorial intervention, the impressionism, the use of scenes to convey meaning, the rendering of an affair. The fact that what is being rendered involves a history with its own momentum and predetermined end increases the harmony between subject and treatment. Ford did not have to worry about his story; he had only to be selective and apply his techniques to it.

The third general aspect is the language Ford uses. He creates a version of Tudor English that is not only effective but does not in any way hinder the sense of reality. This is a considerable achievement; the use of a dated form of one's own language almost always sounds the contrivance it is, unconvincing, artificial and slow. In order to work it needs to sound natural and in order for that to happen the author needs to have created a world or an atmosphere in the context of which it can be natural. Having done that, he needs to use it naturally – directly, informally, selectively, slangily – much as Ford said in his letter to Wells. The result in *The Fifth Queen* is vigorous and convincing, sometimes compressed poetic speech.

All three aspects – power, impressionism and language – are evident in the following scene. The King wishes Archbishop Cranmer to help him write a letter to the Pope, which necessitates careful phrasing:

> 'The Bishop of Rome –' Thomas Cranmer began a hesitating speech. In the pause after the words the King himself hesitated, as if he poised between a heavy rage and a sardonic humour. He deemed, however, that the humour could the more terrify the Archbishop – and, indeed, he was so much upon the joyous side in those summer days that he had forgotten how to browbeat.
>
> 'Our holy father', he corrected the Archbishop. 'Or I will say My holy father, since thou art a heretic –'
>
> Cranmer's eyes had always the expression of a man who looked at approaching calamity, but at the King's words his whole face, his closed lips, his brows, the lines from his round nose, all drooped suddenly downwards.
>
> 'Your Grace will have me write a letter to the – to his – to him –'
>
> The downward lines themselves, and from amongst them the panic-stricken eyes, made dumb appeal to the griffins and crowns of his dark green hangings, for they were afraid to turn to the King. Henry retained his heavy look of jocularity: he jumped at a weighty jibe –
>
> 'My Grace will have thy Grace write a letter to his Holiness.'
>
> He dropped into a heavy passivity, rolled his eyes, fluttered his swollen fingers on the red and gilded table, and then said clearly, 'My. Thy. His.'
>
> When he was in that mood he spoke with a singular distinctness that came up from his husky and ordinary joviality like something dire and terrible – like that something that on a clear, smooth day will suggest to you suddenly the cruelty that lies always hidden in the limpid sea.

'To Caesar – Egomet, I mineself – that which is Caesar's: to him – that is to say to his Holiness, our lord of Rome – the things which are of God! But to thee, Archbishop, I know not what belongs.'

He paused and then struck his hand upon the table: 'Cold porridge is thy portion! Cold porridge!' He laughed: 'For they say: Cold porridge to the devil! And, since thou art neither God's nor the King's what may I call thee but the devil's self's man?'

A heavy and minatory silence seemed to descend upon him; the Archbishop's thin hand opened suddenly as if he were letting something fall to the ground. The King scowled heavily, but rather as if he were remembering past heaviness than for any present grief.

'Why,' he said, 'I am growing an old man. It is time I redded up my house.'

If you were an actor you would know from that scene how to play Henry. In fact, the whole book has the atmosphere and particularity of film. It is set in static scenes and drenched in suggestions of power, fear, sex, longing, guile and fate. Bearing in mind Ford's habit of visualising everything in a room before setting a scene, then not mentioning it, it is interesting to observe how he conveys the room – 'gets the room in' is how he would put it – with mention only of the griffins, the hangings and the table.

You would also know from this what it is to deal with an absolute monarch and something of what it is like to be one; so you have the idea of power. The feel of the scene – background, atmosphere, the past, the uncertain future – comes from what Henry James called 'solidity of specification'. This is the 'air of reality' that James regarded as 'the supreme virtue of the novel', and it is the ideas similar to those expounded in James's 1884 essay, 'The Art of Fiction', that Ford is here putting into practice. It is this, the careful selection of visual detail, that gives the book its cinematographic effect. The observations of each man's hands in that scene are like a camera focusing. There is enough description for the hands to be particular and vivid but room is left for the suggestion of what they indicate. The balance is right.

This is the first of Ford's books of which one can say with

reasonable confidence that, if he had written nothing else, it would still have a good chance of being in print today. Is it a masterpiece? Yes, of its kind – which brings us back to the problem of the historical novel. Whatever the resolution of that is, this is one that should be read.

FOURTEEN

The acceleration in the pace of his life continued through 1908. There were two particularly significant developments: the literary magazine, *The English Review*, and Violet Hunt. There was also a new novel, *Mr Apollo*. This was a Utopian fantasy, satirical, too obviously contrived, but with some good scenes and overall a considerable technical accomplishment. It is probably of interest mainly to the enthusiast and the fact that Ford should turn to this after his successful *Fifth Queen* trilogy suggests that he thought he still had not found his subject, or his voice. If he had been less energetic and less variously talented he might not have attempted such books, saving himself for better ones, but as we know he needed the money and he hoped for good sales. As usual, he was disappointed: about seventeen hundred copies were sold. Violet Hunt liked it, though: 'the most passionate, poetical piece of work of his hand there is. He [Wells] was scornful. I honestly don't think he thinks it is good. It is too poetical for him – A poetical lapse.' To be passionately poetic was high praise in Violet's terms. The phrase probably says more about how she was feeling about Ford at that time than about the novel; it may also suggest something about her, in that she had earlier used the same phrase in praise of one of Wells's books.

'There entered then into me', Ford wrote, 'the itch of trying to meddle in English literary affairs.' The precise origins of *The English Review* are not clear – perhaps they were, quite simply, never precise – but it evolved in discussions between Ford, Conrad, Wells, Edward Garnett and Marwood. According to Ford, it had 'the definite design of giving imaginative literature a chance in England'; also, more fancifully, it was to publish Hardy's poem,

'A Sunday Morning Tragedy'. This poem had been turned down by another magazine and the story soon got about that it had been rejected everywhere. Its last line – 'But pray God *not* to pity me' – would have scandalised many. Ford and Marwood were indignant and they determined to start a magazine in order to get it published; that at least is how Ford put it later. It is true that the poem appears in the first issue but it is unlikely that the background was as clear-cut as that. The poem may have been a factor but the magazine was probably going to happen anyway. Ford put up £500, which was all the money he could raise and included some borrowed from Elsie. Wells was supposed to put up half the money and do half the editing, but later backed out. Marwood put up £500. Ford tried to get the American, S. S. McClure, to finance it, without success. Conrad, who had suggested the title, disliked Americans and was wary of the implied threat of commercialism.

Not that commercialism was ever a real threat to *The English Review*. It is generally accepted that the first eight or nine loss-making months of the magazine's life, which was the period of Ford's editorship (though his influence, because of what he had commissioned, extended for some months longer), made it one of the best literary magazines ever to appear in these islands. It is equally generally accepted that it was a financial disaster, roughly to the tune of £500 per issue, and that Ford's business mismanagement was largely responsible. It would be fairer to say 'partly'; no literary magazine has ever been anything else unless it either broadened its appeal or had a backer to sustain loss. Ford's aims were noble, impractical and unselfish: 'I am an idealist and my ideal is to run the ER as far as possible as a socialistic undertaking.' He gave up his weekly article for the *Daily News* and threw himself into the work. He expected writers who could afford it to sacrifice their own money and time in the cause of literature just as he had, principally by not demanding commercial fees. If they did so demand – and most, apart from Wells and Galsworthy, did – he paid a standard rate of a guinea per five hundred words, which was generally unpopular. He fell out with Arnold Bennett over this, though made it up. On the other hand, he was unreasonably generous to writers he knew to be poor and who did not try to be commercial, paying them over the rate. Conrad and James both fell into this category.

The first issue included contributions from Conrad, Wells, James, Hardy, W. H. Hudson, Cunninghame Graham, W. H. Davies, Tolstoy (a translation of *The Raid* by Constance Garnett) and Galsworthy. There was also the first instalment of Marwood's 'A Complete Actuarial Scheme for Insuring John Doe against all the Vicissitudes of Life', which anticipated measures introduced by the Liberal government and which may have influenced Pound in his unfortunate enthusiasm for economics. The issue ran to 192 pages. Subsequent issues added Bennett, Lawrence, Wyndham Lewis, Pound, Yeats, Chesterton, Belloc, George Moore, Rupert Brooke, E. M. Forster, Lowes Dickinson and Norman Douglas to the contributors. It sold for half a crown.

While Ford was in charge and for as long as his influence was continued the *Review* attracted virtually all the leading literary figures of the day and launched or helped launch a number of unknowns, such as Wyndham Lewis, Lawrence and Pound. Conrad even moved back from Bedfordshire to Aldington partly to be nearer Ford so that Ford could help him with the reminiscences he was to include in the *Review*. Like a theatrical production, it infected everyone with excitement. There were feuds, fallings-out, makings-up – or not – and love matches. It is a reassuring testimony to the impact of the individual upon affairs that the personality of the editor, his enthusiasm, knowledge and judgement made the difference it did. No other literary magazine matched it.

He was, of course in his element. The *Review* was a success in every sense but the commercial; it brought him recognition and even fame. David Garnett described him as 'arrayed in a magnificent fur coat; – wore a glowing topper; drove about in hired carriages; and his fresh features, the colour of raw veal, his prominent blue eyes and rabbit teeth smiled benevolently and patronisingly upon all gatherings of literary lions.' Wells's German governess, on the other hand, described long hair and a black, braided velvet jacket that made him look like a German student.

Douglas Goldring was then a young man working on *Country Life* and was hired by Ford to sub-edit the *Review* in the evenings at 84 Holland Park Avenue. Ford's rooms were the editorial office. Goldring had to share them not only with Ford, but on a Box-and-Cox basis with a very efficient secretary called Miss Thomas, who subsequently worked for Lloyd George. There was a constant flow of visitors with manuscripts and propositions. There were also beggars who 'with the unerring instinct of their tribe . . . had discovered that Ford could be touched and, in consequence, swarmed all day around his ever open front door, the bolder spirits even coming up the stairs to the office. If they encountered Ford and told him their hard luck stories they never failed to receive at least a shilling. If they encountered Miss Thomas, on the other hand, they received a stern warning that the police would be informed if they ever appeared again.'

Ford must have changed his costume regularly because Goldring found him a tall, thin man with fair hair and a blond moustache which imperfectly concealed defective front teeth, wearing a grey-blue swallow-tail coat of uncertain cut, carrying a leather despatch case of the kind the French call a *serviette* and possessing an 'important' manner which in some ways suggest an under-secretary of State. It seems that the grand manner, which at twenty had appeared an affectation, was now, at thirty-five, beginning to wear more comfortably – though he was still slim.

The *Review* has stood the test of time and is still a good read, a big, vigorous, confident and original production such as we would now term heavyweight. The contributions are substantial; there seems to have been no problem about space and social as well as cultural matters are considered. Most of the editorials were by Ford although they were not among his most charming pieces. Apart from fulsome yet graceful compliments to writers such as James, they are rather ponderous and portentous but they are not egocentric and they do display a serious concern for their subject. It is a lively magazine with, for all its seriousness, frequent light touches. It gives the air of it knowing itself to be something special, which it was. In terms of its encouragement for new writing by unknown writers, the only serious equivalent now would be Alan Ross's *London Magazine*.

Ford's style of editing entailed a constant round of breakfasts, lunches, dinners and parties. Goldring witnessed most if it and left the impression that it was one long party with only a few brief interruptions. As word spread, more people wanted to be published, or to talk about who should be published, and the callers at Number 84 proliferated. One of the unknowns was Wyndham Lewis, whose call was described by Ford to Goldring later the same day:

> Lewis, tall, swarthy and with romantically disordered hair, wearing a long black coat buttoned up to his chin, arrived at Number 84 with the MS of a character sketch called 'The Pole'. Getting no answer to his ring he walked up to the editorial sanctum and found it deserted. Undeterred, he climbed another flight of stairs and, hearing at last sounds of human life, knocked at the door from which they came and marched in. It happened to be the bathroom, and there, reclining on his back in the bath, in two feet of hot water, with a large sponge in one hand and a cake of soap in the other, was the missing editor. Disregarding any unconventionality in his surroundings, the 'Enemy' at once proceeded to business. After announcing in the most matter-of-fact way that he was a man of genius and that he had a manuscript for publication, he asked if he might read it. 'Go ahead,' Ford murmured, continuing to use his sponge. Lewis then unbuttoned his coat, produced 'The Pole' and read it through. At the end, Ford observed, 'Well, that's all right. If you leave it behind we'll certainly print it.' The interview then terminated.

Goldring adds that he cannot vouch for the accuracy of the story 'but if it didn't happen it ought to have done. Events of this description occurred daily, almost hourly, during the twelve months of Ford's editorship of the *Review*. Looking back, it seems amazing to me, that so much could have happened in so short a time. It was only a year: but *what* a year!'

At the parties they played party-games, of which Ford was a life-long enthusiast, such as chumps, honey-pots, hunt-the-slipper, *bout-rimes* and 'Ah Gods' sonnets (sonnets beginning with 'Ah God') at which 'no one in London could touch him for speed and brilliance'. One evening when Goldring arrived at Number 84 he found Ford alone and playing the grand piano which was there, humming a song from the sheet before him. It was a music hall song. '"One of my few popular successes, my dear Goldring," Ford remarked as he got up from the stool and shut the piano. "I didn't put my name to it out of respect for my father's reputation, but it was sung everywhere for a couple of seasons."' Goldring comments that Ford's stories had always to be received with caution, although he was very unlikely to have claimed authorship where it wasn't his due and some recently discovered musical compositions by him add credence to this claim. Also, Mrs Chandler, in the poulterer's and fishmonger's below, told Violet Hunt how when Ford was alone he would sometimes thump out on his piano the music hall song, 'Madam, Will you walk?'[1]

René Byles was back from Japan and came along to help out. Ezra Pound appeared and scandalised many by wearing one ear-ring, startling others by springing to his feet and bowing stiffly. D. H. Lawrence was discovered. This happened because Jessie Chambers sent some of Lawrence's poems, and possibly *The Odour of Chrysanthemums*, to the *Review*; Ford, recognising talent as quickly as he always did, plucked Lawrence out of the school where he was teaching in Croydon and introduced him to literary London. If Lawrence is to be believed, Ford had metamorphosised in those few months from a still youthful slim figure into the more familiar man of mature estate: 'He is fairish, fat, about forty, and the kindest man on earth . . . he keeps the doors of his soul open, and you may walk in.' Ford asked to see *The White Peacock*, read it immediately, 'and in his queer voice, when we were on an omnibus in London, he shouted in my ear: "it's got every fault that the English novel can have . . . But you've got GENIUS."' Lawrence adds disingenuously: 'I always thought he had a bit of genius himself. Anyhow, he sent the MS of "The White Peacock" to William Heinemann, who accepted it at once.' Lawrence was later to turn against him and transfer his allegiance to Edward Garnett but he did not deny that he was Ford's discovery: 'FMH discovered

[1] A popular duet of the period. The refrain was:

> Madam, Will You Walk,
> Madam, Will You Talk,
> Madam, Will You Walk and Talk with Me?

He had probably sung it with Elsie.

I was a genius – don't be alarmed, H would discover *anything* if he wanted to.'

In the gaps between the people and the parties the mechanics of editing still had to be done. Ford's method may have something to commend it. Goldring describes how during the day the office was

> . . . perpetually inundated with visitors, so that it was chiefly at night that the actual job of editing the Review could be carried on. But even at night, callers dropped in casually to see how the work was going forward. In order to avoid them, at least for an hour or two, it was Ford's singular practice to attend the 'second house' at the local music hall. At least once a week, my first task on arriving at Holland Park Avenue, was to secure a box or two stalls at the Shepherd's Bush Empire. After dinner I went out and stopped a hansom and editor and 'sub' drove down to Shepherd's Bush with the MSS which had accumulated during the day. During the performance, or rather during the duller turns, Ford made his decisions, and I duly recorded them. But when someone really worth listening to – the late Victoria Monks for example, or Little Tich or Vesta Victoria – appeared on the stage, the cares of editorship were for the moment laid aside. After the show we went back to the flat and worked on, sometimes till two in the morning.'

And still he wrote. Goldring remembers recovering manuscripts of poems from his waste-paper bin and one night he ventured to show Ford one of his own: 'He laid it on the writing desk which had been Christina Rossetti's and read it with care. "I'm afraid, my dear Goldring," he said as he gave it back to me, "you will never be a *real* poet. You have just about as much of the poetic gift as I have myself."' It took Goldring time to appreciate the response: 'To my shame, I must admit that instead of beaming with pleasure at what I have long since come to regard as the greatest compliment ever paid me, I felt, and perhaps looked, rather crestfallen.'

Somewhere, meanwhile, was the solitary, the man whom Mrs Chandler said sometimes sat staring into his fire, sometimes hummed and played his own tunes quietly, sometimes thumped out 'Madam, Will you Walk?' This man, contemporaneous with the busy, obliging editor, was also the one who visited his convalescent wife at weekends, reassuring her and no doubt feeling guilty because of the affair he was then beginning with Violet Hunt.

Thanks to her diaries, we know that Violet became his mistress on 10 June 1909 but their acquaintance, and the real infidelity, began long before that. 'I just met a Miss Violet Hunt. She says she was at school with my mother and used to see me in my perambulator,' Ford announced to Goldring one day. Mrs Hueffer and Violet had indeed been to the same school, though not at the same time, the two families did know each other – Violet 'had often to rap the fingers of the two high-spirited Hueffer boys for playing ball with the penny buns' – and she probably had seen him in his pram; she was eleven years older. She was also, by this time, a well-known literary figure, regarded, says Goldring, 'as an English Colette . . . very French and fast, a fashionable and faintly vicious blue-stocking . . . [who] was never notable for emotional reticence and had already wept copiously on several famous shoulders, so had only herself to blame for being talked about. Even in her girlhood her friends had nicknamed her "the immodest Violet".'

David Garnett thought her 'something of an Elizabethan pirate . . . a thin viperish looking beauty with a long pointed chin and deep-set burning brown eyes under hooded lids. There was a driving force within her, which I afterwards recognised as insatiable ambition.' Mizener, rather harshly, calls her 'a middle-class Moll Flanders' and a snob, adding that she had 'distraught gold hair' (more often described as auburn), was acute, inconsequential, indiscreet, and a lover of drama and clothes. She described herself as 'sensualist of the emotions'; she would break off any anecdote to say what she had been wearing. Garnett's point about ambition is good though not sufficiently specific. When at the age of forty-five she established relations with Ford her driving ambition was social: she wanted to be a married lady. What had complicated previous attempts was that she had also wanted to be wildly in love. She still did. Her beauty, perhaps always a quality more vivid than sensual, had not been helped during recent years by the arsenic she had been taking on medical advice. She might have felt this was her last chance.

Violet's family had, like Ford's, been part of the Pre-Raphaelite and artistic Victorian Great scene. Her father, Alfred, was an Oxford don persuaded by Ruskin to become a watercolourist. She had two sisters, Venice and Silvia. Her mother, whom Ford admired, is thought to have been the original for Valentine Wannop's mother in *Parade's End*. Though sharing Pre-Raphaelite associations, the Hunts were socially smarter than the Hueffers, as well as wealthier. They mixed regularly in high society in a way that Ford did only intermittently, usually when he was with someone like Violet. Despite being a writer and one of the advanced intellectual women of her day (she was also a suffragette), Violet had about her that beguiling whiff of society, of the smart set, of knowing people everywhere, which Ford probably found both attractive and a strain. Elsie, as we have seen, thought she and her like were demented.

In her youth she had charmed Oscar Wilde (he had, perhaps half seriously, proposed) but her first serious lover was the painter George Boughton. The affair began in 1884 when she was twenty-two and he fifty-one. He married three years later but the affair continued for some time after that. She learned from him about painting and was later rumoured to be always prepared to 'drop her dress to the waist for a painter'. There followed an enthusiasm for an Etonian called Eustace Strickland and pursuit by another older man called Walter Pollock. It was at about this time that, worried about her looks, she began taking arsenic. She had several offers of marriage and one admirer, a Dr Cholmeley, patiently pursued her into her forties. When she did fall in love, though, it was with men who would not or could not marry her.

Oswald Crawfurd was the great passion of her thirties. He was the British Consul at Oporto who very pleasantly spent the six summer months each year at his London flat in Queen Anne's Mansions, and he began to take an interest in her some time during the summer of 1890 when he was fifty-six and she twenty-eight. He was handsome, something of a man of letters and married to an invalid. He had many mistresses, often friends of his wife and among them two friends of Violet's. For some time she resisted his advances and it is possible that he didn't pursue her very hard because he already had some reservations about her ability to remain discreet, but they became lovers in 1892. The affair lasted until 1898, by which time he seems to have wearied of her possessiveness and indiscretion. She was in love with him throughout and after.

The year after the affair ended his wife died. This must have renewed Violet's hope but she had made the mistake meanwhile of pursuing him in public and talking about him. He first had an affair with one friend of hers, then married another. When he died in Switzerland at the beginning of 1909 she pasted his obituary in her diary and wrote of the news: 'I have just heard of the death, far away in Switzerland, of such a one as we women, roughly, and tenderly speaking choose to call "the only man we have ever loved"'. She was probably in a susceptible state, therefore, when Ford began his pursuit at about this time. The passing of her great love had left her with longing for another.

It was not all that Crawfurd left her with. In 1905 Dr Chomeley, 'with tears in his eyes', told her that she had syphilis, though probably not in so few words: 'I had a disgraceful illness, in fact tertiaries only he did not name it or do more than hint.' Neither did another doctor, Archie Propert, who had been also courting her but who did not now come forward with the expected proposal. A third doctor, Stephen Paget, was not an admirer and found it easier to be franker. She didn't like it – 'looked at me and spoke to me as something unclean, I never went again' – and she probably tried to ignore what she was told. She did not write about these diagnoses until many years later, in 1936, when her mind was already going. It is difficult to know how much she understood at the time. The likelihood is that she understood more than she wanted to acknowledge but that she did not know all the implications. Whatever her reasons, she was in no hurry to tell Ford when their affair began.

She had written six books between 1898 and 1907, including a novel about her affair with Crawfurd called *Sooner or Later.* She did a fair amount of literary journalism and was widely known and admired. She was an energetic literary hostess but also a fond aunt to her nephews and nieces. She and her mother lived at South Lodge, 80 Campden Hill Road, not far from Ford's rooms in Holland Park Avenue.

Affairs, attempted or avoided, occupied a large part of her energies. In 1906 the novelist and lesbian Marguerite Radclyffe-Hall fell in love with her. She lavished gifts upon Violet but to no avail – 'goods unpaid for, not the wages of sin', Violet said, while describing herself as having 'the airs of a Sultan . . . shows how easily one is corrupted by adoration . . . there is a cruelness only because she loves me so hotly, poor darling . . .' She did, however, indulge in a brief affair with Somerset Maugham and avoided one with Edward Heron Allen, blaming the unexpected assault from this old friend on the hansom cab, which 'I say and think breeds all the evil passions in the other sex. But I can manage Edward.' There was a flirtation with Wells which involved her being pursued in and out of the house at Sandgate but she seems to have stopped just short of becoming his mistress. During the course of one of her visits she observed that Wells's wife, Jane, looked overworked, was no longer so pretty and did her hair wrongly. She obligingly told her so, then noted in her diary: 'I don't think she likes me.'

One weekend she attempted a mild seduction of Henry James at Lamb House. It didn't help that she had to go to her room after dinner and be sick, blaming the bisque. This meant changing her 'pink new Goupy chiffon', which was two shades of red with white embroidery. She put on her 'white Liberty Chinese dressing gown . . . very pretty and drifted as I know how, into the drawing room where he was all solicitude and I do believe pleasure and we discussed Mrs Humphry Ward's books . . .' James made no advances, however. She was ill again the following morning but managed breakfast while watching him eat a plateful of cereals with poached egg on top. They discussed Oswald Crawfurd, James saying he couldn't understand 'how anything so vamped-up such a thin mentality, could have absorbed any of the women whom common report gave to him for conquest . . .' Violet, annoyed, impulsively confessed that she loved Crawfurd 'and poor HJ got up from the table like a dog that has had enough of its bone and closed the discussion . . . He "skoots" from passion as if he had been once bitten by it and yet I am sure that in *my* sense of the word he never has . . . he is incapable . . .'

She seems to have been an impetuous, tactless, lively woman, both arch and naive, with a darting intelligence remarkable more for its insight and quickness than for sustained concentration. Time and again in her diaries she gives herself away artlessly and completely, though her touching openness is tempered by shrewdness. By the time she and Ford were re-establishing their acquaintance one observer thought her 'fashionable, brilliant, daring; a leading spirit . . . glamour personified', and another, 'coarse and plain with a skin like leather'. There was probably truth in both; her skin was perhaps beginning to show the ravages of syphilis but her presence, informed by her personality and illumined by her energy, was glamorous.

Their relationship began some two years before they became lovers. In March 1907 they both had dinner at Galsworthy's and walked home through Kensington, discussing common Pre-Raphaelite memories. A month later they met again in Heinemann's office where she asked Ford to 'boom' her new book, *The White Rose of Weary Leaf*. In July he was invited to her annual garden party (she noted that he came alone) but there was little or no contact throughout the rest of the year until well into 1908, perhaps partly because she was busy with suffragette matters. When the *Review* was going Wells suggested she get Ford to publish some of her stories. She took them to him in October 1908 and over tea he selected *The Coach*. He did so, she records, without seeming to do any more than shuffle the papers as they talked.

This was something that others observed in him at various times throughout his life. He had an unerring knack for picking the best of what was before him and he sometimes spoke of all manuscripts as having a 'feel' which he could get straight away. He told Janice Biala that he could tell what he needed to know from the first paragraph. In his own writing he always stressed the importance of the first paragraph in setting the tone of a book and in *Portraits from Life* he gives an example of how he chose Lawrence's *Odour of Chrysanthemums* for the *Review* on the basis of reading that first paragraph only. The story begins, 'The small locomotive engine

Number 4 came clanking, stumbling, down from Selston'; Ford comments

> . . . at once you know that this fellow with the power of observation is going to write of whatever he writes about from the inside. 'Number 4' shows that. He will be the sort of fellow who knows that for the sort of people who work about engines, engines have a sort of individuality . . .'
>
> '*It appeared round the corner with loud threats of speed . . . But the colt that it startled from among the gorse out-distanced it at a canter.*'
>
> Good again . . . anyone knows that an engine that makes a great deal of noise and yet cannot overtake a colt at a canter must be a ludicrously ineffective machine . . .
>
> '*The gorse still flickered indistinctly in the raw afternoon . . .*'
>
> Good too, distinctly good. This is the just-sufficient observation of Nature that gives you, in a single phrase, landscape, time of day, weather, season.
>
> Your mind does all this for you without any ratiocination on your part. You are not, I mean, purposefully sleuthing.
>
> And if you are an editor . . . you can pitch the story straight away into your wicker stray with the few accepted manuscripts . . .

His assessment of Violet's story – perhaps also of Violet – was probably as rapid and detailed as that. They had tea again three days later, lunch at South Lodge the following week and regular meetings thereafter. She was introduced to Marwood and enrolled as one of the supporters of the *Review*. Her contacts could be useful, as she realised herself. Ford also introduced her to McClure, the American whom he hoped would provide finance for the magazine. He began signing his letters extravagantly – 'Yours till death and after' – while addressing them, 'Dear Miss Hunt'. They were seeing each other two or three times a week and by May 1909 he was telling her that he was 'abominably' in love with her. At the end of the month he contrived a reason to follow her to her cottage at Selsey in West Sussex where over the Irish stew he asked if she would marry him 'if I am ever a divorced man'. She was pleased and flattered but affected not to take him seriously: 'It was an essay in pre-Raphaelite crudity of expression, as if a Madox Brown heavy oil painting or an early Elizabeth Siddall watercolour had been suddenly turned into speech . . . He returned to it again, and I got cross.' But they continued seeing each other frequently. Unknown to him, she had already been indiscreet about their relationship with many others, including Wells. Most of the people in London who knew them knew what was going on.

In *The Flurried Years* Violet describes some of the evenings she spent at Number 84. Ford, it may be observed, was undergoing yet another metamorphosis of figure and dress:

> He was by way of himself preparing little dinners . . . I found him upstairs in the little kitchen, with a nice Japanese silk dressing-gown over his shabby morning suit to preserve it from the grease of the frying-pan. And, after all, the cutlets were burned. Some meringues from the confectioner's next door followed . . . Then we went down and he began to tell me the plot of his new book . . . As he read I looked at him critically. He was no longer so dreadfully thin, since the cough had gone, but he was white like a stick of asparagus grown in a cellar; at any rate, rather pasty. He smoked incessantly, and it made his teeth black. His cuffs wanted trimming . . .
>
> It was rather cold. The light was not good. Shadows were encroaching on the little oasis of light in which we sat, he on a hideous red plush Victorian arm-chair . . . and I on a *chaise longue*. The depression was so thick you could cut it with a knife.

The book he was talking about was probably *A Call*, published the following year. During one of their sessions he talked of suicide and left the room. When he returned she found a bottle labelled POISON in the pocket of (this time) his brown velvet jacket:

> 'Were you?' I said; and he answered, 'I was.'
>
> 'Donkey' I said and, keeping the bottle in my hand, sought for my cloak and shouldered it . . . and, for the first time after one of our dinners he walked home with me – and it was only half-past ten when all was said and done.

It was shortly after this that they became lovers. After the event Ford thanked her for 'the tenderness that saved one's reason and one's life'. She changed her mind about marriage; by the end of the month she was taking him to talk to her lawyer about divorce.

What was he up to? The depression, the soulful talks, the threat of suicide are reminiscent of his talks with Olive and Elsie during his first courtship. But he was nineteen then whereas with Violet he was thirty-five and probably not embarking on his first infidelity; though it perhaps was his first serious relationship since Elsie. Was it meant or was it a pose, a tactical ploy in the wooing process? Towards the end of his life he told Janice that he was a changed man with her. She didn't believe him though it may have been partly true; what is certainly true is that there were common themes throughout his relations with women; dependency and need. The drama he created might have been fuelled by Violet's own enthusiasm for the same thing but it may also have been necessary for him to work himself into that state in order to proceed, as if the simple desire to do it were not enough, or were not simple. He was a sensitive man, vulnerable, imaginative, emotionally highly-charged; it may have been that the revs needed to be high for his emotions to become engaged.

Nor may this have been unusual behaviour. People do sometimes conduct their intimate relationships in ways that would be unguessed at from outside and it may be normal for someone who reacted as Ford had at nineteen to respond in a similar way in early middle age. We know he was subject to periodic depressions, particularly during times of stress and exhaustion, and he had by then been having rows with Conrad, Marwood, Wells, Arnold Bennett and Olive Garnett, not to mention Elsie. The lover's suicide talk is not necessarily cynical simply because there is no attempt to put it into practice. It may be more an expression of feeling than statement of intent. Nonetheless, concealing a handy bottle labelled *POISON* about your person in such a way that the woman you hope to make your mistress will find it is not something anyone does without an eye to effect. It is difficult not to feel that he was a bit of an old rogue on this occasion, and Violet a willing (and older) dupe. It must have made everything more heady and intense. Indeed, it was intensity that characterised this stage of the relationship – the walk home at ten-thirty makes it clear that there wasn't any licentiousness. Nor was the infidelity quite as blatant as it might seem; Mizener believes there are indications that Ford and Elsie had discussed divorce and suggests that she may have offered him a separation. When he asked Violet if she would marry him if he divorced, Ford may have done so in the belief that this was the state towards which he was heading. It was not to be, but neither he nor Elsie nor Violet was to know that at the time.

We see, therefore, the busy, party-throwing editor who edits brilliantly with, as it were, his left hand while at the music hall; we see the writer who is getting on with it quietly during some undiscovered hours of the twenty-four; we see the lover who talks of suicide to his mistress, the father who dotes on his children (when he is with them), the unfaithful husband who nurses his wife, the tenant who sits gazing into the fire or playing the piano, the friend who keeps his friend going, taking his reminiscences at dictation; but in none of these does the man express himself fully. Nor quite in all of them together: there was more to come and, unceasing acceleration being impossible on this earth, the centre was starting to break up again.

FIFTEEN

The major problem was the *Review*. There was a series of disagreements which, as is often the case with such episodes, seem in retrospect to be as petty, wasteful and unnecessary as they seemed weighty and inevitable at the time. Wells, for example, worried about the effect on his *Tono-Bungay* book sales of the possible failure of the magazine that was serialising it, and began pulling out. He was already doing and contributing far less than Ford thought they had agreed and he didn't at first come clean about his *Tono-Bungay* worries. There was an exchange of letters after the Grand Manner following which, as is the way of these things, it was harder to recover close relations than after an oral exchange. Putting it on paper no doubt made everything seem more considered and final, detached from the heat of the moment which actually makes it possible to take angry words less seriously.

Ford also fell out with Edward Garnett over critical remarks Garnett made about the *Review* – which, Ford said, 'I am doing absolutely for the love of Literature and without any idea of advancement or profit for myself'. That was true but it did not make editing and financing the magazine any easier. He also fell out temporarily with Robert, Edward's solicitor brother, while relations with Olive, cooling for some time, did not improve: 'To tea with Ford and stayed on till midnight listening to his new novel: & discussing all sorts of questions . . . Am not now keen on appearing in the Review.' She disliked his 'secretaries & friends'. On the other hand, if she went to tea and stayed till midnight they must have been getting on reasonably well, whatever her private reservations. He read to her from *A Call*, and she did permit one of her stories to be published in the *Review*. But, as we have seen, when he and Elsie drifted apart her sympathies moved farther towards Elsie and in early 1910, by which time the break had become public, her comment on a novel of Violet's was: 'read a novel by Miss Violet Hunt as a specimen and don't wish to read another.'

For all his sociability, Ford seems to have thought of himself as a solitary who was not good at dealing with people. This may seem surprising, given the life he led, but it is less so if regarded as a description of how he felt rather than how he appeared to behave. In fact, he listened more than he spoke. He rarely writes about himself directly in any intimate way but he does offer insights into his fictional characters which may, with some caution, be applied to himself. For instance, he says of the character Count Macdonald in his novel *The New Humpty-Dumpty*: 'A constitutional dislike of talking about his own affairs, and a strong determination to let no other person talk to him about them, rendered [Macdonald] really rather solitary.' The problem for Ford was that public and the private lives overlapped. Marriage, separation and insolvency may have private origins but they are acted out on the public stage. Ford was good at getting on with people, generous, warm, sensitive and interested; he was less good at managing affairs, something that also calls for sympathy but of a more strategic sort. He was too involved and found it difficult to separate himself from what he was doing. He could view something as if he were detached but he could not *be* detached, for all his assumed aloofness of manner. He was never cold.

More serious were his breaches with Marwood and Conrad, the two men – perhaps the two *people* – whose opinions meant most to him. Both breaches were in part brought on by over-work and his unsatisfactory marital state, leading both men – particularly Conrad – to change their attitudes towards him. There were prior indications which, if Ford had been less busy and tired, he might have heeded. In March 1909, for instance, a dramatised version of *The Fifth Queen* was staged. It was advertised as a collaboration 'By the author and F. Norreys Connell' but the MS is in Ford's hand. It was staged by Ada Potter who, according to Violet, adored Ford. It fared no better than Conrad's and James's attempts for the stage. Ford later said that he spent the evening underneath the bar in the pit refreshment saloon. Conrad wrote to him: '. . . you are prodigal of both your toil and your talent. Yet one would like to see your largeness used respectfully.'

It was good advice and it was true. It also implied a warning: Conrad had withdrawn somewhat and was prepared to withdraw farther. They had been close again for some months while Ford helped him compose his reminiscences for the *Review* but a problem had arisen involving Marwood. Ford seems to have felt that Marwood was getting more than his fair share of credit for the *Review* and himself more than his fair share of the blame, especially with regard to financial management. Then Elsie reported that Marwood had for some time been making advances towards her, which included reminding her that he had saved her life by paying for her operation. She had incriminating letters from him. It is significant that she did not complain of this when it happened but chose the time when Ford was already in some disagreement with Marwood. Perhaps she was jealous.

Ford was in an awkward position. He seems to have wanted to doubt neither his friend nor his wife. He distanced himself from Marwood but did not break with him and he involved Robert Garnett as a kind of adjudicating authority. It is a frustrating affair because it is not known precisely what was done and said, yet it is precisely that detail that is needed for any judgement to be made. Not surprisingly, the participants differ as to what went on but that *something* went on there is no doubt. The incriminating letters were actually seen by Robert Garnett. His judgement was that Ford should not break with Marwood: 'Elsie forgot that not only Marwood was flesh and blood but a highly impressionable and *unhappy* person upon whom her confidences were certain to make the greatest mark. You and Elsie both make the same mistake: in your troubles you become self-concentrated and oblivious of how you affect others. Your letters to me showed this.'

Elsie's confidences were presumably about her marriage but the reason for Marwood's unhappiness is not clear, possibly his illness or his own marriage. Without those letters we cannot say much more except to note Ford's own reactions. He wrote to Elsie that he was astonished, adding: 'If it true that he has attacked Yr virtue and my honour (which is what it amounts to) I cannot for the sake of business have any friendly relations with him . . . If I see him he will try to persuade me that your accusations were untrue – so that to have to do with him must mean breaking with you . . . It is a horrible and very ticklish matter for me. On the one hand I do not like you to be misjudged: on the other certain very ticklish negotiations are just being consummated, involving Marwood, Soskice, Robert and myself . . .'

What is missing from this letter is any feeling that he actually minds, or that he might even be jealous. He is concerned about the relative positions of the three and about the proprieties but not, it seems, about the main fact. It is tempting to think that if Marwood had made off with her and Elsie had asked for a divorce, Ford would have been content.

This all happened in March 1909 – that is, before he had become Violet's lover but while he was pursuing her. He mentions her later in the same letter: 'However, I plug along. "I think I ought to tell you" (as the friend of yrs puts it) [Marwood?] that Violet Hunt is coming to dinner. She is really doing her best to get the Monds to take up the Review. If they wd, there wd be an end of all these worries. And, so far I cannot observe in the lady any sign of desiring more of a quid pro quo than the material desire to keep going a magazine in which she hopes to "appear".'

This is disingenuous, to put it kindly, particularly as he probably felt a thrill of excitement at writing Violet's name. He signs off: 'Well good bye old thing – Preserve Yr tranquillity FMH.'

Relations with Marwood were patched up after a while but at the time it meant that Ford was more desperate than ever for financial backing for the *Review*. He borrowed a further £500 from his Münster relatives but refused to borrow Elsie's last £600 – 'if anything happens to me you would certainly need all you can get and keep.' (Could this be a reference to further thoughts about suicide?) The negotiations he referred to in his letter to her began the process which eventually led to his own ousting from the *Review*.

That was not the only lasting effect of the Marwood affair. Elsie told Conrad about it, which again suggests that she wanted to damage Marwood. Conrad was shocked and, like Ford, reluctant both to believe it of Marwood and to doubt Elsie. As before, we do not know exactly what was alleged and therefore what led

Conrad to say of the Marwood family that he 'could not believe these people were as black as they appeared to her'. He says this in a letter to Ford which also records Elsie's suggestion that Ford should come down and stay with the Conrads for a week rather than with her, at the same time as she was saying that she and Ford were reconciled. Conrad's response was firm: 'That cannot be. If you are reconciled so completely, Ford's place, when he is in Aldington, is in the cottage.' What purpose, he asks Ford, 'can be served by re-creating an equivocal situation? By such juggling with the realities of life, an atmosphere of plots and accusations and suspicions is created . . .'

This last is a good phrase, suggestive of the author's knowing his subject – with, one suspects, the added insight of a Polish understanding. Conrad seems sincerely concerned about both his friends. He says that Marwood is unhappy and looks ill – 'I can't give him up for a ruffian' – and suggests that Ford might have over-reacted to what were really faults of tact; that he might, in fact, have treated 'men who *were* admiring friends, with an Olympian severity'. In another vivid phrase he warns: 'You will find yourself at forty with only the wrecks of friendship at your feet.'

He also wrote to Galsworthy of the 'execution' of Marwood by Ford and Elsie: 'I have seen a man guillotined thirty years ago but it hasn't made me feel half as sick as the present operation . . . We couldn't keep the horrid affair off us anyhow – what with E coming with horrid details and revelations (I told her plainly I could not believe what she said – and she only smiled) . . . and the poor M's who we *had* to listen to out of common humanity.'

Again, it seems that not only Marwood himself was involved. Speculation is unlikely to be very useful but it is worth noting that there appear to have been three elements: the letters, incriminating to a degree but, judging by Robert Garnett's reactions, stopping well short of 'horrid details and revelations'; what Elsie told Conrad; what Elsie told Ford. The last two may have been identical but Ford's lack of personal reaction and his apparent lack of any dislike of Marwood contrast with Conrad's shock, which suggests that he might not have heard the same details or that he didn't believe them. Many years later Elsie told her daughter Katharine that Marwood had made earlier advances to her, while Katharine was a little girl sitting in her lap, but there is no indication that Ford knew about these at the time. Also noteworthy is Elsie's reaction to Conrad's saying he could not believe her. Was she smiling at the effect her words were having? The tentative conclusion of all this is that something happened between Marwood and Elsie and that Elsie, seeking to save her marriage, made out to her husband that Marwood was his rival, and made the most she could of it. That may be unfair but what little is known does not suggest that she tried to play it down.

That she was in a fraught state at the time is clear. She had reason to be but she also found reasons where there were none. She thought she was the model for the character Bianca in Galsworthy's *Fraternity*, a woman whose pride and desire to be loved are what kill her husband's inclination to love her. Galsworthy was earnest to assure her that she wasn't but it is significant that she herself made the link. She had better reason for seeing elements of herself in Countess Macdonald in Ford's *The New Humpty-Dumpty*, in which the woman resents the smarter life her husband is leading and insists he should like what she likes. If it were a portrait it would be unfair but Ford probably did what most novelists do: take a colour from here, a colour from there and mix or heighten them. That colour might well have been taken from Elsie because it touched on what, sadly, had happened to their marriage. She had remained much as she had been but he, an undeveloped youth of twenty when they married, had gone on developing.

There is no doubt that the affair played a large part in Ford's losing the intimacy of the two friends he valued most and it may well have played a part in Elsie's losing her husband. The real triangle, as Moser points out, was not Ford – Elsie – Marwood, but Ford – Conrad–Marwood. It was each man's position with regard to the others, not with regard to Elsie (let alone Marwood's wife, who is never mentioned) that is the real subject of their concern. Violet noted this: 'Poor Marwood was a nervous man, full of feeling, but not endowed by nature with the means of letting off steam possessed by the two doyens of the pen . . . in his noble simplicity [he] was caught between two deeply sophisticated personalities, and went about looking ill and unhappy.'

Conrad's attitude towards Ford is often said to change from this time though it would be more true to say that aspects that were always present come more to the fore. For instance, there followed an unfortunate episode involving a Dr Mackintosh, a friend of both families who was to be entertained by each until Ford, according to the Conrads, tried to take over the entertaining. Conrad wrote of Ford to Galsworthy: 'He's a megalomaniac who imagines that he is managing the Universe and that everybody treats him with the blackest ingratitude. A fierce and exasperating vanity is hidden under his calm manner which misleads people . . . I do not hesitate to say that there are cases, not quite as bad, under medical treatment.' The last sentence was more true than perhaps Conrad realised. Ford was beginning to go to pieces again and the managing of affairs, in that harassed state, did not bring out the best in him. He was confused and probably silly. As usual, we do not know his side of it, because he did not write letters criticising his friends.

Conrad's *Reminiscences* were a significant part of the *Review*. They were produced in close collaboration with Ford but following all this disagreement Conrad decided not to write any more. He did not say so to Ford but said instead he was unwell, therefore unable to keep up the instalments. Not unreasonably, Ford announced in the magazine that the series would be resumed when Conrad was better. Conrad was furious with this and said bluntly that there would be no more. There was an exchange of letters during which Conrad pretended that what was so far published was intended all along as a unit, that this was therefore a natural break. Later, he told Galsworthy that he was *prevented* from adding to his reminiscences. This could have been a veiled admission of the fact that he couldn't do them without Ford's help.

Word got around that Conrad would have nothing more to do with Ford and the *Review*, which was damaging to both. It was also rumoured that he was offended by Ford's relationships with women, which was offensive to Ford and was, of course, the kind of rumour that it is impossible to refute. Ford was still upset about it when he wrote to Edward Garnett after Conrad's death in 1924. It remains likely, however, that Conrad had said something on the subject since he did not respond kindly to Violet's subsequent attempts at peace-making between him and Ford.

All this was happening at the time when Ford was losing control of the magazine. His financial difficulties were well known and were getting worse. David Soskice, the Russian who had married his sister Juliet, planned for a group with common political interests to take over. They would control the political content but keep Ford as editor. This did not find favour with Marwood, still involved because of his earlier investment, and the arguments dragged on for some time. Compromise was reached in May 1909: the business side was to be taken over by the Soskice group, who hoped eventually to buy the *Review*, and Ford was to continue with it but no longer was he to write his political editorials or to control the content. Like almost any editor who had such conditions imposed upon him, he felt it as editorial castration.

He rushed off to Aldington that night, not entirely sober, arrived in a downpour and had to walk from the station. He set out again for London the next morning, no doubt calmer and drier but probably with a gloomy sense of finality. While waiting on the platform he asked Elsie for a divorce. Her response was to plead with him to leave London and return to Kent and his writing. He caught the train.

It is interesting that during this crisis of failure and rejection he should have bolted to his wife and home rather than back to 84 Holland Park Avenue, and that he should have waited until he was leaving before asking for a divorce. It may be, of course, that he had already determined on this course of action but it is odd that he should not have sent notice that he was coming so that he could be met. That he should then have waited until the last minute so that discussion would not be prolonged is perhaps less an indication of lack of intent than of Fordian – but by no means exclusively Fordian – dislike of confrontation. This was shortly before he became Violet's lover and, despite Elsie's strong desire to remain married to him, he might have boarded the train believing that divorce was at least a possibility. He was in a confused and unhappy state, bordering on desperation.

There was more. Violet's niece, Rosamond, conceived a passion for him. There is no suggestion that this was in any way returned, although he was doubtless flirtatious and charming, and Violet was in any case confident enough of herself and her ability to cope with her niece, of whom she was fond. After she and Ford had become lovers she wrote to him: 'I have not told her [Rosamond] anything except that you are *not for her* . . . And she tosses her head and says she knows that.'

And more. Gertrud Schlabowsky was the daughter of a Konigsberg tailor and was picked up – or rescued, depending on the point of view – by Ford in the 'Empire lounge' (very probably the Shepherd's Bush Empire). Most of what we know about her comes from Violet, though Goldring also mentions her. Both regarded her as a prostitute and Violet says that Ford set aside thirty minutes every night around midnight for talking to her. Goldring speaks of her in terms of the Victorian cult of saving the fallen woman, making a comparison with Gladstone. He described her as a 'pallid waif', says that Ford let her sleep in his spare room because she had nowhere else to go and recalls only vaguely how she used to 'slink about at night'. He thinks it improbable that there was anything between them.

Violet paid her rather more attention. She describes her as having a 'white, heavy moon-face, short Calmuck nose, wide red mouth, and loops of black hair falling over a rather brutish forehead.' This unflattering but not unappealing picture is put in a different light by Violet's friend, May Sinclair. At one of the parties in Number 84 Gertrud wore one of Violet's best dresses ('grey mock fur made tight and plain in the new mode') and May much annoyed Violet by wondering 'who the beautiful, pale, Russian princess was'. It is easier now to imagine Gertrud's appeal and tempting to speculate on the circumstances of her meeting Ford: did he regard her as a prostitute, was that why he befriended her, how good was her English, was the fact that he also spoke German what brought them together, what did they discuss during their thirty-minute sessions?

There may, of course, have been a sexual relationship between them but it is perhaps more likely that there was not. She called Ford 'Papa' and he apparently did his best to push her forward on social occasions as he might a young niece or daughter whom he was trying to make feel at home in the world. Violet thought of her as 'bored, pining, discontented, dying to get away, with nowhere else to go . . . wanting luxury, gaiety, new clothes

. . . always leaving paper patterns and powder-puffs about the room . . .' Ford wrote a satirical poem about his nightly conversations and published it in the *Review* under the pseudonym Francis M. Hurd: 'And both with a most ancient work to do,/ You selling worthless love; I modern rhyme'. Goldring recalls having recovered it from the *Review* waste-paper basket in Ford's handwriting.

Calmuck noses on Russian princesses were perhaps just tolerable but the increasingly public irregularity of Ford's relationship with the girl – complicated, of course, by the irregularity of Violet's own position – was not. In 1910, by which time she had assumed roughly the position of Official Receiver in Ford's financial affairs, Violet paid for Gertrud to return to Germany and a month or two later for her to go to New South Wales; where, with luck, she might have prospered.

Ford's back was broad and as he humped whale-like through the sea all sorts of flotsam and jetsam would cling to him. He was perpetually, almost compulsively and nearly always to his own disadvantage, helpful. This would be enough to account for Gertrud's presence but it makes all the more surprising the cynical use that was made of her in July 1909; Ford may have been desperate or it may not have been his idea, but it must have had his willing compliance. In that month Violet and Rosamond visited Aldeburgh. Ford followed with Gertrud, thus managing to unite three of the four women then known to be involved with him. Gertrud was described as his secretary but her presence in church in those circumstances scandalised the local congregation. This might have been explained as part of his campaign to introduce Gertrud to the world and make her feel included were it not for the fact that later in the month he wrote a description to Elsie of how Gertrud had been living with him at Number 84 and how he had travelled about with her. The idea was to provide evidence for divorce and perhaps to anger Elsie into agreeing.

Divorce was by then under discussion. He had offered her £400 a year, presumably guaranteed by Violet since he had no money, but her brother Harri had advised her to ignore the offer. The letter about Gertrud was handed over by Ford to the children's nanny, Edmée van der Noot, on the Medway at Tonbridge. Elsie reacted to the news as the lovers had hoped: angered, she started divorce proceedings. On the night of the handover he and Violet had a celebratory supper at Number 84. Violet's devoted maid, Annie Child (to whom Ford had had to declare, in writing, the honour of his intentions towards her mistress), helped prepare it. They must have been quite sure that Elsie would divorce; and so, at first, was she.

It was never very easy for the lovers to make love. Violet felt uncomfortable in South Lodge while Ford's rooms were cramped and hardly private. They tried renting somewhere but that too was unsatisfactory. Probably it felt sordid. Also, Violet was very keen to establish the regularity and legitimacy of their relationship. She had Christina and Katharine to tea at South Lodge, introduced Ford to her relatives and took him to stay with her mother and her sister, Silvia, in Co. Durham. The visit was not a success. Silvia was irritated by the way her daughter Rosamond sat on a stool at Ford's feet and gazed adoringly. She also felt he made no effort with the family and none to hide his boredom. 'I think it really was a mistake my coming here,' he said afterwards to Violet. '. . . I fancy I have made your sister dislike me.' Significantly, in view of future deceptions and self-deceptions, Violet had given Silvia the impression that Ford was already divorced. Silvia discovered he wasn't.

Word of the impending divorce spread quickly through the family and beyond. The German Hueffers urged Elsie not to on the grounds that her Catholic daughters would be compromised and that Violet was anyway likely to prove a passing fancy. Harri believed Mary was still eager to marry Ford should he become available, which presumably was more than the Martindale family felt they wanted to cope with. Ford's affair with Mary – if that is what it was – had not survived the introduction of Violet into his life but her interest in him was maintained for some time, as is evident from her later antipathy. A further point was that Elsie herself became worried that Ford might abduct the girls during the course of divorce. He was fond of them and there is evidence that his possible estrangement from them was the aspect of divorce that most worried him from the start; he was not the man to abduct his children, though, as Elsie later realised. In the event he was to have neither divorce nor his children. Elsie stopped the proceedings and subsequently went to court with a successful petition for restitution of conjugal rights.

Ford was thus in the unusual position of having been made subject of a court order forbidding intercourse at the start of his marriage, then made subject to another tantamount to insisting on it at the end. There was publicity about this case, as there had been about the first. While Elsie was worrying that Ford might seize the girls, Violet was worrying that Elsie would seize the furniture, some of it valuable, in Number 84. Between them, Ford broke down. He wrote a rather frenzied letter to his mother: 'Yet really without exaggeration Elsie has ruined me so that I am mentally a wreck. My work is all going to pieces and I cannot even place the last book but one that I wrote incredible as that seems.' He wrote to Pinker that he was 'practically at starvation point'.

Violet believed that it was these events that brought on in him 'a fresh attack of neurasthenia that lasted three whole years, and was responsible for many things, and much private and particular misery'. She added, accurately, that the effect of emotional events such as these was to give him 'such severe shocks as to render him really ill. His mind was too sensitive to stand it, and for the time being he could be deprived almost of his senses and his power to control himself.' In such matters Ford was an oyster without shell, all vulnerability, unable to fight back, unable to present his case, unable to cope. It is significant that most of the male protagonists in his novels are men who for one reason or another are unable or unwilling to engage in the intimate cut and thrust of life. Their creator was a feeler who wished also to be a doer, and that is always difficult.

Violet's birthday was the 28th September. She and Ford fled secretly to France to stay with friends of hers. His attempts to conceal what they were doing not only brought it to light but had unforeseen and unfortunate consequences. The story he gave David Soskice led Soskice to believe that they had fled the country because there was not enough copy for the November issue of the *Review*. He therefore appointed Galsworthy temporary editor.

There is an inevitability about the rest of the episode reminiscent of classical tragedy, except that instead of catharsis there is confusion, instead of death, mess. The two-week escape was a success, though not without quarrels (their first was in the fly on the way to the station). They stayed at Beaumont-le-Roger with the Farleys, friends of Violet's. Ford's state improved and he began working regularly again in the mornings, always a good sign, dictating *The Portrait* to Violet and to Agnes Farley. In the afternoons they walked.

Back in London the *Review* secretary, Miss Thomas, had received a letter from Violet, posted in Paris, about some stays Violet had promised her. She had also received a telegram from Ford saying he would return on the train arriving at Charing Cross at 10.45 p.m. on 14 October. Earlier on the 14th Miss Thomas was called on by Elsie, Edmée van der Noot and Elsie's lawyer, asking where the missing couple were. Miss Thomas produced Ford's telegram though not Violet's letter. Edmée was sent to South Lodge to enquire when Violet would return and learned that she would be back on the same train as Ford. The trio went to Charing Cross and waited. They were not disappointed.

Violet's later reaction was that it was their own fault for being relaxed, that one of them should have got off at Hither Green. Ford's reaction at the time was to say to her: 'It's all up, old girl! You will see. There will be no divorce.' He knew his wife well enough. Other women might have made this red-handed catch the reason for divorce but for Elsie possession of Ford, in whatever form, became a matter of pride. If she couldn't have him she would still insist on her rights to his name, to his support, to call herself his wife. Years later she said she wished she had agreed to divorce but in 1909 such calm consideration was probably impossible.

Ford's position at the *Review* collapsed in neat parallel. He resumed the editorship but under such restricted conditions that he tried to persuade Sir Alfred Mond to buy the magazine so that he could get rid of David Soskice, with whom he had quarrelled and whom he now regarded as a 'revolutionary extremist'. He would then, he hoped, regain full editorial control. Mond did buy the paper but it was Ford he fired, replacing him with Austin Harrison. (The magazine continued until 1937 but it was never the same). Ford was desolated. The *Review* had been his great enthusiasm, his contribution to the cause of good letters, his brief

– so it must have seemed – hour upon the stage. Violet recorded: 'And we walked as usual in the Park treading the dead leaves like faded hopes under our feet, in silence. For a week of mornings he did not address more than three words to me.'

The *Review* had been much more than a job; it had been a fulfilment in which Ford, perhaps for the first time in his life, had felt he was doing what he should be doing. He was still uncertain about his own writing – his sales did nothing to reassure him – but his editing was widely acknowledged as brilliant. It had put him centre-stage and earned him more recognition than all his books together. But everything had gone wrong. He and everyone else involved had lost money, he had lost the equilibrium he had gained so slowly after his 1904 breakdown, he had lost or was losing friends and he had lost all chance of ending his marriage in such a way as to make possible a new one. Everything had gone wrong except the quality of the magazine, which remained unsurpassed. Had he known at the time that the fire that seemed to consume everything he touched was a transforming fire, that it would fuse within him the strata from which great art would come, even he would probably have remained unconsoled. Near the end of his life, following a second magazine venture, he was still unrepentant: 'If I had a million dollars, I would start a magazine and print all the real talent from here to Baton Rouge and back . . . What a six months that would be!' He had no illusions about it; he simply loved it.

Violet and he still took care to behave with decorum even after their discovery at Charing Cross but they could not stop the news spreading. Ford complained to Pinker for telling Wells (to whom it was unlikely to have been news), also to Galsworthy about what he had been saying. In what Violet called 'a mad letter' he offered to break with Galsworthy but fortunately Galsworthy responded with generous apologies and recognition that Ford's work would outlive his. More significantly, as an indication of the view that a number of people would take, Violet was cut by Henry James. She was to have gone to Lamb House for the weekend but after hearing from Ford about the divorce James wrote to put her off. The circumstances of the divorce struck him as 'painfully unedifying, and that compels me to regard all agreeable or unembarrassed communication between us as impossible'. He signed himself off 'in very imperfect sympathy'. Violet attempted to remonstrate in a letter which suggested that her capacity to change her view of reality according to her wishes was no less than that sometimes claimed of Ford. It did no good.

Following Elsie's petition for the restitution of conjugal rights and the subsequent press stories, Ford did not call at Violet's house for some time. She was in any case worried about facing the servants but to Ford, with his horror of even discussing his private life let alone seeing it turned into public fodder, the situation must have been almost unbalancing. 'I never,' wrote Violet, 'to this day, knew how he was taking it.'

This was not the only effect of the court case. Since the beginning of December 1909 he had been paying Elsie £3 10/- a week. (Like most of his expenses over the next few years, the money was probably Violet's. She had a bill of sale taken out on his furniture, partly in case Elsie should snatch it. It was not sold until 1942, after her death, by which time it was worth considerably more than it had raised on valuation.) When the court subsequently ordered Ford to pay what was in fact a lesser weekly sum to Elsie he refused to comply because to have done so would have been to accept the implication that he was not already paying her that and more (which had not come out in court). He was sentenced to ten days in Brixton gaol, commuted to eight as it spread over a weekend. Unfortunately, he left no record of his time in prison nor of his reason for choosing to go. It is likely that there was more than one. He may have thought it would make Elsie more inclined to divorce him and he may have wanted to arouse sympathy amongst those he had fallen out with over the *Review*. It is perhaps more likely that the point of honour was a real one: that he didn't want to go to prison at all but on this as on other occasions was very resentful of any suggestion that he was not trying to support his wife and children. It is also slightly reminiscent of his week-long sulk at school after losing the fight. Finally, it is not entirely facetious to suggest that he may have welcomed prison as a rest: he didn't have to cope with anything there.

Violet had already decided to move him to South Lodge as a paying guest at £3 a week and while he was in Brixton she removed his possessions from Number 84, selling some of his books to raise money, returning the borrowed ones and securing the furniture. One room, however, was kept for the ever-faithful René Byles who wished to start a literary agency. Gertrud was still in residence and so she too was moved to South Lodge. Violet wrote later that she found she could tolerate her because she was going back to Germany.

Violet was helped in these removals by Mary. She had a knack for getting on with – or at least getting to know – her lovers' wives or former girlfriends, perhaps even an enthusiasm for it. Quite what passed between her and Mary, like what passed between Mary and Ford, we do not know. There was, however, yet another unfortunate consequence: Harri Martindale called while they were both at Number 84 and reported his sister's connivance with Ford and Violet to Elsie, which may have made her even more determined not to grant divorce. When Ford was released Violet took him, her mother, and Gertrud to Fordingbridge in Hampshire for a short holiday. There Ford began *Lady Whose Bright Eyes* (the heroine is modelled on Rosamond and her name is taken from a tablet that Violet saw in the porch of Salisbury Cathedral).

With Ford now resident in South Lodge, Violet's sister Silvia removed Rosamond because she feared the effect Ford would have on her. In Münster Tante Laura died but the legacy Ford had long hoped for was not to be his: it had been contingent on his good behaviour. In his depression he convinced himself that it was the news of his imprisonment that had killed Tante Laura. Yet early in 1910 Edward Garnett reported him to Olive as saying that he was more at peace than he had been for twenty years. It may have been true. He was thirty-six and the first major stage of his adult life was ended. He did not know what was to come but he knew that, whatever it was, it would be different. Perhaps that was what he had wanted.

SIXTEEN

From this time on Violet's dominant desire was to establish a respectable position for herself and Ford. This meant marriage but, if they could not marry, they must at least be accepted as married. She embarked upon a campaign of energetic calling on friends and acquaintances, often with Ford in obedient attendance, smartly dressed and subdued. She got Mary to move into South Lodge with them and, later, Mrs Hueffer.

It is reasonable to consider the years 1910 to 1914 in terms mainly of Violet's aspirations because for much of the time Ford had almost no will of his own. He played the part of husband, he travelled, he tried to keep in touch with his children, he wrote, often in exorcism of his past; he survived; but Violet's was the shaping will, making things happen, while he was the passenger. He was nonetheless a feeling, observant passenger, absorbing, reflecting, re-creating within himself that which was to come. With Violet running his life, he could manage most things so long as he was not thrust upon the public stage. Unfortunately and typically, he was.

Violet decided that they should mount a fence-mending expedition amongst the Hueffer relatives in Germany. She provided herself with a chaperone, Lita Crawfurd, her successor but one in Oswald's arms and his second wife. The widowed Lita was then taking the baths at Bad Neuheim, a place and life that Ford was to use to good effect in *The Good Soldier*. They cruised up the Rhine. He irritated Violet because he would sit silently over patience while working out what he wanted to write, impervious to everything until he had done his day's stint. He would generally think out about a thousand words at a time, dictate or write at a single go and then, as noted earlier, usually leave it unaltered.

Often he did not even read through the typescript and he rarely made notes.

It is curious that Violet, another writer, was not more tolerant of his habits. She was irritated by his refusal 'to be confronted with any of the problems that beset an author unfortunately doubled with a man'. She seems not to have appreciated that such regular work was partly his salvation, that it was also indicative of unusual concentration and dedication. It was not always what he was doing that was important, so much as that he was doing it. Almost all his lesser work would have benefited from revision. Sometimes he wrote slackly and often in short scenes which, though well enough imagined, do not cohere sufficiently to support the meaning of the whole. On the other hand, some of his best writing is, as Pound observed, to be found in obscure paragraphs in little known books.

It also irritated Violet that he did not seem to be making sufficient financial contributions. She was contributing the lion's share, certainly, but in fairness to Ford it should be said that he wasn't being mean; he simply didn't have it. He was free enough with it when he did. Also, he was at this time making over a considerable proportion of what he did earn to Elsie and the children. Perhaps behind Violet's irritation was a growing sense that he might not have been as committed as she. It would not have been necessary for him to display any lack of enthusiasm for her to get this impression; merely the suspicion that his want might not have been as desperate as hers. It wasn't.

This did not stop them coming up with a hare-brained scheme. They talked to a German lawyer who thought it would be a fairly simple matter for Ford to acquire German citizenship in about six months. Then, they thought, they could have a German wedding and Ford's marital problems would be solved. It may be that Holman Hunt's Dutch marriage to his dead wife's sister was at the back of their minds, but there was a difference: Hunt's wife was dead. Quite how they thought a marriage in Germany would mean that a previous marriage in England would cease to count, is not clear. Robert Garnett and others in England were dismissive of the idea, as was Ford's German cousin Hermann, but they went ahead. It was a small but significant departure from reality, a failure to see the links between causes and effects. At the same time Violet became involved in lengthy legal action with her sisters over her mother's affairs. She had to return to England to see to it and Ford went on to Giessen where he hoped to fulfil the requirements of citizenship. It was a miserable period for him; he was lonely, his rooms were depressing, the food bad. He must have eaten a lot of it, though, because from this time onwards it is no longer possible to call him slim: he increased to about sixteen stone and, though he lost some weight later, his youthful form was never recovered. He might also have been having second thoughts about citizenship. He was a prescient man and, as we have seen, had earlier sensed the probability of war in Europe. He could not have been reassured by the children who set off percussion caps outside his window and shouted 'Tag! Engländer'. It was not long before he was saying to Violet that German nationality could mean that either he was shot as a traitor or he would be forced to fight against France (that Britain would be involved was not, at that time, a foregone conclusion).

He managed to relieve his time in Giessen by going to Jena to lecture on the Pre-Raphaelites to his friend Levin Schüking's students. He enjoyed lecturing. He also made a quick trip back to England after Mary had surreptitiously telegraphed him to the effect that Violet was to have a minor operation; he arrived in time for her to come out of the anaesthetic. He visited his daughters, then at school in St Leonard's, and took them amber necklaces that Violet had made. D. H. Lawrence sent Violet three plays of his to be read, which she forgot about. Lawrence became convinced that Ford had taken them back to Germany and lost them – not an unreasonable supposition since Ford was generally awash with manuscripts – and wouldn't believe his denials. Ford actually got Violet to find and return them but by then the damage had been done: Lawrence had already turned against Ford partly, as he saw it, for having abandoned him by leaving the country after discovering him. He transferred his allegiance to Edward Garnett. The misunderstanding over the plays may or may not have been central, but it did not help.

Because of his citizenship application Ford was not supposed to leave Giessen, so his trips had to be semi-clandestine. They spent

Christmas together at Spa, which he thought 'the quietest place . . . that God ever forgot to finish'. He enlivened it a little by making one of his famous punches. They attended Mass in the cathedral at Aix-la-Chapelle and took part in a ceremony that Violet found moving. However, she wrote later, she felt that the man kneeling at her side 'was in a sense unsympathetic to me. A cold, patient man without fire, lazy of habit: his heart dull-beating, was perhaps more faint about it all than he was willing to let appear.' These words were written long after the events but her judgement was sound.

Ford was supposedly trying to convince the German authorities that he was a respectable citizen worthy of German nationality and, not surprisingly, he found the legal pretences wearisome and trivial. He wanted to get on with his writing. Everything else was a charade. But he was tied to Giessen by more than naturalisation requirements since he could not afford to be there unless Violet paid the bills and he could not afford to get away unless she paid his expenses. The court case about her mother's affairs (her mother was no longer able to look after them herself) meant that she was now not as well off as she had been and there began to be arguments between them about money – his accommodation, for instance, the question of a new pony and cart for Christina and Katharine, his teeth. These last probably preoccupied him more than any biography can show, partly because – as many people are now fortunate enough not to know – when teeth are a problem they are ever-present and partly because when they are mentioned they are never taken seriously. Violet paid for him to have most of those that were left after his previous German 'cure' removed, at the very high cost of £8 each. While he was toothless he hid from people; then, of course, there were problems with the false ones.

With Mrs Hueffer Violet adopted the role of daughter-in-law and also dedicated a book to her. Mrs Hueffer chaperoned them in Germany for a while and stuck by them unquestioningly through all the trouble that was to come. Olive Garnett had now finally sided with Elsie. In 1911, for the first time in nearly two years, Ford and Conrad again exchanged letters. The old trouble was not forgotten but relations could be maintained. At times Violet was chafing because Ford seemed not to be getting on with things: for all the talk, naturalisation and divorce were always in progress, always about to happen, but there was never actually anything to show. She sought and got reassurances from Ford, and in his letters to friends in England (and presumably during his not infrequent trips home) he gave the impression that citizenship was virtually granted, divorce a formality.

Did he believe it? Like Violet, he probably wanted to, although unlike her he was in a position to know the details. It is hard to imagine that he had utterly convinced himself. More likely there were two levels of belief: one within himself, just possibly to be shared with someone who knew him well and yet put no pressure on him, at which the truth was unspoken but acknowledged; the other which surfaced the moment any public acknowledgement was required and which construed intentions into facts. Not to have made this transposition would have forced him and Violet to acknowledge the real facts, central among which was the impossibility of their marrying. This was something that Violet, who wanted it so badly, was probably not prepared to face in herself; while Ford, who probably wanted it less badly, was not prepared to face her with it.

Not that all was gloom and illusion. In August 1911 Pound visited Ford at Giessen. Friendship and mutual admiration had developed between them since the start of *The English Review* days and they were to become life-long champions of each other and of each other's work. It has been described as a literary friendship in, for instance, Brita Lindberg-Seyersted's *Pound/Ford, the Story of a Literary Friendship*, and that it certainly was. Each sympathised with what the other was trying to do in his work, never uncritically and never unhelpfully, and each could assume in the other the same dedication to the cause of good letters. To call it a literary friendship ought to suggest deep levels of sympathy, respect and understanding but sadly the phrase normally implies something more limited – a friendship without the personal. Their relationship has been described as just that since their letters do not discuss personal and family issues. It may be that they did not much discuss these in conversation, though it is not known, but that is not the point. A friendship is not less full because its commerce is poetry rather than divorce. It might, indeed, be fuller because much of what is discussed will rest on shared assumptions which do not need to be spoken and on knowledge and understanding without which neither could have reached a common starting point. Pound said that he was interested in the virtues and achievements of his friends, not in their failings and vices, and the same could be said of Ford. At the risk of making an absurdly exalted parallel, the conversations of angels may not dwell at all on men's failings but that does not mean that they are not well understood.

Besides, it *was* personal. They liked each other. Pound's energy and zaniness, which to many was unsettling, found ample space and acceptance in the broad tolerance of Ford's humour. Their letters are quirky and joky and to the end of Ford's life they helped each other. When Ford was in America he went out of his way to visit Pound's parents; when money was needed it was sent, publishers were lobbied, articles written. As a factor in both their lives, their friendship is probably nearly always underestimated. This is partly because nothing went wrong with it; it was two-sided, loyal and lasting; it is easier to make books out of loves that fail. When in the late thirties Pound was criticised for his political views, Ford supported him. Not that he supported Fascism – he detested it – but, as Janice Biala told Pound, 'Ford always said that you had carried the aesthetic burden of English letters for the last thirty years entirely by yourself.' Pound believed that Ford did much the same in the early years of the century and after Ford's death he was one of the first to seek to preserve his memory and to inform opinion.[1] He remained fond of him to the end of his own life in 1972, aged eighty-seven.

It was during Pound's August visit to Giessen that Ford took a roll on the floor, groaning, his hands over his head. He was, said Pound, 'trying to teach me how to speak for myself'. The roll was prompted by Pound's *Canzoni.* As Pound suggests, that a grown man should so behave might seem ridiculous, perhaps particularly to some of the professors of literature whom both so despised, but it was an indication of how much language mattered to Ford. As we have seen, he was one of the very few in England at that time to advocate the use of natural unadorned language in verse. He was the first bridge to the modern; Pound crossed it and, through

[1] See obituary, page 446.

him, Yeats (Pound said that he and Yeats had evening conversations in which he relayed to Yeats what Ford had said in the afternoons), after them practically everyone, but before Ford practically no one. That roll is also an indication of their humour and understanding. It is hard to imagine more arresting criticism of one's work than to see the audience reduced to physical distress.

During that visit they sent a card signed by both to Ford's daughter, Christina, and Ford tried to interest his guest in the sights. 'I had very little time to myself while with Hueffer,' Pound wrote afterwards to his mother, 'not that there was much work done, but we disagreed diametrically on art, religion, politics and all therein implied; and besides he's being married this afternoon or else this A.M. and going to the dentist's in the P.M. I was dragged about to a number of castles etc., which were interesting and about which I persistently refused to enthuse.' He seems also to have acted as Ford's amanuensis, taking at dictation at least one letter to Pinker. Ford had a general and indiscriminate need for amanuenses. Almost anyone who came to stay, particularly if they were female, was likely to find themselves acting secretary. Had he been able to afford it he would probably have lived amidst a disorganised and talented retinue of people who were both friends and servants, a continuous travelling party with himself at the centre, dictating, editing, reading, discussing, encouraging and flirting; and somehow, invisibly, he would have continued to produce novels and poems.

Pound thought Ford's poem 'On Heaven' 'the most important poem in the modern manner', but it was Ford's talk on poetry that he valued more than his achievement. Yeats he thought 'the only poet worthy of serious study in London' but added that he 'would rather talk about poetry with Ford Madox Hueffer than with any man in London.' Ford's writhing had made the point that decoration was not the point. Pound wrote in Canto LXXII:

> and for all that old Ford's conversation was better,
> consisting in *res non verba*,
> despite William's anecdote in that Fordie
> never dented an idea for a phrase's sake
> and had more humanitas.

Asked, after the deaths of both, whether there was ever any hostility between Ford and Yeats, Pound replied: 'There was the matter of "visions". There is no doubt whatever that Ford, from time to time, used to have visions without any effort at all: this was a little humiliating to dear Yeats, who spent a lifetime trying to have visions: he did have some, I think, but he would keep trying to have more than nature allowed him.' These visions, summarised by Pound as 'Venus immortal crossing the tram tracks', may be a neglected aspect of Ford's life. They are important not only for what they showed but for what they did to his sense of reality. If you actually see Venus crossing the tram tracks your sense of reality has either to admit to the possibility of other realities or it has to include the visions as part of the everyday. Either way, your perspective is different and you probably always have one eye on something else. This renders more vivid and real the sort of 'emotional vision' that informed Ford's creation of characters such as Tietjens, the left-over gentleman type. They felt as their creator felt and to him their reality may have been no less than much of what he saw around him. Perhaps it was then only a small step to a different sort of 'emotional vision', that of German nationality and re-marriage. Talking about it, as he clearly did with Pound, might have made it seem – or *feel* – as real as everything else.

In September 1911 he and Violet went to Paris where he had new porcelain teeth fitted. In October they were accosted by a *Daily Mirror* reporter in Spa. The reporter had been following them and had previously pestered Robert Garnett. Violet saw to it that they gave him nothing but he hung around and later that night found Ford at the place where, according to Violet, he went to play billiards most nights. Ford must have been in an expansive mood. The resulting article quotes him as saying that he and Violet were married, that he was heir to Prussian estates, that he had 'retained' his German nationality, had offered himself for service in the German Army but was not required and was now lecturing in history in German universities. It made a good story.

Meanwhile, Ford had written privately to Lawrence telling him that they were married and Violet had written to Mrs Hueffer saying that no one now would see them until they were. On 5

November they attended a religious ceremony which Violet later described as their marriage. The power of mutual illusion must have been very great since it enabled them to overlook Ford's never having appeared before a divorce court, his having no evidence of German nationality and the absence of a marriage certificate.

Not only that, but the illusion seemed to harden under attack. They were back in England in December and began a busy social life. Violet was keen to establish herself in what she saw as her new status. Friends were more cautious. Both the Conrads and Marwood – good relations now having been re-established – tried to warn them, Marwood sensibly suggesting that they should return to Paris. If they were not aware that Elsie could at any time issue a writ, then others were.

Whatever private realities may have been constructed, the ordinary everyday one, with its inexorable double-hammer blow of cause and effect, was not to be denied. That they knew what they were doing, albeit at some deeper level than they were prepared to admit, is evident from what happened to Annie Child, Violet's maid. It was now her turn to have a vision and she saw what Violet described as 'an Implacable Face'. Annie talked about it while serving dinner. Afterwards, Ford imagined he heard the doorbell ring violently, and panicked; he tied up the doors with anything he could lay his hands on and put a bicycle across the front door. When he came to bed, Violet said, he was pale and frightened. It was from then that she dated the three-year attack of neurasthenia.

Lawrence saw them a few days afterwards. He found Ford fat but 'rather nicer than he was', adding, 'He seems to have had a crisis.' Violet he liked – 'she's such a real assassin' – but:

> She looked old, yet she was gay – she was gay, she laughed, she bent and fluttered in the wind of joy, she coquetted and played beautifully with Hueffer: she loves him distractedly – she was charming, and I loved her. But my God, she looked old . . .
>
> I think Fordy liked it – but was rather scared. He feels, poor thing, the hooks are through his gills this time – and they *are* . . .

Had they died then or, better still, been hanged for the crime of love, it would have made an excellent romantic story. Instead, it dwindled into confusion and unhappiness and took a long time doing so.

In April 1912 Violet's mother's novel, *The Governess*, was published. The author had been unable to finish it before losing her mind and Ford and Violet wrote the ending. Violet's sisters tried unsuccessfully to get an injunction preventing publication. In the introduction Ford referred to Violet as Mrs Hueffer. René Byles, who had been staying with them at Violet's Selsey cottage, was now business manager of a magazine called *The Throne*. He wrote a publicity piece for the book in which he also referred to Violet as Mrs Hueffer.

Threat of legal action had previously won Elsie an apology from the *Daily Mirror*, which had also referred to Violet as Mrs Hueffer. Elsie now sued *The Throne*. After news of this new court case Ford broke down again, though he blamed the breakdown on *The Panel*, a novel he had written in about a month during the winter. At the same time he was publishing *The New Humpty-Dumpty* under the pseudonym Daniel Chaucer. This was a satire in which there are not very heavily disguised portraits of a number of his friends and relatives including himself, Violet and Elsie, and an account of his time with the *Review*. It followed *The Simple Life Ltd.*, another satire featuring some of the same people. Neither had done anything to sweeten Elsie. She may even have heard echoes of her own words. In *The New Humpty-Dumpty* the Countess Macdonald's tirade in a railway compartment against her weak and groaning husband sounds only too true to life:

> . . . You are hankering after another woman . . . Do you suppose that I have not any eyes in my head? Do you suppose that if it had not been for her you would ever have had the courage to tell me that you wanted to separate? . . . I dare say you will tell me that you never so much as wanted to kiss the doll of a creature that it is. And I dare say that is true enough. This is the sort of effeminate creature that you are, and you will call it chivalry or honour.

In the novel the marriage is failing because the Countess cannot keep up with her husband's intellectual progress while the Count himself is a 'hopeless neurotic' incapable of dealing with the problems of money or sex. Elsie wouldn't have needed much imagination, any more than Ford did in the writing of parts of it.

No doubt Elsie would have continued with the court case without all this but it had another consequence: Marwood was offended, and this time the break was to become final. He believed that the character of the promiscuous Lord Aldington was a reference to himself. Perhaps it was, in part, as also it is likely to have been part Ford. Indeed, the attractive and honourable Duke of Kintyre might also have been based partly on Marwood (he has the best line in the book: '"Any man," he said slowly, "is any sort of man, some time or other, you know."') Marwood was not a writer and did not see that a fictional character grows away from its human inspiration. As the one evolves, so identity with the other becomes increasingly tenuous. Not surprisingly, other writers understood this better and were generally less offended even by caricatures than were non-writers. Ford, for instance, was used by Wells, Conrad and James in various books and he put them in his, but in no case was this taken very seriously.

But Marwood did take it seriously. He at first demanded repayment of the four hundred guineas he had lent for Elsie's operation four years previously. Conrad became involved as mediator. The Marwood family has subsequently said that the money was never repaid but Violet, who was handling Ford's affairs, said it was, 'on the nail'. Marwood's reason for wanting the payment may not have been simply his quarrel with Ford, though: his health was worsening and he wanted to put his affairs in order. As the break with Ford widened into permanence, Marwood and Conrad continued to meet weekly. Ford felt, and was, excluded. He had also heard what was most hurtful to him: that Marwood believed he was neglecting his children. The youthful Rebecca West, who was an early admirer of Ford and had got to know him as a result of her reviews, was told by Violet that Marwood was so painful a subject that no one dared mention him to Ford.

After the death of her mother Violet become increasingly involved with litigation against her sisters. Ford, on medical advice, was supposed not even to dictate a letter and was on the verge of bankruptcy. He was also drinking heavily. They spent most of the summer of 1912 at Selsey, drugged by the adalin which Dr Tebb had prescribed (Ford took four a night). He played golf with Masterman, however (in the pouring rain, Violet wrote to his mother), befriended Katherine Mansfield and Middleton Murry and saw a fair bit of Pound and Wyndham Lewis. And he worked: 'with aplomb', said Violet, 'dictating his daily screed of typewritten pages which he scorned to look over . . .'

He wanted to spend Christmas 1912 with his daughters but Elsie refused, saying it would unsettle them. Instead, he and Violet borrowed a cottage near Burnham Beeches and invited several guests, among them Mary – still very much a part of the scene – Pound and the Compton Mackenzies. Faith Compton Mackenzie left an account of the festivities in her book, *As Much As I Dare*, according to which Ford spent all Christmas Day locked in his bedroom while Violet ran upstairs and down entreating him to come out and 'speculating loudly as to why he was up there at all'. Pound talked unceasingly from dawn to dusk. On Boxing Day Ford re-appeared, benevolent and lively, and Violet was 'flushed with excitement'. Pound went on talking.

Elsie's case against *The Throne* came up in February 1912. René Byles and W. C. Beaumont, the editor, had been ready to apologise to her provided she really was married to Ford and that they would not by apologising lay themselves open to a similar claim by Violet. According to Beaumont's *A Rebel in Fleet Street*, the two men consulted Ford and Violet in Hanover and were told they were married. According to Violet, she pleaded with Beaumont not to defend the suit but he, on his 'high editorial horse', refused to apologise. It is quite possible that both accounts were true since they do not conflict. Judging by what Ford and Violet had already said about themselves, they were far enough gone in delusion to take this one further step.

The trial was a walk-over, the defence having no evidence. Neither Ford nor Violet was there. Elsie was awarded £300 plus costs, which put the already shaky *Throne* out of business. The press had a good day.

Ford was in Boulogne during the trial. Violet had been with him but returned for it. She heard the result in South Lodge. Although she had been warned that things were not going well and although she was sitting at home in a darkened room dreading the worst, she nevertheless later wrote that when she heard the news, 'I realised that I had not for a moment supposed that "The Throne" would lose – not for one moment.' It was a curious dichotomy. The verdict was, she thought, 'Joseph Leopold's funeral' (those were Ford's Catholic baptismal names).

Violet returned to Boulogne, seen off by a weeping Mary. Ford already had a letter from Dr Tebb confirming that he was neurasthenic and advising that he should not be asked to testify if called. It was fortunate that he was not since when Violet took him the news he lost his voice and it was some days before he was well enough to move. Again, what hurt him most was the prosecution's allegation that he had neglected to provide for his children. The court was left under the impression that he had provided them and Elsie with far less money than he (and Violet) actually had. During the proceedings Elsie testified that she had complained to the Postmaster General about Violet's being listed in the London telephone directory as Mrs Hueffer and that the Postmaster General had promised to attend to the matter. When Violet died nearly thirty years later she was still listed as Mrs Hueffer. The two women continued their fight over the name long after its original owner had abandoned it and them. In 1925 there was further court action because Violet had referred in print to one of her 'husband's' books and had signed herself Violet Hunt Hueffer. It was during that latter case that Elsie's counsel referred to her in her absence as a Catholic, citing that as her reason for refusing divorce. This error became part of Fordian mythology and flourishes to this day. It is typical of much in Ford's life that he, a Catholic who wanted to divorce and re-marry, was prevented by his Anglican wife who was widely believed to oppose it because she was Catholic.

When Ford was well enough they travelled. They went to Montpellier, a favourite with the Conrads, but it was 'a wash out', Violet said, 'ugly and ordinary'. At Carcassonne there was rabies and snow. Ford made the hotel bathroom his study, his desk the bathtub lid. Les Baux 'depressed us immeasurably', at St Remy the mistral was 'a knife-blade of cold'. There was a letter from Elsie demanding more money, another from Conrad concerning Marwood's implacable hostility; he was never to have anything to do with Ford again. Violet kept up a vigorous and cheerful exchange of letters with Mrs Hueffer, whom she addressed as Dear Mother, but between her and Ford there was little vigour and less cheer. She wrote: 'We forced a calmness that spoke less of emotions controlled than of an utter atrophy of all the springs of feeling. We hardly spoke to each other that month . . .' The charge of neglecting his children caused Ford to weep 'as only a German can'.

On that bathtub in Carcassonne he was writing *The Young Lovell*, the last novel he wrote before *The Good Soldier*. It is a novel of fantasy and solitary despair in an historical setting, with visions of Venus. He described it to Pinker as 'rather like *The Fifth Queen*, but, in a sense more romantic. I don't want to let it go to just any publishers, because, if it is anything at all, it is really literature and I have spread myself enormously over it, but of course I leave that to your discretion. '

However fine the writing, this is another example of how the fertility of his imagination wrought much out of little. He deals with big themes but in a realm of fantasy; they are something to which the book is grafted rather than the sap which should nourish it. Unlike *The Fifth Queen*, it is not about real people. It is not yet 'the real right thing'.

SEVENTEEN

They moved back to England in May 1913. Ford had already tried to recompense René Byles for the loss of *The Throne* by letting him have his latest novel, *Mr Fleight*, without an advance for the publishing venture that she was trying to set up. This was another book in which the Marwood strain ran strongly, in the character of Mr Blood. Mr Blood was a favourite of Ford's and he continued to use him in his journalism, making it clear that he admired him. Moser thinks that the book could be read as Ford's plea to Marwood 'for forgiveness and renewed friendship', and in a sense it can; it also represents a further development of a character-type that Ford was to make great use of later.

He did not relish his home-coming. As nearly always, his instinct was to say nothing about personal affairs and for once this did not do him any disservice. It was a wise and practical policy: 'I hold very strongly the view that friends are people before whom one does not need to justify oneself, and personally, I am absolutely determined to speak to no one on these matters.'

Unfortunately, not all the friendly are friends and Violet's inclination was to persuade as many as possible of the justice of their case. She had been urged by real friends to stay abroad longer but she wanted to re-establish her position in society. She embarked on another energetic round of calling, had cards printed naming herself as Mrs Hueffer and gave parties attended by some of her old friends, but not by most. Adultery was acceptable but losing a court case was not. Many of her calls were not returned. May Sinclair, a close friend, advised them to stay away for another six months; another, Mrs Clifford, testified to the strength of feeling the case had aroused and said: 'I would do a good deal for you but I simply should quake if you came here on Sundays, and I believe other people would walk out – *Go away for three years!* and trust to your old friends to smooth things over as far as they can for you.' But Violet fought on; position was of the greatest importance to her.

Masterman was one of those who did not keep away but otherwise their circle tended to be more literary than social. Pound was a tenacious and dependable supporter though his pretty well daily company was a trial for Violet. He was a tyrant on the tennis court, never stopped talking, dressed bizarrely and was a careless breaker of chairs (Gertrude Stein was later to make the same complaint). With him, Wyndham Lewis and others they became involved in the Vorticist movement and its new magazine, *Blast!*

There was further confirmation of the change in Ford's shape. An American observer, Kathleen Cannell, noted that his 'almost huge pink roundness, his silky straight, canary-coloured hair and moustache and very pale blue eyes give him the air of an English country squire . . .' This moustache became a considerable part of him. Many years later, long after his death, Pound wrote of him to Brigit Patmore: '. . . he had all his faults, like his moustache, out in front where everyone cd/see Yum. au fond a serious character as J. J. the reverend Eliot and even ole Unc Wm/the YeAT were NOT.'

Brigit Patmore was a close friend of Violet's. An alluring woman, she inspired Pound and Richard Aldington as well as Ford. He may have had a brief affair with her at about this time. She denied that anything happened between them and Rebecca West said in 1975 that although Ford had a passion for Brigit she doubted that Brigit reciprocated. On the other hand, Ford later gave the impression that there had been some involvement and at the time annoyed Violet by wearing a pectoral cross which he said Brigit had given him. Violet complained that it obtruded during their intimate moments; Brigit denied having given it. Some four years later, however, Violet's diary entry for 20 April 1917 records Brigit admitting to having made love with him. It is, of course, quite possible that they did, that the incident did not lead to a full affair and that Ford's passion was not reciprocated. There is no doubt that he felt it, though; he later told Janice Biala that he had been in love with Brigit. Moser is right, therefore, in asserting that Brigit meant much more to Ford than a friendly flirtation or passing love affair. Not only might she have been the White Lady that the Young Lovell seeks but she might also have been partly responsible for *The Good Soldier*: 'For Ford the courage to start every new, serious novel about modern love had to come from a new woman. In the case of *The Good Soldier* it was Brigit Patmore.' Moser points out that this was five years after Ford had fallen in love with Violet and this fact reminds him 'once more of the appalling regularity with which his [Ford's] phases coincided with the decades and half decades of his life'. Less speculative and more salty was Rebecca West's comment in a letter to Moser: 'You say as a total outsider that "usually Ford could stay in love five years and stay attached only ten." This seems to me characteristic of many of your sex and cannot, I think, be counted as an idiosyncrasy of Ford.'

They saw much of Wyndham Lewis – Violet furnished his flat in Augustus John's Fitzroy Square studio – and Ford got him work wherever he could. Lewis was never particularly grateful, saying that Ford was 'never a favourite of mine', and he criticised him in print, but that changed nothing. Ford was already thinking of himself as a man whose time had passed, a champion of the younger generation who at the same time as trumpeting them would have to make way for them. In many writers modesty is a pose, authorial vanity requiring an affected indifference to their own work, but in Ford it seems to have been genuine. He spoke rarely of his own best achievements and qualities, drawing attention instead to his not always serious acts and poses, to his friends and to life as it felt.

After finishing *The Young Lovell* he wrote a short book on Henry James, possibly meant for James's seventieth birthday though not published until the following year. It was hastily written and although intended as recognition of James's achievements – 'the greatest of living writers, and in consequence, for me, the greatest of living men' – it was never read by its subject. James had continued to see a little of Ford and Violet, taking the occasional brief tea, but he really wanted no more of them. They were a mess in his eyes, Ford never a serious writer. It is possible that James never read any but Ford's early books and the collaborations with Conrad, of which he disapproved so strongly.

In September 1913, when the James book was finished, they went on a trip down the Rhine with Masterman and his wife, Lucy. They found the Germans surly and xenophobic and there was even a suggestion that Masterman might have been mistaken for Churchill. Ford was oppressed by the ominous signs. Violet urged him to visit his relatives but he was not keen – 'Do you want to see me shot or forced to fight against France?' – though he was prepared to do it if she insisted. German nationality was no longer an issue.

When he got back he was thrust into a row between Pound and Harriet Monroe, the editor of *Poetry*. Pound had resigned in a huff and had asked that Ford take over. It was a small enough incident but Ford's letter to Monroe is a good example of his tact, his real self-effacement and his humorous tolerance of Pound. He encloses Pound's letter to him, which simply reads:

> Dear Ford,
>
> Will you please take over the foreign correspondence of 'Poetry' & communicate with them to the effect that I have turned it over to you.
>
> Yr. E. P.

Ford wrote to Harriet Monroe:

> Dear Madam,
>
> I have received the enclosed letter from Mr Ezra Pound who has gone away into the country without leaving me his address. I don't know whether he has the literary advisership of your organ to dispose of, but I am perfectly certain that I could not do his job half so well as he has done. Could you not make it up with him or re-instate him – or whatever is the correct phrase to apply to the solution of the situation, whatever that may be? I really think he has applied himself to your service with such abounding vigour and such very good results that it is a great pity that you should part company. Besides, if I tried to help you that energetic poet would sit on my head and hammer me till I did exactly what he wanted and the result would be exactly the same except that I should be like the green baize office door

that everyone kicks on going in or out. I should not seriously mind the inconvenience if it would do any good, but I think it would really be much better for you to go on with Ezra and put up with his artistic irritations: because he really was sending you jolly good stuff. That is the main thing to be considered isn't it?

Over twenty years later he was still writing letters about jobs for Pound, fixing the job and then trying unsuccessfully to persuade Pound to take it. Another letter, unimportant in subject but revealing, is the one he wrote a few months after this to R. A. Scott-James, who had founded the *New Weekly*:

My dear Scotty,

I suppose I may now congratulate you, as I do very heartily at having got your foot into what appears to be such a very gold-plated stirrup. Violet told me all about it sometime ago, but she forbade me to write to you congratulatorily saying that you had told her in confidence, so that presumably I was not to know anything about it. I really am as sincerely glad about it as you can be yourself; do believe that. I think the programme looks excellent from a solid paying point of view and you can rely on V. and myself doing all that we can to spread your fame.

I do hope you will not forget les jeunes – the quite young and extravagant; it is only in them that you can put your trust. And I dare say you will not. Your list of extinct and semi-extinct volcanoes, alarming though it be, is I know only window-dressing. But you *cannot* go too far in the other direction. Simply because your fat tol-lol goshawks will give you tired stuff, and tired stuff and again tired stuff; whereas the tassel-gentles, though they may fly at the moon – and very probably will fly at the moon – will yet give you the only casts that in ten years' time you will not be ashamed of having promoted.

However, you will not want to be preached to, like this. Anyhow, all good luck go with you.

Not only is this generous encouragement from a man who had not long before been ousted from his own magazine but it is also good advice. It is an indication of Ford's own editorial policy, past and to come, and of an attitude that was to be his for the rest of his life. He always trusted and encouraged the young, often, as Pound pointed out, more kindly than critically. At the same time, he venerated age and literary position; had it been an English custom he would always have addressed such writers as James and Hardy as Master. He would have been happy to be so addressed when he was older. Meanwhile, it is striking that in his fortieth year he saw himself no longer as one of the literary young. There are few novelists nowadays who would be easy with that.

The Young Lovell was published in October 1913 and a month later Ford's *Collected Poems* were issued. This latter was due to the efforts of Douglas Goldring who had then taken over a nearly defunct publishing company called Max Goschen, and who owed Ford money. This was a way of repaying him, along with an advance of £30. The book had practically no sales but helped, Goldring thought, to 'gild the list'. Many of the poems are reminders that Ford was in origin and early literary influences a man of the nineteenth century, a Victorian and a Pre-Raphaelite whose achievement it was to grow from that into a properly twentieth-century writer. Most of them were early but some were more recent, written in a voice that was musing, monotone and reflective. 'The Starling' is an example. Ford was not an extractable poet and this, like much of his work, needs to read in full:

THE STARLING

It's an odd thing how one changes . . .
Walking along the upper ranges
Of this land of plains,
In this month of rains
On a drying road where the poplars march along,
Suddenly,
With a rush of wings flew down a company,
A multitude, throng upon throng,
Of starlings,
Successive orchestras of song,
Flung, like the babble of surf,
On to the road-side turf –

And so, for a mile, for a mile and a half – a long way,
Flight follows flight
Thro' the still grey light
Of the steel-grey day,
Whirling beside the road in clamorous crowds,
Never near, never far, in the shade of the poplars and clouds.

It's an odd thing how one changes . . .
And what strikes me now as most strange is:
After starlings had flown
Over the plain and were gone,
There was one of them stayed on alone
In the trees; it chattered on high,
Lifting its bill,
Distending its throat, crooning harsh note after note,
In soliloquy,
Sitting alone.
And after a hush
It gurgled as gurgled a well,
Warbled as warbled a thrush,
Had a try at the sound of a bell
And mimicked a jay . . .
But I,
Whilst the starling mimicked on high
Pulsing its throat and its wings,
I went on my way
Thinking of things,
Onwards and over the range
And that's what is strange.

I went down 'twixt tobacco and grain,
Descending the chequer-board plain
Where the apples and mays are;
Under the loopholed gate
In the village wall
Where the goats clatter over the cobbles
And the intricate, straw-littered ways are . . .
The ancient watchman hobbles

Cloaked, with his glasses of horn at the end of his nose,
Wearing velvet short hose
And a three-cornered hat on his pate,
And his pike-staff and all.
And he carries a proclamation,
An invitation,
To great and small,
Man and beast
To a wedding feast,
And he carries a bell and rings . . .

From the steeple looks down a saint,
From a doorway a queenly peasant
Looks out, in her bride-gown of lace
And her sister, a quaint little darling
Who twitters and chirps like a starling
And this little old place,
It's so quaint,
It's so pleasant; and the watch bell rings, and the church bell rings
And the wedding procession draws nigh,
Bullock carts, fiddlers and goods.
But I
Pass on my way to the woods
Thinking of things.

Years ago I'd have stayed by the starling,
Marking the iridescence of its throat,
Marvelling at the change of his note;
I'd have said to the peasant child: 'Darling
Here's a groschen and give me a kiss' . . . I'd have stayed
To sit with the bridesmaids at table,
And have taken my chance
Of a dance
With the bride in her laces
Or the maids with the blonde, placid faces
And ribbons and crants in the stable . . .

But the church bell still rings
And I am far away out on the plain,
In the grey weather amongst the tobacco and grain,
And village and gate and wall
Are a long grey line with the church over all
And miles and miles away in the sky
The starlings go wheeling round on high
Over the distant ranges.
The violin strings
Thrill away and the day grows more grey.
And I . . . I stand thinking of things.
Yes, it's strange how one changes.

Not all poems benefit from being read aloud but many of his do, this particularly. Repetitions of rhythm and rhyme produce the mood which is integral to image.

His most significant poem of the period, 'On Heaven', was written after *Collected Poems* came out and was published separately. It was composed at the request of Violet, who said one day at Selsey, 'You say you believe in a heaven; I wish you'd write one for me. I want no beauty, I want no damned optimism; I just want a plain, workaday heaven that I can go to some day and enjoy it when I'm there.' A very understandable desire, particularly if Ford had been carrying on to her along the lines of one of his letters to Lucy Masterman: 'I am a tempestuously religious sort of person and I do not think any clearness of thought is possible unless one either is or has been intensely religious.' He set Violet's heaven in Provence, where his was, and read the poem to her a few days later:

ON HEAVEN

To V. H., who asked for a working Heaven

I

That day the sunlight lay on the farms;
On the morrow the bitter frost that there was!
That night my young love lay in my arms,
  The morrow how bitter it was!

And because she is very tall and quaint
And golden, like a *quattrocento* saint,
I desire to write about Heaven;
To tell you the shape and the ways of it,
And the joys and the toil in the maze of it,
For these there must be in Heaven,
  Even in Heaven!

For God is a good man, God is a kind man,
And God's a good brother, and God is no blind man,
And God is our father.

I will tell you how this thing began:
How I waited in a little town near Lyons many years,
And yet knew nothing of passing time, or of her tears,
But, for nine slow years, lounged away at my table in the
  shadowy sunlit square
Where the small cafés are.

The *Place* is small and shaded by great planes,
Over a rather human monument
Set up to *Louis Dixhuit* in the year
Eighteen fourteen; a funny thing with dolphins
About a pyramid of green-dripped, sordid stone.
But the enormous, monumental planes
Shade it all in, and in the flecks of sun
Sit market women. There's a paper shop
Painted all blue, a shipping agency,
Three or four cafés; dank, dark colonnades
Of an eighteen-forty *Mairie*. I'd no wish
To wait for her where it was picturesque,
Or ancient or historic, or to love
Over well any place in the land before she came
And loved it too. I didn't even go
To Lyons for the opera; Arles for the bulls,
Or Avignon for glimpses of the Rhône.

Not even to Beaucaire! I sat about
And played long games of dominoes with the *maire*,
Or passing *commis-voyageurs*. And so
I sat and watched the trams come in, and read
The *Libre Parole* and sipped the thin, fresh wine
They call Piquette, and got to know the people,
The kindly, southern people . . .

Until, when the years were over, she came in her swift red car,
Shooting out past a tram; and she slowed and stopped and lighted absently down,
A little dazed, in the heart of the town;
And nodded imperceptibly
With a sideways look at me.

So our days here began.

And the wrinkled old woman who keeps the café,
And the man
Who sells the *Libre Parole*
And the sleepy gendarme,
And the fat *facteur* who delivers letters only in the shady,
Pleasanter kind of streets;
And the boy I often gave a penny,
And the *maire* himself, and the little girl who loves toffee
And me because I have given her many sweets;
And the one-eyed, droll
Bookseller of the *rue Grande de Provence*, –
Chancing to be going home to bed,
Smiled with their kindly, fresh benevolence,
Because they knew I had waited for a lady
Who should come in a swift, red, English car,
To the square where the little cafés are.
And the old, old woman touched me on the wrist
With a wrinkled finger,
And said: 'Why do you linger? –
Too many kisses can never be kissed!

And comfort her – nobody here will think harm –
Take her instantly to your arm!
It is a little strange, you know, to your dear,
To be dead!'

But one is English,
Though one be never so much of a ghost;
And if most of your life has been spent in the craze to
  relinquish
What you want most,
You will go on relinquishing,
You will go on vanquishing
Human longings, even
In Heaven.

God! You will have forgotten what the rest of the world is
  on fire for –
The madness of desire for the long and quiet embrace,
The coming nearer of a tear-wet face;
Forgotten the desire to slake
The thirst, and the long, slow ache,
And to interlace
Lash with lash, lip with lip, limb with limb, and the fingers
  of the hand with the hand
And . . .

You will have forgotten . . .
        But they will all awake;
Aye, all of them shall awaken
In this dear place.
And all that we then took
Of all that we might have taken,
Was that one embracing look,
Coursing over features, over limbs, between eyes, a making
  sure, and a long sigh,
Having the tranquillity
Of trees unshaken,
And the softness of sweet tears,

And the clearness of a clear brook
To wash away past years.
(For that too is the quality of Heaven,
That you are conscious always of great pain
Only when it is over
And shall not come again.
Thank God, thank God, it shall not come again,
Though your eyes be never so wet with the tears
Of many years!)

II

And so she stood a moment by the door
Of the long, red car. Royally she stepped down,
Settling on one long foot and leaning back
Amongst her russet furs. And she looked round . . .
Of course it must be strange to come from England
Straight into Heaven. You must take it in,
Slowly, for a long instant, with some fear . . .
Now that *affiche*, in orange, on the kiosque:
'*Six Spanish bulls will fight on Sunday next*
At Arles, in the arena' . . . Well, it's strange
Till you get used to our ways. And, on the *Mairie*,
The untidy poster telling of the *concours*
De vers de soie, of silkworms. The cocoons
Pile, yellow, all across the little *Places*
Of ninety townships in the environs
Of Lyons, the city famous for her silks.
What if she's pale? It must be more than strange,
After these years, to come out here from England
To a strange place, to the stretched-out arms of me,
A man never fully known, only divined,
Loved, guessed at, pledged to, in your Sussex mud,
Amongst the frost-bound farms by the yeasty sea.
Oh, the long look; the long, long searching look!
And how my heart beat!
Well, you see, in England
She had a husband. And four families –

His, hers, mine, and another woman's too –
Would have gone crazy. And, with all the rest,
Eight parents, and the children, seven aunts
And sixteen uncles and a grandmother.
There were, besides, our names, a few real friends,
And the decencies of life. A monstrous heap!
They made a monstrous heap. I've lain awake
Whole aching nights to tot the figures up!
Heap after heap, of complications, griefs,
Worries, tongue-clackings, nonsenses and shame
For not making good. You see the coil there was!
And the poor strained fibres of our tortured brains,
And the voice that called from depth in her to depth
To me . . . . my God, in the dreadful nights,
Through the roar of the great black winds, through the sound
  of the sea!
Oh agony! Agony! From out my breast
It called whilst the dark house slept, and stairheads creaked;
From within my breast it screamed and made no sound;
And wailed . . . And made no sound.
And howled like the damned . . . No sound! No sound!
Only the roar of the wind, the sound of the sea,
The tick of the clock . . .
And our two voices, noiseless through the dark.
O God! O God!

(That night my young love lay in my arms . . .

There was a bitter frost lay on the farms
In England, by the shiver
And the crawling of the tide;
By the broken silver of the English Channel,
Beneath the aged moon that watched alone,
Over the dreary beaches mantled with ancient foam
Like shrunken flannel;
The moon, an intent, pale face, looking down
Over the English Channel.

But soft and warm She lay in the crook of my arm,
And came to no harm since we had come quietly home
Even to Heaven;
Which is situate in a little old town
Not very far from the side of the Rhône,
That mighty river
That is, just there by the Crau, in the lower reaches,
Far wider than the Channel.)

But, in the market place of the other little town,
Where the Rhone is a narrower, greener affair,
When she had looked at me, she beckoned with her long
white hand,
A little languidly, since it is a strain, if a blessed strain,
to have just died.
And, going back again,
Into the long, red, English racing car,
Made room for me amongst the furs at her side.
And we moved away from the kind looks of the kindly people
Into the wine of the hurrying air.
And very soon even the tall grey steeple
Of Lyons cathedral behind us grew little and far
And then was no more there . . .
And, thank God, we had nothing any more to think of,
And, thank God, we had nothing any more to talk of;
Unless, as it chanced, the flashing silver stalk of the pampas
Growing down to the brink of the Rhône,
On the lawn of the little château, giving onto the river.
And we were alone, alone, alone . . .
At last alone . . .

The poplars on the hill-crests go marching rank on rank,
And far away to the left, like a pyramid, marches the ghost
of Mont Blanc.
There are vines and vines and vines, all down to the river
bank.
There will be a castle here,
And an abbey there;

And huge quarries and a long, white farm,
With long thatched barns and a long wine shed,
As we ran alone, all down the Rhône.

And that day there was no puncturing of the tyres to fear;
And no trouble at all with the engine and gear;
Smoothly and softly we ran between the great poplar alley
All down the valley of the Rhône.
For the dear, good God knew how we needed rest and to be alone.
But, on other days, just as you must have perfect shadows to make perfect Rembrandts,
He shall afflict us with little jets and hindrances of His own
Devising – just to let us be glad that we are dead . . .
Just for remembrance.

III

Hard by the castle of God in the Alpilles,
In the eternal stone of the Alpilles,
There's this little old town, walled round by the old, grey gardens . . .
There were never such olives as grown in the gardens of God,
The green-grey trees, the wardens of agony
And failure of gods.
Of hatred and faith, of truth, of treachery
They whisper; they whisper that none of the living prevail;
They whirl in the great mistral over the white, dry sods,
Like hair blown back from white foreheads in the enormous gale
Up to the castle walls of God . . .

But, in the town that's our home,
Once you are past the wall,
Amongst the trunks of the planes,
Though they roar never so mightily overhead in the day,
All this tumult is quieted down, and all
The windows stand open because of the heat of the night

That shall come.
And, from each little window, shines in the twilight a light,
And, beneath the eternal planes
With the huge, gnarled trunks that were aged and grey
At the creation of Time,
The Chinese lanthorns, hung out at the doors of hotels,
Shimmering in the dusk, here on an orange tree, there on a
  sweet-scented lime,
There on a golden inscription: 'Hotel of the Three Holy Bells'.
Or 'Hotel Sublime', or 'Inn of the Real Good Will'.
And, yes, it is very warm and still,
And all the world is afoot after the heat of the day,
In the cool of the even in Heaven . . .
And it is here that I have brought my dear to pay her all that
  I owed her,
Amidst this crowd, with the soft voices, the soft footfalls,
  the rejoicing laughter.
And after the twilight there falls such a warm, soft darkness,
And there will come stealing under the planes a drowsy
  odour,
Compounded of all cyclamen, of oranges, or rosemary and bay,
To take the remembrance of the toil of the day away.

So we sat at a little table, under an immense plane,
And we remembered again
The blisters and torments
And terrible harassments of the tired brain,
The cold and the frost and the pain,
As if we were looking at a picture and saying: 'This is true!
Why this is a truly painted
Rendering of that street where – you remember? – I fainted.'
And we remembered again
Tranquilly, our poor few tranquil moments,
The falling of the sunlight through the panes,
The flutter for ever in the chimney of the quiet flame,
The mutter of our two poor tortured voices, always a-whisper
And the endless nights when I would cry out, running
  through all the gamut of misery, even to a lisp, her name;

And we remembered our kisses, nine, maybe, or eleven –
If you count two that I gave and she did not give again.

And always the crowd drifted by in the cool of the
even,
And we saw the faces of friends,
And the faces of those to whom one day we must make
amends,
Smiling in welcome.
And I said: 'On another day –
And such a day may well come soon –
We will play dominoes with Dick and Evelyn and Frances
For a whole afternoon.
And, in the time to come, Genée
Shall dance for us, fluttering over the ground as the sunlight
dances.'
And Arlésiennes with the beautiful faces went by us,
And gipsies and Spanish shepherds, noiseless in sandals of
straw, sauntered nigh us,
Wearing slouch hats and old sheep-skins, and casting admiring
glances
From dark, foreign eyes at my dear . . .
(And ah, it is Heaven alone, to have her alone and so near!)
So all this world rejoices
In the cool of the even
In Heaven . . .
And, when the cool of the even was fully there,
Came a great ha-ha of voices.
Many children run together, and all laugh and rejoice and
call,
Hurrying with little arms flying, and little feet flying, and
little hurrying haunches,
From the door of a stable,
Where, in an *olla podrida*, they had been playing at the *corrida*
With the black Spanish bull, whose nature
Is patience with children. And so, through the gaps of the
branches
Of jasmine on our screen beneath the planes,

We saw, coming down from the road that leads to the olives
and Alpilles,
A man of great stature,
In a great cloak,
With a great stride,
And a little joke
For all and sundry, coming down with a hound at his side.
And he stood at the cross-roads, passing the time of day
In a great, kind voice, the voice of a man-and-a-half! –
With a great laugh, and a great clap on the back,
For a fellow in black – a priest I should say,
Ormay be a lover,
Wearing black for his mistress's mood.
'A little toothache,' we could hear him say; 'but that's so good
When it gives over.' So he passed from sight
In the soft twilight, into the soft night,
In the soft riot and tumult of the crowd.

And a magpie flew down, laughing, holding up his beak to
us.
And I said: 'That was God! Presently, when he has walked
though the town
And the night has settled down,
So that you may not be afraid,
In the darkness, he will come to our table and speak to us.'
And past us many saints went walking in a company –
The kindly, thoughtful saints, devising and laughing and
talking,
And smiling at us with their pleasant solicitude.
And because the thick of the crowd followed to the one side
God,
Or to the other the saints, we sat in solitude.
In the distance the saints went singing all in chorus,
And our Lord went by on the other side of the street,
Holding a little boy.
Taking him to pick the musk-roses that open at dusk,
For wreathing the statue of Jove,
Left on the Alpilles above

By the Romans; since Jove,
Even Jove,
Must not want for his quota of honour and love;
But round about him there must be,
With all its tender jollity,
The laughter of children in Heaven,
Making merry with roses in Heaven.

Yet never he looked at us, knowing that would be such joy
As must be over-great for hearts that needed quiet;
Such a riot and tumult of joy as quiet hearts are not able
To taste to the full . . .

. . . And my dear one sat in the shadows; very softly she
 wept: –
Such joy is in Heaven,
In the cool of the even,
After the burden and toil of the days,
After the heat and haze
In the vine-hills; or in the shady
Whispering groves in high passes up in the Alpilles,
Guarding the castle of God.

And I went on talking towards her unseen face:
'So it is, so it goes, in this beloved place,
There shall never be a grief that passes; no, not any;
There shall be such bright light and no blindness;
There shall be so little awe and so much loving-kindness;
There shall be a little longing and enough care,
There shall be a little labour and enough of toil
To bring back the lost flavour of our human coil;
Not enough to taint it;
And all that we desire shall prove as fair as we can paint it.'
For, though that may be the very hardest trick of all
God set Himself, who fashioned this goodly hall.
Thus He has made Heaven;
Even Heaven.

For God is a very clever mechanician;
And if He made this proud and goodly ship of the world,
From the maintop to the hull,
Do you think He could not finish it to the full,
With a flag and all,
And make it sail, tall and brave,
On the waters, beyond the grave?
It should cost but very little rhetoric
To explain for you that last, fine, conjuring trick;
Nor does God need to be a very great magician
To give to each man after his heart,
Who knows very well what each man has in his heart:
To let you pass your life in a night-club where they dance,
If that is your idea of heaven; if you will, in the South of France;
If you will, on the turbulent sea; if you will, in the peace of the night;
Where you will; how you will;
Or in the long death of a kiss, that may never pall:
He would be a very little God if He could not do all this,
And He is still
The great God of all.

For God is a good man; God is a kind man;
In the darkness He came walking to our table beneath the planes,
And spoke
So kindly to my dear,
With a little joke,
Giving Himself some pains
To take away her fear
Of His stature,
So as not to abash her,
In no way at all to dash her new pleasure beneath the planes,
In the cool of the even
In Heaven.

That, that is God's nature.
For God's a good brother, and God is no blind man,
And God's a good mother and loves sons who're rovers,
And God is our father and loves all good lovers.
He has a kindly smile for many a poor sinner;
He takes note to make it up to poor wayfarers on sodden
roads;
Such as bear heavy loads
He takes note of, and of all that toil on bitter seas and frosty
lands,
He takes care that they shall have good at His hands;
Well He takes note of a poor old cook,
Cooking your dinner;
And much He loves sweet joys in such as ever took
Sweet joy on earth. He has a kindly smile for a kiss
Given in a shady nook.
And in the golden book
Where the accounts of His estate are kept,
All the round, golden sovereigns of bliss,
Known by poor lovers, married or never yet married,
Whilst the green world waked, or the black world quietly
slept;
All joy, all sweetness, each sweet sigh that's sighed –
Their accounts are kept,
And carried
By the love of God to His own credit's side.
So that is why he came to our table to welcome my dear,
dear bride,
In the cool of the even
In front of a café in Heaven.

Violet didn't much like it: 'Love without breadth, depth or thickness, without dimension. Subjective purely . . . Not . . . the love that moves mountains, faces the 7 seas of boredom, but the mild, watery variety . . . repeats the great word Agony 3 times, taking up all one line.' She has a point about Agony; like 'joy' or any similar evocation it doesn't often do for the reader what it does for the writer. Also, their time together in Provence had been less than heavenly and it seems to have been the place that inspired the poem rather than she who shared it with him. If, however, what Violet really wanted was a love that would move mountains (not in fact a work-a-day heaven), neither this nor anything else was likely to please. It is not very difficult to imagine her frustrations and anxieties but it is a pity she did not like the poem better; it is a great and graceful compliment, even if not a very personal one; and it is more. Anyone who doubts should try writing on the same theme.

He later said that he sat down to write *The Good Soldier* on 17 December 1913, his fortieth birthday. Some authorities argue for an earlier date, such as in the summer after finishing the James book, while others opt for autumn or winter. It doesn't matter; the point was that he had reached the age at which people take some stock of life, feeling that this might be their last chance to claim that long-promised future but fearing that the pattern might be already set. *The Good Soldier* was the novel into which he decided he would put everything he knew about novel writing. It was, he said, his Great Auk's egg, the last he would do. In two articles in *Poetry and Drama* he announced his farewell to literature and said that he was 'relatively speaking, about to die'. Olive Garnett mentions a letter he wrote in May 1914 to his daughter Christina in which he said that he was dying. His involvement with Pound, Wyndham Lewis and the young literary and artistic scene then making all the noise in London seems to have convinced him, at least for the time being, that he was past it. Even his hallowed Impressionism was under attack from Imagists and Vorticists, presumably also from any other ists who were that week's news. There didn't seem to be much of a future.

Nor was a survey of the past very encouraging. His marriage was dead, he was apart from his children, living with a woman who wanted the one thing he could not give her, alienated from one of the great friends of his life and in only limited communion with the other. The circumstances of his separation had become a public scandal with a virulence which is hard to imagine now. For instance, Goldring recalls that as late as 1936 – a quarter of a century after the events – he returned one of Violet's books to the London Library and referred to her as Mrs Hueffer only to be seriously corrected with, 'You mean Miss Hunt.' Additionally,

Ford's health had suffered to the extent that he was sometimes incapable of coping with anything, and drink (Dr Tebb thought whisky helped him keep going and was probably right) was causing him to put on a great deal of weight. He was also broke. Twenty-one years of full-time authorship had yielded some forty books, a large number of articles and many poems; the result was bankruptcy in all but name. He had a reputation as a literary figure based partly on his editorship of a magazine from which he was known to have been ousted. His books were quite often admired but few people bought them. His journalism, such as his series of Literary Portraits in *Outlook*, was more widely read but it didn't earn enough money. The occasional sub-title of *The Good Soldier* – originally its title – is *The Saddest Story*. This is the story of how love can kill, when it is not itself still-born. Additionally, he had felt love die around him. Conrad's warning about wrecks of friendship was indeed prophetic.

The view of the longer term in many lives is similarly bleak but, depending on the personality, there may be daily compensations. Ford's personality ensured that there were. He had the knack for living, that relish for each minute that brings riches to some where others find only drudgery and despair. Janice Biala recounted an incident from the 1930s when she and Ford were living in the South of France. Her account was published by Sondra Stang in *The Presence of Ford Madox Ford*:

> Once the wolf nearly got us. Ford was writing a series of articles for *The American Mercury* which later came out in book form as *Portraits from Life*. Each month, on receipt of the manuscript, *The Mercury* paid for it and cabled the money to Toulon. All went well for some time, and then for three months running no money turned up. Rather hopeless enquiries were made at the bank, but the answer was always no; no money had come. So many firms were failing that Ford was afraid to confirm his fears that this one too had gone bust and hadn't bothered to explain. Week after week the worry and tension mounted; finally the situation got so bad that Ford blew the last five dollars on a cable to New York. The answer came back that the money had been paid regularly each month. Restored to life, with the

telegram in my hand, I went to the bank and this time refused to take the usual no. After much running around and looking up of books, it was discovered that the money was there all right, I asked to see the Director, to tell him what I thought of his bank, but I was so enraged that I could only open my mouth, and not a word came out. I took the tram home to Cap Brun. It was winter and quite dark by then. There was an accident. Part of the platform I was standing on got ripped off. I didn't even notice it. When I finally got to my stop, I found Ford waiting for me with the announcement that there was to be a total eclipse of the moon in about ten minutes. So we walked up the road until we got into a comfortable-looking bush. We sat down in the damp grass in front of it and waited for the eclipse of the moon.

The point of this, as Janice explained to the present writer, is that, for all the worry about money, it was the moon that Ford thought they should attend to at that moment. That was what was worth looking at; money should not be allowed to interfere. That is how he got, and gave, so much pleasure from life.

There were plenty of day-to-day pleasures in the year leading up to the war – to Armageddon, as Ford termed it. Goldring recalled that no amount of neurasthenia prevented him from being a genial and generous host, dispensing his famous punch. Nor did he ever cease to feel the charm of women. He dictated part of *The Good Soldier* to Brigit Patmore who stayed with them at Selsey where, Violet wrote, 'like all other pretty ladies she played secretary to Joseph Leopold'. She also stayed with them in London and Violet also wrote, 'To see his happy face when he came down to breakfast next morning ought to have told me.'

It was also the time of the Futurists and Vorticists. Ford noted that in May and June 1914 there were only six days on which he did not have at least three dinner and after-dinner engagements. There were evenings at the Cave or the Golden Calf, a nightclub in Heddon Street, just off Regent Street, run by Strindberg's Viennese second wife. She was chalk white and wore a fur coat. Ford described her and the club in *Return to Yesterday* and in *The Marsden Case*: 'for she was a kind, voluptuous, abstracted creature

. . . She had that wonderful dark hair, a hook nose, and eyes that blazed out and then went in again, brown, like a hawk's. I know she was very benevolent . . .' People danced 'those obsolete Vorticist dances, the Turkey Trot and Bunny Hug', and Ford wrote a shadow play with which, predictably, everything went wrong, so that he was forced to act it himself. He said later that on one occasion the future Edward VIII was there.

It was the time of Futurists and Vorticists, a hectic, egotistical, hedonistic time in which Wyndham Lewis was prominent. Viewed from this distance, it has a sad charm because of the earnestness with which things that now seem of so little consequence were pursued and because the participants appear now like children happily playing, all unaware, in the deepening shadow of Armageddon. Perhaps they weren't really so unaware; perhaps they sensed it and therefore did everything with a more frenzied energy.

Ford was involved in the new movements although his position was ambiguous. He was mocked and used, listened to and scorned at the same time. He was of the older generation, a writer whom Lewis said could no longer write; he was also their friend, he accepted their madnesses and vanities, he helped them (Lewis particularly, whose rudeness he repaid by getting him commissioned to do the design for his (Ford's) poem 'Antwerp', published by the Poetry Bookshop in January 1915). It later seemed to him that he had been everyone's Dutch uncle in those days and that he was again the green baize door which everyone kicked on entering or leaving.

Violet went further. She commissioned Lewis to re-decorate Ford's comfortable pipe-strewn study in South Lodge (complete with tobacco-cutting machine) in Vorticist style, which turned out to be predominantly crimson. Even more surprisingly she began wearing what she still regarded as ugly Vorticist clothes. She must have been very keen to appear 'in'. Ford, on the other hand, compromised neither his identity nor his sense of style. Invited to lecture at Lewis's Rebel Art Centre in Great Ormond Street, he did so in tails.

For all that, it appears that Lewis's criticisms hurt and discouraged him. His confidence in his own good work was always rather shaky – unlike his confidence in his judgement of other people's good work – and he was easily wobbled. He coped with it but for a while he was prepared to believe he really was finished. The difference between himself and Lewis was essentially an artistic one and, though Ford never allowed it to become personal, it went deep. He summarised Lewis's argument in *The March of Literature*:

> . . . Or the matter may be more comprehensively put by a speech addressed to the present writer early in this century by a young lion then expecting to supersede him in the public favour. Said he:
>
> 'Old fogeys like you and Conrad and Henry James go to unending trouble to kid the public into the idea that you provide them with vicarious experience. You efface yourselves like ostriches, never let yourselves appear through a whole, long blessed story, go to enormous trouble to get in atmospheres, to invent plausible narrators, old colonels, ships' captains, priests, surgeons – what do I know all . . . Oh, yes, "above all to make you *see*" . . . But that sort of stuff will never succeed. It isn't what the public wants. What the public wants is to see monstrous clever fellows' – and here he slapped himself on the cheek – 'monstrous clever fellows like *me* . . . Handsome, elegant figures, striding, posturing, pirouetting, moustache-twisting, cane-twirling, gold-ball juggling, tight-rope dancing, trapezists . . . You're all done with, I tell you. To me the far-flung future . . .' Well, Fielding might have said as much to Defoe and Richardson . . . even to Smollett.

Ford greatly disliked Fielding for his authorial interventions.

It is not that other arguments or schools of thought caused him to doubt the rightness of what he believed in so much that they made him doubt the success of it. When, in 1923 Stella Bowen was depressed by Pound's criticism of her painting Ford detected behind what Pound had said the Lewis approach to art; he refuted it in the same way that he had rebutted the Lewis approach to literature:

> Of course if he doesn't depress you too much it is a good thing to listen to gramophonic records of Lewis's dicta (in wh. Lewis

himself doesn't for a moment believe) but if you get too depressed by it, just don't listen . . .

. . . the prevalence of any type or other of Art – *any* Art – is merely a matter of cycles . . . there are certain axioms, one of which is that good drawing will also cause emotions to arise; so will good colours and good patterns. And goodness means observation rendered – in each case . . .

. . . You must remember that the Present School is largely a reaction against the Instantaneous photograph. It doesn't say so – but it is hypnotised and afraid of that phenomenon . . . and this leads . . . into a desire to be hyper-human – to the point of producing work that is not a rendering but a comment on the inspected object. And that is a foredoomed fallacy! . . .

Again, it is the rendering of reality that he insists on; but not all reality. His achievement and his limitation was that he sought to render impressions and states of mind. He often did this brilliantly and at his best there is no one to touch him but it remains a limitation because of its tendency to solipsism. Some of the descriptions and observations in his non-fiction – in *The Soul of London* or *The Heart of the Country*, for instance – make it a matter of regret that such an eye should, in the novels, have turned so often inwards. He could have been a great 'realist' novelist if he had been colder towards his own emotions.

In 1913 and 1914 he still lacked confidence, though not belief, in what he was doing. That was why Lewis's criticisms clung sufficiently for him to recall them many years later, although by then he could do so with detachment. He later took a similarly relaxed attitude towards what he saw as his isolation in English letters on the question of Art versus Science as the saviour of mankind, and of conscious Art versus haphazard Inspiration as the way to proceed. Writing of himself and Wells in *Mightier than the Sword*, he said:

Mr H. G. Wells and I must have been enemies for more years than I care now to think of. And the situation is rendered more piquant by the fact that one or the other of us must by now [the 1930s] be the doyen of English novelists – though I prefer not to discover which of us it is. At any rate in the kingdom of letters Mr Wells and I have been the leaders of opposing forces for nearly the whole of this century.

I do not think it is immodesty in a man to claim that he is a leader of forces when his military unit is indeed a unit. One may be allowed, I mean, to say that one is one's own leader . . . for it is getting on for a great number of years since I could say that I had in England even a comrade in arms, so complete has been the triumph in that country of Mr Wells's forces . . .

In that summer of 1914 there was even talk of another magazine to be started by Amy Lowell and involving Pound and Ford. It got as far as a couple of dinners in London, at the first of which Ford had a row with Amy Lowell and at the second, an '*Imagiste*' dinner, he caused offence and embarrassment when, disliking the way her guests aimed their speeches at Amy's pocket, he said he had no idea what an imagist was and suspected no one else did. Intellectual pretension was never one of his vices.

In late July 1914, just before war broke out, he and Violet spent a few days with friends near Berwick-upon-Tweed. There was a weekend house-party and Ford remembered the occasion with nostalgia. It was a fine ending to the old world. They read aloud on the lawns – '. . . the turf of the Scottish lawns', he wrote, 'was like close, fine carpeting and the soft Scottish sunshine and the soft Scottish showers did the heart good . . .' – Ford from *The Good Soldier* and Mary Borden, their American novelist hostess (whose married name was Turner), from a little-known writer called James Joyce.

There was argument at breakfast about the chances of war. Wyndham Lewis was there and later described the argument.[1] Mrs Turner is speaking:

'There won't be any war, Ford. Not here. England won't go into a war.'

Ford thrust his mouth out, fish-fashion, as if about to gasp for breath. He goggled his eyes and waggled one eyelid about.

[1] *Blasting and Bombadiering*

Ford, perhaps as Henry James saw him – 'too young for the Commons, too loose for the Army, too refined for the City, too sceptical for the Church . . . too much in his mere senses for poetry and yet too little in them for art . . .'

Below: Elsie Hueffer in the early 1900s. A quiet life after marriage on elopement; but she never let go.

Below right: Mary Martindale, Ford's vivacious and obsessive sister-in-law – and possibly his mistress.

a

b

c

d

Some of the women in his life: (a) Violet Hunt, who wanted to marry; (b) Brigit Patmore, who didn't; (c) Stella Bowen, honest and courageous, artist and writer, mistress and friend; (d) Rene Wright – two husbands and three marriages.

ord, described by Graham reene as the survivor of a niddle life made miserable y passion . . . with his umour intact . . . and the ind of enemies a man ought › have.'

.t dinner with the ıshionable novelist Dorothy Speare, Murray Hill, 1937. Olive Garnett, a lose friend, described his onversation as being 'like aviar'.

Ford, probably at Cooper's Cottage, Bedham *c.* 1920. He is still wearing his Sam Browne, and is pictured with Penny, the goat which reminded him of Pound.

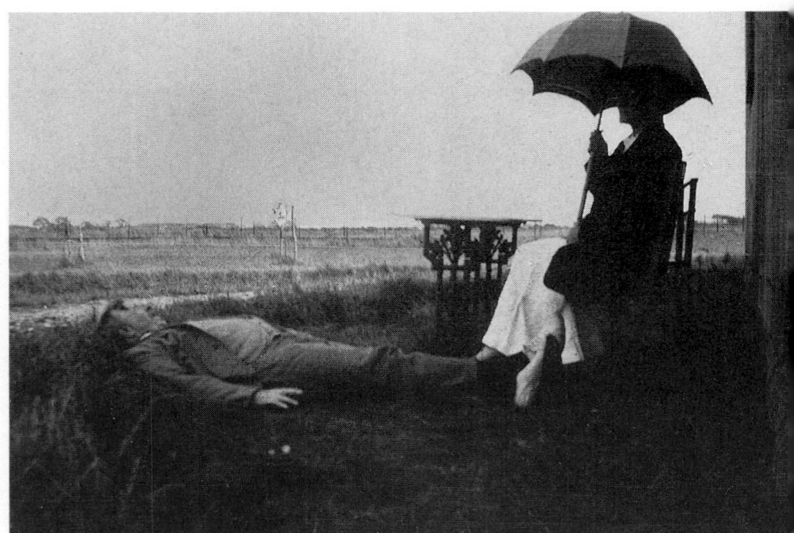

Down but not out; with Violet Hunt, probably at Selsey.

Pound, John Quinn, patron of the arts, Ford and Joyce at a *Transatlantic Review* conference in Pound's Paris studio, *c.* 1923.

'They continued to have limitless tolerance of each other . . .' Ford and Pound at Rapallo, *c.* 1932.

With Janice Biala at Cap Brun, *c.* 1934. Their relationship was, she said, 'a long, passionate dialogue'.

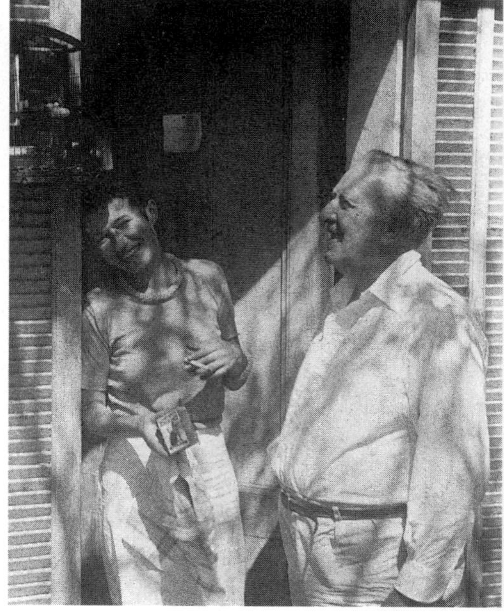

'The great grey behemoth in tweeds' on board ship with the Loewenfeld twins, *c*. 1935.

In the garden of the Tates' house in Tennessee, *c*. 1935. 'He took up', said Janice Biala, 'a great deal of space.'

Ford Madox Ford

He just moved his lips a little and we heard him say, in a breathless sotto voice –

'England will . . .'

'England will! But Ford,' said Mrs Turner, 'England has a Liberal Government. A Liberal Government cannot declare war.'

Ford sneered very faintly and inoffensively: he was sneering at the British Government rather than at us. He was being omniscient, bored, sleepy Ford, sunk in his tank of sloth. From his prolonged sleep he was staring out at us with his fish-blue eyes – kind, wise, but bored. Or some such idea. His mask was only just touched with derision at our childishness.

'Well, Ford,' said Mrs Turner, bantering the wise old elephant 'you don't agree!'

'I don't agree,' Ford answered in his faintest voice, with consummate indifference, 'because it has always been the Liberals who have gone to war. It is *because* it is a Liberal Government that it *will* declare war.'

Even in late July 1914 the view that there would be war was not as common as might now be thought. Asquith's cabinet had recently met and had anticipated that there would be no continental war involving Britain. Ford, though not alone in his opposing view, was one of a minority of odd-men-out.

What lay behind his calm assertion, at breakfast that day, was his opinion that the Germans might have been less likely to attack Belgium if there had been a Tory government in Britain; because the Government was Liberal the Germans would take advantage and the Government, fearing to confirm the idea that it could be taken advantage of, would feel obliged to respond. This was part and parcel of his long-held doubts about the consequences of institutional good intentions. In his poem, 'Süssmund's Address to an Unknown God', he had written in favour of

> Adultery, foul murder, pleasant things
> A Touch of incest, theft, but no Reformers.

Whatever the rights or wrongs of that, he was, like Aesop's hedgehog, right about the big thing: beyond that Scottish lawn lay Armageddon.

It also appears from Lewis's account that Ford's state of mind and bodily health may still not have been very good at that time. He goes on to say:

> After breakfast Ford read the other papers in the Hall. Coming down from my room and going towards the main house-door, Ford put down his paper and held out his hand.
>
> 'Help me up, there's a good chap,' he panted, with a pained discomfort. He liked being helped up from chairs by people over whom he exercised any authority, by nobodies or juniors. He got on his feet with a limp, as though he had stuck together. He shook. He stood still, his feet pointing flatly to the right and left.
>
> 'When will the car be ready?' he asked, in his soft-painting 'diplomatic' nasal undertone.
>
> 'I'm just going to see.'
>
> 'I'll come with you,' said Ford.
>
> The car was just outside the door. Ford lit one eye, his teeth appeared through his walrus moustache, he nodded, and went and had a jolly companionable talk with the chauffeur.

It is of passing interest to note that in his account, which was not published until 1937, Lewis still refers to Violet as Mrs Hueffer, describing her as 'the once famous author of *White Rose of Weary Leaf*'.

The Good Soldier has led to the making of many books, not in a genealogical sense but in commentaries and criticisms. Its entrails have been picked over, its epistemology and chronology dissected and wondered at; there have been arguments about its humour, its irony, its point of view, its biography; other novelists have proclaimed it a masterpiece, academics have battened upon it. The best known of Ford's books, it is only now becoming well known.

He thought it technically his best and 'something of a race that will have no successors'. That is probably true. He didn't try himself and it would be very dangerous for anyone else to do so, however tempting. There is no reason to take anything other than literally his claim that he put into it all he then knew about writing. It is the marriage of how he thought novels should be written and what they should be about with the deep well-springs of his own life. That 'solidity of specification' that made *The Fifth Queen* trilogy so good is here almost entirely and deliberately lacking. The novel deals in states of mind, attitude, belief and illusion, shifting things, with not many facts to go on. He used to insist that states of mind mattered more than facts, being the regions within which people felt and thought, and this exemplifies it. Yet the tale is told in a precise, quiet manner by a narrator who is not only seeking to establish the facts but is himself part of the reason why there is so little that can be finally known. This is what puts the tension in the watch-spring, driving the tale to its unfolding with a relentlessness that is beguilingly concealed by the apparent leisure of the telling.

Very briefly, the book is about permutations between Edward Ashburnham, soldier and gentleman, his wife, Leonora, Dowell, the American narrator, his wife, Florence, and Nancy, a young girl. Nothing in human relations, we learn, is quite what it seems, being both more subtle and complex and more brutally simple than appears. Having a heart does not make for a better, and certainly not for a happier, life; not having one means one lives less. It has been suggested that there may be conclusions to be drawn about Ford from the sexually neutered character of Dowell. This is a waste of time but it might just be worth asking whether Ford really liked sex. That may seem an odd question to ask of a man with his history but there is a certain ambiguity, as there is not with – say – H. G. Wells. There is no doubt that he liked women (did Wells?) and it may be that what he most sought was the emotional intensity, intimacy and dependence engendered by sexual relationships rather than sex itself. Although we should not conclude too much from the character of Dowell, what he says on the subject of sex may well be a partial representation of Ford's own views:

> I have come to be very much of a cynic in these matters; I mean that it is impossible to believe in the permanence of man's or woman's love. Or, at any rate, it is impossible to believe in the

permanence of any early passion. As I see it, at least, with regard to man, a love affair, a love for a definite woman – is something in the nature of a widening of the experience. With each new woman that a man is attracted to there appears to come a broadening of the outlook, or, if you like, an acquiring of new territory. A turn of the eyebrow, a tone of the voice, a queer characteristic gesture – all these things, and it is these things that cause to arise the passion of love – all these things are like so many objects on the horizon of the landscape that tempt a man to walk beyond the horizon, to explore. He wants to get, as it were, behind those eyebrows with the peculiar turn, as if he desired to see the world with the eyes that they overshadow. He wants to hear that voice applying itself to every possible proposition, to every possible topic; he wants to see those characteristic gestures against every possible background. Of the question of the sex instinct I know very little and I do not think that it counts for much in a really great passion. It can be aroused by such nothings – by an untied shoelace, by a glance of the eye in passing – that I think it might be left out of the calculation. I don't mean to say that any great passion can exist without a desire for consummation. That seems to me to be a commonplace and to be therefore a matter needing no comment at all. It is a thing with all its accidents, that must be taken for granted, as, in a novel, or a biography, you take it for granted that the characters have their meals with some regularity. But the real fierceness of desire, the real heat of a passion long continued and withering up the soul of a man is the craving for identity with the woman he loves. He desires to see with the same eyes, to touch with the same sense of touch, to hear with the same ears, to lose his identity, to be enveloped, to be supported. For, whatever may be said of the relation of the sexes, there is no man who loves a woman that does not desire to come to her for the renewal of his courage, for the cutting asunder of his difficulties. And that will be the mainspring of his desire for her. We are all so afraid, we are all so alone, we all so need from the outside the assurance of our own worthiness to exist.

So, for a time, if such a passion come to fruition, the man

will get what he wants. He will get the moral support, the encouragement, the relief from the sense of loneliness, the assurance of his own worth. But these things pass away; inevitably they pass away as the shadows pass across sundials. It is sad, but it is so. The pages of the book will become familiar; the beautiful corner of the road will have been turned too many times. Well, this is the saddest story.

And yet I do believe that for every man there comes at last a woman – or no, that is the wrong way of formulating it. For every man there comes at last a time of life when the woman who then sets her seal upon his imagination has set her seal for good. He will travel over no more horizons; he will never again see the knapsack over his shoulders; he will retire from those scenes. He will have gone out of business.

Although these words are spoken by a character in a novel, they read as if they are pretty close to a statement of Ford's views. The passage convincingly suggests the background to much of what happened to him, as also to what he did, both before and after the time of writing. The effect is to demote the purely sexual to a status below that which it is often given in contemporary writing, while stressing the generality of desire and the mutal dependency of men and women. It may not be a complete statement of human sexual relations but it indicates much of what is most important and its emphasis, though it may have particular reference to Ford, touches more widely. It has been suggested that his comparison of sex with regular meals means that he did not much value sex, but that is to ignore the context within which the comparison is made (it also fails to take into account the Fordian appreciation of a good lunch).

If asked why he didn't write about sex (a narrowly contemporary question), Ford's answer might have been three-fold. Firstly, there was no reason why he should – writers could choose what they want to write about and there is no syllabus, nor any need for one. Secondly, he might have objected that explicit descriptions of sex were distasteful, citing the occasion when he fell out with Frank Harris over his refusal to publish a 'lewd' story of Harris's in the *English Review* – the only time, he said, he ever rejected anything on other than literary grounds. Thirdly, he might have argued that he did write about sex, that he wrote very much about it, but that he concentrated on what was important, the passions it aroused, the states of mind it provoked and what people did as a result of it. This was consistent with the rest of his artistic canon, in that to describe sexual acts would have been to concentrate on physical events which were not themselves the point.

The Good Soldier was, as earlier mentioned, originally to be called *The Saddest Story* but the publisher, John Lane, felt that it would be hard to sell such a title in 1915 when there was more than enough sadness about. How the alternative title came to be is evident from a letter Ford sent from South Lodge in December 1914. He probably dictated it to Violet:

> My Dear Lane,
>
> I should have thought that you publishers had had eye-openers enough about monkeying with authors' titles, at the request of travellers. 'The Saddest Story' – I say in all humility – is about the best book you ever published and the title is about the best title. Still, I make it a principle never to interfere with my publisher, but I take it out in calling him names. Why not call the book 'The Roaring Joke'? Or call it anything you like, or perhaps it would be better to call it 'A Good Soldier' – that might do. At any rate it is all I can think of.

Despite some similarities with James's *The Golden Bowl*, *The Good Soldier* was not widely understood when it first appeared. It was a great novel that differed from preceding great novels and some people did not know what to make of it. There were critics who thought it a sordid and rambling tale of adultery and Chesterton's *The New Witness* printed a vicious and anonymous personal attack on Ford. The signature, J. K. Prothero, concealed the identity of Ada Elizabeth Jones, subsequently Chesterton's sister-in-law. This attack probably owed something to the scandal of Ford's non-divorce – he was referred to as a stallion, a coward and, oddly, a Jew. He was subject to such attacks at various times in his life from quite disparate people. Perhaps it was because he was himself a man of extremes, never studied, academic or detached, but where he liked, liking warmly, and where he disdained, disdaining absolutely, so provoking similar reactions in others.

Nevertheless, there were those who liked the book. Wells wrote to Chesterton that he would not let *The New Witness* into his home again: 'Some disgusting little greaser . . . has been allowed to insult old [*sic*] FMH . . . His book is a great book . . . the whole attack is so envious, so base, so cat-in-the-gutter-spitting-at-the-passer-by . . .' Rebecca West was another ally. She wrote of the book in her review: '. . . It is as impossible to miss the light of its extreme beauty and wisdom as it would be to miss the full moon on a clear night.'

The Good Soldier marked the culmination of his pre-war novels. It would be possible to write many pages on its ancestry among his earlier novels and on whom the various characters were based, but the time spent reading those pages would really be better spent reading the book. In accordance with Ford's own beliefs, you can tell from the first paragraph whether you are going to like it.

Of the earlier novels, apart from *The Fifth Queen*, too many were, as Pound said, hastily written and 'unachieved'. There are good ideas and good passages, but he wrote too much, partly for want of money, and too often tried to force it, yoking plots and characters into scenes that he had apprehended intellectually but had not yet lived through.

The Good Soldier has been described as bringing the Jamesian tradition to a close. It certainly draws on James's world of hesitation, innuendo, suggestion and moral void, but it goes to the heart of the matter in a way that James never did: it takes that final step. That is why it can have no direct successors, though other books can approach the same truths and same uncertainties from different angles. He must have dipped his pen in his heart's blood to write it but, like all great art, it is independent of that which gave it rise. As in a perfectly executed gymnastic movement, ideal form and the particular body are for those moments inseparable; and the performer may be left not knowing quite how he did it, nor why it worked then and not the other times, nor if he can ever do it again.

EIGHTEEN

They were at Selsey when war was declared on 4 August 1914. Two days before they had been in London where Ford had discussed the likelihood of war with Masterman at the Foreign Office. He said the discussion had included Asquith and Grey and had involved consideration of peace terms. This is normally taken as Fordian exaggeration but it is worth bearing in mind that peace terms *were* under consideration, that he may have been told about them by Masterman and may just possibly have seen Asquith and Grey. It is unlikely that the conversation took place as he related it. When war was declared he sought and received assurances from Masterman regarding his British status.

Among Violet's friends at Selsey was Edward Heron Allen, no friend of Ford's and a disapprover of her association with him. During a meal he told scaremongering stories about landings from German submarines, invasions and so on, probably relishing the effect on his audience. Ford was not one of the affected. He thought it was rubbish and said so – 'remonstrated in a friendly way with him', Violet put it.

They were more hard up than usual. In a morning, for £10, Ford wrote a satirical short story called 'The Scaremonger' with obvious (to those who had been there) reference to Allen. Allen was outraged and there was a war of words; Ford apologised 'on the wrong side of his face'.

Not long after he received a letter from the Chief Constable of West Sussex: 'I have been requested to prohibit your residing in the area of the Chichester Division. I therefore give you notice that you must leave this County.' He got it quashed, no doubt by Masterman, but saw Allen's hand behind it. Following the German atrocities in Belgium, his German ancestry and name attracted unpleasant attention. He was insulted in the street in Selsey and word got about, even among some of Violet's educated friends, that he was a German spy. There was thus another paradox to add to the list: having not many years before been pilloried in the courts partly for trying to be German when he wasn't, he was now under police and public suspicion that he was.

Masterman, meanwhile, was put in charge of the Wellington House operation, a ploy to counter German propaganda in the United States by sending to influential Americans copies of secretly sponsored books by respectable British professors. Ford was asked to write a propaganda book about the Germans. He set to in September 1914 and the book was published by Hodder and Stoughton six months later. It is no mean book: three hundred and forty-three pages, dictated to Richard Aldington at between six and eight thousand words a week. Presumably it eased his financial position somewhat. The title, *When Blood Is Their Argument*, is taken from *Henry V*: 'For how can they charitably dispose of anything, when blood is their argument'. Not the normal run of propaganda, it is balanced, informed, lucid, wise and readable. The argument is that it is not German-ness but Prussia that is the demon, that German culture ceased with the ascendance of Prussia and that what is admirable about Germany (also what is German in Ford) is the south. Six months later he wrote another propaganda book, *Between St Dennis and St George, a Sketch of Three Civilisations*. In this he was able to give rein to his francophilia and was very pleased when the book was later taken up by the French government and translated. It is a looser, wider-ranging work than the first, more general and discursive, less informative. His francophilia was, as we have seen, an inherited love subsequently reinforced by contact with Conrad and by admiration of French writers. France provided a refuge from domestic troubles and later became the country in which he could live more congenially than in England. If it is not at once too extravagant and too simple, it could be said that France was always a woman for Ford and that the two other strains of his inheritance, Germany and Britain, he increasingly lumped together as Nordic, a stern, dour, cheerless, masculine amalgam.

He followed the first year of war with even more attention than most people. It must have been as if he had three parents, two in uneasy alliance against the third. He was patriotic but at the same time culturally and linguistically European. He had been used to moving from one country to another with the ease of travelling across English counties. Now he had the prospect of his countrymen killing his cousins. The place where the Germans had invaded Belgium – 'Near a place called Gemmenich', he usually called it, giving to the word an apocalyptic ring – was very near the spot where he and Violet had first proclaimed their marriage.

The fate of the all too often forgotten Belgians – he saw the refugees in London – prompted his poem, 'Antwerp'. It is therefore a civilian's war poem and it is likely that events and scenes such as he describes played a significant part in his, and many other people's, reasons for forsaking their naturally peaceable inclinations:

ANTWERP

I

Gloom!
An October like November;
August a hundred thousand hours,
And all September,
A hundred thousand, dragging sunlit days,
And half October like a thousand years . . .
And doom!
And then was Antwerp . . .
                In the name of God,
How could they do it?
Those souls that usually dived
Into the dirty caverns of mines;
Who usually hived
In whitened hovels; under ragged poplars;
Who dragged muddy shovels over the grassy mud,
Lumbering to work over the greasy sods . . .
Those men there, with the appearances of clods
Were the bravest men that a usually listless priest of God
Ever shrived . . .

And it is not for us to make them an anthem.
If we found words there would come no wind that would fan them
To a tune that the trumpets might blow it,
Shrill through the heaven that's ours or yet Allah's
Or the wide halls of any Valhallas.
We can make no such anthem. So that all is ours
For inditing in sonnets, pantoums, elegiacs, or lays
Is this:
'In the name of God, how could they do it?'

II

For there is no new thing under the sun,
Only this uncomely man with a smoking gun
In the gloom . . .
What the devil will he gain by it?
Digging a hole in the mud and standing all day in the rain by it
Waiting his doom,
The sharp blow, the swift outpouring of the blood,
Till the trench of grey mud
Is turned to a brown purple drain by it.
Well, there have been scars
Won in many wars . . .
Punic,
Lacedaemonian, wars of Napoleon, wars for faith, wars for honour, for love, for possession,
But this Belgian man in his ugly tunic,
His ugly round cap, shooting on, in a sort of obsession,
Overspreading his miserable land,
Standing with his wet gun in his hand . . .
Doom!
He finds that in a sudden scrimmage,
And lies, an unsightly lump on the sodden grass . . .
An image that shall take long to pass!

III

For the white-limbed heroes of Hellas ride by upon their horses
For ever through our brains.
The heroes of Cressy ride by upon their stallions;
And battalions and battalions and battalions –
The Old Guard, The Young Guard, the men of Minden and of Waterloo,
Pass, for ever staunch,
Stand for ever true;
And the small man with the large paunch,
And the grey coat, and the large hat, and the hands behind the back,
Watches them pass
In our minds for ever . . .
But that clutter of sodden corses
On the sodden Belgian grass –
That is a strange new beauty.

IV

With no especial legends of marchings or triumphs or duty,
Assuredly that is the way of it,
The way of beauty . . .
And that is the highest word you can find to say of it.
For you cannot praise it with words
Compounded of lyres and swords,
But the thought of the gloom and the rain
And the ugly coated figure, standing beside a drain,
Shall eat itself into your brain.
And that shall be an honourable word;
'Belgian' shall be an honourable word,
As honourable as the fame of the sword,
As honourable as the mention of the many-chorded lyre,
And his old coat shall seem as beautiful as the fabrics woven in Tyre.

V

And what in the world did they bear it for?
I don't know.
And what in the world did they dare it for?
Perhaps that is not for the likes of me to understand.
They could very well have watched a hundred legions go
Over their fields and between their cities
Down into more southerly regions.
They could very well have let the legions pass through their woods,
And have kept their lives and their wives and their children and cattle and goods.
I don't understand.
Was it just love of their land?
Oh poor dears!
Can any man so love his land?
Give them a thousand thousand pities
And rivers and rivers of tears
To wash off the blood from the cities of Flanders.

VI

This is Charing Cross;
It is midnight;
There is a great crowd
And no light.
A great crowd, all black that hardly whispers aloud.
Surely, that is a dead woman – a dead mother!
She has a dead face;
She is dressed all in black;
She wanders to the bookstall and back,
At the back of the crowd;
And back again and again back,
She sways and wanders.

This is Charing Cross;
It is one o'clock.
There is still a great crowd, and very little light;

Immense shafts of shadows over the black crowd
That hardly whispers aloud . . .
And now! . . . That is another dead mother,
And there is another and another and another . . .
And little children, all in black,
All with dead faces, waiting in all the waiting-places,
Wandering from the doors of the waiting-room
In the dim gloom.
These are the women of Flanders.
They await the lost.
They await the lost that shall never leave the dock;
They await the lost that shall never again come by the train
To the embraces of all these women with dead faces;
They await the lost who lie dead in trench and barrier and
  foss,
In the dark of the night.
This is Charing Cross; it is past one of the clock;
There is very little light.

There is so much pain.

L'envoi
And it was for this that they endured this gloom;
This October like November,
That August like a hundred thousand hours,
And that September,
A hundred thousand dragging sunlit days,
And half October like a thousand years . . .
Oh poor dears!

He was pleased to do the propaganda work, no doubt anxious to be useful, but it wasn't enough; he was a romantic and nothing less than the whole hog would do; he had to be there, which meant joining up. He wrote to his mother: 'I cannot imagine taking any other course. If one has enjoyed the privileges of the ruling class of a country all one's life, there seems to be no alternative to fighting for that country if necessary.'

There were, of course, plenty of alternatives and many of his friends and acquaintances had no difficulty finding them. An exception was Wyndham Lewis who, much given to artistic blasting and bombardiering, now opted for the other sort and joined the Royal Artillery. He described a conversation he had with Ford about joining. They were talking of the death in action of the young sculptor Henri Gaudier-Brzeska, whom they had both much liked and admired; '. . . so wise, so old, so gentle, so humorous, such a genius, . . . he had great personal beauty' Ford was to write of him in *No Enemy*. London, he observed, had up to 1914 been host to swarms of foreign writers and artists '. . . because London was unrivalled in its powers of assimilation – the great, easy-going, tolerant, lovable old dressing-gown of a place as it was then.' Things were changing and Lewis wrote:

> When I had first attested, I was talking to Ford Madox Hueffer about Gaudie's death. I had said it was too bad. Why should Gaudier die and a 'Bloomsbury' live? I meant that *fate* ought to have seen to it that it didn't happen. It was absurd . . .
>
> It was absurd, Ford agreed, but there it was, he seemed to think. He seemed to think *fate* was absurd . . .
>
> . . . The 'Bloomsburies' were all doing war-work of 'national importance', down in some downy English county, under the wings of powerful pacifist friends; cooling cheese, planting gooseberry bushes, and hay-making doubtless in large sun-bonnets . . .
>
> . . . But the 'Bloomsburies' all exempted themselves, in one way or another. Yet they had money and we hadn't; ultimately, it was to keep them fat and prosperous – or thin and prosperous, which is even worse, that other people were to risk their skins. Then there were the tales of how a certain famous artist, of military age and militant bearing, would sit in the Cafe Royal and, addressing an admiring group back from the Front, would exclaim '*We* are the civilisation for which you are fighting' . . . Ford Madox Hueffer looked at me with his watery-wise old-elephant eyes – a little too crystal gazing and claptrap, but he knew his stuff – and instructed me on the very temporary nature of the hysteria. I was too credulous! I *believe* that he tipped

me the wink. He was imparting to me I believe a counsel of common sense.

'When this War's over,' he said, 'nobody is going to worry six months afterwards what you did or didn't do in the course of it. One month after it's ended, it will be forgotten. Everybody will want to forget it – it will be bad form to mention it. Within a year "disbanded heroes" will be selling matches in the gutter. No one likes the ex-soldier – if you've lost a leg, the more fool you!'

. . . This worldly forecast was verified to the letter.

Ford took a commission in the Army at the end of July 1915 and was gazetted to the Third Battalion, the Welch Regiment on 13 August. He joined up after lunch with Lucy Masterman, who was to prove his most faithful correspondent throughout the war. Taking a commission was a simpler matter then than now, or than in the Second World War. He wrote to Lucy: 'You may like to know that I went round to the WO after seeing you and got thrown into a commission in under a minute – the quickest process I have ever known.' He was forty-one. He didn't tell Violet until it was safely done and they were on their way to Selsey with a secretary. 'Then, as now', Violet wrote, 'he sheltered behind the presence of a third person that precluded cross-questioning.' (It is reminiscent of his asking Elsie for a divorce while waiting for the train.) Violet cried for three days and probably cross-questioned for about the same period; she must have realised that it marked the end of their 'marriage'. To his mother he wrote: 'I wanted to get a commission without talking about it, & a commission in the Regular Army, not in any of the fancy services which are only a form of shirking . . . V takes it rather hard, poor dear, but I hope she will get used to the idea.'

Motives are mixed more often than not and we should not always assume that the worthy are automatically invalidated by the less worthy. There is little doubt that Ford, like many who enlist in mature years, was taking the opportunity to escape from a domestic situation. There is even less doubt that Violet took it as desertion. She was lonely and upset, particularly as her niece, Rosamond, put her off from visiting for fear of compromising the position of her clergyman husband. Violet appended a note to Ford at the end of the letter Rosamond had sent her: 'This is what you have brought on me, dear Ford, and you are happy in Cardiff and leaving me to bear it alone. It is this sort of thing all the time, and loneliness – and I wish now I was out of this world you have made for me, or that you will say we made, so that we could live together. That's the joke! And this is the last straw, more than I can bear. Don't write to Rosamond on any account. You have done me enough harm already. V.'

She never sent the note but the same histrionic tone is evident in a number of notes and memoranda she kept amongst her papers. Going through them after her death, Douglas Goldring concluded that she wanted the world to know she suffered. Perhaps she did; that doesn't, of course, mean that she did not suffer. If, as some critics believe, the character of Florence in *The Good Soldier* was inspired by Violet, it is also easy to see why Ford was not happy. But it is nearly always too easy to pigeon-hole relationships; in 1915 Violet published *Zeppelin Nights*, partly composed of vignettes which Ford had written in 1913 and which she – possibly with his help – joined up. They were co-authors. However, their growing unhappiness with each other had, according to Wells, been notorious for some time. It seems to have been at about this time that Ford learned of Violet's syphilis when the doctor who was treating her insisted on talking to her 'husband'. Ford might also then have learned hitherto unknown chapters of her romantic history.

Another possible reason for his taking a commission was that he may have felt he had to overcome or atone for his German ancestry. It cannot have been very pleasant to be insulted in the street nor to have the police alerted to his presence. To his credit, it doesn't seem to have made him bitter – we have seen that he experienced similar reactions in Britain and Belgium during the Boer War. He does not seem to have had any such problem once in the Army. Later he wrote of Violet's friends: 'I found that she had been entertaining at Selsey the various gentlemen whose chief claim to patriotic activities, as you know, had been the denouncing of myself to the police as a German agent.'

Mizener sees the whole thing, as he sees Ford, negatively. He thinks Ford enlisted because he was a passed-over middle-aged writer, barely tolerated by the younger generation, oppressed by Violet and South Lodge and driven by a 'Tory feeling of obligation to his country'. Such a view is unfair. Ford was middle-aged and he may well have felt finished as a writer but he was not passed-over. In March 1915 he had published what he knew, and what the perceptive few recognised, to be a great novel. Marwood he never heard from again but the book prompted Conrad to break a long silence: 'The women are extraordinary – in the laudatory sense – and the whole vision of the subject perfectly amazing. And talking of cadences, one hears all through them a tone of fretful melancholy, extremely effective. Something new, this, in your work, my dear Ford – c'est très curieux et c'est très bien, très juste.'

Even while dictating it he had evidence of its power. H. D., the beautiful poetess wife of Richard Aldington, took over from Brigit Patmore but had to stop because she was too upset by the book, leaving her husband to continue. (In fact, the history of that little trio is similar to some of the events in the book, as if *The Good Soldier* carried a curse into the lives of those who helped to bring it to life. Brigit first became a very close friend of H. D.'s, then an even closer one of her husband's. She lived with him for a decade, the happiest of her life, till he ran off with her daughter-in-law, breaking Brigit's heart.)

It is true that the younger generation had a mixed reaction to Ford but to say that he was 'barely tolerated' is playing it down somewhat. They used him, certainly, but he was admired and respected by some, fondly regarded by others. Even Wyndham Lewis, one of the least tolerant, had some respect and liking for him, as is evident in the extract quoted. Admittedly, he fell out rather badly with Lawrence but that was a curious episode about which there are contradictory accounts by himself, Violet and Frieda.

To write off the rest of his motivation as a 'Tory feeling of obligation to his country' is misleading. There was a sense of obligation, as he said to his mother, and he was far from alone in feeling it; he shared it with many in Kitchener's Army and it was by no means a party political matter. But there was more than that. His poem, 'Footsloggers', written at the end of 1917, gives as good an account of his and others' motivation as anything else written:

FOOTSLOGGERS

To C.F.G.M.

I

What is the love of one's land? . . .
I don't know very well.
Is it something that sleeps
For a year – for a day –
For a month – something that keeps
Very hidden and quiet and still
And then takes
The quiet heart like a wave,
The quiet brain like a spell,
The quiet will
Like a tornado; and that shakes
The whole of the soul.

II

It is omnipotent like love;
It is deep and quiet as the grave
And it awakes
Like a flame, like a madness,
Like the great passion of your life.
The cold keenness of a tempered knife,
The great gladness of a wedding day,
The austerity of monks who wake to pray
In the dim light,
Who pray
In the darkling grove,
All these and a great belief in what we deem the right
Creeping upon us like the overwhelming sand,
Driven by a December gale,
Make up the love of one's land.

III

But I ask you this:
About the middle of my first Last Leave,
I stood on a kerb in the pitch of the night
Waiting for buses that didn't come
To take me home.
That was in Paddington.
The soot-black night was over one like velvet:
And one was very alone – so very alone
In the velvet cloak of the night.
Like a lady's skirt,
A dim, diaphanous cone of white, the rays
Of a shaded street lamp, close at hand, existed,
And there was nothing but vileness it could show,
Vile, pallid faces drifted through, chalk white;
Vile alcoholic voices in the ear, vile fumes
From the filthy pavements . . . vileness!
And one thought:
'In three days' time we enter the unknown:
And this is what we die for!'
For, mind you,
It isn't just a Tube ride, going to France!
It sets ironic unaccustomed minds
At work even in the sentimental . . .
Still
All that is in the contract.

IV

Who of us
But has, deep down in the heart and deep in the brain
The memory of odd moments: memories
Of huge assemblies chanting in the night
At palace gates: of drafts going off in the rain
To shaken music: or the silken flutter
Of silent, ceremonial parades,
In the sunlight, when you stand so stiff to attention,
That you never see but only know they are there –

The regimental colours – silken, a-flutter
Azure and gold and vermilion against the sky:
The sacred finery of branded hearts
Of generations . . .
            And memories
When just for moments, landscapes out in France
Looked so like English downlands that the heart
Checked and stood still . . .
            Or then, the song and dance
Of Battalion concerts, in the shafts of light
From smoky lamps: the lines of queer, warped faces
Of men that now are dead: faces lit up
By inarticulate minds at sugary chords
From the vamping pianist beneath the bunting:
'Until the boys come home!' we sing. And fumes
Of wet humanity, soaked uniforms,
Wet flooring, smoking lamps, fill cubicle
And wooden-walled spaces, brown, all brown,
With the light-sucking hue of the khaki . . . And the rain
Frets on the pitchpine of the felted roof
Like women's fingers beating on a door
Calling 'Come home' . . . 'Come home'
Down the long trail beneath the silent moon . . .
Who never shall come . . .
            And we stand up to sing
'Hen wlad fy nadhau . . .'
            Dearest, never one
Of your caresses, dearest in the world,
Shall interpenetrate the flesh of one's flesh,
The breath of the lungs, sight of the eyes, or the heart,
Like that sad, harsh anthem in the rained-on huts
Of our own men . . .
That too is in the contract . . .

V

            Well, of course
One loves one's own men. One takes a mort of trouble

To get them spick and span upon parades:
You straf' them, slang them, mediate between
Their wives and loves, and you inspect their toe-nails
And wangle leaves for them from the Adjutant
Until your Company office is your home
And all your mind . . .
               This is the way it goes:
First your Platoon and then your Company,
Then the Battalion, the Brigade, Division,
And the whole BEF in France . . . and then
Our Land, with its burden of civilians,
Who take it out of us as little dogs
Worry Newfoundlands . . .
               So, in the Flanders mud,
We bear the State upon our rain-soaked backs,
Breathe life into the State from our rattling lungs,
Anoint the State with the rivulets of sweat
From our tin helmets.
               And so, in years to come
The State shall take the semblance of Britannia,
Up-borne, deep-bosomed, with anointed limbs . . .
Like the back of a penny.

VI

               For I do not think
We ever took much stock in that Britannia
On the long French roads, or even on parades,
Or thought overmuch of Nelson or of Minden,
Or even the old traditions . . .
               I don't know,
In the breathless rush that it is of parades and drills,
Of digging at the double and strafes and fatigues,
These figures grow dimmed and lost:
Doubtless we too, we too, when the years have receded
Shall look like the heroes of Hellas, upon a frieze,
White-limbed and buoyant and passing the flame of the torches

From hand to hand . . . But today it's mud to the knees
And khaki and khaki and khaki . . .
        And love of one's land
Very quiet and hidden and still . . . And again
I don't know, though I've pondered the matter for years
Since the war began . . . But I never had much brain . . .

VII

I don't know if you know the 1.10 train
From Cardiff:
        Well, fourteen of us together
Went up from Cardiff in the summer weather
At the time of the July push.
It's a very good train;
It runs with hardly a jar and never a stop
After Newport, until you get down
In London Town.
It goes with a solemn, smooth rush
Across the counties and over the shires,
Right over England past farmsteads and byres;
It bubbles with conversation,
Being the West going to the East:
The pick of the rich of the West in a bunch,
Half of the wealth of the Nation,
With heads together, buzzing of local topics,
Of bankrupts and strikes, divorces and marriages;
And, after Newport, you get your lunch,
In the long, light, gently swaying carriages
As the miles flash by,
And fields and flowers
Flash by
Under the high sky
Where the great cloud towers
Above the tranquil downs
And the tranquil towns.

VIII

And the corks pop
And the wines of France
Bring in radiance;
And spice from the tropics
Flavours fowl from the Steppes
And meat from the States,
And the talk buzzes on like bees round the skeps,
And the potentates
Of the mines and the docks
Drink delicate hocks . . .
Ah, proud and generous civilisation . . .

IX

For me, going out to France
Is like the exhaustion of dawn
After a dance . . .
You have rushed around to get your money,
To get your revolver, complete your equipment;
You have had your moments, sweeter – ah, sweeter than
  honey;
You have got your valise all ready for shipment:
You have gone to confession and wangled your blessing,
You have bought your air-pillow and sewn in your coat
A pocket to hold your first field-dressing,
And you've paid the leech who bled you, the vampire . . .
And you've been to the Theatre and the Empire,
And you've bidden goodbye to the band and the goat . . .
And, like a ship that floats free of her berth,
There's nothing that holds you now to the earth,
And you're near enough to a yawn . . .
'Good luck' and 'Good-bye' it has been, and 'So long, old
  chap'
'Cheerio: you'll be back in a month' – 'You'll have driven the
  Huns off the map.'
And one little pressure of the hand
From the one thing you love next to the love of the land,

Since you leave her, out of love for your land . . .
But that little, long, gentle and eloquent pressure
Shall go with you under the whine of the shells,
Into the mire and the stress,
Into the seven hundred yells,
Until you come down on your stretcher
To the C.C.S. . . .
And back to Blighty again –
Or until you go under the sod.

X

But, in the 1.10 train,
Running between the green and the grain,
Something like the peace of God
Descended over the hum and the drone
Of the wheels and the wine and the buzz of the
talk,
And one thought:
'In two days' time we enter the Unknown,
And this is what we die for!'
And thro' the square
Of glass
At my elbow, as limpid as air,
I watched our England pass . . .
The great downs moving slowly,
Far away,
The farmsteads quiet and lowly,
Passing away;
The fields newly mown
With the swathes of hay,
And the wheat just beginning to brown,
Whirling away . . .
And I thought:
'In two days' time we enter the Unknown,
But *this* is what we die for . . . As we ought . . .'
For it is for the sake of the wolds and the wealds
That we die,

And for the sake of the quiet fields,
And the path through the stackyard gate . . .
That these may be inviolate,
And know no tread save those of herds and hinds,
And that the south-west winds
Blow on no forehead save of those that toil
On our suave and hallowed soil,
And that deep peace may rest
Upon that quiet breast . . .
It is because our land is beautiful and green and comely,
Because our farms are quiet and thatched and homely,
Because the trout stream dimples by the willow,
Because the water-lilies float upon the ponds,
And on Eston Hill the delicate, waving fronds
Of the bracken put forth, where the white clouds are
flying,
That we shall endure the swift, sharp torture of dying,
Or the humiliation of not dying,
Where the gas cloud wanders
Over the fields of Flanders,
Or the sun squanders
His radiance
And the midges dance
Their day-long life away
Over the green and the grey
Of the fields of France . . .
And maybe we shall never again
Plod thro' our mire and the rain
Of the winter gloaming,
And maybe we shall never again
See the long, white, foaming
Breakers pour upon our strand . . .
But we have been borne across this land,
And we have felt this spell . . .
And, for the rest.

L'envoi

What is love of one's land?
                    Ah, we know very well
It is something that sleeps for a year, for a day,
For a month, something that keeps
Very hidden and quiet and still,
And that takes
The quiet heart like a wave,
The quiet brain like a spell,
The quiet will
Like a tornado, and that shakes
The whole being and soul . . .
Aye, the whole of the soul.

24/12/17 – 1/1/18

That, surely, is the way it often is with patriotism: starting with the immediate, the platoon, or, before that, the family, it embraces the bigger entities which are almost abstractions. You cannot love what is far from you unless you have learned to love what is close, and if you cannot love that you probably cannot love. It is hard to imagine that Ford would have had much sympathy with E. M. Forster's assertion that if he had to choose between his friends and his country he would choose the former; this posing of a false opposition and evasion of responsibility, with the consequent betrayal of his friends' friends, would have seemed to Ford a dereliction of duty. When he talked about duty, about being a gentleman and a member of the ruling class and so on, it was not a pose but a part of his moral universe.

'Footsloggers' not only crystallises many people's vaguely patriotic feelings but is also a true-to-life picture of the Army. Ford's war poems give a better picture of actual military experience than most. The wet humanity, soaked uniforms, wet flooring, the rush to complete kit, the trance-like floating free, nostalgia for what is being left, the quiet thoughts of what's to come, are all true. Observations of external detail tend to play a greater part in his war poems than in his novels. (Eliot, incidentally, thought 'Antwerp' the only good poem he had met with on the subject of the war.)

In one of his first books written after the war, *No Enemy*, he explores his own motivation farther. It is not simply a question here of love of people:

> . . . The trees again became the foreground and there was the feeling that Gringoire could never get away from – that they would be personally humiliated, shamed, abashed; as if they would wrathfully bow or avert their heads if ever field-grey troops passed down the Broad Walk, or the park keeper at the gate wore a Uhlan uniform! That was in the early days of the war – August 1915, I think. The feeling that there might be an invasion was still, and was strong, in the air. There was no knowing, still, where the dam might give way and the mud-coloured tide pour towards us . . .
>
> . . . 'I wonder' Gringoire said again that evening, 'if other people had like myself, that feeling that what one feared for was the land – not the people but the menaced earth with its familiar aspect. I dare say it was just want of imagination: one couldn't perhaps figure the feelings of ruined, fleeing and martyred populations, and yet, when I had seen enough of those, the feeling did not alter. I remember what struck me most in ruined Pont de Nieppe, by Armentières, was still the feeling of abashment that seemed to attach to furniture and wall-paper exposed to sky . . . what struck me as infinitely pathetic was lace curtains, fluttering from all the unroofed walls in glassless window-frames. They seemed to be more forlornly ashamed than human beings I had ever seen. Only brute beasts ever approach that: old and weary horses, in nettle-grown fields; or dogs when they go away into bushes to die . . .
>
> . . . There were in those days, you will remember, no more sanctuaries. All the nooks of the world were threatened by the tide of blue-grey mud. We were out there to hold it back on the Somme, but could we?'

No Enemy contains a sensitive and detailed probing of what one feels *for* and there is no reason to doubt that the reactions described were Ford's own. It is his account of how the war affected his sensibility and shaped his future beliefs and actions. The autobiography is only slightly disguised.[1]

The night before Ford left London for Tenby Violet gave '. . . Not a party – only whisky, and sandwiches and a few old friends.' Goldring was invited: 'We all knew, by then, that the Ford-Violet affaire was practically over and that this was probably the last time that they would entertain their friends as "Mr & Mrs Hueffer". The evening was a hectic one – Violet was always lavish with her drinks – but the departing guests did not take Ford with them, as seemed to be anticipated. He lingered behind, finished off the remaining whisky with Violet and her secretary – so the latter has since informed me – and after a violent quarrel was finally "hoofed out" in an advanced state of what is politely called "fatigue".'

An inglorious but probably by no means unique send-off; it is not known where he spent the night. It seems, though, that he was already in uniform. He did the 'Chelsea Course' with the Irish Guards at the Chelsea Barracks. This sounds like a basic introductory and drill course for officers and it might have been what he was referring to in the dedication to Stella Bowen he wrote for the 1928 edition of *The Good Soldier*:

> . . . I was on parade again, being examined in drill, on the Guards' Square at Chelsea. And, since I was petrified with nervousness, having to do it before a half-dozen elderly gentlemen with red hat bands, I got my men about as hopelessly boxed as it is possible to do with gentlemen privates of H.M. Coldstream Guards. Whilst I stood stiffly at attention one of the elderly red hat bands walked close behind my back and said distinctly in my ear, 'Did you say, The *Good* Soldier?'

Once he had joined the Welch Regiment it is unlikely that he would have had any occasion to drill guardsmen. In a letter to

[1] It is also a scandal of English letters that the book is not simply underrated here, not simply not included in the rich canon of Great War literature, not simply unknown but, like much of his poetry, not published. As often with Ford, we have the Americans to thank for bringing it to light – some years after it was written – in 1929 – and for keeping it alive now. It is an Ecco Press paperback, ISBN 0-88001-062-2, and it should be read.

Arthur Mizener, Iris Barry wrote of him in those days: 'He was then always in uniform – impressive with all that rosy colour and blue eyes, moustache, drooping lip.'

He was ready for the move in just about every way. In one of his regular *Outlook* articles, dated 10 July 1915, he wrote: 'If not today, then tomorrow, I hope to be up and away to regions where I shall be precluded from uttering injunctions to find le mot juste.' He was not the first to seek escape in war but this should not be allowed to count against the fact that he did it. After all, he didn't have to go at all. He was far too old and unfit to go to the Front as an infantry subaltern and it is typical of his career that he seems never to have received due credit for it. Further, in *Parade's End* he wrote what is perhaps the best novel in English that deals with that war, yet he is not generally known for having written about war at all. His donning uniform is sometimes assumed to be yet another persona he was adopting for the time being, like cricket, smallholding or clubs. The point is that they all hang together: men who are captains of cricket at school, who try their hands at farming, who like clubs and who believe in the ethic of the gentleman are very likely to find commissioned military life not too uncongenial and to join armies in time of war; they are not generally accused of pretending to these things. That Ford was also a poet with pacifistic inclinations and wrote novels which showed the limitations of the gentlemanly ethic – to be more precise, the limitations of the gentlemen – does not mean that his other aspects were vanities. They were a part of him.

It would be easy to conclude that the extent to which he has been misunderstood or underestimated in this and other areas is really a reflection of his own contradictions. After all, he sometimes appears contradictory about his main passion, literary art. On the one hand, he writes that the ideal style should be unnoticeable and the author invisible; on the other that 'imaginative literature' is that writing that most reveals the personality of its author. These seem to lead to contradiction even if it is not inherent. He says both that the imaginative author should not let himself speak in his own person and that 'his whole book, his whole poem is merely an expression of his personality'.

There is, however, less contradiction than appears. What he means is that the personality of the author should inform the book while its shape, construction and style should be so worked as not to draw attention to themselves but to focus all upon the matter. Personality is like spirit. There is in his book on Holbein a suggestion of how it should infuse a work: 'Great art is above all things generous, like the strong and merciful light of the sun that will render lovable the meanest fields, the barest walls.' What he meant by good style is clearly stated in his own article on Dostoievsky:

> . . . What is to be aimed at in a style is something so unobtrusive and so quiet – and so beautiful if possible – that the reader should not know he is reading, and be conscious only that he is living in the life of the book . . . a book so quiet in tone, so clearly and so unobtrusively worded, that it should give the effect of a long monologue spoken by a lover at a little distance from his mistress's ear – a book about the invisible relationships between man and man; about the values of life; about the nature of God – the sort of book that nowadays one would read in as one used to do when one was a child, pressed against a tall window-pane for hours and hours utterly oblivious of oneself, in the twilight.

Nor does it matter that his practice did not always conform to his ideals. He often exaggerated and used superlatives, particularly in his journalism, and even in some of his more careful writing he made rather too obvious his use of strange plurals, the thicknesses, finesses and heavinesses. The effect of these is to introduce a note of passivity and vagueness. The words probably conjured up something for him – heavinesses might recall specific periods of despair – but they are too lacking in specification to do anything for the reader. He was being lazy.

It is not really his contradictions, such as they were, that are the problem; rather, it is the effect they have on others. Perhaps he was less inhibited than most people, or showed things more easily, because small incidents of his behaviour seemed to have disproportionate effects. Edward Crankshaw, for instance – a good friend – wrote of Ford that he '*was* a problem, and one which he was the last person to solve. How could he, indeed? He did not know from minute to minute who he was . . .' Crankshaw goes on to cite an occasion when they were out walking and Ford suddenly knocked a mushroom from Crankshaw's hand, warning of anthrax and adding: 'There is only one thing I am more afraid of than anthrax, and that is being savaged by a stallion.' Crankshaw commented: 'this completely dumbfounded me and we walked on in silence'. Ford was not necessarily being entirely serious here but even if he were – so what? Many people have particular fears.

The trouble is that the cumulative effect of such incidents and comments leads intelligent and earnest critics to pose such non-questions as Moser's: 'the real question is this: could an agoraphobic, neurasthenic, impressionistic solipsist – with, surely, a schizoid personality – write a good novel? It seems unlikely, except that Ford did it.'

It can lead to worse, too. Ford's well-intentioned supporters have not always been over-endowed with humour, with the result that they miss his own. For instance, he has a little joke in *The Good Soldier* at the expense of the Anglican Church. Dowell, the narrator, says that he would marry Nancy 'if her reason were ever sufficiently restored to let her appreciate the meaning of the Anglican marriage service. But it is possible that her reason will never be sufficiently restored to let her appreciate the meaning of the Anglican marriage service.' Why, asks Moser, 'this daft repetition?' He concludes that it is 'to convey the hellish ennui of life at Branshaw Teleragh.' With supporters like that, poor Ford has no need of detractors. Appreciated by too few in his life, it has been his fate in death to be imprisoned by some of his admirers.

It is yet another irony that serious-minded, analytical academics were among those he most despised – they laid, he thought, a dead hand upon literature – but it is to just such academics, particularly American, that to a large measure he owes his literary survival. They kept his books in print and made study of him respectable during decades when, apart from isolated efforts by other writers such as Graham Greene, Anthony Burgess, Basil Bunting and C. H. Sisson, he would probably have gone under. As it is, his very considerable super-structure is now emerging from the waters. He would have hated aspects of the critical approach to him and would have mocked its earnestness, but he would have thanked his critics because, though they may not all have been merry, they trusted to good letters, as he did.

NINETEEN

He liked the Army; it suited him and he it, more or less. It was another sort of love affair which had its bad patches but which never really died. After the war he was in no hurry to leave and years later wrote that the two institutions he thought most ideally shaped to their purposes were the Holy Roman Catholic Church and His Britannic Majesty's Army. It was, of course, the first time he had had a job.

Nor should it be surprising that he liked it. The notion that poets and writers are too sensitive and imaginative to be military would have sounded as strange to – say – Shakespeare and his contemporaries, as to Horace, Chaucer and Tolstoy, not to mention such as Wilfred Owen and Keith Douglas to whom war gave subjects in exchange for their lives. A substantial portion of the men of English letters have borne arms. (It would be of passing interest to count them since it is possible that, conscription apart, the proportion of combatants to non-combatants would be higher than in the male population as a whole.)

He spent most of the rest of 1915 training at either Tenby or Cardiff Castle. The Army, he found, was one of a large number of occupations whose regime was less harsh and whose demands were less exacting than writing. In September 1915 he wrote to his mother: 'I have never felt such an entire peace of mind as I have felt since I wore the King's uniform. It is just a matter of plain sailing doing one's duty, without any responsibilities except to one's superiors and one's men.' There were weekend leaves when he could get away to London or stay elsewhere with friends. Pound wrote to Harriet Monroe: 'Hueffer was up in town on leave yesterday . . . He is looking twenty years younger and enjoying his work.' Like George Heimann in *The Marsden Case*, he probably felt 'fit and with a place in society'. Low enough, but still a place.

The hours were long – six a.m. to seven p.m., sometimes – but the days passed. He wrote to Lucy Masterman, whose brother-in-law, Sixtus, was one of his fellow officers: '. . . It is astonishing how the day slips round from Coy. 6/R to dinner and bed and back again, as if one were in a sort of closed ball of dreams. It is probably very good for me – a sort of progression of little incidents that suggests nothing so much as a mist of bluebells in a wood. That may seem a queer simile, but it is fairly exact . . . I go down to Porthcawl every Sunday to play golf with an old major who is a soothing person. I wish you wd come down there. Couldn't you? & we cd. have a day or two together. Some of those places are *wonderfully* beautiful just now: if ever I wrote poems now they wd. be full of celtic twilight – with your beautiful hair to give them colour.' He was the sort of correspondent every married lady needs.

His only complaint was the lack of social life and he asked Lucy if there was anyone in the neighbourhood to whom she could introduce him. But he had not been able to leave everything behind: Violet got Wells to write to him about her. In what must have been a rather difficult letter of reply he told Wells, rather disingenuously, that he 'hadn't the least idea there was any difference between Violet and himself – or at least anything to make her face the necessity of talking about it.' He asked Wells to explain that he was always at her disposal except when the demands of regimental life came first, and those couldn't be cut. He had, he said, 'the greatest possible affection and esteem for her' and bore no grievance. He wanted nothing better than 'to live with her the life of a peaceable regimental officer with a peaceable wife'. For a soldier seeking a peaceable life and wife, there were better choices than 1916 and Violet Hunt.

Although a junior subaltern (second lieutenant) he was, of course, more than twice the age of the great majority of subalterns and older than most commanding officers. Appropriately enough, his duties seem to have been more concerned with administration than with running around at the head of a platoon, although he was later to lecture on weapon training and specialised in the

Ross rifle. He enjoyed having to write a memorandum about a prostitute, Violet Heyman, who was 'introduced by Lance-Corporal Plant, Fifth Welch' into the men's quarters: 'They lived – these desperadoes – in a tumble-down skating rink . . . a great cavern of a place that was laid out in stalls like a cattle market . . .' Violet Heyman was chased around the rink and over the beds by the sergeants and, when caught, was improperly handed over to the civil authorities. Ford had to demonstrate the impropriety of this in order that neither she nor her military accomplices should be brought before a civil court. He argued that 'the charge wd. not lie because the lady had not come into the Rink *proprio motu* but had been introduced . . .' The Garrison Commander returned the memorandum for re-writing on the grounds that it was both illegible and illiterate. This latter point amused Ford and he commented, accurately, 'and so everybody strafes everybody else in this microcosm & without doubt discipline is maintained.' He had grasped the essence of garrison life.

In his biography of Ford, Frank MacShane quotes a letter he received from one of Ford's brother officers, Thomas Lloyd: '. . . We all liked him in the mess, and for my own part I always found him most kind and helpful, like an elder brother or a senior boy at school. I well remember his initiating me into the onerous duties of Orderly-Officer which, as I was young and inexperienced, was then something of an ordeal. Little did I appreciate the fact that I was being instructed by so celebrated an author, a fact that he kept to himself. The thing that struck me most, perhaps, was the "softness" of his voice. He always spoke very quietly, it seemed. Posted to France again I lost touch with this good friend, but later I heard that he followed overseas and was at the Base, interrogating German prisoners.' He would have been a good man in the mess, an agreeable, amusing, capable and – in the good sense – patronising companion for the younger officers.

In one of his 1916 letters to Lucy Masterman he comments on the situation in Ireland. He was sympathetic to the cause of Irish nationalism and this letter follows the Easter Rising. It is the same letter in which he recounts the Violet Heyman incident and is in response to one from Lucy: 'I don't know: one can't comment on

Ireland. At least I can't. As for shooting the rebels: I wish it had been done *in situ*; I suppose it had to be done, tho' I don't know why . . .' It was a shrewd point.

Military life in South Wales had its compensations apart from the chasing of prostitutes around ice-rinks. He wrote three poems referring to this period – 'The Iron Music', 'The Silver Music' and 'What the Orderly Dog Saw'. The first two refer to a visit to Chepstow in female company while the latter is dedicated to a Mrs Percy Jackson, to whom he gave the manuscript. Whether she is also the lady of the first two, or whether there wasn't a lady, is not known. Like any poet, he was quite capable of writing nostalgic pieces to an imaginary female presence, though these do appear to point to a particular experience. 'The Iron Music' was written at Albert on 22 July 1916, after he had seen action:

The French guns roll continuously
And our guns, heavy, slow;
Along the Ancre, sinuously,
The transport wagons go
And the dust is on the thistle
And the larks sing up on high . . .
But I see Golden Valley
Down by Tintern on the Wye.

For it's just nine weeks last Sunday
Since we took the Chepstow train,
And I'm wondering if one day
We shall do the like again;
For the four-point-two's coming screaming
Thro' the sausages on high;
So there's little use in dreaming
How we walked above the Wye.

Dust and corpses in the thistles
When the gas-shells burst like snow,
And the shrapnel screams and whistles
On the Bécort Road below,
And the High Wood bursts and bristles

Where the mine-clouds foul the sky . . .
But I am with you up at Wyndcroft,
Over Tintern on the Wye.

This is strong on psychological truth, especially the last stanza. The rhythm and rhyme and the wistful tone echo earlier verses but the subject is new and the tension thus created is effective. The image of the gas-shells bursting like snow – powder-soft, continuous, seemingly gentle and harmless – is aptly contrasted with the screaming and whistling shrapnel 'On the Bécort Road below'. It is the short hard look and sound of 'Bécort' that makes that line, suggesting the violence of metal ringing off the road. No doubt he wrote it quickly, as he did all the others, and never revised it. (There is a similarly effective use of a place name in Sassoon's 'Blighters', where the line 'To mock the riddled corpses around Bapaume', suggests in its last word the ominous double report of big guns.)

Mrs Percy Jackson remains a mystery, though there is an Eleanor Jackson mentioned shortly after a couple called 'Nel and Percy' in Violet's diary for April 1917 (she later mentions a Miss Ross with whom Ford seems to have got involved). One very long shot for the truly indefatigable researcher is that at the end of *No Enemy* the Ford figure – Gringoire – has dinner not only with his mistress and the narrator but also with the wife of the local headmaster, who appears as admirer of Gringoire and reciter of his verses. Perhaps Mrs Jackson fulfilled the same role and had the same provenance. (Another typically Fordian touch is that Gringoire ends up holding hands with both women.) Violet must have been aware of having more than just the Army in competition with her, although in those last weeks in Wales he was correcting the proofs of her novel, *Their Lives*. He wrote of it to Lucy: 'I have been correcting the proofs of V's novel wh. is really very good. She seems to be absolutely untouched, mentally, by the war – wh. is no doubt a blessed state . . . I am writing in the Coy office with a number of people telling indecent stories wh. is trying to a letter-writer – so, in the Tommies' way, I shall conclude.'

His reference to Violet's mental remoteness from public affairs became more true than he could have realised, although it might be another example of his prescient instinct. As time went on she showed increasing signs of being concerned only about what touched most nearly; public events, apart from her suffragette involvement, became as remote as another country's weather report. This may have been partly temperament although in her later years it had physical causes as well. In the Second World War Ford's words were fulfilled to a chilling degree: she became senile and was so far from reality as to think the bombs falling around South Lodge were thunder in the Welsh mountains, where she thought she was walking with her father. (Ironically, South Lodge now displays a blue plaque commemorating Ford's brief occupancy, without mentioning Violet.)

Ford was warned for France on 1 June 1916 but was delayed for over a month. This was the beginning of the Battle of the Somme. There were loose ends to be tied before he went, the sort he had mentioned in 'Footsloggers'. Because we know he came back, it is easy to forget that he did not know he would and that for him this was quite possibly the end of his story rather than a part. There were wills to make, letters to write, faces to be seen for perhaps the last time. He wrote asking if he could borrow Conrad's old binoculars to take into action with him. Conrad appreciated the gesture but it was too late – the binoculars had disintegrated: 'Yes, *mon cher*! Our world of fifteen years ago is gone to pieces: what will come in its place, God knows, but I imagine doesn't care. Still what I always said was the only immortal line in "Romance": "Excellency, a few goats," survives – esoteric, symbolic, profound and comic – it survives.' This re-affirmation of their friendship must have greatly pleased Ford. Conrad was patriotic and war brought them closer. His son, Borys, was also serving in France and Violet had helped him on his way through London. Ford was to help him out there, continuing the tradition he had begun when Borys was a baby. Ford saw his own going to war as similar to Conrad's going to sea and he was pleased when Conrad agreed with Violet to be his literary executor. They met when he travelled down from Wales for what he called a 'valedictory interview' in which they 'cleared up a number of outstanding matters, he consenting to become my literary executor and asking me to write a memoir of him if I survived . . .'

No such reconciliation was possible with Marwood, however, who had died of cancer that May – in fact, on the 13th, the day that Ford had written to Lucy about Ireland and the girl in the ice-rink. In *Thus to Revisit* Ford attempted his own posthumous reconciliation by writing fondly of Marwood as if there had been no breach at all. It was a generous gesture because, apart from Marwood, *Thus to Revisit* is solely about writers and writing. He also wrote of him in articles. He liked, he said, Marwood's generalising habit: 'For myself, I love, sweeping dicta; the more obviously sweeping they are, the less they need to be taken *au pied de la lettre* . . .' It is possible that the process of idealising Marwood in his fiction was facilitated by Marwood's early death. It freed Ford's imagination from the foundation of his original inspiration and allowed him to shape the character he wanted. It probably also helped him feel he was making amends to his old friend.

He saw his daughters. They travelled to London from Kent and he took them to lunch in a Lyons café. Christina was seventeen, Katharine fifteen. Christina was determined to become a nun and she refused her father's and her mother's urging that she should delay doing so at least until he returned from France, if he did. She said that waiting would make no difference. Ford must have recalled his warning of a decade or so before that if she went to the Rye convent there would be no knowing what the nuns would do with her – 'she's such a loyal little thing.' Katharine was shy at being in a restaurant and said little.

It cannot have been an easy lunch and there was probably much unsaid, at least on his part. He never saw either again. Christina went to her nunnery but with Katharine he kept in touch at least until the death of his mother in 1924, after which, Katharine said, her letters went unanswered. (This is odd, if true, since he several times tried to arrange meetings and he was always an assiduous correspondent. Neither Stella nor Janice would have kept such letters from him, and Janice is sure that he never had any during the decade that she knew him.)

It was on 13 July 1916 that he entrained at Cardiff for Rouen. The waiting had been enervating and nerve-racking. He was learning that war, as he was to observe in *No Enemy*, is '112/113ths waiting'. He was also poor again. He couldn't do the journalism he had used to do, his books were earning little and he was still paying for Christina and Katharine. In the last days in Wales he was too broke to leave Cardiff Castle.

The draft that arrived at the base camp at Rouen was dispersed among the Welch Regiment's battalions. Ford was sent to the Ninth Battalion, part of 58 Brigade, Nineteenth Division, on 16 July. The battalion was not far from Albert (formerly Ancre) in the area of the notorious Mametz Wood and had played a part in the attempts to advance up Sausage Valley (so called because of the German observation balloons that hung over it) towards La Boisselle. It was big rolling country, for the most part bare; troop movements were exposed, shelling constant. The fighting in the labyrinth of trenches and dug-outs of Mametz wood had been vicious. Near La Boisselle the Lochnager Crater, the largest on the Western Front, may still be seen. It was blown with 60,000 lb of gun cotton on 1 July 1916 and the shock was allegedly felt hundreds of miles away. Even now it measures some 300 ft across and 90 ft deep.

Ford was attached to the battalion's first line of transport before Bécort Wood at the bottom of Sausage Valley. The battalion was commanded by Lieutenant-Colonel Cooke, formerly an Eastbourne town councillor who had, apparently, a dislike for officers of the Special Reserve, of which Ford was one. The adjutant was Captain R. R. Whitty, in civilian life a post office clerk. Ford's duties appear to have been those of transport officer and general administrative dogsbody, responsible for bringing new drafts up to the line, for helping with supplies, billeting when in reserve and performing tasks such as Mess Officer, an onerous and unpopular appointment which usually earns blame for everything and thanks for nothing (the green baize door again).

Colonel Cooke may have been one of those who took against Ford on sight. His later actions certainly suggest it. Leaving aside the personal elements, though, it is likely that few commanding officers would have welcomed an elderly and possibly eccentric subaltern, as inexperienced as he was enthusiastic, at a time when the battalion was hard-pressed and when the commanding officer himself was probably exhausted and under constant pressure. Also, Cooke had actually stated that he did not want an elderly officer in the line. Thomas Sugrue, a brother officer and Ford's closest companion during those days in France, wrote to Arthur Mizener in 1966 that Ford '. . . took no active part in the fighting . . . He was most anxious to obtain front line experience . . . but Colonel Cooke would not allow him, on account of his age.'

This unintentionally reinforced a misleading view of Ford's part in the war, to the effect that he was hardly in it at all, spent all his time 'behind the line' and afterwards grossly inflated his own role. Goldring observed that this view was current even in Ford's lifetime. It was lent credence by his later exaggerations, though he exaggerated no more than many. Mizener mentions his talk of marching 'my battalion' into the lines and of his being gassed when probably, Mizener thinks, he was not. The point is that these were *only* exaggerations. He did march drafts into the lines and later he did briefly command a labour battalion which he quite likely would have marched into the lines since that is where it would have done some of its work. Mizener is right to point out that he didn't have a 'glorious war' but, like most men out there, he wasn't in it for that. It was not, anyway, a very glorious affair.

The gas incident may or may not have happened. Ford seemed genuinely to believe that it had. He wrote to his mother in December 1916 of 'the touch of gas I got at Nieppe' and he often referred to it later. He also told his friend Edgar Jepson how he had packed a portmanteau at the front and, when opening it on leave, had got a breath of gas. There were gas attacks in his sector and it is possible that he was affected, perhaps not seriously but enough to worry him since his breathing was not in any case very good. Nor is the portmanteau story necessarily impossible, though it may be that he did not expect it to be taken seriously. It is plausible that a whiff of the stuff might remain in the contents of a locked case for a while. Other whiffs do. It could also be that he imagined it. The deterioration in his lungs – which certainly happened – was probably due mainly to smoking and to living and sleeping in wet clothing, but being in the region of gas attacks and seeing gas casualties may have encouraged him to associate the deterioration with that.

A more general point concerns the nature of the war itself. Briefly, this is that being 'behind the line' did not mean that one was not involved in the action. The great majority of troops at any time were behind the front line and many never saw it at all. There is an assumed analogy with the days of hand-to-hand fighting which does not hold, even though soldiers did sometimes shoot an enemy they saw, throw grenades or kill with bayonets. Guns enable men to kill at a distance and big guns enable them to kill an enemy who is too far away to be seen. The majority of casualties in that war were from shell-fire; although being shelled may not have been very dashing it was, for very many soldiers, what being in action meant.

There is the difference, too, of singular and plural: Ford was in the lines but only not in *the* line, i.e. the front line. An infantry battalion's transport would usually be two or three miles behind the front, still within the range of bigger guns, and a transport officer would have to make regular supply runs up to the front, often along routes that were singled out for shelling. In or behind those transport lines was where most soldiers spent most of the war. Battalions would spend about seven to twelve days manning their portion of the front and would then be withdrawn, rested, re-equipped and put in reserve for a couple of weeks before being sent to another part of the front. If, like Ford's, they had had a busy time, they might be sent to a quieter part. The high casualty rate for which the war is notorious – battalions of eight hundred wiped out in hours, subalterns' life expectancy of about three weeks and so on – was true only of certain sectors at certain times. Despite the slaughter, the great majority of men under arms were uninjured. The night raids across No Man's Land, the stumbling over the parapet amidst the numbing noise of an attack, the sudden eruption of mortar bombs along a trench, the bodies twitching on the wire to the tap-tap of machine-guns – these were, in a sense, the pinnacles of the experience, not its general characteristics. The latter comprised waiting, being shelled, administering, training, being ordered somewhere, ordered back, waiting, administering, being shelled, waiting. That was Ford's and many other men's predominant experience of war:

> That damned truck had stayed under that bridge for two hours and a half . . . in the process of the eternal waiting that is War.

> You hung about and you hung about, and you kicked your heels and you kicked your heels: waiting for Mills bombs to come, or for jam, or for generals, or for the tanks, or transport, or the clearance of the road ahead. You waited in offices under the eyes of somnolent orderlies, under fire on the banks of canals, you waited in hotels, dug-outs, tin sheds, ruined houses. There will be no man who survives of His Majesty's Armed Forces that shall not remember those eternal hours when Time itself stayed still as the true image of bloody War! . . .[1]

But he wanted to go into the front line, as Thomas Sugrue said. It was natural; having let himself in for it, he would want to get as far as he could. Also, he was all his life a man who wanted to contribute, to join in, to be there; so to be denied, to be pushed back, to be made to feel an unwanted supernumerary in a strange battalion must have been deeply and continuously hurtful.

It was unlikely to have been simply a question of his age. He was by no means the only elderly subaltern on the front: the oldest Somme casualty, killed near Mametz, was Lieutenant Harry Webber, of the Devonshires, aged 67. Ford and Colonel Cooke saw very little of each other, not enough for Cooke to have formed a bad opinion of his work. It may have been something more personal. He might, for instance, have made Cooke feel socially inferior, which would be all the worse for being unintentional. It is also possible as already noted, that the battalion may not have been in a very good state and likely that Cooke himself was stretched to cope.[2] Ford got on with subsequent, though less crucial, commanding officers.

He wrote frequently to Lucy Masterman from his position before Bécort Wood. On 28 July he wrote:

> . . . We are right up in the middle of the strafe, but only with the 1st line transport. We get shelled two or three times a day, otherwise it is fairly dull – indeed, being shelled is fairly dull,

[1] *A Man Could Stand Up*

[2] The 9th Welch war diary for the month of July shows approximately twenty killed, thirty-one missing and three hundred and fifty-four wounded; bad enough, though July 1916 had worse stories to tell.

> after the first once or twice. Otherwise it is all very interesting – filling in patches of one's knowledge & so on, but it isn't more than interesting, because one gets no news. Absolutely none, except gossip. One hears that such and such a division has taken such and such a place – then that it hasn't; such and such a regiment has been wiped out, then that its casualties are one accident. The landscape here is long downland, the sun blazes down & then gets obscured by haze, blazes down & is then obscured again. There are trees in rows; in little copses – each copse with a name – La Boisselle, Mametz, Pozières, & so on. But there isn't a village any more to bear any of the names . . . The noise of the bombardment is continuous – so continuous that one gets used to it, as one gets used to the noise in a train and the ear picks out the singing of the innumerable larks . . . I see that . . . the Rt. Hon DLG [Lloyd George] still has his back to the wall & will fight to the last drop of our blood. I wonder what he wd. say if he were out here for a week! . . . Poor V. I wonder what is happening to her. I have not had a line from her since I started . . . the off'rs here are a terrible lot, without a soul that one can really talk to except little boys . . .

A few days later he wrote that he had hopes of a staff job – he was known to one or two generals – but meanwhile '. . . The work is interesting in the extreme & one gets a certain amount of fun out of oneself. This morning, for instance, I was standing in a pail like Adam before the fall when some shrapnel burst overhead – & I was amused to discover that I grabbed for a shirt before a tin hat.'

The staff job never happened. It was not necessarily a case of the Army's neglecting to make use of his talents since there are indications that he was considered, but by then Colonel Cooke's bad reports had done their damage.

War didn't stop him reading, or even writing. He sent for a number of books he admired with the idea of re-reading them in order to see how they stood the test of an extreme experience, among them Conrad's *Heart of Darkness* and *Youth* and, probably, James's *What Maisie Knew*. He began a French translation of *The Good Soldier*, from memory. Thirty-seven pages survive at Cornell University, but there is evidence that the entire book was completed and the manuscript lost, probably during the Second World War. He is believed to have done it all from memory, quite plausibly. As Allen Tate recalled: 'He said then that he had the entire novel – every sentence – in his head before he began to write it in 1913. He had the most prodigious memory I have encountered in any man. And *The Good Soldier* is not only his masterpiece, but in my view the masterpiece of British fiction in this century.' (Two subsequent translations, not by Ford, are apparently inferior and capture little of the feel of the book.) He wrote most of the poems subsequently published in *On Heaven*. Two weeks on the Somme could be a long time and he was, in any case, a man who could put a lot into one.

There was an interruption, however. Just before the battalion was withdrawn he was blown up by a near-miss. Concussed, he suffered almost total loss of memory for about thirty-six hours. Those expensive porcelain teeth were damaged and weeks later he wrote that they were still 'literally bleeding'. He was sent back to No. 36 Casualty Clearing Station at Corbie, which wasn't much better than the Front:

> After I was blown up at Bécort-Bécodel in '16 and, having lost my memory, lay in the Casualty Clearing Station in Corbie, with the Enemy planes dropping bombs over all over it and the dead Red Cross nurses being carried past my bed, I used to worry agonisedly about what my name could be – and have a day-nightmare. The night nightmare was worse, but the day one was as bad as was necessary. I thought I had been taken prisoner by the Enemy forces and was lying on the ground, manacled hand and foot . . . Immense shapes in grey-white *cagoules* and shrouds, minching and mowing and whispering horrible plans to one another! It is true they all wore giant, misty gas-masks . . .

His memory was not fully recovered for a long time and he later wrote that it was 1923 before he 'got over the nerve-tangle of war'. This experience increased the fear of madness which had been with him since at least 1904. He was in fact shell-shocked (another non-specific description which is nevertheless apt) and was to remain so for most of the rest of the war. Pound wrote to Lewis at about that time: 'Met Hueffer's brother-in-law [David Soskice] on the plaisaunce. He said a shell had burst near our friend and that he had had a nervous breakdown and was for the present safe in a field hospital.'

He spent a week there and by the time he was out the battalion had moved with the rest of the 19th Division to the Ypres salient, a quieter section at that time but still the Front. He wrote to Lucy Masterman in August:

> Using a good deal of determination, I have got out of the nurses' hands and back to duty, after an incredibly tortuous struggle across France. I rather begin to think I will not begin to be able to stick it – the conditions of life are too hard and the endless waitings too enervating . . .

It sounds as if he had discharged himself, after which it could not have been easy to admit to his doubts about seeing it through. It was a depressing home-coming since Colonel Cooke and the adjutant were disagreeable and unwelcoming. The Germans, however, 'seem to have nothing but minenwerfers & little or no artillery – only occasionally a shell comes over here – so that it seems wonderfully like Heaven . . . it is very interesting, all of it – if not gay'.

His next letter complained of being over-worked because of his Flemish: '. . . I have to buy straw and pacify infuriated farmers as well as attending all parades and fatigues . . . the CO says I am too old and the Adjt. thanks me all day long for saving the HQ Mess 2frs 22 on turnips & the like. I don't know which I dislike most.'

He saw King George V and the Prince of Wales when they visited and he expressed further hopes of a staff job: '. . . because I have had my week in the Somme & three weeks here & a week in Field Ambulance & a week draft conducting.' He thought the staff were 'nibbling' at him. He goes on to describe what seemed, in comparison with the Somme, the quiet of the new sector: '. . . It is – tho' you won't believe it – a dreamy sort of life in a grey-green country & even the shells as they set out on their long journeys seem tired. It is rather curious, the extra senses one develops here. I sit writing in the twilight &, even as I write, I hear the shells whine and the M.G.'s crepitate & I see (tho' it is hidden by hill) the grey-flat land below & the shells bursting & I know that in all probability W.63 or some such section has just phoned to the H.A. & that the Bosche are getting cheeky with [illegible] and need suppressing . . . Thanks so very much for the Echo de Paris . . .'

'Crepitate' is a good word for machine-gun fire. He ended the letter by observing that 'V seems very queer' and urges Lucy not to repeat anything to her 'because she does so worry'. One of the things that had worried Violet, and about which she harried him, was that somewhere in France he had lost his bicycle.

Towards the end of August he wrote with some excitement that *Between St Dennis and St George*, translated by Mary Butts, was to be published in Paris, though he bemoaned the fact that no one seemed to publish the poems he was writing. He was sending them back to Violet whom he half suspected of 'suppressing them for ends of her own'. In fact, the March 1917 edition of *Poetry* published Ford's 'What the Orderly Dog Saw' with, after it, Violet's 'What the Civilian Saw'. He might have been half right.

Relations with Colonel Cooke were worsening: 'With the labour of 184 men I have today drained a considerable portion of this country & I have also marched 12 miles to bring up a draft. So I have not been idle. But the CO continues to impress on me that I am too old for this job. I think he wants to force me to relinquish my commission . . .' That was not all. Within two weeks – the 6th September – he was complaining, firstly, that he had no correspondence but notes from Violet about the bicycle; secondly that 'We are in a h-ll of a noise, just now – my hand is shaking badly – our guns are too inconsiderate – they pop up out of baby's rattles & tea cosy & shake the rats thro' the earth.'

Apart from Lucy's sympathetic letters and some from Conrad, much of the news from England served only to reinforce all the old worries. Money was still a problem. War was not, after all, the clean-cut thing, the break, the escape he might have hoped it would be. This theme is most powerfully evident in the *Parade's*

End books where Tietjens's wife, Sylvia, contrives even to pursue him to the Front, not satisfied with harassing him from a distance, overdrawing his bank account, spreading lies about him and so on. It was evident too in *The Marsden Case*:

> I used to think that, once out there, we should be surrounded by a magic and invisible tent that would keep us from all temporal cares. But we were not so surrounded and it is not like that. The one nail does not knock out the other. There is that never ceasing waiting about; and the cold and the long depressions. Now and then there is terrible noise – wearing, lasting for days. And some pain. All that is bearable. But what is desolating, what is beyond everything hateful, is that, round your transparent tent, the old evils, the old heart-breaks and the old cruelties are unceasingly at work.

When the old evils from home combined with the new evils closer to hand the regimental strafing became worse than more conventional shelling. He later wrote a short story, *The Colonel's Shoes*, in which there is a character from an unpopular reserve battalion who is the victim of gossip about himself and women and his previous German connections.

After his return to the battalion in August he was sent for by Cooke who read to him a letter which he was sending to Brigade Headquarters, copied to Ford himself at South Lodge: 'I consider that he is quite unsuitable to perform the duties required of an officer in this campaign. He would not inspire his men with confidence and his power as a leader is nil . . . I recommend that he be sent home as early as possible as there is no use to which I can put him. I could not place him in command of men in the field. I cannot recommend him for employment at home.'

They were hard words. Ford did not protest – he was too ill to do so, he wrote to Masterman – but he requested transfer to some post in which he could use his languages. He also told Masterman that at the date of that interview he had met Cooke only once 'and that I have certainly committed no military offence of any kind; that I have carried out punctually and exactly any military duties

I have had to perform & that, at the time of his writing his first comm.n to me the C.O. had not so much as shaken hands with me nor had the Adjutant & that neither of these officers or any other had seen me in contact with the men – simply because I had not been in contact with the men, but only in the 1st line transport wh. is composed mostly of mules.'

In Wales Ford was described as being good with the men and with the younger officers, helpful and interested, even learning some Welsh; later on in France, another colonel under whom he served asked to have him back; later still he was promoted; but there is little doubt that at his age and in his condition he should not have been in a front line infantry unit. He might have got on better as a gunner, like Wyndham Lewis or Edward Thomas, or in one of the corps.

He was probably a brave man. This does not, of course, mean that he was not frightened but it is suggested by what he says about failure and by how his concern is always for getting on with the job, which is what bravery means in such circumstances. When he writes about the war in his fiction he is normally trying to convey the state of mind of his hero – usually a mind harassed like his own by the devils from back home. However true this may be of many men at war, for those of us who were not there it is the physical description that is often of greater interest. It may be unpleasant to recall or merely banal but to the outsider the setting seems, perhaps misleadingly, to be of the essence. This may be one reason why Ford is not better known as a war writer; his subject was not war but the people, the people war produced. He offered his own explanation in *A Day of Battle*, a manuscript fragment:

> I have asked myself continuously why I can write nothing . . . about the psychology of that Active Service of which I have seen my share. And why I cannot even evoke pictures of the Somme or the flat lands around Ploegsteert . . . Today, when I look at a mere coarse map of the Line, simply to read 'Ploegsteert' or 'Armentières' seems to bring up extraordinarily coloured and exact pictures behind my eyeballs – little pictures having all the brilliant minuteness that medieval illuminations have – of

> towers, and roofs, and belts of trees and sunlight; or, for the matter of these, of men, burst into mere showers of blood, and dissolving into muddy ooze; or of aeroplanes and shells against the translucent blue. – But, as for putting them – into words! No: the mind stops dead, and something in the brain stops and shuts down: precisely as the left foot stops dead and the right foot comes up to it with a stamp upon the hard asphalt – upon the 'square' after the command 'Halt', at Chelsea!

He could not bring himself to expatiate upon horror. Probably he felt enough anyway in the daily course of life and had no desire for a surfeit. Also, he was a man of essential goodness and like other such people he turned away from anything gratuitously bad or horrifying because he loved it not at all, not even enough to exploit it for art. Nor was he ever a hypocrite: he would have known that the evocation of violence in the name of peace is never quite the whole story. He could not even bring himself to believe in atrocities. When the reports of German atrocities in Belgium had reached England, he had rejected them. Not finding that in himself which would permit such actions, he could no more believe it of others than some people who, finding nothing in themselves to echo it, can believe in human generosity and goodness. He was lucky, perhaps, to die in June 1939.

We know from Pound that Ford's view of Yeats was that Yeats must have been an emotionally cold man since he thought no one could have made such powerful use of emotion in his verse if he really felt it. He might have argued similarly if asked why he didn't do more to dramatise suffering in war. It was with this as with confrontations of all sorts: he felt collisions with the world too much to dramatise them directly, yet felt their effects too deeply to write seriously about anything else. Thus his letters were sometimes more straightforwardly revealing than his books. In the first week of September he wrote three to Conrad which are interesting not only for their description of what was going on but also for the affection they show and for what they tell us about how he was coping. They are worth quoting in full:

Attd. 9/Welch
19th Division., B.E.F.
(September 1916)

My Dear Conrad—

I have just had a curious opportunity with regard to sound wh. I hasten to communicate to you – tho' indeed I was anyhow going to write to you today.

This aftn then, we have a *very* big artillery strafe on – not, of course as big as others I have experienced – but still *very* big. I happened to be in the very middle – the centre of a circle – of H. A. and quite close to a converted, naval how[itzer]. The [illegible] last for about an hour – incessant and to all intents and purposes a level pitch of sound. I was under cover filling up some of the innumerable A.F.'s [Army forms] that one fills up all day long even here – & I did not notice that it was raining and suddenly and automatically I got under the table on the way to my tin hat. – Out there, you know, you see men going about daily avocations, carrying buckets, being shaved or reading the D'ly Mail &, quite suddenly, they all appear to be pulled sideways off their biscuit boxes or wagon shafts. I mean of course shrapnel or minen.

Well I was under the table and frightened out of my life – so indeed was the other man with me. There was shelling just overhead – apparently thousands of shells bursting for miles around and overhead. I was convinced that it was all up with the XIX Div. because the Huns had got hold of a new & absolutely devilish shell or gun.

It was of course thunder. It completely extinguished the sound of the heavy art[illery], and even the how about 50 yds. away was inaudible during the actual peals and sounded like *stage thunder* in the intervals. Of course we were in the very vortex of the storm, the lightning being followed by thunder before one cd. count two – but there we were right among the guns too.

I thought this might interest you as a constatation of some exactness. And, for the matter of that, when the rain did come down the sound of it on the corrugated iron roof of the dugout also extinguished the sound of gun-fire tho' that is not so remarkable. It probably stopped the guns too, but that I don't know. At any rate they are quiet now, but the rain isn't.

The mud and rain here are pretty bad – after about a fortnight of wet – but they are not really much worse than Stocks Hill – *t'en souviens tu*? – used to be and I bear them with more equanimity than most of my brothers in arms – I daresay because of that early training. I certainly remember worse weather experiences between the Pent & Aldington. But I have lain down wet in the wet for the last three nights and do not seem to have taken any harm except for a touch of toothache. And I am certainly in excellent spirits tho' of course it is not yet cold and that may prove too much for me. I daresay eulogia of the French Press which continues to blaze and coruscate about my gifts has remonte my morale. It *is* gratifying, you know, to feel that even if one dies among the rats in these drains one won't be – if only for nine days – just like the other rats. Of course these salvos are a little machined by the French Govt. – but still, some of them are genuine – and Genl Bridges who kindly commended me on Bn Parade the other day – tho' God knows my [illegible] was dilapidated enough with seven smoke helmet buttons and three cap badges missing!! – tells me that he has written to Genl Plumer to say that I ought to have a staff job so I may get one – and I don't know *what* I should be sorry. I have been for six weeks – with the exception of 24 hours – continuously within reach of German missiles &, altho' one gets absolutely to ignore them, consciously, I imagine that subconsciously one is suffering. I know that if one of the cooks suddenly opens, with a hammer, a chest close at hand, one jumps in a way one doesn't use when the 'dirt' is coming over fairly heavily.

An R.F.A. man has just come along & explained that the 'rain has just put the kybosh on the strafe' – so there, my dear, you have the mot juste. But it is fairly sickening all the same.

I hope you are all right: Drop me a line now & then. There are no goats here – but 40,000 mules – mostly from Costaguana! Yrs always,

I have been re-reading *Pierre Nozière* at intervals; it's thin; it's *thin*, my dear. I wonder the old man won't appear like thread paper after all this. *C'est la son danger*, as far as the future is concerned.

9/Welch
19th Div., B.E.F.
6.9.16

My dear,

I will continue 'for yr information and necessary action, please' my notes upon sounds.

In woody country heavy artillery makes *most* noise, because of the echoes – and most prolonged in a *diluted* way.

On marshland – like the Romney Marsh – the *sound* seems alarmingly close: I have seldom heard the *Hun* artillery in the middle of a strafe except on marshy land. The sound, not the diluted sound, is also at its longest in the air. [An arrow is drawn from the 'e' in the following paragraph to the 'e' in this paragraph.]

On dry down land the sound is much *sharper*; it hits you & shakes you. On clay land it shakes the ground & shakes you thro' the ground. A big naval (let us say) gun, fired, unsuspected by us out of what resembled (let us say) a dead mule produced the 'e' that I have marked with an arrow.

In hot, dry weather, sounds give me a headache – over the brows and across the skull, inside, like a migraine. In wet weather one minds them less, tho- dampness of the air makes them seem nearer.

Shells falling on a church: these make a huge '*corump*' sound, followed by a noise like crockery falling off a tray – as the roof tiles fall off. If the roof is not tiled you can hear the stained glass, sifting mechanically until the next shell. (Heard in a church square, on each occasion, about 90 yds away.) Screams of women penetrate all these sounds – but I do not find that they agitate me as they have done at home (Women in cellars round the square. Oneself running thro' fast.)

Emotions again: I saw two men and three mules (the first time I saw a casualty) killed by one shell. A piece the size of a pair of corsets went clear thro' one man, the other just fell – the mules hardly any visible mark. These things give me no *emotion* at all – they seemed obvious; rather as it wd. be. A great many patients on stretchers – a thousand or so in a long stream is very depressing – but, I fancy, mostly because one thinks one will be going back into it.

When I was in hospital a man three beds from me died *very* hard, blood passing thro' bandages and he himself crying perpetually, 'Faith! Faith! Faith!' It was very disagreeable as long as he had a chance of life – but one lost all interest and forgot him when one heard he had gone.

Fear;

This of course is the devil – & worst because it is so very capricious. Yesterday I was buying – or rather not buying – flypapers in a shop under a heap of rubbish. The woman was laughing & saying that all the flies came from England. A shell landed in the château into whose wall the shop was built. One Tommie said, 'Crump!' Another: 'Bugger the flies' & slapped himself. The woman – about thirty, quick & rather jewish – went on laughing. I said, 'Mais je vous assure, Madame, qu'il n'y a plus comme ça de mouches chez nous.' No interruption, emotion, vexed at getting no flypapers. Subconscious emotion, 'thank God the damn thing's burst.'

Yet today, passing the place, I wanted to gallop past it & positively trembled on my horse. Of course I cdnt. gallop because there were Tommies in the street.

Attd. 9/Welch
19th Div., B.E.F.
7/9/16

Dear Conrad,

I wrote these rather hurried notes yesterday because we were being shelled to hell and I did not expect to get thro' the night. I wonder if it is just vanity that in these cataclysmic moments makes one desire to *record*. I hope it is, rather, the annalist's wish to help the historian – or, in a humble sort of way, my desire to help you, cher maître! – if you ever wanted to do anything in '*this line*'. Of course you wd. not ever want to do anything in this line, – but a pocketful of coins of a foreign country may sometime come in handy. You might want to put a phrase into the mouth of someone in Bangkok who had been, say, to Bécort. There you wd. be and I, to that extent, shd. once more have collaborated.

This is a rather more accidente portion of the world: things in every sense 'stick out' more in the September sunlight. The Big Push was too overwhelming for one to notice details; it was like an immense wave full of debris. It was France, of course – and this too is France. But this is France of tapestries – immense avenues along the road, all blue in the September twilight & the pleasant air that gives one feelings of bienaise. It is curious – but, in the evenings here, I always feel myself happier than I have ever felt in my life. – Indeed, except for worries, I am really very happy – but I don't get on with my superior officers here & that means that they can worry me a good deal in details – there are almost endless openings for the polite taquineries called 'strafing' in a regiment – especially if one has had a Regular training & gets attached to R.A. Bn, where all the details are different. However, these things, except in moments of irritation, are quite superficial – and it is all matter for observation. One of these days I daresay I shall fly out at someone & get into trouble – tho' not the sort of 'trouble' one minds. But indeed I hope I shan't – because discipline is after all discipline & [I] begin to believe it is the first thing in the world.

God bless you, my dear. Love to Jessie. I hope you have good news of Borys.

Yrs.

The way he referred to his troubles with Cooke is typical where personal troubles were concerned. The understatement which makes the whole business sound impersonal and detached – 'all a matter for observation' – as if he was taking the wider view, is both revealing and misleading. It is the former because he really did take that wider view, and not only in recollection, and it is the latter because it conceals how at the same time he really was hurt by such things. It should also be noted that he had one day in six weeks away from the shelling.

He was, however, to have some more days. The translation of *Between St Dennis and St George* brought him modest recognition from the French Government which, at that time particularly and as he had indicated to Conrad, pleased him enormously. He was invited to Paris for the publication and to be thanked by the Minister of Instruction, and he put in for leave from the 9th to 11th September. He hoped at the same time to sort out his financial affairs (one of the old evils that still pursued him) and get permission to see a dentist in Paris so that his bleeding teeth could be 'pumped out'.

He wrote a good impressionistic description of his time in Paris in *No Enemy*, where he has Gringoire respond to the Minister's asking him whether there is anything he needs with the single word, 'Ferrets'. The battalion wanted them to keep down the trench rats. It is not known whether Ford actually made such a request though it would be in character; the result, for Gringoire at least, was polite acknowledgement but no ferrets.

He was by this time in eager correspondence with Masterman about getting himself moved away from the influence of Cooke, a move that would have pleased all parties but which, as is the way with bureaucracies civil or military, was not to go quite as planned. He was also writing to Conrad about *Chance*, the book that brought Conrad widespread fame. Ford had predicted it would and he said Conrad sent him a fiver in the trenches as settlement of their bet. When he reached Paris, though, he broke down. What exactly happened is not entirely clear, not even from his unpublished writings about the war such as *True Love & A G.C.M.* (General Court Martial). He wrote to Masterman that he spent thirty-six hours cutting *Between St Dennis and St George* and writing an epilogue in French, after which, 'I collapsed and was made to see the M.O. who said I was suffering from specific shell-shock & ought to go to hospital. However, I wdnt, & got back here' (to the battalion).

Whatever work he did on the book has never come to light but there is no doubt that he experienced a collapse. In December 1916 he wrote to his daughter Katharine that he had been 'blown up by a 4.2 & shaken into a nervous breakdown which has made me unbearable to myself & all my kind.' For how long he was with the battalion after Paris is unclear because the records are themselves contradictory. His personal service record gives him as wounded on 16 October 1916 but by then he was already writing to Masterman from the Welch Regiment's 3rd Battalion in Wales, whither he had returned. This move was very probably the result of Masterman's machinations on his behalf but he had been hoping for a move elsewhere in France rather than back to Wales. As he explained to Masterman, he was paid less back in Wales and couldn't really afford to be there. He tried writing articles again 'but it is rather difficult to write in an ante room with 40 officers'.

Soon he was feeling that he had no purpose in life and might as well resign his commission and 'disappear into a decent obscurity'. Money was becoming ever more a problem. 'One can't,' he wrote to Lucy, 'with my age & disposition, run up bills at shops without any possibility of meeting them & so on. I cd. get along personally on my pay – but I have outside liabilities too, you see. And V's campaign of vilification makes people very shy of publishing my work, even if I cd. write, so I shd. really be much better off if I relinquished my commn. & enlisted. It isn't depression or pique, but just commonsense.'

As with others who were in the trenches and survived to write about it, when he was away from the horror he wanted to be back. He was probably quite serious about enlisting in the ranks and, like Gringoire in *No Enemy*, he now felt uneasy with civilians back home. The only people who would understand were the people 'out there'. By the end of November, his and Masterman's machinations had worked again, up to a point. He was ordered back to France, asking only that he should not be returned to the 9th Welch – 'I don't at all want not to be killed – but I don't want to be straffed unjustly as well.'

At the base camp at Rouen he learned, like many in the British Army before and since, that his destination was precisely that which he had striven to avoid. It must have been equally unwelcome news to Lieutenant Colonel Cooke. Ford protested and asked to be sent elsewhere – anywhere. Meanwhile he was employed 'writing proclamations in French about thefts of rations issued to

H.B.M.'s forces & mounting guards over German sick.' In another letter addressed 'My dear' (French writers of the period commonly addressed each other as 'Mon cher') he wrote to Conrad about one of the sick prisoners:

> As I had to wait for some papers and it was snowing I went into a tent. I asked one of the prisoners – who was beautifully warm in bed – where he came from and what he did before the war. I was wet thro' and coughing my head off – not in the least interested anyhow. So I don't know where he came from – somewhere in Bavaria. But as for his occupation, he said, 'Herr Offizier, *Geisenhirt*!' So there was our: 'Excellency, a few goats!' quite startlingly jumped at me. And then, it may interest you to know, he smiled a fatuous and ecstatic peasant boy's smile and remarked: 'But it is heaven here!'

Though still at Rouen when he wrote that letter he was by then in Number 2 Red Cross hospital. While waiting for the matter of his return to the 9th Welch to be resolved his lungs had 'intervened', as he put it, 'with extensions at the bases & solidifications and all sorts of things – partly due to a slight touch of gas I got in the summer & partly to sheer weather.' Not surprisingly, his condition was not only physical. He suffered hallucinations in which the ward was peopled by German soldiers: 'I am in short rather ill & sometimes doubt my own sanity – indeed, quite frequently I do. I suppose that, really, the Somme was a pretty severe ordeal, though I wasn't conscious of it at the time. I find myself suddenly waking up in a hell of a funk – & going on being in a hell of a funk till morning. And that is pretty well the condition of a number of men here. I wonder what the effect of it will be on us all, after the war – & on national life and the like. I fancy amenity of manners will suffer a good deal . . .'

His reference to the Somme is surely right. He began to crack up when the strain eased – that is, when he went to Paris – as is the way with many people. When there is no longer a pressing need to keep going and the pressure drops the accumulated effects of strain bubble to the surface. No doubt he was also right about the physical causes of his worsening lungs – 'what I was doing [in

Rouen] meant getting wet through & coming in to write for a couple of hours in a stifling room, often getting wet through some more & then sleeping in a dripping hut –' and his overall physical condition was probably further weakened by the strain. Nor is it too far-fetched to suggest that his not being able to contribute to the battalion as he would have liked might have played a part: few experiences are more debilitating than the contemplation of one's own unwanted and unavailing endeavours.

His experiences in the hospital, a former seminary, were not such as to encourage speedy recovery. He wrote in a December 1932 article in *Harper's*:

> . . . We occupied small white priests' cells, two to a cell, a camp bed in each corner. Diagonally opposite me was a Black Watch 2nd lieutenant – about twenty, wild-eyed, black-haired. A shell-shock case. He talked with the vainglory and madness of the Highland chieftain that he was, all day. Towards ten at night he would pretend to sleep.
>
> As soon as the last visit of the V.A.D.'s was over he would jump out of bed and rush to a wall-press with sliding doors. He took out a kilt and a single shoe. His face assumed a look of infinite cunning. He would fix his black, shining maniacal eyes on mine and, stealthily stretching out an arm, would extract from the press a *skene dhu*. A *skene dhu* is the long, double-edged dagger that Highlanders carry in their socks. From the creasing of his lips, you could tell when he had put a sufficient edge upon that instrument. He would be sharpening it on the sole of his single shoe. He never removed his eyes from mine. He would rub his thumb along the edge of the blade and with a leering, gloating look he would whisper
>
> 'We know who this is meant for'.
>
> I never ascertained. Delirium would then come. I was delirious most nights.

There are reflections of this unsettling companion in MacKechnie in *Parade's End*.

Fortunately, his successor was less alarming:

> One night he had disappeared and the convoy whistle blew – towards four. It was always disagreeable to be awakened by the convoy whistle. It meant that the Enemy, far away in the black and frozen night, had been pushing an inch or two farther towards the Mediterranean. Wounded were coming down.
>
> Tweedledum in a steeple-crowned hat burst in. He had two fleeces bound round his khaki stomach. He pitched his hat onto a nail in the wall and exclaimed disgustedly:
>
> 'H'or caows 'as better 'ouses in Horsetrileyer!'
>
> That was tragedy. I said, 'It is all over. They are putting Tommies in with the officers. The Germans have burst through. They will be here any day. They will be on the Mediterranean in a week.'
>
> That was not snobbishness. It was despair at the thought that there had been so much slaughter. There had been no time to sort the wounded . . .
>
> Well, next morning, after a night of delirium, I saw across the cell a little, fat, rumpled dumpling of maybe forty, leaning over the end of his pillow, looking with disgust at his breakfast. He spat out to my pet V.A.D.:
>
> 'We get heggs from h'our 'ens in Horsetrileyer.'
>
> He was an officer all right. The line still stood. The Côte d'Azur did not need to tremble. He was a field officer who in civilian life supplied milk to a great city where they walk upside down and have retained since 1840 the purest Cockney language . . .

On 15 December he wrote to his mother: 'It wd. really be preferable to be dead – but one is not dead.' He received news that brother Oliver, also in uniform, had been badly wounded. He sent £5 to Katharine for Christmas.

The medical board at Rouen found him in a bad enough state to order him home. Offered what many in the Army longed for, he yet again protested. The board relented and assigned him to limited service in France. On Christmas Eve he had a serious relapse and two weeks later was ordered to Menton in the South of France in order to rest at Lady Michelham's convalescent hospital.

By the time he left Rouen he had written a number of poems, some in the trenches and some at the hospital. He told Conrad that of the fourteen officers with whom he had travelled from Wales in July, he alone was left (it is not clear whether he meant left at Rouen, or left alive and relatively well), while of the sixty who had joined the Welch battalions since July, eleven were already dead. These deaths, especially of young subalterns (whom he usually referred to as 'poor boys' or 'little boys') moved him in ways that surprised him: '. . . one gets a feeling', he wrote to Conrad, 'of sombre resentment against the nightmare population that persists beyond No Man's Land. At any rate it is horrible – it arouses in one a rage unexpressed and not easily comprehensible – to see, or even to think about, the dead of one's own Regt, whether it is just the Tommies or the NCOs or one's own felllow officers.' In the *A Day of Battle* fragment he wrote: 'For I do remember all the wounded of my own Bn. that I have seen. The poor men, they came from Pontypridd and Nantgarw and Penarth and Dowlais Works and they have queer, odd, guttural accents like the croaking of ravens and they call every hill a mount*ain* . . . and there is no emotion so terrific and so overwhelming as the feeling that comes over you when your own men are dead . . . It shakes you like a force beyond all other forces in the world . . .'

These feelings were resolved into, among others, the poem 'One Day's List':

(Killed. – Second Lieutenants unless otherwise stated.
Arnott, E. E. – Welch Regt.
Jones, E. B. D. – Welch Regt.
Morris, J. H. – Welch Regt.
And 270 other ranks, Welch Regt.

Died of Wounds.

Knapp, O. R. – 2nd Lieut. Welch Regt.)

My dears . . .
The rain drips down on Rouen Town
The leaves drip down
And so the mud
Turns orange brown . . .
A Zeppelin, we read, has been brought down.
And the obscure brown
Populace of London town
Make a shout of it,
Clamouring for blood
And reductions in the price of food . . .
But you – at least – are out of it . . .

Poor little Arnott – poor little lad . . .
And poor old Knapp,
Of whom I once borrowed a map – and never returned it.
And Morris and Jones and all the rest of the Welch,
So many gone in the twenty-four hours of a day . . .
One wonders how one can stay . . .
One wonders . . .
For the papers are full of kelch,
Finding rubbishy news to make a shout of it,
But you at least are out of it.

One wonders how you died . . .
The mine thunders
Still where you stuck by Welch Alley and turned it . . .
The mine thunders
Upwards – and branches of trees, mud, and stone,
Skulls, limbs, rats, thistles, the clips
Of cartridges, beef tins and wire
Belch
To the heavens in fire
From the lips
Of the craters where doubtless you died,
With the Cheshires and Wiltshires and Welch
Side by side.
One wonders *why* you died,

Why were we in it? . . .
At home we were late on parades,
Seldom there to the minute,
When 'B.' were out on Cathays
We didn't get much of the lectures into the brain . . .
We talked a good deal about girls.
We could all tell a story
At something past something, Ack Emma!

But why? why? Why were we there from the Aisne to
  Mametz,
Well – there's a dilemma . . .
For we never talked of glory,
We each thought a lot of one girl,
And waited most days for hours in the rain
Till she came:
But we never talked of Fame . . .

It is very difficult to believe
You need never again
Put in for week-end leave,
Or get vouchers for the 1.10 train
From Cardiff to London . . .
But so much has the Hun done
In the way of achievements.

And when I think of all the bereavements
Of your mothers and fathers and sweethearts and wives and
  homes in the West,
And the paths between the willows waiting for your tread,
And the white pillows
Waiting each for a head,
Well . . . they may go to rest!

And, God help me, if you meet a Hun
In Heaven, I bet you will say, 'Well done,

You fought like mad lions in nets
Down by Mametz.'

But we who remain shall grow old,
We shall know the cold
Of cheerless
Winter and the rain of Autumn and the sting
Of poverty, of love despised and of disgraces,
And mirrors showing stained and ageing faces,
And the long ranges of comfortless years
And the long gamut of human fears . . .
But, for you, it shall be ever spring,
And only you shall be for ever fearless,
And only you have white, straight, tireless limbs,
And only you, where the water-lily swims
Shall walk along the pathways, thro' the willows
Of your West.
You who went west,
And only you on silvery twilight pillows
Shall take your rest
In the soft sweet glooms
Of twilight rooms . . .

No. 2 Red Cross Hospital, Rouen, 7/1/17

Menton was a good rest. 'A peeress of untellable wealth and of inexhaustible benevolence had taken, for us chest-sufferers of H.M. Army . . . for us alone all the Hotel Cap-Martin . . . one of those great, gilded caravanserais that of my own motion I should never have entered . . . We sat at little tables in fantastically palmed and flowering rooms and looked from the shadows of marble walls over a Mediterranean that blazed in the winter sunlight. We ate *Tournedos Meyerbeer* and drank *Château-Pavie* 1906 . . . 1906, think of that . . . We slept in royal suites; the most lovely ladies and the most nobly titled elderly seigneurs walked with us on the terraces over the sea . . . Sometimes we looked round and remarked for a second that we were all being fattened for slaughter . . . But we had endless automobiles at our disposal and Monte Carlo was just around the corner . . .'

As before, and as was often to be again, Provence became his haven and his saviour; Château-Pavie was one of his favourite wines. An officer with him at that time, Claude Lewis, showed Douglas Goldring an inscribed copy of *Between St Dennis and St George* that Ford gave him and 'remembered Ford very clearly as an agreeable companion, in spite of the disparity between their ages, and was greatly impressed by the respect in which he was held by the Provençal people with whom, on various expeditions, they came in contact.'

Ford went with other officers to Monte Carlo where they did some small-scale and apparently successful gambling – 'I tried out poor Marwood's system' – after changing into civilian clothes because officers were forbidden to use the tables. It was probably on the way back from one of these trips that he ran into a little of the trouble he seemed so often to court. His motives were, as usual, better than his tactics:

> I had a disagreeable affair one day coming back from Monte Carlo – in a tram. There were two very very senior officers in that vehicle and a number of French civilians. The senior officers did not belong to any fighting branch: they were civilians given rank so as to have authority when making inspections of military stores. But they were just as bedizened in scarlet and gold as if they had commanded in chief all the troops of the Principality of Monaco. They had with them a lady whom each in turn addressed at the top of his voice. They said, 'Mwor cooshay avec voo!' . . . The French civilians mostly got up and left the tram.
>
> I took the view that my own fortunes were relatively unimportant. I was witnessing the sort of thing that makes us Anglo Saxons not so popular on these shores. It is the duty of junior officers to put their seniors under arrest when they have exceeded. So it became a disagreeable affair.
>
> To console me, I suppose, I was put in charge of a body of my comrades a day or two later . . .

This was to undertake one of the expeditions to which Claude Lewis refers, a visit to a village in the mountains where Ford had to make a speech in Provençal. On their return they were all examined for syphilis since the Army believed that the inhabitants suffered from a strain 'that was to them innocuous but that was extraordinarily malignant to anyone else'. Ford was indignant that they should not have been told until afterwards (though there is no indication that he had personal cause for alarm). Not that Menton was all pleasure. They saw a large number of French Senegalese who were dying of consumption: 'The spectacle of several thousand moonlit negroes lying tuberculous, motionless, and fatalistic along the shores of the Mediterranean sometimes made us not sleep too well.' He had been followed to Menton by Horsetrileyer who

> embarrassed me a good deal, poor fellow. He stuck to me like a shadow when I was in the mood for elegant acquaintance amongst the staid opulences of Menton. But he saw me off. He went rolling like a porpoise to the bookstall to buy me a *Vie Parisienne*. One of my books was in those days covering the whole of France [presumably *Between St Dennis and St George*]. 'Horsetrileyer' came running breathless back to me, his eyes sticking out of his head. He squeezed my fingers into jam and shouted:
>
> 'Oofer, if ever Hi'd known you'd written a book I'd never'f spoken to you as I 'ave!'
>
> It was typical that the sincerest of all tributes to literature should come from an Antipodean mouth beneath the palms of these shores . . .

(It is typical, too, of so much of Ford's writing that the *Harper's* article from which these extracts have been taken should seem so like a delightful conversational meander; and yet, at the end, it is apparent that he never really left his subject – the Côte d'Azur – at all, but was all the time taking you through it. The article is particularly good on how to order meals and how to protest about the bills – 'very, very sorrowfully' – as well as on the importance of garlic: 'The *aïoli* was magnificent: we did not dance with lay partners for three days after eating'. It ends with a hint of sombre prophecy: '. . . regions that have produced the Forum Romanum, the Colosseum, the Campanile of Venice, *aïoli* . . . and the uniform worn by the *fascisti*.')

By early 1917 he was back at Rouen, where there was cold and snow. He had left the warm country 'where the Mediterranean spouts up into the rosemary & lavender . . . for the bare, cold & trampled North, with nothing but khaki for miles & miles . . . Bare downs, & tents . . . & wet valleys . . . & tents . . . & AAC guns . . . mud . . . & bare downs . . . & RFC . . . & mud . . . & motor lorries . . . & mud . . . & bare downs'. It was not good for his lungs but in other respects things were better than when he was last there. He was no longer threatened with return to the 9th Welch but was, he wrote to the poet F. S. Flint, promoted to adjutant and was running a Canadian casual (labour) battalion. It was not glamorous but it was a proper job. He thought it rather like running *The English Review*, only easier, and he was 'personally very happy in this sort of life: in the end it suits me better to write: "O. C. Canadous will detail a fatigue party of 1 NCO & 10 men at 4:30 a.m. . . ." than to watch the Mediterranean foam spattering over rosemary & lavender – for I don't believe I am really, really Highbrow . . .'

The point of that letter was not, however, to describe his own experiences but to ask Flint to gather and publish the war poems he had been writing 'before the war ends or I am killed'. He had some himself and had sent others to Mrs Jackson, Mrs Masterman and Mrs Wells, but not, it seems, to Violet. He and she were still in correspondence but the signs were of increasing resentment on her part and on his of increasing suspicion that she was more interested in damaging than supporting him.

He was with the labour battalion only a few weeks but he could at least feel himself to be properly in harness. It was the commanding officer of this battalion who, after Ford had returned to Britain, applied for him to be posted back. Near the end of February he was sent to Abbeville, another region of mud and bare downs, to command prisoners of war. It was a task to which he was probably well-suited, having their language, a sense of fairness and decency and a belief in the necessity for discipline, but it was not a congenial one. It did not last long because the doctors intervened again and in mid-March he was invalided home on account of his lungs. He was given light duties as a captain attached to the 23rd King's Liverpool Regiment at Kinmel Park, though he was officially under medical treatment until mid-May.

Here he found another commanding officer, Lieutenant Colonel G. R. Powell, with whom he got on. When *On Heaven* was published he dedicated the book to Powell and gave him an inscribed copy as a wedding present. Powell wrote a recommendation on Ford's service record: 'Has shown marked aptitude for grasping any intricate subject and possesses great powers of organisation – a lecturer of the first water on several military subjects – conducted the duties of Housing Officer to the unit (average strength 2,800) with great ability.' Ford must have been very pleased with this measure of official vindication, as well he might have been because Housing Officer is another of those detailed, untidy and thankless tasks, particularly with so large a unit. He was promoted substantive lieutenant on 1 July 1917, being already Acting Captain.

Money again became a serious problem. On active service in France the pay was better and expenses negligible; it wasn't much but he could survive, while in Britain the pay was reduced and the expenses, particularly for officers, increased dramatically. He was no longer able to supplement his income with journalism, having neither the time nor, he felt, the contacts he had had before the war. He may have exaggerated his own literary eclipse caused by war service but it was understandable that he felt out of the swim: those of his books that were in print were not selling well, he had little on the stocks and for the first time for many years he did not sleep, eat and drink Literature; his contacts with literary people were mainly by letter. In the long run it was no bad thing since literature is not made by being literary but it had been his daily bread, such as it was, and the future was not encouraging. It was at this time that he tried to return to France, with the help of the obliging colonel of the labour battalion, but the medical board would not pass him fit for General Service. 'I have a desire to be out there which is almost nostalgia,' he wrote to Lucy Masterman. '. . . It is annoying because a Labour Bn is just as dangerous & uncomfortable as a Service one, yet the credit is less. However, I don't mind that.'

He was sent instead to join the staff of a training command at Redcar in Yorkshire where he inspected, trained and lectured throughout the north of England. In January 1918 he was promoted from acting to substantive captain, which must have eased financial pressures a little. He told his bank, Cox & Co., to send £2 a month to Katharine and he put some money into the War Loan for her. In March 1918 he was promoted to temporary brevet major. More, perhaps unexpected, money came from his share of the advance of the new Nelson edition of *Romance*. Nevertheless, typically Fordian incidents continued to occur. In August 1918 he was to defend a man at a court martial (mentioned earlier) but before the man came to trial he 'rushed into my tent, having escaped from his escort: tried to strangle his father, bit me, and has just been carried off to an asylum . . . If there is anything of that sort going on, I am usually in it!' He liked his job and when the Armistice came in November 1918 he was in no hurry to leave the Army. In fact, he hoped to stay on and secure promotion to lieutenant colonel as Education Adviser to Northern Command, but it was not to be. When he did leave, officially on 1 January 1919, he found he was in discharge category 19 '– authors, gipsies, travelling showmen, unemployables. We were non-productives and so to be discharged last!' He thought this a disgraceful display not so much of Army bureaucracy as of English philistinism, and often quoted it.

Not many established writers went into that war and though he knew two that had – Wyndham Lewis and Edward Thomas – he may have been right in his belief that he was the only established and well known novelist to bear arms. The canon of Great War literature, especially the poetry, is deservedly appreciated now but most of it was written by men for whom the war was their first, great and sometimes only subject. Perhaps if Ford had had no reputation at all his war poetry and subsequent novels might have become as well known as others. It may have been that very reputation, the fact that he *was* a literary figure, not new and more than slightly soiled, that meant that people did not look for anything new in what he wrote.

What the war gave him was not only a subject and a bigger background for his themes (as did its continuation for later writers such as Evelyn Waugh and Anthony Powell), nor simply an enlargement of his already generous sympathy, but confidence. For all the shell-shock, the neurasthenia, the memory loss, despite the conviction that he was a forgotten writer and the occasional protestations that he had abandoned literature, it gave him the confidence that a writer was what he really was, conclusively and absolutely. He may have been a failed one but there was no longer any question as to the nature of his existence on earth. He had been through the fire and everything inessential had been burned off. He also learned what he had always known – how to live simply – but he had learned it more thoroughly after two to three years of living largely in the open air. A few vegetables, a rabbit, a leaky hut and an upturned ammunition box would do for him now. He needed someone to share it, of course, in the same way that he needed a readership. After discharge he lived in a single room at 20a Campden Hill Gardens – not at South Lodge – where, as he said of one of his characters, 'his dressing-gown was his overcoat. Beneath this . . . a blue-grey army shirt and a pair of khaki slacks . . . blue-grey woollen socks and scarlet, heel-less Turkish slippers.' Like Tietjens, he slept on a 'camp-bed for the use of officers, G. S. one'. No longer the man-about-town, no longer the would-be squire, no longer the dashing editor – and no longer the agoraphobic. He had shed much.

Wells wouldn't have agreed. He wrote to Goldring: 'The pre-war FMH was tortuous but understandable, the post-war FMH was incurably *crazy*. He got crazier and crazier.' He caricatured Ford in *The Bulpington of Blup*. Wells's view was influenced by the volume of reminiscences Ford wrote immediately after the war, *Thus to Revisit*. He wrote this before he was recovered, as he later acknowledged, but Wells did not distinguish between the anecdotal rambler and the author of *Parade's End*. The one was an extension of table-talk, fed by a generous imagination and an enthusiasm for Château-Pavie, the other a product of a view of life that was deep and sane. It may be that the mad can paint great paintings, write great music or perhaps even write great poetry – it *may* be – but to write great novels it is necessary, at least at the time of writing, to be uncommonly sane. You need to see clearly, to see through, to perceive relations, to make them clear to others and to see with the eyes of others. Solipsists and mad people do not do that. Great writers may go mad but great literature is written sanely.

For Ford, meanwhile, that last year of the war was bringing changes not apparent from its beginnings.

TWENTY

After he was posted back to Britain in 1917 and after the failure of his attempt to return to France, he and Violet began to see more of each other. Most of his mail still went to South Lodge, where Violet got her maid, Annie Child, to open it. She thus maintained what became an increasingly vindictive watch over him, at one point humiliating him by drawing out all £72 in his bank account on two forged cheques, so that his own were dishonoured. Even many years later this could be a serious matter for a commissioned officer; Ford was always conscious of the need to behave honourably and never referred to her having done it – referring instead to it having been done by 'a friend' – but he would have been deeply embarrassed. It was also during this period that Mary, now much more Violet's friend than his, followed him up Campden Hill, cursing him.

Although he and Violet spent some of his leaves together at Selsey, by January 1918 he was asking Lucy Masterman if she knew of any cheap lodgings he could take in her part of London for his next leave since 'South Lodge does not seem to be available'. Yet in that year Violet spent time with him up in Redcar, where he irritated her by eating all the cream and going on duty during air-raids when she thought he should have stayed with her. She was probably more seriously annoyed to discover that in selecting the pieces to go in *On Heaven* and *Poems Written on Active Service* (published in 1918 by John Lane) he had sought the help of his colonel's wife (whether the newly married Mrs Powell or whether another is not clear and in a sense didn't matter: he *had* to have sympathetic female companionship, and he could always find it). What might further have annoyed Violet was the inclusion in the volume of what she called 'some cheap silly pieces', probably the poems written for that earlier sympathetic companion, Mrs Jackson. Also, Violet felt that the preface belittled 'On Heaven', the poem dedicated to her. It was not a very happy stay.

At the same time as saying and perhaps feeling that he would abandon literature, which was probably a reaction to the more worrying feeling that it was abandoning him, he was writing when he could and urging Pinker to publish whatever could be published. He was very keen to have a collected edition of his works and remained so throughout his life, without ever achieving it. In 1919 he spoke of himself as having written nothing for seven years, probably meaning nothing worthwhile since *The Good Soldier* in 1913. Perhaps by his standards he hadn't but the seven years following 1912 produced what most writers even in peacetime would consider a respectable bag: two novels, two Wellington House books, two unfinished novels, over one hundred articles (mostly in *Outlook*) and the *On Heaven* poems. Friends were active on his behalf: Pound got the fragment *Women and Men* published and Pinker did what he could; but money was still the problem. *The Good Soldier*, his great work, had earned him just £67 11/11d and the publisher, John Lane, lost £54 10/-. Ford was both disbelieving of and dismayed by these figures.

But he remained ever-helpful to the aspiring, revealing in the process something of his own aims and approach, particularly in poetry. In July 1918 he wrote from his sick-bed in Ripon (he had 'neuritis') to Iris Barry about the poem she had sent him. Referring to himself as an extinct volcano, he praised her for writing *things* rather than *about* things: 'There is a certain I was going to say ferocity – but let us say determination of attack on visible objects that I have always tried to get at myself – without much success – but that you seem to get in your stride . . .' There, in a sentence, is a statement of his inability to confront, an inability that encompassed physical objects, marital rows, scenes of all kinds and courts of law. Perhaps he was of too human kind to bear very much reality; his responses to confrontations were so overwhelming that he made his subjects the moods, feelings and states of mind that the confrontations provoked rather than what was being confronted. If he had written murder stories there would have been plenty of horror, long aching silences, much anguish and words and gestures that were small and terrible, but not many corpses and hardly any ice-axes.

He goes on to say to Iris Barry that a volume of poems 'isn't a set of cubes or mosaics exhibited in the black velvet of museum cases. It is a quiet monologue during a summer walk during which one seeks to render oneself beloved to someone one loves. It is a revelation of personality that wants sympathy from men of good-will – not a bludgeoning of Times Literary Supplements or a display of dexterity. That is what, for the time being, is wrong with yr. Imagiste & Cubist associates. They are too much "out" for the purpose of expressing scorn, & try to be lovable in original media – too little. Of course that is a phase that will pass with youth – which eventually sees that clubbing one's grandfather is only a means to an end. One wd. have done more if one had perceived that truth earlier.'

It was in the spring of 1918 that he met Stella Bowen. She was twenty-three, attractive, enthusiastic, unattached, an Australian studying art in London and relishing the cosmopolitan intellectual world into which she had fallen. He was forty-four, married, involved in a dying and joyless affair, shell-shocked, unsure that he could write again and very hard up. She wrote of their meeting:

> Ford was an innovation in our circle because not only was he in khaki but he actually liked it. He was the only intellectual I had met to whom army discipline provided a conscious release from the torments and indecisions of a super-sensitive brain. To obey orders was, to him, a positive holiday, and the pleasure he took in recounting rather bucolic anecdotes of the army was a measure of his need for escape from the intrigues and sophistication of literary London.
>
> Ford was considerably older than the rest of our friends, and much more impressive. He was very large, with a pink face, yellow hair, and drooping bright blue eyes. His movements were gentle and deliberate and his quiet and mellow voice spoke, to an Australian ear, with ineffable authority . . .
>
> He had known everyone, and was full of stories . . .
>
> I reacted violently against him at first on the grounds that he was a militarist. But I soon found that if he was a militarist, he

was at the same time the exact opposite. When I got to know him better, I found that every known human quality could be found flourishing in Ford's make-up, except for respect for logic. His attitude to science was very simple. He just did not believe a word of it! But he could show you two sides simultaneously of any human affair, and the double picture made the subject come alive, and stand out in a third-dimensional way that was very exciting. What he did not know about the depths and weaknesses of human nature was not worth knowing. The hidden places of the heart were his especial domains, and when he chose he could put the screws upon your sense of pity or fear with devastating sureness.

The stiff, rather alarming exterior and the conventional, omniscient manner, concealed a highly complicated emotional machinery. It produced an effect of tragic vulnerability: tragic because the scope of his understanding and the breadth of his imagination had produced a great edifice which was plainly in need of more support than was inherent in the structure itself. A walking temptation to any woman, had I but known it!

To me he was most simply the most enthralling person I had ever met.

It is not easy to say much that is new about their relationship because Stella told it all so well in her autobiography, *Drawn From Life*. She was an understanding, generous and honest woman with that naïvety that is temperamental rather than intellectual, more a matter of trusting than of not seeing, a quality that in time matured into shrewdness and realism. The book is worth reading for her and its sake quite apart from the unmatched portrait of Ford which it offers.

She came from Adelaide, the daughter of an estate agent who had died when she was three. Her education and upbringing were sound and respectable within quite narrow limits, a healthy, tennis-playing, church-going, good sort of life. Her artistic talents, probably inherited from her father, led her firstly to art school and then, following the death of her mother, to England in 1914. She needed her guardian's permission to travel and was supposed to stay only a year until her younger brother finished at school. She boarded with a family in Pimlico and then with an artist, Peggy Sutton, in Chelsea. This and the people she met at the Westminster School of Art, where she was taught by Sickert, led her into an artistic milieu that soon broadened to include Pound, Eliot, Wyndham Lewis, Yeats, Arthur Waley, G. B. Stern, Mary Butts, May Sinclair, Violet Hunt and, eventually, Ford. By this time she had established an independent life in Pembroke Studios with a beautiful drama student, Phyllis Reid, and they entertained most of the above, and others, at what Stella called 'beer and gramophone parties'.

It seems extraordinary good luck to have arrived in a city where so many people lead lonely and frustrated lives and to have fallen straight into its literary and artistic heart at a time when there really was such a life and it had a real heart. It is always, of course, a question of knowing whom rather than what, and Stella was fortunate in her early contacts. She could so easily have spent a friendless and confusing year and then returned to Adelaide. But it probably wasn't entirely adventitious: nearly everyone welcomes attractive young women and she had about her a kind of vital, unaggressive openness that warmed people to her. That ability to make friends never left her and her life was her personality writ large. Her daughter, Julia Loewe, wrote that Stella's favourite proverb was the Spanish one that was also Ford's favourite: 'Take what you want,' said God, 'take it, and pay for it.' She did both and she never went back to Adelaide.

They met through Ezra Pound. He used to go to the Pembroke Studios parties and in return invited the two girls to his weekly lunch at Bellotti's in Soho. She knew Ford by reputation because 'he was one of the writers whom Ezra allowed us to admire'. He

> revealed himself as a lonely and very tired person who wanted to dig potatoes and raise pigs and never write another book. Wanted to start a new home. Wanted a child . . . I said 'yes', of course . . . I was ready, I felt stalwart and prepared for anything . . . I did not realise to what extent he would be putting his clock back, whilst I put mine forward . . . It was what he wanted, and when Ford wanted anything he filled the sky with an immense ache that had the awful simplicity of a child's grief,

> and appeared to hold the same possibilities of assuagement . . . our union was an excellent bargain on both sides . . . Ford got his cottage, and he got the domestic peace he needed, and eventually he got his baby daughter. He was very happy, and so was I. What I got out of it, was a remarkable and a liberal education, administered in ideal circumstances. I got an emotional education too, of course, but that was easier. One might get that from almost anyone! But to have the run of a mind of that calibre, with all its inconsistencies, its generosity, its blind spots, its spaciousness, and vision, and its great sense of form and style, was a privilege for which I am still trying to say 'thank you'.

That was written after Ford's death and more than a decade after their 'union' ended.

They were corresponding by June 1918 and it is usually assumed that they became lovers during that summer. Possibly they did, though the change of address in his letters from 'My dear' to 'My dear darling' occurs only after her visit to Redcar in October. Until that point Violet still seems to have been involved. In August Ford wrote to Stella: 'I am sorry you are not coming to Runswick Bay with V' and in October, when she did visit, Stella telegraphed Violet at Selsey: 'Shall stay here till you come or he leaves as doctor says he must have nursing.' Perhaps we should not look for anything too clear-cut in Ford's relations with women; after all, the relations he wrote about were often far from clear-cut. In September 1918 he returned to an old theme unconnected with either women: 'The poor old Welch have been getting chawed up in France. My own battalion had four officers killed and eight wounded last week – so a lot of us will be going at once. I hate not being there.' He still wanted to join in.

Just before the armistice he fell out with Arnold Bennett who, as Director of Propaganda in France, had asked him to write about the British peace terms but had been presented instead with Ford's plan for the entire peace settlement. Ford believed that his views had been censored and, later, that he had even been refused a passport for France and possibly prevented from staying on in the Army, all for this. It is unlikely that Bennett did any more than ignore the views offered him and Ford's reactions are probably more indicative of his sense of estrangement from the literary and semi-public world that had once been his than of any reasoned hypothesis. He was not, as he later said of himself, quite normal at that time; indeed, he made an eloquent plea to the effect that all those returning from the Front should be regarded as mad for two or three years and therefore not subject to the normal processes of law. He attended or heard about the trials of one or two people with whom he had served.

It did not help when he came to London in December 1918 for a Christmas party given by the French Embassy for British writers who had furthered the French cause. The only face he recognised was the round ruddy one of Bennett which contrasted with the 'pallid and misshapenly elongated' faces that seemed to be standard for other British writers – 'they seemed all unusually long, pale and screwed to one side or the other.' Bennett appeared 'like a round red sun rising from among vertical shapes of cloud' but he and Ford were not by then on speaking terms. Ford, still in uniform, stood alone, feeling conspicuous. 'Pale faces swam, inspectantly, towards me. But, as you may see fishes do round a bait in dim water, each one checked suddenly and swam away with a face expressing piscine distaste. I imagine that the barb of a hook must protrude somewhere from my person . . .' Eventually he was approached by a large black figure with 'the aspect of an undertaker coming to measure a corpse . . . "You used to write," it intoned, "didn't you?"' This disagreement over the peace terms was almost certainly the material he transformed into Mark Tietjens's renunciation of public service in *Parade's End*.

At Redcar in October he and Stella watched what they believed was the last convoy to sail for France from Tees Bay. When the armistice came she was in London, he at Easton in Yorkshire. She spent part of the day on top of one of the old open buses with Ezra Pound, who banged his stick on the side and harangued passengers in other buses. Ford wrote from Easton: 'Just a note to say I love you more than ever. Peace has come, and for some reason I feel inexpressibly sad. I suppose it's the breaking down of all the old strain.' She visited him for his birthday on 17 December. Interestingly, his letters still refer to her 'talking to V' about coming up.

The letters he wrote to Stella while he was still in the Army are unfortunately too long to quote in full. They are amusing and very true to British Army life. There is, for instance, an account of what happened when he appropriated the brigadier's car after a dance, mistaking the brigadier for the driver, for the purpose of taking home his companion, the quartermaster's daughter. This meant that his colonel's lady was deprived of a lift home since she was unwilling to squeeze in with the quartermaster's daughter. The repercussions were outrageous and wholly credible. Several officers requested transfers, resignations were tendered, there were scenes, Ford delivered perorations to the left and the right of him, there was talk of involving the commander-in-chief and the adjutant was seen to pale; finally, all was settled amicably. It was a typically Fordian business, he having been the unwitting agent who had then inflated it hugely because of a point of principle which had bubbled to the surface – in this case, the social equality of officers. Having won his point he concluded his account: 'I tell you all this because it strikes me as comic – I mean my bothering my head and getting into the most frightful tempers on the surface, over such matters. But still it *is* a serious thing for the Army, wh. is the only thing I care much about, when Colonel's wives won't ride with Q.M.'s daughters.' (It is tempting to wonder whether there wasn't also some inwardness over his taking the Q.M.'s daughter to the dance. The colonel's lady, Mrs Pope, might have felt put out because he had previously been attentive to her – in the matter of his poems, for instance. That would make the whole affair yet more thoroughly and satisfactorily Fordian.) The episode is instructive because it is reminiscent of some of the literary rows he had; there being no equivalent of Army Council Instructions to regulate civilian behaviour, no commander-in-chief to act as final arbiter and no possibility of resigning from civilian life, such rows had scope to matter more. He was aware of this himself:

> I have been having a most frightful strafe all this morning and afternoon with the Quarter Master (the father of the girl) – not a quarrel but an endless argument before the C.O., the adjutant

and the P.R.I.[1] as to where 'postings' are to go on arrival – and, as no one in H.Q. knows anything about it, we both invented A.C.I.'s[2] and authorities as hard as we could go and roared at each other and grew purple in the face with rage – and then went off arm in arm to the mess and had drinks.

It is funny how you can get into the most violent rages over duty and yet be the best of friends in the Mess two seconds later, without a syllable about what went on over the road. I wonder if it wouldn't be possible to conduct married life on that sort of line: it wd. be a tremendous solution.

Perhaps he could manage this sort of confrontation because he was acting a part, because he wasn't himself involved, and perhaps that was one reason why the Army suited him: it provided him with a role, a costume and, as it were, a stage-name, all of which he lacked until then. It gave him an identity which meant he could rest from his uncertainties as well as shield them from public view, but at the same time it did not attempt to take over his private life and reflections. He could still be himself underneath that shield.

The letters show how genuinely he relished much of what he was doing. He played golf, billiards, bridge, hockey (aged forty-five now), got drunk in the mess sometimes, went to Mass sometimes, prepared the cookhouses for inspection, lectured on tactics and calmly noted that half the battalion was deployed in Middlesbrough 'to be prepared for election riots'. At his C.O.'s request, he even stayed on for a week after he had been gazetted out of the Army.

It pleased him greatly one day to overhear three junior officers – 'little boys' – talking about who was the coolest person 'on a certain night in Jy. 1916 when we were suddenly shelled from behind Bécort Wood'. They agreed it was 'Old Hoof' and that 'Old Hoof ought to have had the M.C. only the C.O. didn't like him.' This caused him genuine, almost boyish delight and his description of what prompted it rings true:

[1] President of the Regimental Institute, concerned with finance and administration.

[2] Army Council Instructions

I remember the occasion quite well: I was so busy looking after an officer who had got very drunk and was trying to expose himself, that I never really noticed the shelling at all except that I was covered with tins of sardines and things that had been put out for our dinner.

That was really the worst of the front from the novelist's point of view. One was always so busy with one's immediate job that one had no time to notice one's sensations or anything else that went on around one.

As with Violet during the early days, it was hard for him and Stella to find anywhere where they could be alone for any length of time. When he left the Army he had his room in Campden Hill with his camp-bed and his kit, then Stella found a cottage at Bottom Farm in Berkhamsted where they spent occasional days. He was much cheered by being able to see her there but was often in low spirits and talked of getting up 'monotonously, and wetly and longly'. Like many soldiers, he had learned to cope with the war but the peace that followed brought its own problems: 'you may say that everyone who had taken physical part in the war was then mad. No one could have come through that shattering experience and still view life and mankind with any normal vision. In those days you saw objects that the earlier mind had labelled as *houses*. They had used to seem cubic and solid permanences. But we had seen Ploegsteert, where it had been revealed that men's dwellings were thin shells that could be crushed as walnuts are crushed . . . All things that lived and moved and had volition and life might at any moment be resolved into a scarlet viscosity seeping into the earth of torn fields . . . We who returned . . . were like wanderers coming back to our own shores to find our settlements occupied by a vindictive and savage tribe. We had no chance. The world of men was changed and our places were taken by strangers.'

No one had taken his place with Violet, though. She still wanted him to appear at South Lodge but when he did she berated him. It seems that she did not at this stage know that he was Stella's lover, though she may have suspected, or might have known but thought it less serious than it was. He told Stella he wasn't worried by Violet's attacks, to which Stella shrewdly responded, 'You know they kill you really.' Pressed by Violet, he told her she did not 'realise how you hurt me. How you drove me out of the house by insults – saying I only lived with you for the sake of your money. I will not, I will not sleep in the house again . . .'

In *No Enemy* Gringoire in the trenches had a sustaining vision of a green nook. It took a variety of forms but it kept him going. The belief in its possibility, that it existed somewhere, that it offered rest and seclusion not only from shell-fire but from the more insidiously worrying and damaging 'strafing' of daily life, largely took the place for Gringoire that burying heads in women's laps had taken for earlier Fordian heroes. It did the same for Ford and in April 1919 he found it at a cottage called Red Ford, near Pulborough in West Sussex. It was a 'leaky-roofed, tile-headed, rat-ridden, seventeenth-century, five-shilling-a-week, moribund labourer's cottage.' One or two ceilings were down, the lath and plaster walls were disintegrating, there was a hole in the roof (which was there for some time: Herbert Read, who came to say, remembered lying in bed and seeing the stars), water had to be fetched from a hole in the garden and its only link to the road was a long and muddy lane. But it was a retreat and he loved it.

So did Stella. She describes it as 'built of old red brick and old red tiles, all greened over with mossy stains, and it was tucked under a little red sandstone cliff, and faced over a lush meadow which sloped downwards to a little stream, and upwards to a wood on the opposite side.' Ford poured paraffin down the rat holes, put in an oil stove for cooking, built a leaky lean-to to go over it, laid some of his precious oak boards (a job-lot in a sale) over the mud on the floor, bought and made furniture, made a pig sty and got the garden going. He was a better gardener than handyman, perhaps even as good a gardener as he was a cook. In *No Enemy* he poked gentle fun at the inspired recklessness of Gringoire's cooking, as Stella did at his own: he 'reduced the kitchen to the completest chaos. When he cooked one kitchen-maid was hardly sufficient to wait upon him.' It wasn't always he who did the cooking, though:

> It was some time before I became skilful enough to deputise for him in the kitchen, but this became necessary when at last I

persuaded him to start another book. Then he would retire upstairs to write, and leave me to wrestle with the dinner. At eight I would say, 'Are you ready to eat?' and he would reply, 'In a minute.' At eight thirty I would say, 'It is eight thirty, darling,' and he would reply, 'Oh give me another twenty minutes,' and I would return to the kitchen and concoct something extra – another vegetable, or a savoury. At nine I'd say, 'What about it?' and he'd tell me to put the meal on the table. At nine thirty I would suggest putting it back on the fire to re-heat. 'What!' he'd cry, 'Dinner on the table all this time? Why ever didn't you tell me?' Well, we'd eat perhaps at ten, with enormous appetite and discuss the progress of his book and of my cooking. We enjoyed ourselves.

His working routine varied at different places and at different times of his life. In Sussex it was gardening and chores in the morning, lunch, a long walk in the afternoon, a late tea and then he would go to his desk. Though the details varied, the existence of a routine was almost life-long.

At the start, however, it hadn't been easy to get there. He had moved in in April 1919, for a while keeping his room on in London, but Stella did not wish her brother, Tom, to know of the arrangement. She did not move down until Tom, who had also been at the Front, was demobbed and returned to Australia. Another complication was that they were trying to keep it secret from Violet. Stella spent only one weekend there during April and May. Meanwhile, Ford busied himself about house and garden, ordering paint, seed-potatoes and coconut matting through Stella, who busied herself with blankets and mattress (Ford still had only his camp bed since what was left of the furniture he owned was at South Lodge). He acquired a mongrel called Beau and at his urging Stella scoured London for a cheap Sealyham. When she found one, a puppy, there was a problem about bringing it to Sussex as 'a 6 month's quarantine is now insisted on. London is now an infected area – there was a mad dog yesterday in Holland Road.' They decided to call it Brigadier as Ford had served under Brigadier Sely.

He was very happy to be pottering about among domestic and

horticultural details. Primitive conditions never bothered him and were more than compensated for by his delight at getting his peas to grow, at buying something cheap in a sale or at building a rickety table. He was proud to enter his potatoes for the Pulborough Annual Show, and, in a matter of weeks, became an enthusiast of the Sussex Large Black Pig. It was the kind of recuperation that he and many others needed but the after effects of the war were still obvious, not only psychologically: he had boils, trouble with one leg and in May a neck-tumour had to be removed.

In one of his volumes of reminiscence, *It was the Nightingale*, there is a memorable description of his first dinner at Red Ford when, with a bottle of port and a leg of mutton, he waited to see whether the skins would come off the simmering shallots as a sign that he should go on living, or not. In *No Enemy* a less despairing state of mind is portrayed: 'When Gringoire entered it [the cottage] in the early spring, there had certainly been the wave-marks of inundations and half-inches of mud on the brick floors. He had come down with his valise contents, his camp-bed, a knife and fork, a paraffin stove and a gallon of oil, determined, as he puts it, to dig himself in in the face of destiny.' Writing to Stella on the actual night of his arrival, however, Ford said: 'My first feelings of dismay at the dilapidation of the house have given way to comparative complacency after a meal of fried chicken and beans and oranges – but *no* drink' (perhaps she had been getting at him about his drinking). These three accounts provide a good example of how Ford dealt with facts in his writing: straightforwardly in the letter, as a novelist would in the novel and still as a novelist in the autobiography where he used the incident to create an impression of how he felt, if not at that time then at others.

The fiction he then began writing was in fact more literally autobiographical than most of his autobiography. He was working on the manuscript that became *That Same Poor Man*, in which Mr Croyd seeks refuge in the life of the Small Producer just as his creator was doing. The landscape articles called 'English Country' which he was writing for the *New Statesman* became chapters two and three of *No Enemy*. He was re-creating, in fact and literature, his own life, a process that could almost be described as natural psychotherapy. He was not yet able to achieve again what he had achieved so triumphantly in *The Good Soldier*: that distance from the raw material of his life that allows it to be transmuted into art. *No Enemy* is only not an excellent war novel because it is hardly a novel at all, but it is excellent war writing and an excellent read.

In June 1919 he changed his surname by deed poll from Hueffer to Ford. He told Pinker that it was 'partly to oblige a relative & partly because a Teutonic name is in these days disagreeable & though my native stubbornness would not let me do it while the war was on, I do not see why I sh. go on being subjected to the attacks of blackmailers indefinitely.' To Masterman he wrote (from the Authors' Club in Whitehall, which he now used on his visits to London) that he 'would not do this out of obstinacy, while the war was still on but I see now no longer any reason to put up with the inconvenience that a Teutonic patronymic causes in the rather humble sphere of life that I now adorn.' Perhaps more importantly, he did not want to risk any repetition of law suits by Elsie in the event of Stella's being referred to as Mrs Hueffer. The name he chose has not, of course, helped him. There are unavoidable associations with motor cars and, if he is not thought to be a relative of Henry Ford, he is often assumed to have been his own maternal grandfather. He chose Ford, it is believed, because it resembled Conrad's name in that it could be used both as first and surname.

Stella joined him that month. She arrived with septic tonsilitis, which he caught, and their first pig died of a chill. But they were happy. 'I even loved the pigs,' she wrote '. . . We took such perpetual and unanimous pleasure in the *look* of everything, the sky and the weather and the view and the garden and the arrangement of our cottage . . .' It was to this period she was referring when she wrote: 'You can live on a view. Almost.' This applied as much to Ford as to herself but that 'almost' is important; for anyone living with him the view was often just about all there was to live on. The green nook was not a complete haven. Pound wrote in 'Mauberley 10':

> The haven from sophistication and contentions
> Leaks through its thatch;
> He offers succulent cooking;
> The door has a creaking latch . . .

But money had still to be earned, articles and books to be written, things made to grow where they hadn't, animals to live when they inclined to die or made to stay where they didn't want. The pigs used to get out and had to be chased up and down the lane, the pony ate enormous quantities of hay and there was a goat named Penny, after Pound. Also, Violet had to be told.

They used an intermediary, Ethel Mayne. Stella urged Ford to continue to appear occasionally at South Lodge and he agreed to do so but insisted to all his correspondents that they should keep his Red Ford address a secret. This may have seemed unnecessarily dramatic but subsequent events again proved his prescience. When Violet was told she unleashed her exasperation on Ford's mother and sister, who were perhaps by this time used to coping with his womenfolk, then took to her bed and summoned Ford to appear. Urged by Stella, he went. They argued it out by her bedside all one Monday morning. Afterwards Violet wrote to Mrs Hueffer that 'he had come at another woman's petition . . . We have agreed to stay together without love . . .' Ford may have been a little tougher than he normally was in such situations because he was genuinely angry that some people were saying that Violet had kept him. Also, his understanding of what they had agreed was not quite hers. When he wrote to his mother about the episode he said he had agreed at Stella's request to appear at Violet's parties 'to save Violet the mortification of appearing officially deserted . . . only it does not make things easier when Violet turned up & made a scene at my Club on the afternoon of her party . . .'

This is further illustration that Violet's principal concern was her position. In the early days of their relationship that concern had been ameliorated by love but it outlived emotion and it is a testament to its strength that it eventually survived even her bitterness. At this stage, though, she would have preferred to have him and hate him than to see him disappear. He did turn up at at least one or two of her parties; Alec Waugh records seeing him 'moon around looking very lost. He did not seem to know if he was a guest or host. He appeared surprised when I went up to say "goodbye" and "thank you".' It is not hard to imagine the state of mind in which he would have got himself up in his white tie.

For all its charms, and even by Ford's standards, Red Ford was not a very practical place to live and they soon began looking round for something to buy in the area. Stella had an inheritance on which they could draw and he had a windfall of £429 from Pinker's sale of the film rights of *Romance*. In fact, Pinker sold the rights for $5,000 but took out of Ford's half what Ford owed him. The amount owing surprised Ford; bad news about money always did. Stella wrote that 'his whole system rejected any knowledge of money matters . . . the smallest unexpected cheque would inspire a mood of ebullient optimism which led to an immediate orgy of spending . . . and a new bill to arrive at the next awkward moment . . .' Nevertheless, with £400 from him and the rest from Stella they were able in August 1919 to buy Cooper's Cottage in nearby Bedham. But they had to wait for the tenants to die before they could move in and then the house needed work to make it habitable, so it was not until September 1920 that they actually took possession.

The intervening year was spent at Red Ford, in winter mud grimly reminiscent of Flanders, and at a farmhouse they rented at Bedham, called Scammell's Farm. That part of Sussex is characterised by wooded downland with wide views, tall beeches, flint farmhouses, dramatic scarps, tiny twisting lanes and great southwesterly rains (they were, in fact, near where Edward Thomas had lived) and during the summers they had no shortage of visitors. But few relished the dark, cold and mud of winter and conditions even in summer were alarmingly primitive to some. Ford and Stella gloried in it until the long winter nights and the seemingly endless wet finally got to them.

His failed attempts to keep their address secret from Violet were vindicated by her actions when she found out. In August 1920 Pound visited them at Scammell's and Ford believed that Violet might have had him followed there by a private detective. Soon after, when they had moved into Cooper's, she 'planted herself in the neighbourhood & runs about interrupting my workmen & generally making things lively'. She did more; with May Sinclair she hung over his gate and watched him feeding his pigs. Next she found someone to spy on him. This was another Mrs Hunt, the wife of the local carpenter who was helping repair Cooper's Cottage. Violet paid her to send reports on what Ford and Stella were doing, though she was a better soul than this makes her sound. She was under the illusion that Ford was Violet's husband but even so there were limits to what she was prepared to do and when Violet pushed her to them, she terminated the agreement.

It seems Ford was aware of what was going on, since in *Parade's End* he has Sylvia spy on Tietjens and Valentine Wannop in just this way. He doesn't seem to have responded to it at the time or been anything other than obliging to Mrs Hunt, but it must have been aggravating, to say the very least, because by then Stella was heavily pregnant (like Valentine Wannop) and such attentions could easily be upsetting. Fortunately, she was robust: their mare could overtake cars on the very steep Bedham Hill and she recalled one occasion 'when we had the pleasure of passing, without a flicker of recognition, a whole car-load of London busy-bodies coming to peep at Ford in his new retreat, gently rolling backwards down the hill!' One of those who pursued them was Mary.

Not content with this, Violet also called on Elsie, who was living at Aldington. She called unannounced, seemingly with no clear aim but presumably prompted by her inability to leave anything to do with Ford alone. She offered to settle a legacy on Katharine, but did not. Afterwards she wrote a rather self-dramatising letter complimenting Elsie on her dignity, self-control and 'wonderful attitude towards F.'. She referred to herself as 'still storm-tossed' and remarked in passing that 'dreadful things have been happening', with no further detail.

Ford was now writing articles for *The Dial* and for his own former magazine, *The English Review*, as well as working on *That Same Poor Man*. The future was resolving itself into writing, Stella, the baby, Cooper's Cottage and the ten acres on which they hoped they would become self-supporting. Nothing in this was certain: he and Stella were living together unmarried – though she was referred to as Mrs Ford – in an age when marriage mattered more; the baby was an unknown quantity, much wanted[1] but an extra mouth to feed; writing was as necessary and continuous as ever but there was no indication that it had any future and for all he

[1] By Ford, anyway. Stella later told Janice Biala that when she found she was pregnant she felt utterly 'trapped'.

knew he had written himself out; finally self-sufficiency on a few acres is an idea that has appealed to many but he might have known, at least in his heart, that it couldn't work. Perhaps he did. Stella said that if confronted with the possibility of failure he would 'collapse into such a misery of despair that our entire lives became paralysed . . . he could not finish a book if his mind was upset . . . I must manage to keep all worries from him . . . I must not let him know how overdrawn we were at the bank, nor how big the bills from the corn mills had become, nor how badly we needed a paraffin tank . . .'

It was a heavy load for her to bear. Without independent money, the combination of farming and writing is likely to be too much for anyone. Both are unremitting and uncertain, demanding daily attendance, acknowledging no limits and significantly influenced by luck. Small family farms survived into recent times but the holdings were larger than ten acres, the living was generally poor, the whole family worked and there was no other full-time continuous activity. Ford and Stella, however, paid wages to Mrs Hunt's husband and son, to an old man called Standing, to a young woman called Lucy and to another man for a little gardening. Ford never paid less than the top rate. They had two sows and their litters, thirty hens, twenty ducks, three goats and the old mare to keep on those ten acres of garden and rough hillside. Even though they killed and dressed their own pigs every animal must have cost far more than it earned. Also, Standing was often observed by Mrs Hunt's sons to take measures of Ford's pig food home to his own pig. But they were happy for much of the time, as is clear from Stella's amused accounts of chasing the old sow down the lane with her pram and of being pulled about by the goats.

Bedham and Cooper's Cottage are much as she described: 'an extravagantly beautiful and quite inaccessible spot on a great wooded hill about ten miles from Red Ford. There was an immense view, and lonely paths winding through beechwoods over the hillside. Our cottage, white plaster and oak beams with a steep tiled roof, was about three hundred years old and had settled well down into its hillside. There was an orchard full of wild daffodils running up to the hard road at the top of the hill, a small wood full of bluebells lower down behind the cottage, and below that,

a big rough field. Ten acres in all, sloping towards the view.'

The house is now called Cotford Cottage and, though enlarged, is recognisable from Stella's descriptions. The improvements they made may still be seen: the porch Ford helped build, the landing where he had his desk and wrote, the straight window that Stella had put in which, being the only straight one, appears crooked. There are also marks on the beams where she cut out woodworm. She stripped thirteen layers of wallpaper from the walls. The orchard is not there now and Elgar's studio – he was a near neighbour and must have recalled the small part he played in the drama of Elsie's flight to Ford nearly thirty years before, when he sent the telegram confirming her disappearance – is above the house where the garden gate originally was, but the beeches are still there and the view is still beautiful.

Since 1984 the house has been owned by the hospitable Mr and Mrs Cook who have a contribution to make to the story. Mrs Cook's sister-in-law had an aunt Marjorie who, as a young girl, spent some of her time at the tiny Bedham School. One year she won a prize for the best handwriting, a book which at the school's request was presented by Ford. When she told her parents, however, she was made to return the book because Ford and Stella were living in sin. She remembered Stella as often wearing a red smock.

This sad little incident was probably even more hurtful to Ford, if he knew of it, than to Marjorie. It would have struck at his fondness for children, his delight in encouraging any form of literary activity, the recognition – however humble – that he was a worthy writer and at his attempt to establish a new life with Stella. It may, however, have been an indication of how they were regarded by some of the locals. An ageing and upper-middle-class London writer who perhaps was known to have left his wife and children, who was followed to Bedham by a smart strange woman claiming to be his wife, who was living with a pregnant Australian girl artist with whom he amateurishly tried to run a smallholding, who entertained strings of London and American literary people and who probably accumulated a disreputable number of empty bottles outside the back door might even now find difficulty in gaining whole-hearted acceptance in some small communities.

Then, there would have been many who were genuinely offended. Nevertheless, neither he nor Stella seemed to have been made uncomfortable by local dislike and presumably whoever asked Ford to give the prize was not too bothered. Also, they were generous, and money buys tolerance.[1] There is a suggestion of resentment, though, in a long poem Ford wrote before they eventually left Bedham, 'Mister Bosphorus and the Muses or a Short History of Poetry in Britain'. To his complaints about the English climate and English criticism he added:

> The lewd, grim prudery; for-ever protracted chases
> After concealed lechery; hog-like dull embraces
> Under a grey-flannel sky . . .

Their daughter, Esther Julia, was born in a London nursing home on 29 November 1920, a few weeks before Ford's forty-seventh birthday. It was with the coming of the baby that Mrs Hunt ceased spying for Violet. She returned what Violet had sent her, saying, '. . . in Mrs Ford's condition I do not think it fair to her, to worrie her so much.' Stella makes no secret that the birth was hard: 'There seems to be a conspiracy of silence about the horrors of childbearing and a pretty legend that the mother forgets all about it as soon as it is over. The hell she does! Nor does she forget the feeling of quivering helplessness both before and afterwards, and the indignity of having been reduced, even for a day, to the status of a squealing and abject animal.'

Ford is usually said to have been disappointed that it wasn't a boy, as they seem to have thought it would be. Maybe he was, although Janice Biala is quite sure he wasn't and there is no doubt that he was immediately fond of his third daughter. As Stella wrote, Esther Julia 'gave him a big new stake in the post-war world where he still felt pretty lost'. He 'simply doted. His large slow person and quiet voice were just what young things liked . . .' Esther Julia was expensive, though. Stella's stay in the nursing

[1] One of Mrs Hunt's sons recalls that they were popular because they were 'the toffs' and, as such, were the only employers in the hamlet. People were very poor and the effect of 'toffs' on the local economy was considerable: the part-time gardener used to walk over from Byworth, about four miles away.

home, longer than expected, dug a deep hole in their savings.

The stream of visitors increased, especially during the summer of 1921 and especially from America, where Ford was beginning to be published. In his usual optimistic way, he exaggerated his American prospects to himself and to everyone, but any entry, however small, into a new market must have been very cheering. A little appreciation can go a long way to those who feel starved of it. Another small cheer must have been when his poem 'A House', won *Poetry*'s poem of the year award.

Visitors were set to work, chopping wood (however inexpertly – Standing confiscated the axe from one American who was in danger of losing his toes), mowing hay or helping with the animals. Supper, especially if Ford was cooking, was likely to be good but late – ten or eleven o'clock. Conditions remained primitive, of course, but the conversation compensated. Ford was busy, relaxed and happy: 'I go about in filth all day,' he wrote to F. S. Flint, '& put on a cricket shirt & very old dress things at night – not for swank but because I have only one other respectable suit which I save for the Metropolis.' His mother visited and wrote to his nephew, Frank Soskice, of Ford's writing and labouring and of his 'two *huge* pigs who to me are hideous but your Uncle stands by them with a bland smile & a straw in his mouth & says they are "beautiful".' The cottage she thought pretty, simple and cosy with good china and silver, but 'it really is the end of the world . . .'

There was a price for this, which Stella paid: 'Ford never understood why I found it so difficult to paint whilst I was with him. He thought I lacked the will to do it at all costs. That was true but he did not realise that if I *had* had the will to do it at all costs . . . I should not have been available to nurse him through the daily strain of his own work . . .' He needed more reassurance than anyone she had ever met: 'That was one reason why it was so necessary for him to surround himself with disciples . . . in exchange for the help he gave Ford received something very valuable and without which he could scarcely live. He received the assurance that he was a great master of his art.'

The disciples, usually aspiring writers, came at weekends and Ford built himself a leaky hut at the top of the orchard in which he could get away to write. *Thus to Revisit*, on which he was by then working, was his first post-war book and was published in 1921. It is not as good as his earlier and later volumes of reminiscence; in fact, he uses much of the same material but to greater effect in *Return to Yesterday*, published over a decade later. The truth was, as he acknowledged, that he was not yet recovered from the war. The book shows it in its short-cuts, its flaccidity, its easy options and assertions. There are some good passages but it is really a rather tired book, written from habit and old memories, its author not fully engaged. When he sent off the manuscript it was still only partly typed.

It was during this period that the writer Anthony Bertram met him. Bertram's account, given to Tony Gould in a BBC Radio 3 interview broadcast in 1974, is interesting not only because of what it says about Ford, but because it shows how even the well-disposed – Bertram became a friend – could fail to understand:

> I was on a walking tour with a friend. We were both at Oxford reading English Literature. We had both gone through the war and were resolved to be writers. We fancied that we were sufficiently mature and bold enough to open the gates to a great writer. There he was in the garden, a large heavy man in rough clothes planting potatoes. Ford at once took us in and it was not long before he invited us to stay the night. He said it wouldn't matter if we hadn't got dinner-jackets in our rucksacks. We hadn't. That evening he appeared in one of great antiquity. I never saw him again in one, a sad little example of his need for unnecessary armour. He talked late into the night and we listened and heard as much as we could from his softly falling voice and the indrawings of breath. He spoke about himself in a sort of myth that revealed the man but not his facts. It was Ezra Pound who said of him that he was 'the helpless victim of his own imagination'. He could not extricate himself from what he imagined. We spotted that from the beginning so it was no shock to us, quite the contrary.

There are several points about this. Firstly, Ford's quip about dinner-jackets in their rucksacks was surely no more than that. Secondly, this was by no means the only time he wore his antique dinner-jacket in the evenings at Bedham. It probably appealed to him to wear a dinner-jacket in what many people would regard as a hovel. It was more a joke than an armour, a bit of self-mockery, and a sign that gentlemen were independent of their living conditions. It also, as his letter to F. S. Flint shows, probably had practical origins.

Nor was it true that he could not extricate himself from what he imagined. In his letters and in his daily life he did: Elsie, Violet, Stella and Janice did not have to put up with daily doses of hallucination; they lived with a man who understood only too well what was going on, whether he coped with it or whether he hid from it. Nor did his colleagues in the Army where, as we have seen, he actually played down his literary achievements. When he played up or boasted, lied or fantasised it was usually in literary company. He was putting on an act behind which there was probably an assumption, not necessarily conscious, that others would see it for what it was and perhaps even join in; even as audience they participated. Thus, when the two young men called on the great writer, it was the great writer act that they got.

At the time of writing *Thus to Revisit* he tried ideas on various publishers, with or without the co-operation of Pinker, but haste and financial worry did not help his judgement. Eventually he had to confess: 'I always get into mysterious rows and misunderstandings with publishers if I deal with them direct.' Not only with publishers: he offended Wells in *Thus to Revisit* by writing of how Wells had lectured him on how to write. He apologised sincerely, though without really seeing why he might have offended. It was one of those unfortunate and unnecessary literary squabbles which left a worse taste than their intention or substance merited, another reminder that the literary world was not like the Army where you adjourned to the mess to drink with your opponents.

With Pound, however, relations remained as good as ever. Pound saw that *Thus to Revisit* was not Ford's best but said that it had in it several pages of 'the only criticism there has been in England'. In 1921 Ford was advising Pound on 'Mauberley' and on what was to become Canto II. The letters between them are facetious and fond but serious and detailed in their criticism.

In January 1922 Pinker died suddenly in New York. This was a blow since he had, like Pound, held Ford's literary welfare at heart. What was more, he knew better than his authors how to deal with publishers and at the time of his death had been trying to secure Ford permanent publication with Macmillan. He also had plans for American publication but it all fell through.

Ford finished *The Marsden Case* in February 1922, having begun it in September 1921, but both Macmillan and Liveright rejected it. He next sent it to Duckworth's. Though quickly written, it is done with more assurance than *Thus to Revisit*. The central character is George Heimann and his experiences draw heavily on Ford's during the time of the court cases with Elsie and of his harassment by Violet during and after the war, but he had still not yoked his own autobiographical material on to a sufficiently convincing and dynamic vehicle. There are interesting scenes, especially of London literary life, but it is a less interesting book than *No Enemy*. Another project that failed during this period was the American Samuel Roth's suggestion that Ford should become British editor of a New York magazine, *Two World Weekly*. Ford spent two months enlisting writers, including the even then neglected A. E. Coppard, but money was not forthcoming and nothing happened. He never, however, lost his willingness to get involved with literary journals.

It was via another magazine editor, Harold Monro, that salvation came. He had stayed at Cooper's Cottage and had offered the loan of his small villa at Cap Ferrat, near Villefranche. The winter of 1921–2 was a wet one in that part of Sussex and had left the Fords 'a household of neuralgics'. Stella wrote of the mud that was all over the back door, of the path down to the house from the road that was 'a long, perilous slide. The pipe that brought our water from the spring would freeze and burst, the kitchen was damp and draughty and it was always cold upstairs. We had no telephone, and [in 1922] no wireless. We were too poor for a library subscription and never saw a cinema. Petworth was five miles away and the only means of transport was the high, open dog-cart. These things did not matter particularly, but the rain did. Day after day without any let-up at all. And the darkness mattered, too. And the mud.'

The prospect of a fourth winter combined with the lure of the sun in Provence. They decided they would let the cottage and winter abroad, taking the girl Lucy to look after Julie so that Stella would have more time to paint. With the enthusiasm that grips people who realise that their lives can be changed by a talk over dinner, they packed, sold the animals at knock-down prices, prepared the house for tenants and – Stella's job – cleaned and patched all their old clothes: '. . . having scarcely seen a well-dressed woman, nor a fashion magazine for three years, my own appearance must have been pretty dismal.' Money was a problem, of course. Ford wrote to Conrad asking for the money he thought was owing from the fire at The Pent many years before. Conrad replied that the damage had been made good and none was owing. It all depended on Duckworth's buying *The Marsden Case*. They had had no word but

> . . . in our usual foolhardy fashion, we went right ahead with our plans, trusting that the Lord would provide. The baggage was packed, the passports obtained, and we were actually piling into the dog-cart to drive to Fittleworth Station when the postman delivered the manuscript – returned. This caught us hard in the pit of the stomach. As we stood on the windy station platform, Lucy and Julie and Ford and I, feeling that it was the height of folly to have burned our boats and to be leaving our blessed home, I managed secretly to undo a corner of the parcel, in case there was a letter inside, for Ford hated opening anything disagreeable. The letter said that Duckworth would like to publish the book if Ford would make certain minor alterations . . .

He was never again to live in England.

TWENTY-ONE

The next five years were among the busiest and most productive he knew. They had been in Sussex for nearly four and, though it may not always have felt like it, the garden, the animals, the rain and mud, the summer visitors, the long winter nights, the cooking on the oil stove under the lean-to, the hours spent writing at the desk on the landing or in the leaky hut, the tall beeches and the long walks had been a healing balm. A few basic present worries, like keeping dry and warm, are a good antidote to deeper neuroses. But when they crossed the Channel it was as if they were emerging from a long hibernation; when they reached the South of France they were, literally, stepping into the light.

First, though, they went to Paris. According to Stella, they were like sleepwalkers from another world:

> Ford and I were both slow people, and our natural slowness had been encouraged by our bucolic existence. Our nerves had been protected by the space and solitude of Sussex from the jostling noises of city life and this physical calm had become to us almost a necessity. We were tired, jumpy and over-worked, and I can remember both of us almost sobbing under the nervous strain of being buffeted along the narrow pavements of the clattering and screaming streets of the Left Bank. Just the noise – nothing else!

It was mid-November 1922. Despite tiredness and money worries, travel always had an invigorating effect on Ford. Also, they found the cheapness of the franc a great comfort. By the 25th he was writing to his friend, Edgar Jepson, from the Hôtel de Blois, asking if any magazines would like 'an article or two about French literary life' and adding:

> Paris, I find, personally, rather fatiguing: but the rest of my small caravan trots around to Museums, parks, parties & so on with great enthusiasm and vigour, Esther Julia having developed such a passion for motor-cars that, if one draws up on the sidewalk near her, she bolts into it before the occupants can get out.
>
> Ezra is here, going very strong; Joyce going rather weak; my brother Oliver enormously fat and prosperous; but there is very little French stuff of much value coming out, & Proust's death has cast an extraordinary gloom on literary parties – tho' he was pretty generally disliked personally. I just missed seeing him & had to content myself with solemnly attending his funeral, which was a tremendous affair, Stella being the only person in the church who did not shake hands with the next of kin, but her shyness made her bolt out of the back door whereat the venerable Suisse nearly wept.

Though he never met Proust (there was at one time the possibility of his beginning the translation of *A la recherche du temps perdu* but he wasn't very keen on the idea), he was pleased to get to the funeral as 'a representative of English letters'. Stella records that they were given details of where and when by a waiter in the café where they were sitting. '"And imagine," said Ford, "if I asked an English waiter about the funeral of, say, Thomas Hardy, I should discover that he had never heard of the fellow."'

The funeral was important not only because it marked for Ford a ritual of welcome on his return to literary life, as it was a ritual of farewell to Proust, but it was also a mark of how things always seemed to pick up for him when he went to France. He immediately felt he was in a culture which valued what he valued, where writers and artists were accorded their proper places. Just as London had, he thought, been the place to be in the decade before the war, so Paris was after it. There is probably truth in that, though a strong claim could be made for Vienna, but it would be interesting to know whether he ever reflected on the fact that the cultural life he so much valued and contributed to in France was far more cosmopolitan than French, just as artistic and literary society in pre-1914 London had been very cosmopolitan. Nearly all the people he mixed with in Paris were English-speaking, many speaking only English, and nearly all the literature he became associated with was produced by Americans, Irish or British. Of course, he would have held it to the credit of France that she had provided the climate in which all this could blossom – and so it was – but he and Stella seemed to have moved in a society that was almost entirely expatriate, and, even in its poorest examples, wealthy compared with the majority of French people.

Proust's funeral may also have prompted Ford to write *Parade's End*: '. . . it was his death that made it certain I should again take up a serious pen,' he wrote in *It was the Nightingale*. '. . . I think I am incapable of any sort of rivalry. There is certain literary work to be done . . . Proust being dead I could see no one who was doing that . . .' This is truer and less conceited than it might sound. *Parade's End* offers a critique of a certain kind of English society in a way similar to that which *Remembrance of Things Past* offers of a certain kind of French society; both are big books spanning years and ranging widely; both show decay in the heart of high society. It is quite possible that musing on Proust might have prompted Ford to attempt his own equivalent and is certainly true that he was not prompted by thoughts of rivalry. As pointed out earlier, he lacked envy to an almost dangerous degree and would no more have asserted himself as pre-eminent among writers than among other officers of his battalion. He wanted status, of course, but the status of belonging and of being recognised amongst those he admired. He wanted community, wanted to be a part.

They found that it rained also in Paris. After three days of it they took a night train south, arriving at Avignon, Stella said 'to that great radiant floodlight which hits the ground and reflects upwards, to fill the shadows with a bubble-like iridescence . . .' She was still very attached to Cooper's Cottage and had never been to France but to Ford it must have felt like coming home. It had never been that but it was to be from now on; although he lived elsewhere for much of the time, this was where he wanted to be and where he always returned. In Kent, in London, in

Flanders and in Sussex there had been the grey days, the wet weeks, the months of mud, the entanglements, depressions and confusions, but here in the clear hard sunlight there would be clarity and kindness and time. It had to be nothing but the sun.

The Villa des Oliviers, Harold Monro's small house, is in the Chemin de Moulins at St Jean-Cap Ferrat. It is bigger now but it still has the vivid view of Villefranche harbour, edged with the old white buildings and the stone fortress. You can still step across the path and see Beaulieu on the other side of the Cap, Monte Carlo and Italy beyond it. Nor is it much less difficult of access than when Stella wrote:

> You climbed to it by a rough mule-track, or alternatively by long flights of stone steps of a giddy and exhausting steepness . . . no wheeled vehicle could reach the place. But this steepness and slowness mattered nothing in comparison with the fact that the path was dry. It had been dry since the dawn of history! And the garden terraces which overhung Villefranche Harbour appeared to have been levelled and stoned up also since the same epoch . . . climate is one of the few things in life that really matter. Other things, friends, fame, or fortune, may elude or dispirit you but a good climate never lets you down . . . life is too short to be struggling perpetually with the weather . . .

Cooking was by charcoal but for once they had water laid on and even electric light. The view across the harbour was of 'a great luminous sky with a Saracen fortress on the sky line opposite . . .'

It is much more built up now but the actual spot is unchanged despite the surrounding Mercedes, Lamborghinis and Jaguars, the marching pylons, large blocks of flats and new hotels, the security systems and warnings of guard dogs. It was rich then, too: 'this is a comic place,' Ford wrote to Anthony Bertram, 'we have the Duke of Connaught on one side of us, & the Rothschilds next door and the Louis Mountbattens with all the wealth of Cassel just above us & all the divorcing duchesses, Westminsters and Marlboroughs in rows along the water's edge below . . .'

On a winter's afternoon, as when they arrived, the sea and sky may change rapidly from azure to dramatic indigo, to purple, to red and gold, and before a storm the smooth water of the harbour resembles a blue-black carpet moved from below by draughts. Ford began writing *Some Do Not*, the first volume of the *Parade's End* tetralogy. He sat, he said, at Monro's grandfather's campaign-secretaire which had been on the field at Waterloo. It was, 'under Monro's olive-trees, a final struggle with my courage'. After making due allowance for dramatic licence, it is likely that what he said was true: it was a struggle to begin. His post-war publishing to date had been either thin or disguised reminiscence or the raking of sparks from old bonfires, but this was the project he must have known would stretch him. For this he would need to bear on his back all the old lumber of the past while simultaneously making it into an enduring artistic form. It was his great work; once started he was to go on as quickly as ever.

Life in his beloved Provence also went on as it should. In March he wrote to Monro that he had 'got the garden here quite tidy & spick & span by now & have tried several experiments with manures'. He worked out a planting scheme and made suggestions for a new path down through the hanging gardens to the road. In the same month Pound and his wife took Stella on a fortnight's picture tour of Italy. She had seen neither the country nor its paintings before and though she greatly missed Ford and Julie – it was her first separation – she also greatly enjoyed what she was seeing. He stayed at Cap Ferrat and wrote. Letters of the period mention a four-act play but there is no other evidence of it.

In late April they left, partly because the area was becoming crowded and Ford thought they should see something of the real Provence of the Rhône Valley, but perhaps also because Monro wanted his villa. They went to Tarascon where they stayed in the small Hôtel Termineuse. It was a warm spring and life was free and easy. They spent a lot of time at the café. Ford became friendly with the local *avoué* and *avocat*, and with the latter would 'discuss the proper use of the subjunctive, in elaborate French prose. Ford really knew French perfectly but he spoke it badly because he never moved his lips enough. I did not know it at all, but I picked up a certain amount of colloquial slang . . . and eventually got more quickly understood than Ford's literary murmurings.' They went to a bull fight which Stella did not much like; she says nothing about Ford's reaction.

In May a noisy fair parked itself beneath the plane trees in front of the hotel and the weather anyway was becoming too hot. They took the advice of the *avoué* and moved to St-Agrève in the Ardèche. There, the Hôtel Poste was empty, the town grim and the weather cold. They had none of their winter clothes and Ford went down with bronchitis, an experience which formed Stella's opinion of French doctors (cupping was still recommended). When the weather changed for the better, everything else followed. Ford had an annexe of the hotel where he could work in silence, the food was excellent and Stella was able to paint outdoors. He wrote cheerfully to Anthony Bertram: 'I hear that Bertram Higgins is wandering over France, exclaiming faintly "Ford! Ford!" in the effort to find me & getting shown into garages – for there is a Ford more famous! . . . tell him I'd be delighted to see him here. It is very cheap working out at less than 4/- a day, all told . . .'

Stella's painting was becoming a more serious part of her life. She had had another fortnight away while they were in Tarascon, taking lessons in Paris. The fact that they still had Lucy to look after Julie, that she had somewhere to work – the open air – and that she was surrounded by new combinations and vividness of colour made for a flowering of her talent. Later that year she had a number of paintings hung in the Salon de Automne in Paris. They stayed in the hotel until September, when they returned to Paris.

They had let Cooper's Cottage for the winter and so hoped to find somewhere cheap in Paris. It was virtually impossible but they did it: 'On one of our first days in Paris we bumped into another large, pink-faced blue-eyed gentleman on an island in the Place Médicis.' It was brother Oliver who wanted to let his small cottage behind some studios at 65 Boulevard Argo while he and his wife went to America. It was damp, of course, and in something of a mess, and they were once more without electricity or gas, but it was a place. It was also picturesque, with greenery, creepers and even a walled garden. There they began their three Parisian years, a hectic, peripatetic life full of people, parties, desperate searches for new flats (the burden of which fell on Stella), battles with landlords, dances, more parties, painting and writing. The gay life of Paris in the 1920s was for them no myth; it was bohemian café society, free-spending, hard-drinking, gossiping, stimulating, cosmopolitan, promiscuous, productive – for those with the self-discipline to work – and impoverished; though, again, not so much that anyone seems actually to have had to get a job.

Ford was in the thick of it, whether at his favourite restaurant, the Nègre de Toulouse in the Boulevard Montparnasse, or in cafés such as the Dôme or the Deux Magots. He would sit on the edge of his chair, his mouth hanging open, talking unceasingly and never, it is said, boringly, draining glass after glass with no apparent effect. He was over-weight, ponderous, his blond hair almost white, his teeth bad, his cheeks rosy and his moustache heavy. He would talk to anyone, would tell tall stories of the Victorians and the Edwardians, pronounce upon style, make astute comments on painting, argue about wines, become sentimental, boast about everything except what he did best, let himself be mocked by the young, encourage anyone in what they were doing, explain the secrets of his trade to any who asked, lend money, borrow it, curse all publishers, bless all the young and tell them always to trust their first reactions. A Falstaffian figure, as indignant about bad food and wine as Falstaff was about small beer, he seemed to some a relic of another age even in that age which he was himself helping to shape. That was not appreciated by most of those who knew him; he wasn't simply a part of the mythology of the past that somehow still survived but was himself doing more than most to create the myths of the future. At nearly fifty, he actually lived the bohemian life that others wrote about or, with the security of money behind them, played at. And all the time, day-in day-out, unlike the great majority, behind the talk and the drink, the parties and dances, he worked. Inside that garrulous, splay-footed sixteen or seventeen stones, inside that mind – 'like a Roquefort cheese,' said Van Wyck Brooks, 'so ripe it was palpably falling to pieces'– was the sharp point of steely purpose that would no more let him rest than he would loosen his grip on his daily routine.

It was not long before Lucy, now homesick, returned to Sussex and Stella had to set about looking for another child-minder. The choice was 'Madame Annie, a lively little widow of forty with a formidable temper.' This was reserved exclusively for Stella: 'For those three years she ruled me with a rod of iron, and at the end of that time, when I had achieved reasonable domestic conditions, and knew I could command the services of someone more domestically congenial, it was all but impossible to get rid of her.'

They decided to live permanently in France, hoping to sell Cooper's Cottage for enough money to buy an apartment in Paris and a small house in Provence. Life was indeed very pleasant: Ezra was on hand, Joyce, with whom Ford was soon on friendly terms (they would argue about the virtues of white wine, which Joyce favoured, and red, upon which Ford insisted), Gertrude Stein and shoals of other unpublished newcomers, amongst them Ernest Hemingway. Ford and Stella were generous hosts and their parties were soon famous. Harold Loeb, in *The Way it Was*, described one he attended:

> . . . The main room was full of dancers, expounders, strollers, music and smoke . . . I could not see Stella, our hostess, but heard her voice in the stair well which led down to the kitchen. As I started down to her, Silvia Goff kicked Mary Butts' behind.
>
> At once Tommy Erp and Wheeler Williams began to fight up above on the main floor. A ring formed about the fighters. Stella roared up from below, 'Miserable man, he's spoiling my party by committing suicide!'
>
> The crowd deserted the fighters and tumbled down the stairs. There was blood but no body . . . I . . . was dancing with a tall, elegant Swedish girl when Berenice Abbott fell on her back in the middle of the floor.
>
> Waldo Pierce looked at her tersely. Some of the guests seemed confused but Ford was quite calm . . .

It sounds as if Stella had a loud voice, though perhaps only when she was excited. There are slight indications – not from him – that she might sometimes have embarrassed Ford. Along with the straightforwardness and openness of her nature there are signs that she may have lacked that quick, intuitive appreciation that he possessed to a remarkable degree. Much as he liked parties, he was nearly always quiet; she probably wasn't. Also, there were aspects of their new society that she found difficult: 'It took me a little while to get used to living among people who, on the whole, had replaced all their moral prejudices by aesthetic ones.'

He finished *Some Do Not* in the walled garden of Oliver's cottage. It was good and he felt it to be so (Pound was later to tell his father that it was the best thing Ford had done since *The Good Soldier*). He wrote to Wells, with whom he was back on terms: 'I've got over the nerve tangle of the war and feel able at least really to write again – which I never thought I should do.' Naturally, they did not get anything like what they had hoped from the sale of Cooper's Cottage but they would still have had enough to buy reasonably had not something else intervened.[1]

Ford was a man who lived more for his imagination than for security or comfort, so that something with imaginative appeal would always triumph over the sensible. The origins of the *Transatlantic Review* are not clear but essential background was provided by Ford's yen for editing literary magazines, by the number of writers he knew in Paris, the lack of any comparable journal and, sadly, his brief possession of £400 or so remaining from the sale of Cooper's. The catalyst seems to have been Oliver, whose idea it probably was and who promised access to sums that would support it. Ford certainly credits Oliver with the idea in a highly-coloured account which is supported in substance by Stella. Pound was also involved at a very early stage. Ford said that people kept stopping him in the street and telling him he should start another *English Review*. He needed little enough urging. Very shortly after he had taken up Oliver's offer, it became apparent that the funds, whatever their source, would no longer be available. By then the story had got around that Ford *was* starting a review and people were approaching him with manuscripts and ideas. He hated to retreat and he felt he was back at centre stage again, no longer

[1] It was sold initially to a Royal Academician called Philpot. Ford is described in the Land Registry document as 'retired captain in His Majesty's Army, C.M.G.'. It is not clear who awarded him the honour but it may well have been one of his own jokes on officialdom. What is clear is that three years earlier, in 1920, he had made over the entire property to Stella 'in consideration of mutual love and affection'.

young himself but still 'the only Uncle of the gifted young', as Lawrence had called him. He couldn't say no.

During the period when he still hadn't fully said yes, Stella was trying hard to buy a house before their money disappeared. Twice she nearly did it and she and Ford came as close to life-long security as they ever would, but the deals fell through. Before she could find another house Pound persuaded an American lawyer, John Quinn, to put up $2,000. There was a meeting at Pound's studio between Quinn, Joyce and Ford at which Quinn formally agreed, provided Ford would do the same. Ford put up what he had – £435 (the additional £35 was Stella's). The magazine was born.

That, of course, was just the start. The magazine had a voracious appetite. Further fodder came from Stella's Australian capital on which she drew in the surprising hope that she was making an investment. She 'could not help seeing how lovely it would be for him if he could have his review' and so 'joined that sad army of Paris wives who spend their days following up vague clues of flats to let.' Flats were made expensive partly by the influx of the very Americans for whom the *Review* was partly intended. In fairness, Ford later did what he could to repay her by making over to her the royalties of a number of his books but neither of them ever really recovered, financially, from this choice.

William Bird of the Three Mountain Press at 29 quai d'Anjou provided an editorial office, in fact a galley at the back of his shop measuring 15 feet by 6 and accessible by flimsy stairs. There was a desk and two chairs and from there Ford edited the *Transatlantic Review*. Pound produced two sub-editors, a starving White Russian officer who suspected Ford of being a Communist agent and who absconded with some proofs, and a bespectacled young Englishman called Basil Bunting. He had nowhere to live and so was put up in a damp storeroom behind Ford's and Stella's kitchen. Another Pound product was an efficient secretary called Marjorie Reid. The aim of the *Review*, Ford wrote for the first edition, was the promotion of good writing: 'The aim of the Review is to help in bringing about a state of things in which it will be considered that there are no English, no French – for the matter of that, no Russian, Italian, Asiatic or Teutonic – Literatures: there will be only Literature.'

He set about recruiting contributors. There was no lack of manuscripts – fortunately, as we have seen and as he told Stella, he didn't have to read thoroughly to know if they were good because 'I know what's in 'em' – but he wanted material from established writers as well as unknowns, as he had with *The English Review*. Always conscious of tradition and of being part of it himself, he wanted others to see its benefits and progress. It was also his preference, he told A. E. Coppard, 'not to have sexually esoteric, psycho-analytic, mystic or officially ethical matter but don't bar any of them obstinately.' From the start there were others, particularly the young Americans – it was a magazine in which everyone felt they had a say – who thought they could break with tradition and weren't interested in anyone older than themselves. Very soon Ford was feeling as he had felt in the *English Review* days and he wrote to Gertrude Stein (who was fond of Julie, and saw a lot of her and Stella): 'I really exist as a sort of half-way house between non-publishable youth and real money . . .' He once again compared himself to the green baize door that everyone kicks on entering or leaving. He remained as helpful as ever to the young, though – untypically for him – he did describe Waldo Frank and Robert McAlmon (who didn't like him) as the two worst writers in Paris. But it is also clear that among his earliest thoughts was a revival of his old friendship with Conrad by publishing accounts of what by now seemed the halcyon days of collaboration. This was of no more interest to the temporarily young than were the manners of Ford's youth akin to their own. As Mizener points out, he had been brought up in a more formal world where it was customary – perhaps a pleasure – to address senior writers such as James as, 'Cher Maître', and he hankered after that. When the odd Frenchman did it to him, Stella recalls, it 'filled his heart with simple pleasure'. He sought to reconcile the two worlds. It was not possible for his success to be apparent at the time since the young did not regard themselves as being within bridging distance, particularly by the fat Falstaffian sentimentalist who, irritatingly, could not be ignored, though he could be further resented because of his unerring, instinctive and exasperatingly casual critical acumen. It is only in retrospect that the bridge can be seen to have existed and that those who crossed it did so by extending the tradition they thought they were opposing; the rest – the majority – disappeared; the span of the bridge was Ford's personality.

Early in 1924 he visited Conrad in England. The occasion was his rush back to London because Mrs Hueffer had developed diabetes and was thought to be dying (in fact, she lived another three years). Though neither knew it, it was to be his and Conrad's last meeting, the one at which Ford thought they had re-established their old friendship. But Conrad wrote to Eric Pinker (son of the original and less successful): 'As we talked pleasantly of old times I was asking myself, in my cynical way, when the kink would come . . . Ford wants to be friendly in his personal relations with me . . . In fact, entre nous, too friendly . . .' They discussed the publication of *The Nature of a Crime*, both its reissue in the *Transatlantic Review* on the basis of the original *English Review* copies and publication as a separate book. They also discussed the attribution of *Romance* which Dent were reissuing without mentioning Ford's name. He had to threaten legal action to get this typically Fordian piece of publishing luck put right. There was also the possibility of further legal action by Elsie against Violet, who, now in her sixties, had signed a letter to the *Weekly Westminster* as Violet Hunt Hueffer. Ford said that he would be willing to drop his preface to *The Nature of a Crime* if Conrad did not want to risk being associated with this further piece of unsavoury publicity but it turned out not to be necessary. Conrad agreed with everything to Ford's face and commented behind his back that he had done so 'in order to conciliate the swell-headed creature who seems to imagine that he will sweep all Europe and devastate Great Britain with an eventual collection of his own works'. War had warmed their friendship but, on one side anyway, there was not enough fire to keep it going.

Conrad was by then an author in decline, not only in the quality of his later work but in literary fashion. Though this latter point found no acceptance from Ford, he was, with his usual insight, aware of the former. Three years earlier he had written to Edgar Jepson: '. . . his later work appealed to me so relatively little that I don't want to write any more about it. I mean, it is difficult to do so without appearing, and for all I know, being, ungenerous.'

When he saw his mother he presented her with a portrait of himself by Stella which she described as 'very clever but *hideous* as a likeness exactly like him and also looking like a Frenchman with a past'. That was more or less what he was becoming.

Owing to Hemingway's interventions and to his own absence in America trying to sort out sales, Ford had less editorial control over the *Transatlantic Review* than over the earlier *English Review*, with the result that some issues dwindled into the self-regarding trickle of a Left Bank coterie. Those that he controlled, however, showed all the old flair and catholicity over the earlier review. The *Transatlantic* included works by Pound, e.e. cummings, Conrad, Gertrude Stein, Hemingway, Joyce, Paul Valéry, A. E. Coppard and William Carlos Williams. There was nothing else like it in 1924 or after its demise.

Joyce's extract from *Finnegans Wake* was something of a coup. An early admirer of *Ulysses*, Ford had several years before accorded Joyce the pole position, as it were, of novelists then writing in English. Now that they had got to know each other they got on well, enjoying their disagreements about red and white wine, agreeing in their condemnation of a de-frocked priest and lunching happily with him afterwards. Ford suggested the title of the extract, 'Work in Progress', and Joyce was sufficiently pleased at Ford's becoming 'godfather' to the book in this way that he made the rare concession of agreeing to become Julie's godfather at her Catholic baptism.

Ford had a less even relationship with Hemingway. It was uneasy from the start: 'he comes and sits at my feet and praises me. It makes me nervous.' They disagreed over the contents of the *Review*. Hemingway, for example, was against the idea of a Conrad supplement after Conrad's death in August 1924 and when persuaded by Ford to write a piece for it he praised Conrad at the expense of Eliot. He wrote that if he had known 'that by grinding Mr Eliot into a fine, dry powder and sprinkling that powder over Mr Conrad's grave Mr Conrad would shortly appear, looking very annoyed at the forced return and commence writing, I would leave for London early tomorrow morning with a sausage grinder.' Ford hesitated over publishing this, since Eliot was a supporter of the *Review*, but felt he ought not to be censorious and so did. In the next issue he apologised to Eliot, which apology enraged Hemingway. That was generally the pattern of their relationship, toleration on one side, irritation on the other. Hemingway was given his early breaks by Ford and took several opportunities to kick him in public for it, most notably in his later caricature of him in *A Moveable Feast*. Later still, Basil Bunting gave his own opinion of that in his introduction to Ford's *Selected Poems*:

> . . . among the young men who owed Ford thanks, few owed more than Hemingway: early publication, a chance to edit in part the *Transatlantic Review* or at least to influence its editing, some introductions, some knowledge of the town, or of that part of the town that Hemingway was least likely to see for himself, gossip no doubt, and perhaps some notions about the structure of novels. Hemingway too was a writer of fiction, entitled to his lies, and to live them as vividly as he dared, for a novelist must inhabit the people he invests to make them convincing. His chronic fantasy was unusually vulgar, the dream so popular with women and womanish men of a magnanimous bully. It brought him readers and prosperity though it obliged him to write what is really the same book over and over again. He had a right to it.
>
> But his sketch of Ford in *A Moveable Feast* is another sort of lie, one deliberately assembled to damage the reputation of a dead man who had left no skilled closed friend to take vengeance; a lie cunningly adjusted to seem plausible to simple people who had never known either Ford or Hemingway and to load his memory with qualities disgusting to all men and despicable to many; yet so false that I, for instance, who knew them both, would never have guessed the unlaughable caricature was meant for Ford if Hemingway had not named it.
>
> Before I had heard of *A Moveable Feast* Hemingway was protected by his own grave from what might have been said about him.

During the 1930s Ford told Janice Biala that he thought Hemingway's bitterness resulted from his telling him once that his (Hemingway's) novels showed that he was weak on construction, and that that was something he would have to learn. Despite the bitterness, which was evident before *A Moveable Feast*, Hemingway continued to send Ford copies of his books for comment. It may be that there were other reasons, too, suggested by Hemingway's attitude and dating from their earliest acquaintance. Ford was not a hero in the Hemingway mould: he was vulnerable, untidy, sentimental, funny in a way that Hemingway could probably sense but not see, and genuinely heroic; he was superior in age, status, experience, knowledge of his craft, sensitivity and ability; he was unaggressive, fat and wheezing, had fought in the trenches and was unaccountably popular with women. There was much that Hemingway might have found hard to forgive.

There are also incidents such as that which Gertrude Stein records. Hemingway was telling her why he couldn't review her book, *The Making of Americans*, and was interrupted: 'Just then a heavy hand fell on his shoulder and Ford Madox Ford said, "Young man, it is I who wish to speak to Gertrude Stein."' He then asked permission to dedicate his book, *A Mirror to France*, to her. She was very pleased, perhaps because Ford had acted to save her from Hemingway's aggression, but it is easy to imagine that Hemingway was less pleased; he probably didn't like being called 'young man'.

Bunting was Man Friday to the *Review*. He was described by Ford in a letter to A. E. Coppard as 'a dark youth with round spectacles in a large Trilby hat and a blue trench coat with belt who shall hold up a copy of the *Transatlantic Review* towards passengers arriving at the barrier and smile.' In Tony Gould's 1974 radio interview Bunting described what he did:

> Besides the obvious duties of assistant editor I did all sorts of other things . . . I corrected not only the proofs of the magazine but those of the current novel, which was *Some Do Not*, and some of Conrad's work. Finally, when there was nothing else that needed doing, I would sometimes bath the baby. In return I got the most friendly and tolerant boss you could possibly have. I occupied a room on one side of the studio, Ford and his wife were in rooms the other side. But if I turned up at breakfast in the morning with an unannounced and unintroduced young

> lady Ford would never turn a hair, merely shout that we wanted another four eggs or something like that. Altogether life could have been very comfortable. I left for a reason which it is a little difficult to explain. The great drawback to working with Ford at all times was that he was overcome so easily by little worries. Small things would go wrong, they would pile up and then instead of doing a little general cursing and getting on with it as most folk do, Ford would weep on your shoulder. It's very uncomfortable for a young man of twenty-two to have someone a generation older than himself and very heavy weeping on his shoulder and in the end I couldn't put up with it and moved on.

It was partly generosity that led Ford to live so public a private life and it was also his misfortune. However, Bunting pinpoints two crucial elements. Firstly, Ford's inability to absorb small worries – it is usually small worries that get to people – which perhaps encouraged his earlier detached omniscience of manner. This was how he tried to distance himself from anxiety and towards the end of his life it led to that broad-minded refusal to be worried, the kind of elder-statesman calm that he achieved. Secondly, as pointed out earlier, his self-parodying humour which was unnoticed not only by Hemingway but also by others more sympathetic. When he told stories he was creating a myth that revealed not the facts of his life but himself. All art is partly self-revelation and Ford's art went as much into his conversation as into his writing. He might have been better understood in the west of Ireland or in Russia than among the literati.

The *Review* was awash with all the problems that usually beset such projects: unreliable printers, proofs going astray, copies lost, quixotic contributors, subscriptions likewise, distribution networks that didn't distribute and all the time the widening gulf between income and expenditure. The title of the first issue was printed in lower case, not in tribute to the forthcoming work of e.e. cummings but because there wasn't room for upper case; this became its trademark. It was a very social time, well remembered by Stella:

> . . . On Thursdays, The Transatlantic Review was at home, and I made tea for all and sundry at the office . . . Ford would first be observed aloft at his desk, narrowly framed by the semi-circle of the arched roof, and talking to a new contributor. Presently he would descend and spread geniality amongst the faithful . . . He really enjoyed himself superbly.

During this period they had to leave Oliver's house, move briefly to a large studio on the Boulevard Argo and then to a tiny apartment in the rue Denfert-Rochereau which had a bed in the kitchen and no bath. Gertrude Stein helped them find a cottage out in Guermantes and there Julie and Madame Annie spent most of their time. In April 1924 *Some Do Not* was published to critical acclaim which, for all that Ford's detached attitudes to reviews was both feigned and real, must have been genuinely pleasing. Hemingway, however, wrote a vitriolic attack on him for the *Review*, to which Ford's friend, Edgar Jepson, replied pseudonymously.

Finances went from bad to worse. He calculated that twenty thousand copies of the *Review* had gone astray in America but John Quinn, the American backer and remarkable patron of the arts, could do nothing to help as he was dying of cancer. Ford tried a new share issue, using more of Stella's money, but it wasn't enough; he decided he would have to go to America himself to try to raise more and to sort things out.

He sailed in late May. When his ship called at Plymouth late at night he was 'seized with an overwhelming conviction that I should never see Conrad again. I got up and desperately scrawled to him a last letter assuring him of my forever unchanging affection and admiration for his almost miraculous gifts.' That was written after Conrad's death but the letter, though less forceful and dramatic than he describes, was sent when he says. Whether he was convinced he would never see Conrad again is an open question but there is little doubt that Conrad was much on his mind as he touched the shore, for the last time, of land where Conrad lived.

He had a very social time in America, was wined and dined and made to feel welcome, all of which contributed to his growing hunch that perhaps his literary future lay there. At a lunch given in honour of an albino monkey he sat next to the hostess and 'seemed to enjoy himself greatly, though at times looked a little bewildered'. John Quinn, however, was too ill to be seen and the *Review*'s future began to look no better than his. While Ford was away Hemingway adapted the August issue to his own American tastes, making it less cosmopolitan. It was too late for Ford to alter when he returned although he added a few ironic words to the editorial, promising that in future editions 'Other works of English and French writers will also be again allowed to creep in.'

While Ford was in New York Elsie, without either author's permission, sold the proofs for *Romance* which he and Conrad had corrected, as well as some letters; at about the same time Violet sold some of his letters to herself. He was upset since he had never sold anything to do with Conrad and he never forgave it. Nearly three years later he wrote to the *New York Herald Tribune*, saying he had never authorised the sale. It would have seemed to him like desecration.

He was back in Paris in good time for Bastille Day, when he and Stella gave a large party at the Dôme. Before that they had to give up the apartment and base themselves largely at the Guermentes cottage but nevertheless contrived a very social summer. In the rue du Cardinal Lemoine was a small dance-hall called the Bal du Printemps. It was the kind of place, Stella said, where chauffeurs and *petits commerçants* would 'bring their girls to dance and drop two sous into the proprietor's cap each time they take the floor. There was always a policeman sitting just inside the door. That is the law. The music was usually provided by an accordionist. This establishment closed on Fridays but Ford persuaded the proprietor to open at 10 p.m. for himself and whoever he invited. These nights became known as Ford's Nights and soon involved a large proportion of the expatriate Left Bank community. The policeman came, too, though the proprietor had no licence for a "bal privé" – and enjoyed it. The proprietor didn't charge his usual two sous.' It was illuminated, she added, by a row of electric lights across an angle of the steep and twisting old street:

Inside, the rough tables and wooden benches were painted scarlet and the walls around the dance floor were set with mirrors and painted pink, with garlands, all done by hand . . . you never knew who would be there . . . You would find yourself dancing with someone. Nothing but the coat sleeve to indicate whether he should be addressed in French or English. You decide to try English.

'I love an accordion,' you say.

He, 'So do I. I have a beauty at home, in carved ivory and pink silk. My wife gave it to me the first time she was unfaithful to me.' Do you ask if he got a piano the second time? Perhaps not.

Herbert Gorman, in *The Bookman* of March 1928, was one of several who described those evenings:

We entered to the whining moan of an accordion and the measured thump of a drum . . . the small square of dancing floor . . . is now crowded with figures hopping up and down in a peculiar rhythmic fashion. Above these syncopating puppets is a small balcony fastened like a bird's nest to the wall and in it are seated two perspiring nonchalant musicians . . .

We notice what at first glance appears to be a behemoth in grey tweeds. He turns in the dance and we recognise him immediately. The blue eyes, the blond hair, the bland cherubic expression, the open mouth . . .

It is the Leviathan of the Quartier Montparnasse, the gentle Gargantua of Lavigne's . . . He plods happily and with a child-like complacency through the dance, his partner swaying like a watch-fob before him . . .'

Douglas Goldring, then in Paris, brought along an American senator he was trying to impress but the company, 'the extreme simplicity of the place, the gloomy, collarless, accordion-player with a perpetual half-smoked cigarette dangling from his lips' and the fact that someone slapped the bottom of the senator's dancing partner did not produce the hoped-for reaction, and they left early.

Like most good things, Ford's Nights had also to come to

an early end. According to Nina Hamnett it was because the intellectuals wanted to talk and the dancers wanted to drink and dance; according to Stella it was because journalists came 'with English-women in evening dress, who thought it fun to go slumming in Paris' and because 'some clean-living Americans wanted to organise the whole thing as a club'. According to Ford, the dances 'gradually became burdensome and then overwhelming'. He had asked about thirty couples to start with, all writers, painters or composers, and he hoped that some publicity for the *Review* would result. The dances were too popular and were ruined by gate-crashers, 'often up-state bankers and publishers who, passing through Paris, came as it were to a dance straight from a boat-train, made themselves offensive, and caught the next morning's train for Monte Carlo, Berlin or Vienna.' But he had no regrets: 'I do not mind giving dances. I can think my private thoughts while they go on nearly as well as in Underground during rush-hours – and if anyone is present that I like and there is a shortage of men, I dance. I would rather dance than do anything else.' (Janice Biala confirmed that he would dance whenever he could. He wasn't actually any good, she said, and she told him so; but he didn't mind that.)

Conrad died suddenly in August 1924 of a heart attack. He was recovering, it was thought, from a less serious attack and died after announcing that he felt better. On hearing the news, Ford dropped everything and began writing *Joseph Conrad: A Personal Remembrance*. He wrote it in two months ('at fever heat') while serialising it in the *Review* and he described it in the following terms: 'This then is a novel, not a monograph; a portrait, not a narration: for what it should prove to be worth, a work of art, not a compilation.' It was criticised for inaccuracy of detail, despite a further introductory statement to the effect that 'Where the writer's memory has proved to be at fault over a detail afterwards out of curiosity looked up, the writer has allowed the fault to remain on the page; but as to the truth of the impression of the whole, the writer believes that no man care – or dare – to impugn it.'

There was some praise for the accuracy of its impression, further criticism for being as much about its author as about Conrad. Perhaps this is an indication of what the friendship did for Ford. He gave freely of himself and in so doing became more purposed, more honed to endeavour, more dedicated to the great cause. He could not have helped writing about himself since it was through that friendship that he found himself. It was indeed a great love and the whole of *Joseph Conrad* is imbued with it: 'In the days here mostly treated of, Conrad had a very dreadful, a very agonised life. Few men can so much have suffered; there was about all his depressed moments a note of pain – of agony indeed – that coloured our whole relationship; that caused one to have an almost constant quality of solicitude . . . But most marked in the writer's mind was the alert, dark, extremely polished and tyrannous personality, tremendously awake, tremendously interested in small things, peering through his monocle at something close to the ground, taking in a characteristic and laughing consumedly – at a laborious child progressing engrossedly over a sloping lawn, at a bell-push that functioned of itself in the door-post of a gentleman (H. G. Wells) who had written about an invisible man – or at the phrase, "Excellency, a few goats . . ."' What damaged him most was a letter that Jessie Conrad wrote to the *TLS* in December 1924. The letter made clear her dislike of Ford and wrongly suggested that virtually all of what he had written about her husband was untrue. It was damaging not so much for its immediate effect but because it became part of the received Fordian mythology of succeeding generations. It is typical of his life that his loving remembrance of his great friend should have been used in evidence against him. Later he got a friend to put flowers on Conrad's grave in Canterbury with the epigraph that had fronted the dedicatory poem in *Romance*, Victor Hugo's '*C'est toi qui dors dan s l'ombre, O sacre Souvenir*'.

It was a summer of deaths: following John Quinn and Conrad it was now the turn of the *Transatlantic Review*. It was kept going for a while by hopes of support from a rich American couple, Mr and Mrs Krebs Friend, but after various toings and froings the money still was not forthcoming. (The Friends had their own sad story: she was forty years older than he and was trying to give him some reason to live which, as a result of being badly shell-shocked in the war, he lacked.) Ford called a wind-up meeting in November and in his last editorial said he hoped the magazine would be re-started and that it had fulfilled its objective of treating literature as international despite the hijacking by the Americans of the Left Bank, who had turned it into a little review. It had run for a year.

Closing had not been an easy decision. It had swallowed virtually all the money that Ford and Stella had, as well as various donations. He felt badly but there was no choice. It was only the ending he regretted, though, since he loved editing as much as he did before. Not that it was as bad this time as after *The English Review*. There was none of the bitterness and he didn't have to endure seeing the magazine continue in someone else's hands. Also, as Stella pointed out, 'the loss of an editorship could not inflict a mortal wound upon a man who is just embarking upon the most creative work of his life.' On 31 October, a few days before his Conrad reminiscence was published, he began *No More Parades*, the sequel to *Some Do Not*. Though they still had the cottage they were camping in the Paris studio that Stella had found (it was her first studio). Within the past year they had lived in three furnished and two unfurnished places, none with what used to be called modern conveniences, and they were both very tired, she with moving and Ford, who minded less about where he lived, with the *Review*. As before, he recovered through work.

It was about this time that he became involved with Jean Rhys. She was not a writer when he first knew her but was more or less down and out in Paris, desperate for money and probably desperate by nature. At sixteen she had left the West Indies to go to drama school in England but had had to leave after her father died. She was good-looking and became a chorus girl and model. Her first serious lover was a man considerably older than herself but the relationship did not work out. She then met and married a Dutch poet. They lived in Paris, where she had a baby that died, and their lives began to drift without much sense of direction or hope of income. They were living in a hotel. She had taken some articles written by her husband to the wife of a newspaper correspondent whom she had known in London. They were not saleable articles but the woman asked whether Jean had herself written anything. She had not except for some diaries which she had kept during her time as a chorus girl. She took those to the woman who, seeing that they might have potential, altered them – introducing chapters and so on – and showed them to Ford. This was while Ford was still editing the *Review* and was on the look-out for new talent. With his usual eye, he saw through the alterations to an original mind and asked to meet the author. Jean was then aged about thirty.

Ford and Stella took her up and had her to live with them while her husband did a short term in prison for a currency offence. She possessed, Stella said, 'nothing but a cardboard suitcase and the astonishing manuscript. She was down to her last three francs and she was sick.' She also possessed physical charm and a dangerous combination of vulnerability, despair and independence; added to that, she had a great unrealised talent which Ford set about bringing out while Stella helped with new clothes. What he taught her was not so much *how* to write, though there was some of that, as that she *was* a writer. He published her in the *Review* and wrote a long and generous preface for her first book, *The Left Bank and Other Stories*. He introduced her to serious reading in French and English and to literary society. Until her re-discovery by Francis Wyndham in the 1960s this was the only time she mixed with literary people. Had she continued to do so she might not have suffered the eclipse that she did. As it was, Nina Hamnett remembered her simply as 'Ford's girl'. He also taught her some tricks of his own: she told Francis Wyndham that when she was worried as to whether a sentence would do she would translate it into French and see if it would work then; if it did, it would also work in English. Many years later she wrote of Ford to Tony Gould: 'When it came to writing he was a very generous man and he encouraged me a great deal. I really don't think that he tried to impose his ideas on me or anyone else but his casual hints could be extraordinarily helpful.'

Their affair is unusual in having been written about directly or indirectly by at least three of the people involved: Jean in *Quarter*, the novel already referred to, Stella in *Drawn from Life* and Jean's husband in a later novel of his own. Also, Ford is thought to have based Lola Porter in 'When the Wicked Man' on Jean. Stella writes perceptively and with her always uncommon frankness and generosity. She thought Jean was 'a really tragic person . . . She had a needle-quick intelligence and a good sort of emotional honesty, but she was a doomed soul, violent and demoralised. She had neither the wish nor the capacity to tackle practical difficulties

. . . [she] showed us an underworld of darkness and disorder, where officialdom, the bourgeoisie and the police were the eternal enemies . . . and was well acquainted with every rung of that long and dismal ladder by which the respectable citizen descended towards degradation . . . It taught me that the only really unbridgeable gulf in human society is between the financially solvent and the destitute. You can't have self-respect without money. You can't even have the luxury of a personality'.

Stella didn't like what happened any more than most people would but she coped with it rather better: 'Life with Ford had always felt to me pretty insecure. Yet here I was cast for the role of the fortunate wife who held all the cards, and the girl for that of the poor, brave and desperate beggar who was doomed to be let down by the bourgeoisie. I learnt what a powerful weapon lies in weakness and pathos and how strong is the position of the person who has nothing to lose, and I simply hated my role! I played it, however, until the girl was restored to health and her job materialised, since we appeared to represent her last chance of survival . . .'

The affair with Ford is usually said to have been partly responsible for two of Jean's novels, *Quartet* and *After Leaving Mr MacKenzie*, both of which have been quoted from already (although, as we shall see, there are grounds for doubting that the latter was in fact inspired by Ford). Certainly, *Quartet* and Stella's *Drawn from Life* are well worth reading back to back since *Quartet* clearly draws on events and describes some of the scenes and incidents mentioned by Stella. The perspective is different, of course. Jean's heroine, Marya, views Lois's (i.e. Stella's) parties with a scathing eye: 'The women were long-necked and very intelligent and would get into corners and say simple, truthful things about each other.' Ford's dances at the Bal du Printemps are described with a practical observation that indicates the trouble that may have stirred up the gate-crashers: '. . . the quality of the brandy left a great deal to be desired. Imagining that it was very weak, people drank a great deal of it, and it generally had a very bad effect on their tempers!' The party at which two men fought, described by Stella as an example of what happened when the Left Bank expatriate crowd were together, becomes in *Quartet* something for Lois to boast about to Marya and to read the descriptions together is to find them compatible in an unsettling way, since it modifies the reader's perception of each writer.

Jean did not like Stella. She didn't dislike women altogether, though she was perhaps rather more of a man's woman, but she particularly disliked the sort of energetic, capable, organising woman that Stella must have appeared. She describes Lois in a paragraph which is convincing and vivid:

> Lois was extremely intelligent. She held her head up. She looked at people with clear, honest eyes. She expressed well-read opinions about every subject under the sun in a healthy voice, and was so perfectly sure of all she said that it would have been a waste of time to contradict her. And, in spite of all this, or because of it, she gave a definite impression of being insensitive to the point of stupidity – or was it insensitive to the point of cruelty? Which? That was the question. But that, of course, always is the question.

That insensitivity may have encouraged Ford to seek its opposite in someone 'needle-quick' and almost crippled by her own sensitivity – almost, since Jean, like her heroine, could in the end always look after herself.

Marya's wooing by Heidler is easy to imagine as Ford's. Some of it is reminiscent of his weeping on Basil Bunting's shoulder in the same year: '"Well, I'm sick of myself," Heidler said gloomily. "And yet it goes on and on. One knows that the whole thing's idiotic, futile, not even pleasant, but one goes on. One's caught in a sort of trap, I suppose."' There are incidents and scenes, apart from those quoted, very likely to have been based on the actual:

> Marya liked the parties best when, about midnight, everybody was a little drunk. She would watch Heidler, who could not dance, walking masterfully up and down the room to the strains of 'If you knew Susie as I know Susie' played on the gramophone, and wonder almost resentfully why his eyes were always so vague when he looked at her. His side-long, cautious glances slid over her as it were.

> 'He looks very German,' she decided. But when they danced together she felt a definite sensation of warmth and pleasure.

She describes elsewhere the feeling of being comforted which his presence gave, something others also mention.

Quartet is a taut, excellent novel from which no one comes out well. The Heidlers are an unpleasantly hypocritical pair and even the fact that Jean is as hard on her heroine as on them does not really balance it because it is the heroine who suffers, and therefore engages our sympathy. As a portrayal of the affair – than which it is more, of course, being also a portrayal of Jean's state of mind afterwards – it lacks two important elements: the extent to which Ford helped Jean and any suggestion of tenderness. The latter is important both in terms of the novel, since without it Marya lacks an important part of her motivation, and in terms of how posterity views Ford. If he was wholly rather than partly like Heidler he would deserve the negative view that Mizener and some others have taken and would probably not have deserved the allegiance which many who knew him – particularly the women – have given. There are, anyway, indications that Jean's view was not Marya's – or not for long, anyway. She told Francis Wyndham that she regretted having written *Quartet* with so much 'spite' in it and she took every opportunity in later years to stress her gratitude to Ford. Wyndham, who came to know her well, believed that she probably had been very much in love with him. Ford had much that she then felt she lacked – reading, culture, erudition, literary experience, confidence, a critical mind – was about twenty-one years older than her and, like a number of her lovers and particularly the first, was a fatherly figure with whom she felt safe. In an unkind passage which reads plausibly, Marya describes Heidler as sexually clumsy:

> He wasn't a good lover, of course. He didn't really like women. She had known that as soon as he touched her. His hands were inexpert, clumsy at caresses; his mouth was hard when he kissed. No, not a lover of women, he could say what he liked.

This would not, Wyndham believes, have troubled Jean in Ford, if it existed; a sexually arousing woman herself, she was quite capable of loving others for quite different reasons. Also, the fact that she continues similar themes in *After Leaving Mr MacKenzie* suggests deep hurt. The heroine there says: 'He sort of smashed me up. Before that I'd always been pretty sure things would turn out all right for me, but afterwards I didn't believe in myself anymore.'

Exactly what happened and when is as unclear as usual. What is known is that Ford got her a job with an American in the South of France, a Mrs Hudnutt whose family were heirs to an American perfumery empire and whose daughter married Rudolph Valentino. Jean told Francis Wyndham that Ford wrote the letter of application for the job on her behalf and that her duties were to write down the dreams and other relevant experiences of the psychic Mrs Hudnutt. She enjoyed it and all went well until one morning when Mrs Hudnutt, still in bed, read aloud to her a letter from Ford accusing Mrs Hudnutt of exploiting her. Both women were puzzled. They returned to Paris and were met by Ford at the station. Mrs Hudnutt cut him but he took Jean off to a hotel. 'It was after this', she told Tony Gould, 'that all the trouble started. It's obvious that I can't elaborate on every detail now.'

It is usually assumed that the physical affair began before Jean went south to Mrs Hudnutt – as happened in *Quartet* – but it seems from this that it might not have. Francis Wyndham was never clear about the precise timing and, as he pointed out, one of the problems about talking to Jean and her contemporaries was that so many of them were drunk for so much of the time that facts are hard to come by. What lay behind Ford's letter can only be guessed at. The incident remained a mystery to Jean for the rest of her life; an example, perhaps, of one of Ford's favourite themes – that the heart of man is a dark forest.

There is some slight room for doubt as to whether or not Ford paid Jean an allowance. Mizener said he did, basing himself on a 29 October 1926 letter from Stella to Ford which refers ambiguously to 'The Richelot cheque'. There is a similarly ambiguous January 1927 letter from Ford to Stella which refers to 'the allowance'. Jean, however – whom Mizener never met – denied it categorically in her letter to Tony Gould: 'It is utterly untrue that I ever lived on an allowance given me by Mr Ford.' There is support for this in a letter from Diana Athill, Jean's editor and close friend of her last years, to Francis Pagan, whose family owned Cooper's Cottage from 1926 to 1984. The letter was written in 1978 when Jean was still alive:

> Only *Quartet*, by the way, is about the affair with Ford. She [Jean] says that the chief way in which it parted from fact on developing into a novel is that 'in real life the unhappiness was *much* more over having no money and my husband being in prison than it was about love. Ford wasn't in the least in love with me – God knows what he felt, he was a mystery to me, but I think he just hated being alone when Stella went into the country – and I wasn't in love with him. It's just that I was stuck and there was no-one else to help me.' Knowing Jean, that last sentence rings very true . . . Also it was someone else, not Ford, who made her a financial allowance for a time . . . She says Ford and Stella sometimes paid for things for her, but never gave her money, and about that sort of thing she is very precise and scrupulous, so I think that would be true . . . Ford wasn't 'Mr MacKenzie' of *After Leaving Mr MacKenzie* by the way, . . . it was her first love of all (see *Voyage In the Dark*) who provides the image of the lover who pensions the girl off, then finally stops sending the cheques . . .

Diana Athill thought Stella's account of Jean 'very convincing'.

Those who were not there are too ignorant to make firm judgements; those who were have fallible memories and cannot avoid special pleading. The difficulty about saying what it was that really happened is that 'it' varied with the actors; only a novel like *The Good Soldier* can show it all.

Apart from Jean's novels, the other major consequence of Ford's relationship with her was the death of his 'marriage' with Stella. It took another three years or so to happen and their friendship survived it, fortunately, but Stella was in no doubt that the dying process began with the affair: 'The obvious and banal business of remaining in love with someone who has fallen for someone else is anybody's experience and no one will deny that it hurts, or that it creates an essential change in the original relationship, however well it may afterwards appear to have been mended . . . To realise that there can be no such thing as "belonging" to another person . . . is surely a necessary part of an adult's education . . . After being quite excruciatingly unhappy for some weeks, I found on a certain day, at a certain hour, that for the first time I was very tired – not to say bored – with personal emotions, my own no less than Ford's . . . I think the exhilaration of falling out of love is not sufficiently extolled . . .' Not surprisingly, she viewed Ford's actions now with a new detachment: 'A man seldom shows to advantage when trying to get rid of a woman who has become an incubus. When Ford disengaged himself from what he called "this entanglement", he announced that having weathered the "pic de tempête" nothing could ever upset us again. But of course he was wrong.'

Without diminishing Stella's account of why the relationship broke up, it might nevertheless be worth considering it from one other perspective. Although she viewed their break-up as an important stage in the development of her confidence in her art, their letters – particularly those written when she was with the Pounds in Italy, in which he urged her to stay on and learn – suggest that he was keen to enhance her confidence and generally did all he could to encourage her. It may be that her tendency to put him first could not be overcome while she was with him and that the resentment this fostered could have been an underlying contributor to the break-up. Her doubts about her own talent may have been as destructive – though less dramatically so – as Ford's waywardness.

As for the man himself, the big portly man who perhaps had, like Heidler, wooed his woman by strolling up and down to the tune of 'If you knew Susie', there is no record of what he felt beyond what is in his books. Personal records designed for posterity found no favour with him. Jean recalled that when *Quartet*, then titled *Postures*, was published in 1928 it caused a lot of upset and trouble but there is no record of Ford's response. He probably quoted to himself that Spanish proverb: 'Take what you want,' said God. 'Take what you want, and pay for it.' Furthermore, we should beware of crediting the affair with a degree of emotional importance – so far as Ford is concerned – that owes more to its having been written about than to anything that happened in it. There is little doubt, for instance, that his affair (or non-affair) with Brigit Patmore meant more to him than that with Jean but because so little is known about it, little is said. Janice Biala once estimated that there had been eighteen women in Ford's life, including one of considerable importance of whom nothing is known except her first name, which was Elizabeth.

TWENTY-TWO

He worked. In January 1925 he finished *A Mirror to France*, which expressed in early form some of the ideas he was to put forward in *Provence* and *The Great Trade Route*. It is not a good book: meandering, over-conversational, uninspired, repetitive. It is of interest only as an early example of his Provence-is-the-home-of-civilisation theme. This had already appeared in the long poem 'Mister Bosphorus' but its interest was his grandfather's French links and his father's interest in Provence and the chivalric tradition. He developed this into something approaching a creed so that by the time of *The Great Trade Route* the spread of civilisation could be traced along a line he drew from the Mediterranean through selected regions of Europe to the south-east of England and across the Atlantic to selected states of America; in other words, all the bits he liked.

Provence and *The Great Trade Route* have much to recommend them; they are the entertaining digressions of a rich and generous mind, crafted so carefully that the craft is hardly noticed. But even so the insistence on France and especially Provence as the home of everything good – chivalry, generosity, art, literature, something he called 'pure thought', wisdom, frugality, the art of living, understanding, tolerance – with the simultaneous blaming of what he calls 'the Nordics' for everything bad, becomes a little much. Allowances may be made for an understandable francophilia, for his feeling that England had rejected his work and therefore him, for the fact that France had from early days been his refuge, for his ancestry and for his natural exaggeration – but he carries it to an extent that might have embarrassed the shade of Monsieur Chauvin himself. It is hard sometimes not to feel that he was lucky to die before Vichy. On the other hand, he did it entertainingly and there is often some truth in his prejudices; also, despite it all, he remained, according to Janice, very patriotic.

In May 1925 he finished *No More Parades*, the second of the Tietjens books, and that summer they moved yet again to a large studio in the rue Notre-Dame-des-Champs which had been found for them by Nina Hamnett. This one had electricity and water, even a sink, but no rooms, only screens. It was large enough, though, for parties. Stella has a good description of Ford playing Père Noël that year, entering by the balcony with sacks full of presents for all the children. After that they wintered in Toulon near Spanish painter friends, Juan Gris and his wife Josette. Stella had hoped they could leave behind their troublesome Alsatian puppy, Toulouse, on the basis that the hotel they were to stay in would not take dogs. 'Nonsense,' said Ford, and the hotel obliged.

They had a very good time in Toulon, with dancing, cinemas, (which Ford enjoyed), good talk and good cafés. Juan Gris, however, observed that Ford 'absorbed a terrifying quantity of alcohol. I never thought one could drink so much.'

They visited Cap Brun and Ford decreed that they should buy a house there. They had no money but he insisted that that was where they must live. It was during this period that they mixed with a number of rich people although Ford, as Stella observed, 'couldn't afford to stand drinks and shoes'; but he was getting past letting that worry him. Style, in life now as in letters, was becoming increasingly important. Besides, *Some Do Not* and *No More Parades* were selling better than anything he had written for years, particularly in America, and it was there that he looked for his future. American reviews were good and one day during their stay in the South he was visited by a number of people from an American liner. This pleased him greatly; America, perhaps, would offer recognition and financial security in degrees hitherto unknown. He started the third of the Tietjens books, *A Man Could Stand Up*, in Toulon that January.

They went to Italy to see Ezra and Dorothy Pound in Rapallo. It is odd that Ford did not show more curiosity about Italy; he went there two or three times and no doubt could have gone more often if he had wanted. Italy, after the Romans, plays relatively little part in his scheme of how civilisation developed. The Pounds lived in a sixth-floor flat overlooking the harbour and the unserviceable lift discouraged visitors so that Pound could get on with his Cantos. When disposed for conversation he would sit outside the quayside café below, and conversation would come to him. They walked and talked; Ford tried to persuade him to visit America again, saying that the literary establishment was not as against him as he imagined, that it would advance his career as it seemed to be advancing his own, but Pound was 'violently averse to anything of the sort'. Everything he wanted was in Italy. He could work there, he was respected in Rapallo, he admired Mussolini and was in touch with him, he was an enthusiast of the principles of the Douglas Credit System (it is possible that his economic interest had developed in part from awareness of Marwood's contributions to *The English Review* many years before).

In succeeding years Pound did much for the cause of international arts in Rapallo but Ford never desisted from trying to persuade him to return to America. It says much for their friendship that it survived Pound's fascist sympathies, for Ford was no fascist. He was a man before and above anything political and the reason he could have friendships with fascists, communists, liberals, socialists and conservatives was that he treated other people as humans first and labels second. Every label was in his eyes a diminution.

This visit to Rapallo was significant. Pound may have developed as he did partly as a result of cutting himself off. He did it in various ways but Rapallo represented the geographical, which is important because it removed him from regular converse with friends such as Ford – perhaps even uniquely Ford – with whom he could disagree without falling out, who could tease him, who could pat him on the shoulder and remind him that they went back a long way, who could, at the same time as accepting him, provide the conflict with other minds without which many good minds are lost. Ford's visit was an attempt not so much to bring Ezra back to what he had left as to point him in the way of the future; he was right, as usual, but it did not work.

When Ford and Stella visited Toulon again in March 1926 the café society they had so much enjoyed had declined into quarrelsomeness and so after Easter they headed for Paris. It was on this journey that they detoured to eat the cassoulet at

Castelnaudary and Stella went on her bucolic rampage in the antique shop. It was still a marriage.

In Paris they lived during the week in the partitioned studio and during the weekends with Madame Annie and Julie at Guermantes. Ford got into tangles with American publishers and, typically, his American royalties on *Some Do Not* were accidentally delayed until late 1927. But he finished *A Man Could Stand Up* on 21 July.

The parties were resumed in Paris. Mizener quotes an account of one by Mary Blomfield[1]:

> Ford had a vast and dismal studio . . . He was a great fat Englishman . . . [who] took into his house a series of mediocre and respectable women who took care of him and were all called Mrs Ford . . . a vast room badly heated by a very small oil stove and furnished with all sorts of uncomfortable chairs and day beds, most of them too far from the stove to be reached by its faint glow . . . making conversation with Ford, who for some occult reason fancied himself a lady-killer, but in spite of this was witty in the best manner of the English and really fun to talk to. Around me was greatness and fame . . . the Hemingways, the F. Scott Fitzgeralds, the Archie Macleishes . . .

From late August into September they went on holiday in Avignon and on 20 October Ford sailed for New York. His idea was to secure permanent publication of his books and to do as much publicity as possible for *A Man Could Stand Up* and its two predecessors. He succeeded in the first in that he was able to negotiate a contract with Albert Boni under which Boni would pay him $400 a month for three years in return for rights on all his novels past and to come. There was to be a uniform edition which Ford hoped one day would lead to a collected edition and, in fact, three books – including the American edition of *The Good Soldier* which had the introduction dedicated to Stella – were published as the Avignon edition, probably in memory of their holiday. It would have been a good deal if it had continued as planned.

[1] *Town and Country*, January 1943

The publicity side – lecturing at universities and to arts clubs and influential ladies' clubs – was not, to start with, encouraging: his lecture agent had arranged only one engagement. But it soon picked up and within a couple of weeks he was being interviewed, photographed and asked out. All this pleased him in an uninhibited, child-like way. Stella, however, in her 29 October letter had already sounded a warning note advising him to tell the Americans about Europe rather than about themselves and to beware of being misquoted. The first was recognition of his tendency to embrace the latest object of his enthusiasm and to tell everyone about it (as he might have gone on to Elsie about Conrad and Marwood). He did not take the hint but began writing a book about America, called *New York is not America*. Her second point was probably a more subtle hint that his delivery in a lecture might not be well understood. His speaking style was quiet and sometimes wheezy and many in his audiences could not hear him. To those who could he wasn't always easy to follow as in the account given to Markham Harris and quoted by Mizener: 'Ford . . . began by requesting that if he did not speak loud enough for those towards the back they let him know by raising their hands. At first people good-naturedly complied (but without appreciable effect) . . . to those down front like myself, the hazy contours of a rambling, soughing, ironic, paradoxical, and blandly egocentric reminiscence took shape . . .'

Nor did those who could hear always understand. He nevertheless secured enough bookings to be able to say that if he were dead he would begin talking again if propped up on a platform. Magazine articles and social and literary engagements also flourished. He was guest of honour with Hugh Walpole and Osbert Sitwell at the P.E.N. Club Dinner. He felt justifiably optimistic about his American publishing career, which now looked better than his European ever had.

There were some problems. He discovered that the reputation he was trying to build up was being damaged from the outset by publicity resulting from Jessie Conrad's letter to the *Times Literary Supplement* about his remembrance of her husband. Also, Violet Hunt's novel about her relationship with him, *The Flurried Years*, was being published (as *I Have This To Say*) by none other than the firm that was also publishing him, Boni. Further, Rebecca

West was in America promoting the image of Violet as martyr at the same time as inviting Ford to lunch. He attempted countermeasures, writing to the *New York Times* about Jessie's erroneous denial that he had suggested the theme of Conrad's *Amy Foster* (with no copy before him and having written the book some twenty-eight years before, he recalled that the relevant passage was on or about page 162 of *The Cinque Ports* – it is page 163) and, less effectively, refusing to dine with T. R. Smith of Boni. This latter contributed to his reputation among publishers as a difficult man to deal with, understandably but perhaps not entirely fairly. Many people might find it hard to sit at table with a man who was publishing a novel about their relationship with a resentful former lover; if the same man is their publisher, it might also be politic to do so. Ford, however, was no more a politician than he was a bore. He didn't like it and said so.

In January 1927 he was in Chicago and, after yet another lecture, was given a party by Harriet Monroe, editor of *Poetry*, at which Harriet reminded him that he had promised her a two-thousand-word article, as yet unwritten. They went to her office after the party where he sat down and dictated it. It is a charming article, a plea for tolerance of modern writers such as Joyce, Stein, Cummings, Tate and Crane. He barely mentions his own poetry and his prose not at all. The critics come in for a few swipes, though: 'I mean that it is an easy job to say that an elephant, however good, is not a good wart-hog; for most criticism comes to that.' (There was at that time, incidentally, a real Tietjens on the advisory committee of *Poetry*, named Eunice.)

While in Chicago he visited Hemingway's parents who lived in 'a particularly Puritan and ridiculous suburb' that their son would have been embarrassed for his friends to know. He must have spoken well of Hemingway junior since Dr Hemingway described Ford in a letter to Ernest as 'your great admirer' who 'came on time and made a very charming guest. He gave us a wonderful word picture of you and your boy . . . Mother was so pleased with the Englishman. He seemed to enjoy his dinner and the Tea and all the other eats.' Neither charm nor appetite ever forsook him.

Stella had taken Julie to England where she saw Mrs Hueffer

and stayed with some friends in Oxford. The letters between her and Ford are long and affectionate, though he felt it necessary to reassure her that she should not 'worry about my success with the ladies. One never sees them twice and the once is always in bevvies of about four hundred or so . . .' Nevertheless, she worried that New York was taking him away from her and probably wasn't greatly reassured at his mention of such small incidents as the use of his flat by an adulterous couple. She was also worried about their dog, Toulouse, who had taken to biting strangers. Ford had given her leave to sell him but she was reluctant because he had said Toulouse was 'the only beautiful thing he had ever owned'. Meanwhile, she was in a domestic quandary because it was proving difficult to get rid of the redoubtable Madame Annie. (Eventually Stella persuaded her to accept an offer of marriage and the problem was solved.)

Before leaving New York towards the end of February he began dictating the fourth and last of the Tietjens volumes, *Last Post*, to Caroline Tate. He dedicated it to Isabel Paterson, its 'fairy godmother' who had entertained him and but for whom 'this book would have only nebularly existed – in space, in my brain, where you will, though it be not on paper or between boards, but, that is to say, for your stern, contemptuous and almost virulent insistence on knowing "what became of Tietjens" I never should have conducted this chronicle to the stage it has now reached.' When he returned they went again to Toulon but Juan Gris was dead and it seemed no longer the town of their first visit. However, he finished *New York is not America* there, went back to Paris and carried on with *Last Post*.

In June 1927 Mrs Hueffer died. Ford returned to England and stayed a week or so after the funeral trying to boost his sales. He continued to try from Paris for some months afterwards, even offering himself to the *Sunday Express* as a boxing reporter for the Dempsey–Tunney fight, claiming that he was a qualified army referee. His promotional efforts were not entirely unavailing. The Tietjens novels did not sell badly in England though never well enough to make significant money.

In July, he heard that Borys Conrad had been imprisoned for a year for gaining money by false pretences. He immediately offered through Eric Pinker to have Borys's wife and child to stay with them at Avignon during August – 'People like to get to France where as a rule nothing is known of their cases', he wrote, perhaps recalling his own experiences of legal affairs. The offer was not taken up but it was not the first time he had helped Borys, having sought him out when they were both on active service in France. Borys may have been no chip off the old block but the memory of his father was sufficient for Ford.

Their stay at Villeneuve-les-Avignon was something of an idyll. Ford typed *Last Post* on his Corona from seven till ten each morning, then they would swim in the Rhône, walk, drink and talk. He would name the herbs and flowers they passed in the fields and one day they danced a round dance on a bridge to the tune of a nursery rhyme. As usual, when work was going well, everything did. The following month he returned to America, sailing on the S.S. *Minnedosa*. The night before they reached Quebec he finished *Last Post*. He had done it in a burst and, relieved at last of the pressure, wrote immediately to Stella announcing the conclusion, then walked into the ship's concert and offered to make a limerick on any passenger's name within thirty seconds.

In New York he concluded his agreement with Albert Boni and even found a possible backer for a revived *Transatlantic Review* which fortunately came to nothing. He had worked hard and played hard and began to get dizzy spells, but it did not stop him. He worked from eight in the morning till lunch and then talked and ate and drank until about two the following morning. He went everywhere he could, met everyone he could and was probably more of a celebrity and more financially successful than at any time of his life. Goldring was there and visited him 'in the small and dingy apartment which he used as an office'. He had a table, a typewriter and two chairs and was dressed only in his under-garments. Goldring never discovered where he actually lived, though not long after he moved in with Caroline and Allen Tate.

Goldring's visit was cut short by the sudden deaths of his sister-in-law and her husband in Paris. His wife, who was new to France, was having to cope. Ford 'sent a long cablegram to his household in Paris, invoking their aid on my wife's behalf'. Goldring booked a berth on the first boat he could afford: 'In the days which elapsed before she sailed, Ford looked after me with a kindness and sympathy which I can never forget. He took me to parties to distract my thoughts and, on the day of my departure, he even came to my little hotel to help me pack. The ship sailed at midnight and, to fill up time after dinner, Ford took me to call on some young friends of his, who were meditating masterpieces in what Londoners would call a slum . . . We drank home-made red wine, out of tea-cups. In these modest surrounds, Ford – who at that time was one of the most prominent and respected men of letters in New York and much sought after by socialites – was perfectly happy . . . he discoursed for several hours on French and English prose, to an audience which hung on his words . . . he was in his element.'

He was approaching fifty-five and was like a puppy on the loose, thoroughly enjoying himself. His reiterations to Stella that he was becoming successful and that his presence in America facilitated his publishing career were not greatly exaggerated: the *Parade's End* books – *Last Post* having been chosen by the Literary Guild – eventually sold, Mizener calculated, about 30–35,000 copies, compared with about 4,000 in Britain. Further, he was a puppy who soon learned to house-train himself: finding New York distressingly short of public facilities, he used the Guaranty Trust Company on Fifth Avenue as his *pissoir.* He had no other business there and no doubt the Grand Manner ensured that he went unchallenged. He had reached that stage of life where his pose was no longer out of keeping with his age or appearance. He was what he seemed. He had achieved himself.

Stella, meanwhile, worked in their large studio and lived in a small flat they had recently acquired in the rue Vaugirard. She was learning to appreciate a room of her own: 'Since I've been working here hard, regularly, I realise how much I count upon being quiet and alone in the studio,' she wrote to him. There is a change in their letters during these few months; although Ford continues to address her as 'darling', their signings-off became less expressions of love than of affection, esteem, admiration, best wishes and God's blessings. 'Falling out of love,' she wrote later, 'is a delicate and important business, and as necessary to the attainment of wisdom as the reverse experience.' They managed it well. Gently, by stages, without any undue ruffles, they reached agreement, as they always had. By the end of the year Ford was able to ask her to rent on his behalf a small flat in the same block as the new one. She did so and responded: 'But your letter and the "Last Post" together, seem to mark the end of our long intimacy, which did have a great deal of happiness in it for me, and which did involve us in a great deal of decent effort . . . I will try to get the electric light put on in the new apartment before you come back. The principal room is a real good size with two dormer windows. I think you will be very happy there.' As with Elsie and Violet, he had brought about the break-up of the relationship by geographical separation. It worked more amicably with Stella because of the person she was and perhaps also partly because of the distances involved: it is easier to feel neglected if someone doesn't visit Sussex from London or London from Cardiff, than Paris from New York.

With hindsight, Stella was also to write:

> Ford was a much larger and more luxuriant plant than I. He required to be well-entwined around the support of his choice, but in due course the roving tendrils began to attach themselves to other supports, without showing any disposition to release the first one. This created a situation which I found too difficult. It brought me into relationship with new elements which I was too tired to cope with.

One of these tendrils had, towards the end of 1927, inched itself around the ample Mrs Rene Wright, a forty-eight-year-old lady whom he had first met over twenty years before when in America with Elsie. She was married then to her first husband, who had died. She and Ford met again during his visit earlier in 1927 and now, with her second marriage breaking up, they saw a good deal more of each other. He began to be seen in public with her and wrote a poem about her, 'Winter-Night Song', beginning;

> My dearest dear, my honey-love
> My brown-eyed squirrel, my soft dove.

He returned to France early in 1928 and told Stella. Stella went to the South to think things over and in April wrote a selfless letter offering a complete break if he wanted it. He did not; he had no wish not to see Stella again and badly wanted to stay in touch with Julie.

Nor was a complete break really possible for Stella at that stage. It was all too close: 'But even when working at my easel, my head was conscious of Ford's needs and wishes and states of mind. This would not have been so if I had been bored by him, but I was not. Nobody could be. They might be exasperated and antipathetic, but never bored.' Nor did she, any more than Rene, want to share. They made reasonable arrangements. Stella would keep the studio and the flat, Ford the newly rented one. He formally acknowledged his financial debts to her, accumulated since Cooper's Cottage, and made over to her his entire British earnings until the debts should have been paid, including interest at 5%. After that she and Julia would continue to receive £200 per year of his British earnings plus half of his American earnings up to a maximum of $4,800. The Depression and the Wall Street crash saw to it that Stella never got anything like what was intended; neither did Ford. He did his best no matter how poor he became and never tried to alter the terms. She lived off the remainder of her capital and what she could make from her painting; he off no capital and what he could make from his writing. Their letters – over 200, mostly unpublished – tell almost the whole story. One of her last ends: 'Do remember sometimes, as I always shall, that we were very happy together and do let us stay friends. God bless you always . . .'; and one of his: '. . . I esteem you and I am attached to you as I have always done and been. It is really the riding that has done it. We grew too tired before the settling down of peace . . . may God bless you at your rising up and your lying down, at your setting out and at your returning . . .' The 1928 and subsequent editions of *The Good Soldier* all carry a dedicatory letter to Stella.

A Little Less than Gods is another historical novel, set in the time of Napoleon and usually referred to by Ford as his 'Ney' novel. Not surprisingly, it does not come up to the tetralogy that preceded it. He should have had a break but felt he couldn't afford one. It was begun in a rush, too – 11,000 words in four days while in New York during the week in which he was looking after Douglas Goldring. It was published in the autumn of 1928, *The Last Post* having been published in January. The previous year he had published a slim volume of poems old and new but called *New Poems*, as well as *New York is not America* and *New York Essays*. This was apart from commissions for articles here and there, such as that for the *Saturday Review of Literature*, prompted by E. M. Forster's *Aspects of the Novel* which Ford – in a rare reference to Forster – called a 'pretty bad' book. The articles prepared the way for his own *The English Novel* published in 1929. Such work was not simply something he was able to fit in to an otherwise hectic life, nor was it even a major part of life; it was, for him, the condition of life. It is not possible to imagine him without work; what he did he was. The rest – the friends, the lectures, his reading, his affairs, the parties, limericks and likely stories – were the overflow of spirit and energy. His faults were those of generosity, always of too much, never of too little.

TWENTY-THREE

Like *The Good Soldier*, *Parade's End* is a book that has spawned other books, usually theses and works of criticism. There is not much point in debating which is the greater since, despite some similarities of theme, they do different things. The one is grand and broad, a picture of a society in peace and war; the other narrow, concentrated, intense, a sounding of the emptiness within. Both successfully marry the individual and the social, both are Ford writ large and not Ford at all; in each he most fulfils and most transcends himself. In years they are separated by little more than a decade but in terms of life lived it is as if he had been allowed a second, building on the first.

It is better to read and re-read *Parade's End* rather than read about it but it is worth saying that in Tietjens Ford at least fully realises his Marwood figure while Sylvia Tietjens is the fullest imaginative re-creation of the women who loved and pursued him to the bitter end. The first is that rarity, a good man who is yet an interesting hero, a man of honour in a fallen world who gains in conviction the more he becomes victim and who doesn't give in. The other is another rarity, a sensitively portrayed she-devil, hard, cruel and persecuting yet sympathetic. She wants to possess and be possessed, to make a man of a martyr:

> And now, walking along the table with her plate in her hand, she could not but acknowledge that, triumphantly – and very comfortably for her! – Tietjens had been right! In the third year of the war it was very convenient to have a dwelling, cheap, comfortable, almost august and so easy to work that you could have, at a pinch, run it with one maid, though the faithful Hullo Central had not let it come to that yet . . .

Being near Tietjens she lifted her plate, which contained two cold cutlets in aspic and several leaves of salad; she wavered a little to one side and, with a circular motion of her hand, let the whole contents fly at Tietjens' head. She placed the plate on the table and drifted slowly towards the enormous mirror over the fireplace.

'I'm bored,' she said. 'Bored! Bored!'

Tietjens had moved slightly as she had thrown. The cutlets and most of the salad leaves had gone over his shoulder. But one, couched, very green leaf was on his shoulder-strap, and the oil and vinegar from the plate – Sylvia *knew* that she took too much of all condiments – had splashed from the revers of his tunic to his green staff-badges. She was glad that she had hit him as much as that: it meant that her marksmanship had not been quite rotten. She was glad, too, that she had missed him. She was also supremely indifferent. It had occurred to her to do it and she had done it. Of that she was glad!

She looked at herself for some time in the mirror of bluish depths. She pressed her immense bandeaux with both hands on to her ears. She was all right: high-featured; alabaster complexion – but that was mostly the mirror's doing – beautiful, long, cool hands – what man's forehead wouldn't long for them? . . . And that hair! What man wouldn't think of it, unloosed on white shoulders! . . . Well, Tietjens wouldn't! Or, perhaps, he did . . . she hoped he did, curse him, for he never saw that sight. Obviously sometimes, at night, with a little whiskey taken he must want to!

She rang the bell and bade Hullo Central sweep the plateful from the carpet; Hullo Central, tall and dark, looking with wide-open eyes, motionlessly at nothing.

Sylvia went along the bookshelves, pausing over a book back, 'Vitae Hominum Notiss . . .' in gilt, irregular capitals pressed deep in the old leather. At the first long window she supported herself by the blind-cord. She looked out and back into the room.

'There's that veiled woman!' she said, 'going into eleven . . . It's two o'clock, of course . . .'

She looked at her husband's back hard, the clumsy khaki back

> that was getting round-shouldered now. Hard! She wasn't going to miss a motion or a stiffening.

Sylvia's physical characteristics were inspired, Ford told Janice Biala, by his seeing Sinclair Lewis's wife in a gold gown like that in which he at one point dresses Sylvia.

Parade's End is remarkable for its war writing. As in *No Enemy*, it is not the individual heroics or actions that come over most strongly as the sense of the individual in the grip of a vast impersonal madness which serves to heighten rather than relieve all the normal worries, in the scale of which death comes fairly low. As an evocation of war in its daily mundanities, confusions, futilities and occasional horrors, it is unsurpassed:

> He remembered being up in the artillery O.P. – what the devil was its name? – before Albert. On the Albert-Bécourt-Bécordel Road! What the devil was its name? A gunner had been looking through his glasses. He had said to Tietjens: 'Look at that fat! . . .' And through the glasses lent him, Tietjens had seen, on a hillside in the direction of Martinpuich, a fat Hun, in shirt and trousers, carrying in his right hand a food tin from which he was feeding himself with his left. A fat, lousy object, suggesting an angler on a quiet day. The gunner had said to Tietjens:
>
> 'Keep your glass on him!'
>
> And they had chased that miserable German about that naked hillside, with shells, for ten minutes. Whichever way he bolted, they put a shell in front of him. Then they let him go. His action, when he had realised that they were really attending to him, had been exactly that of a rabbit dodging out of the wheat the reapers have just reached. At last he just lay down. He wasn't killed. They had seen him get up and walk off later. Still carrying his bait can!
>
> His antics had afforded those gunners infinite amusement. It afforded them almost more when all the German artillery on that front, imagining that God knew what was the matter, had awakened and plastered heaven and earth and everything between for a quarter of an hour with every imaginable kind of

missile. And had then, abruptly, shut up. Yes . . . Irresponsible people, gunners!

The incident had really occurred because Tietjens had happened to ask that gunner how much he imagined it had cost in shells to smash to pieces an indescribably smashed field of about twenty acres that lay between Bazentin-le-petit and Mametz Wood. The field was unimaginably smashed, pulverised, powdered . . . The gunner had replied that with shells from all the forces employed it might have cost three million sterling. Tietjens asked how many men the gunner imagined might have been killed there. The gunner said he didn't begin to know. None at all, as like as not! No one was very likely to have been strolling about there for pleasure, and it hadn't contained any trenches. It was just a field. Nevertheless, when Tietjens had remarked that in that case two Italian labourers with a steam plough could have pulverised that field about as completely for, say, thirty shillings, the gunner had taken it quite badly. He had made his men poop off after that inoffensive Hun with the bait can, just to show what artillery can do.

It is also the book in which Ford describes violent events and death with a directness that is uncharacteristic of much of his writing. 'O Nine Morgan', for instance, is a company runner to whom Tietjens had recently forbidden leave on the grounds that he was likely to be hurt by his wife's prize-fighter lover. Morgan makes his final appearance when Tietjens and another officer are talking in a shed some way behind the lines during not very serious shelling:

A man, brown, stiff, with a haughty parade step, burst into the light. He said with a high wooden voice:

''Ere's another blooming casualty.' In the shadow he appeared to have draped half his face and the right side of his breast with crape. He gave a high, rattling laugh. He bent, as if in a stiff bow, woodenly at his thighs. He pitched, still bent, on to the iron sheet that covered the brazier, rolled off that and lay on his back across the legs of another runner, who had been crouched beside the brazier. In the bright light it was as if a whole pail of

> scarlet paint had been dashed across the man's face on the left and his chest. It glistened in the firelight – just like fresh paint, moving! The runner from the Rhondda, pinned down by the body across his knees, sat with his jaw fallen, resembling one girl that should be combing the hair of another recumbent before her. The red viscousness welled across the floor; you sometimes so see fresh water bubbling up in sand. It astonished Tietjens to see that a human body could be so lavish of blood.

It is a long and masterly scene in which the business of clearing up the bits is convincingly interspersed with Tietjens's random private reflections. It ends:

> Two men were carrying the remains of O Nine Morgan, the trunk wrapped in a ground sheet. They carried him in a bandy chair out of the hut. His arms over his shoulders waved a jocular farewell. There would be an ambulance stretcher on bicycle wheels outside.

But because it is a book that deals also with peace and with the more familial tortures of life at home, because the focus is not that of the gun-sight but rather the view from the upturned ammunition box in a wet steaming tent during a strafe while trying to write a letter home, it is not normally appreciated as war writing.

There is disagreement among Fordians about the final volume, *The Last Post*. As is clear from his dedication to Isabel Paterson he had not intended to write it when he began the series. The book was to be a trilogy, ending with Tietjens and Valentine dancing on Armistice Night amidst the confusion and yelling and prancing of that time out of time, caught between the unburied past and the unknown future, with Sylvia, the tigress, still at large. Later, in a letter to Eric Pinker about a possible collected edition of his works he wrote: 'I strongly wish to omit *The Last Post* from the edition. I do not like the book and have never liked it and always intended the series to end with *A Man Could Stand Up*. Please consult Duckworth's about this. I am ready to be guided by them but should much prefer the above course.' This is unequivocal and is partly why Graham Greene omitted *The Last Post* from his Bodley Head edition of *Parade's End*. Greene had, however, another reason: 'This is a better book, a thousand times, which ends in the confusion of Armistice Night 1918 . . . and this – not the carefully arranged happy *finale* of *The Last Post* – was the true conclusion . . .'

It is clear from its first page that *The Last Post* is different. Tietjens is off-stage for nearly all of the book and most of the narrative is from the point of view of his brother, Mark, who took to his bed and would not speak because of the peace terms and who now lives in a make-shift shelter in the garden, as Elsie had when convalescing in Kent. But, unlike Elsie, Mark is waiting to die, and the house and garden are modelled on Cooper's Cottage, not Aldington. His musings and observations provide a perspective both on what has gone before and on the post-war world and the post-war Tietjens. It also, incidentally, enables Ford to describe the unfolding of the drama of Tietjens's marriage without having to dramatise it.

It would be possible to debate at some length the merits of including or excluding *Last Post*. On the one hand, there is some contrived arranging to let us see that Tietjens and Valentine are doing all right, that they are surviving and that Sylvia has given up her vindictive pursuit in favour of blessing their union. It might be argued that this is sentimental and weakens what comes before it, adding too much water to the whisky. On the other hand, *A Man Could Stand Up* does not end in the cathartic quiet of passion spent; because the war is over, because the world has changed and the new peace cannot be as the old, we do ask – as we see Tietjens and Valentine dancing a cumbersome shuffle into the future – what then? Are they going to make it? To leave them clasped to each other is not quite enough because we know that the peace to come will in some ways be harder than the war. Tietjens tried to support the old world on his shoulders, only to watch it cascade in feathery fragments about his feet. He was changed, too: how will he cope with the new? Because he was not destroyed, because he is going to go on – into our world – it is a legitimate question. Nor does the ending of *The Last Post* leave us or the characteres with a too-contrived finality; it is not unequivocal, no one has arrived finally and safely but they do have a determination to go on, which is a kind of arrival.

There is also the question of whether we should heed an author's wish not to include work about which he has changed his mind; what is more, work which – whatever his feelings before and after – he did at the time intend to include. Janice Biala's impression was that he never either fully repudiated nor fully endorsed it, but was certainly keen enough on selling it. The answer, surely, is no; once an author has placed his work in the public domain it is no longer his judgements that count. He has views that may be noted but the power to withhold should be no longer his; he built the craft and handed her over; where she sails is up to those who would sail her. Furthermore, if readers are deprived of the book they have no chance to make up their own minds. In the end, it is a matter of taste. Most probably feel, like Isobel Paterson, that *A Man Could Stand Up* does call for a sequel even if it is not essential. Those who do not so feel have the choice of ignoring it. What is important is that neither party be deprived of the choice.

But the main question about *Parade's End* is: does it *really* work? This is not to question its status as a major novel, but to ask whether, like others in the great league of great novels, it defines the terms by which we judge it; as when, for example, we are confronted by a personality so outstanding that though we say others are like him or her in this or that particular, we feel that he or she is like no one else and cannot be compared. For instance *The Good Soldier* fulfils its own artistic intention so completely and latches on to its bit of the world so surely that it is impregnable, but it is hard to have quite the same feeling about *Parade's End*. The reason is the twin notions of the gentleman and of seventeenth-century spirituality that are the mainspring of Tietjens' character, the source of his conflict with the Edwardian world. These provide the contrast by which the moral pretensions of the Victorian and Edwardian times were judged and, in part, the reason why the author wrote the book. Both are myth: there never was an English gentleman quite like Tietjens (perhaps Sir Thomas Fairfax, the young commander-in-chief under whom Cromwell was content to serve, comes closest to it; but he did not suffer passively like Tietjens) and there never was quite such a state of spiritual purity to which we can confidently look back. Both are products of an Anglo-German romantic imagination, of someone who had painstakingly learned the rituals only to find that they were just that, and who spent much of the rest of his life trying to put meaning into them.

Though hard to imagine Tietjens without all this mythological baggage it is possible because Ford has created a character sufficiently convincing for us to talk about him as if he were real, and for real people we can always imagine alternative motives and actions. If he had been an honourable man by the standards of his time rather than by invented ones, the point of conflict between him and a dishonourable world would have been that much more central; he would then have fought the battle for all decent men and women of all times, including our own, rather than the battle which no one else is fighting because, although we know the world is often as bad as that, we also know it was never really very good. In most great novels in which the protagonist is an idealist – Dostoievsky's *The Idiot*, for instance – he is either tragic or ridiculous, but Ford doesn't want Tietjens to be either. He wants Tietjens to be reasonable, honourable and wise but what motivates Tietjens is something that most honourable men of his time would not have recognised as reasonable. Perhaps in the end it is because Ford is a realist who wants to be an idealist; to return to Aesop, he was a fox knowing many things who wanted to be a hedgehog and know one big thing.

Which is not to say, after all, that the book doesn't work. Perhaps it should not but Ford gets away with it. He does so not because his major characters are all strong, nor because the minor characters are so memorable (Perowne, for instance, Sylvia's lover, is a beautiful evocation of a nonentity), nor because his portrayal of the world he is describing is so real – though all are true – but because the force of his own vision, which is at the heart of the book, is so great and so vividly dramatised that we *are* convinced. It is an artistic triumph despite the limitation that is also the source of its energy – Ford's exorcism of himself in Tietjens.

In the spring of 1928, when he and Stella had put their separation into effect – he in his flat, she in hers, and she anyway away in the South – he worked on *A Little Less than Gods*. In the evenings he could be seen in the Deux Magots, a fat man looking rather older than his years, sitting at a table waiting for a familiar or at least obliging face to whom he could talk; once talking, he had no further need of stimulation. Within a few years he would be writing of Henry Martin Smith, the hero of *The Rash Act*: 'He went out for most of his meals. Sometimes he found an acquaintance to talk to him. As often as not he did not. He imagined that some people still avoided him – but he might have been mistaken . . .'

He started his Thursday afternoon teas again, keeping open house. It was not, however, simply that he wished to see people; it was also a way of ensuring that he did not have to see them all the time. At one time he was even, he said, 'coerced into learning a number of Charleston steps'. In May he went to a dinner given for Pound, whom he was to eulogise, but the eulogy was never heard because a surrealist pulled a knife on Pound and the dinner broke up. At 3.15 one morning he wrote to Stella about Julie's education. He wanted Julie to be 'a real Catholic for as long as it lasts', but added, 'If you regard Romanism in Julie from now till eighteen or so as you now regard her belief in fairytales it will go perfectly happily.' If, on the other hand, Stella wanted not to 'cut her off from the free-thinking influence' it would be better to bring her up an atheist since 'A clean Catholic will jump straight off when the time comes, if it does. A child who has been all mucked up always ends by compromise after compromise and that is fatal for the intellect.'

Late in May he left for New York, giving a large party the night before at which all the glasses were broken; he counted it a success. He arrived in New York within days of Rene Wright's divorce, only to find that she would not live with him as his mistress unless they were to marry. He had, perhaps, counted on her weakening now that he was no longer living with Stella but she did not. She wanted marriage, as Violet had, but was not prepared to commit herself until she knew she could have it, and Ford was still a married man. She was not prepared simply to be his American wife. (Eventually, she got her marriage, though not with Ford: she re-married her second husband.) They went about together but it was probably an anguished time for both. He could not really live without a woman and must have wanted her very much.

She, Harold Loeb recalled in *The Way it Was* and in the *London Magazine*, seemed 'touchingly fond' of him and in the taxi Loeb shared with her she was on the verge of tears. She told him that Ford could not marry her and she could not live with him unmarried. Loeb had the impression that Ford was not allowed into her hotel bedroom. As usual, Ford's own reactions were not recorded. Meanwhile, Rene's former husband, Guy, had better luck: he married within a month, though it was another five years before he was free to marry Rene again.

Ford returned to Marseilles in July, dedicating *A Little Less than Gods* to Rene. Between leaving for New York in May and returning to France he wrote over one hundred thousand words. He didn't get back to Paris until October, but travelled slowly up through France. It was unusual for him to be so much alone and there may have been an element of recuperation, a much-needed marking of time. He may also have been more fond of Rene than is known and was perhaps feeling his age: he was fifty-five and had burnt his boats only to find that the new coastline was not as hospitable as he had thought. At the hotel in Marseilles he had not even enough money for the bill and could not leave until some arrived from New York.

In November Caroline and Allen Tate arrived in Paris from New York on the Guggenheim fellowship for which he had recommended them. He revived his sonnet contests at which the prize, Allen Tate told Mizener, 'was always stale cake provided by Ford which he always won, but gave to the runner-up'. The contests involved his preparing in advance many copies of the last word in every line of a sonnet – he particularly used those by Shakespeare and Christina Rossetti – and the copies would be passed round the guests so that everyone would try a sonnet based on the same rhyme words. Mary McIntosh described the parties to Sondra Stang, saying that Ford always composed his efforts on the typewriter in the adjoining study. They were warm and lively occasions with a nucleus of regulars and a changing stream of visitors. McIntosh recalls Hemingway being present 'long after the period he refers to when he wrote about Ford in his *Moveable Feast.* He didn't act as if his sense of smell was being offended by the presence of Ford in that small, warm room. That chapter about

Ford in Hemingway's book is inexcusable. I can't help feeling that Hemingway wrote it from some unworthy, petty motive of personal revenge . . .' The cakes that she remembers, though, were 'delicious petit fours . . .'

In Janury 1929 Stella moved out of her flat so Ford moved back in and the Tates had his. Despite the parties and the dinners he was still probably rather lonely, with plenty of time for wondering what he had made of his life and what, if anything, was to come. He was working on a new novel, *When the Wicked Man*, and trying to establish himself not simply as a writer who sold in America but almost as an American writer (*When the Wicked Man* is set there).

Things must have brightened, though, when Rene arrived in Paris 'to buy clothes' and they returned to New York together at the end of the year. Once there he was mugged on New Year's Eve but reported the experience with the cheerfulness that was his custom during physical adversity, saying he had 'got off rather successfully with a little damage to my teeth and throat'. Never for long could he forget those teeth that Violet had paid for.

In January he tried for the last time to persuade Elsie to agree to divorce, no doubt so that he could marry Rene. Elsie wouldn't, strongly suggesting via Robert Garnett that her reason was the children. This is unlikely, however true it may have been before. Both were well into adulthood, Christina a nun and Katharine, since 1927, the wife of the Irish painter Charles Lamb, with whom she lived in County Galway. It may have been that Elsie was annoyed by Ford's letter in which he said, wrongly, that he had only just heard that she wouldn't divorce because he was a Catholic. This was a variant of the 1924 error on her barrister's part when she was bringing proceedings against Violet, about which Ford had heard at the time. He also told Robert Garnett that he remained 'solemnly resolved' not to pay any more money to her unless they were divorced. It may have been that this combination served only to harden her in her own solemn resolve never to grant the one thing she could still deny him. Whether she was really as bitter as this suggests is not known but her life-long refusal can hardly be accounted for by the reasons she gave. Perhaps it was the name: having fought for and won it, she wasn't going to give up her sole right to be Mrs Hueffer for anyone, even though Mr Hueffer had ditched his name a decade ago. This indirect contact was the last they had. For Ford and Rene it meant there could be no marriage and therefore no Rene Ford.

He stayed in New York till August, finishing *When the Wicked Man*, writing the essays for *The Bookman* which became *The English Novel* and articles on cookery and wine. These latter were successful; he knew his subjects and he knew how to write about them. *The English Novel* is a little-known good book which was, he tells us, written in New York, on board the S.S. *Patria*, and in the port and neighbourhood of Marseilles during July and August 1927, though Mizener thinks, possibly rightly, that it was in fact the year after. It is short, accessible and now safely back in print, thanks to Carcanet. It is also unashamedly unacademic, unobjective, biased and personal, almost more an after-dinner conversation than a book, during which your cigar goes out unnoticed in your fingers and your brandy remains unfinished at your elbow. The voice that addresses you is warm and intelligent, its judgements made more definite – for good and ill – by an overwhelming love for its subject. The author speaks as if in the secure knowledge of certain verities, knowledge which he knows you share and which therefore needs no demonstration. He treats Shakespeare as a novelist, wondering that 'the greatest writer of all time should not have taken the trouble ever to read his own works in print'. In fact, he doesn't often write about Shakespeare, seeing him perhaps as the highest and most isolated peak, leading nowhere. It may be that contemporary productions were a discouraging influence: 'On the face of it, the plays of Shakespeare read extravagantly well but, on the modern stage, play extravagantly badly. I have never in my life been more bored and appalled than at having to sit through an uncut performance of Hamlet, given by one of the most noted performers in the world in front of a gigantic real castle. It was terrifying and it lasted from six at night till four in the morning.'

He considers Chaucer, Bunyan and Defoe before settling upon Richardson as the first example of a novelist who is truly modern in the sense that form and perspective are shaped so as to marry with the narrative and bring out its meaning. The pure line then crosses the Channel to mainly French writers (no German, interestingly), culminating there in Turgenev and Flaubert before crossing back again to James and Conrad. These apart, most English novelists have shown, he thinks, a distressing lack of any appreciation of form and indeed of any real seriousness about what they are doing:

> Any sort of English writer takes any sort of pen and on any sort of paper with in his hair whatever sort of vine-leaves you will and at his elbow any nectar from metheglin to Château Yquem or pale ale, writes any sort of story in any sort of method – or in any sort of mixture of any half dozen methods. So if he have any of the temperament of an artist, you have a Fielding or a Trollope, a Samuel Butler or a George Meredith, each rising as a separate peak but each absolutely without an inter-relation with any other.

Fielding and Thackeray were the worst offenders, the former – with the exception of *Jonathan Wilde* – not even a serious writer for grown-up people. Ford particularly disliked *Tom Jones*:

> For myself, I am no moralist: I consider that if you do what you want you must take what you get for it and that if you deny yourself things you will be better off than if you don't. But fellows like Fielding, and to some extent, Thackeray, who pretend that if you are a gay drunkard, lecher, squanderer of your goods and fumbler in placket-holes you will eventually find a benevolent uncle, concealed father or benefactor who will shower on you bags of tens of thousands of guineas, estates and the hands of adorable mistresses – those fellows are dangers to the body politic and horrible bad constructors of plots.

The Fielding/Thackeray tradition led to what he called 'the nuvvel', which was really the literature of escape. Thackeray was the greater criminal because Fielding could at least tell good stories of people running into and out of each other's bedrooms, whereas Thackeray was hampered by the curse of many English novelists: the aspiration to the status of gentleman. 'The dread spectre of the Athenaeum Club was ever in his background' – but he did worse than that:

> And I imagine that the greatest literary crime ever committed was Thackeray's sudden, apologetic incursion of himself into his matchless account of the manoeuvres of Becky Sharp on Waterloo Day in Brussels . . . The motive of most crimes is so obscure, so pathological or so fatalised by hereditary weakness that there is almost nothing that cannot be pardoned once one has dived beneath the calm surface of things. But Thackeray as a child-murderer can never be forgiven: the deeper you delve in the hidden springs of his affairs, the more unforgivable does he appear.

Again, Thackeray has introduced

> his broken nose and myopic spectacles into the middle of the most thrilling scene he ever wrote, in order to tell you that, though his heroine was rather a wrong 'un, his own heart was in the right place.

Fortunately, not all English novelists were thus affected:

> Trollope and Miss Austen – like Shakespeare and Richardson – stand so absolutely alone that nothing very profitable can be said about them by a writer analysing British fiction in search of main-currents of tradition. They were both so aloof, so engrossed, so contemplative – and so masterly . . . as in the case of Turgenev, the aspiring writer can learn very little of either. These novelists write well, know how to construct a novel so as to keep the interest going with every word until the last page – but after that all you can say is that they were just temperaments, and quiet ones at that. Inimitable – that is what they are. You could imitate Oscar Wilde – but never Trollope giving you the still, slow stream of English country and small-town life.

Smollett is also praised, Marryat more so:

> . . . I re-read *Peter Simple* for my pleasure. It was to come into contact with a man who could write and see and feel. For me, nothing in *War and Peace* is as valuable as the boat cutting-out

expedition of Marryat and for me he remains the greatest of English novelists. His name is not even mentioned in the manual of literary dates with which I have just been refreshing my memory.

But the real tradition was with the French. They were consistently writing novels the aim of which was 'to produce the effect of being there'. James, Conrad, and Stephen Crane would inherit this tradition when it died in France and subsequent writers of English would be more concerned with form and with producing novels that were more than chronicles of 'characters', of tales or of comforting moral illustrations. But Ford was aware that it might not always be thus:

> There are probably – humanity being stable, change the world how it may – there are probably eternal principles for all the arts, but the application of those principles is eternally changing, or eternally revolving. It is, for instance, an obvious and unchanging fact that if an author intrudes his comments into the middle of a story he will endanger the illusion conveyed by that story – but a generation of readers may come along who would prefer witnessing the capers of the author to being carried away by stories and that generation of readers may coincide with a generation of writers tired of self-obliteration . . . then you will have a movement towards diffuseness, backboneless sentences, digressions, and inchoatenesses.

Prophetic words, though it is probably the case that as long as there are novels there will be authors who intrude directly and authors who do not. What is rare is excellence in either.

On his way back to Europe he stopped off in London and renewed his lapsed relations with Pinker's two sons, Eric and Ralph. He also began complicated negotiations with Cape about various books. His relations with his numerous publishers, British and American, varied from uneasy to fraught and it is noticeable that the more worried he was about money the more difficult he became. Nor, to be fair, was he always well served; but money worries seem in him to have been the main corrosive.

It is hard not to conclude that he would have been better served with fewer publishers and fewer agents. The result of being spread over so many was that no one firm had an interest in keeping him going; also, those were more than usually difficult times for anyone trying to make a living from writing and he was never able to bargain from a position of strength. It was a great pity that Pinker died before *Parade's End* because he might have made that the foundation stone of all that followed. As it was, the good reputation the series earned for Ford was largely, though fortunately not wholly, frittered away amongst various projects and publishers.

He went again to New York in the autumn and was back by December. It is tempting to see this peripatetic life as an indication of loneliness and restlessness but it was a pattern that continued throughout his last years, when he was not at all lonely. It might be more accurate to see it mainly as his attempt to earn a living west of the Atlantic, though it is also true that he liked America and was probably stimulated by switching from one life to another.

It was at this time that Hugh Walpole became a good friend. In December 1929 he wrote to Walpole from Paris that he had recently had an operation and that 'Except for a troublesome form of blood-poisoning I am pretty well and in spirits.' The letter ends: 'Excuse pencil; I am dictating on my back. Thank you!' There is no other indication as to what was wrong. That Christmas was the last at which he played Père Noël for Julie and her friends.

During the spring he helped Richard Aldington prepare an anthology of Imagist poets. These, now sufficiently in the past to have anthologies compiled, had been the young bloods before Armageddon, a time when Ford already felt passed-over and spent, yet here he was helping, as it were, to conduct the memorial service. It was not the only time he found himself in this position: he had done it for the Pre-Raphaelites, for the generation of Conrad and James and by the time he died the young Turks of his *Transatlantic Review* were middle-aged and being spoken of as a previous generation. He kept going, never out of date because never quite in fashion, and because he never stopped.

May Day 1930 coincided with one of his Thursday teas. Janice Biala, who wanted to meet Ezra Pound, was taken along by a friend. Janice was a young and attractive painter with the same sort of fearless honesty as Stella. She was Polish-American-Jewish and had been born Janice Tworkov but had changed her name to that of her home town in order to avoid confusion with her painter brother, Jack. It was, of course, through Pound that Ford had met Stella and the same happened with Janice that May Day, except that Pound was not there and she met Ford instead. Mary McIntosh and Willard Trask were sharing Ford's flat with him (Mary noted that at that time he was writing from 5 a.m. until noon and that this routine was invariable no matter how late he had stayed up the night before). She later described to Sondra Stang the meeting between Ford and Janice:

> Willard's friend, Eileen Lake, from America, had come for a visit to Paris, bringing her best friend, Janice. Willard had invited the two girls to one of Ford's Thursdays, and soon after we asked them for supper and, of course, invited Ford to join us. We had a lively supper, the liveliest our little salle à manger had contained. There were many questions to ask about America and much to tell about our new life. Ford was at his best, appreciative in listening and joining in enthusiastically. In the living room after supper he sat between the girls on the sofa and I sat facing them in my big chair. Ford did most of the talking then – leading it anyway, and I felt that they all had quickly become friends. They laughed and talked easily, delighted with each other. Then it was that I had one of the strangest experiences of my life: I saw, literally *saw*, the transformation of Ford, as though he were a monarch moth shedding his cocoon. We had always thought of him as an old man (he was then fifty-eight). But here he was, become a young man. Ford, of course, always liked women and I knew that he was especially fond of one of the women in our group in that year; but never had I seen him like this. He was ardent, he was charming, he was a man in love.
>
> Later that evening Ford took Eileen and Janice out to see some *boîtes* and to do some dancing, and the girls told us later that he danced with them all night long. I heard him come in after dawn; nevertheless, he met Willard and me for our noon dinner. Our conversation that day was entirely about the night before

and the two girls from New York. Eileen was really the showpiece of the pair. She was a poet, tall, blonde, and fascinating, born and raised in Antigua, which fact always seemed to increase her interest for everyone, and we thought that naturally she would be the one that Ford would be taken with. So we started talking about her – wasn't Eileen charming, wasn't she attractive, and so on? Ford listened and agreed with all we said, and then paused and said very quietly, 'And the little dark-haired one is nice.' And, just from the way he said it, I knew instantly that he was in love with Janice, that it was for her that he had been transfigured the night before.

Ford was in fact fifty-five, Janice twenty-six. From the earliest days with Elsie he had sought intimacy, sympathy, communion and closeness. He was not promiscuous in the way that most men are but he was promiscuous in his intimacies. He sought a woman who would give him final rest and peace and, as is often the case, it was the search itself that rendered the end for long unattainable. The need that drove him to one woman was also the need that drove him to the next. When finally he was found by what he sought – Janice – it was his grown-up mind, she said, that drew her to him. She later told Mary: 'I have looked all my life for a man with a mind as old as my own, and what difference does it make if, when I find the man, he has a pot belly!' There thus began what Janice called their 'long passionate dialogue' which lasted until his death; although, talking to her now, it feels as if it is not finished yet. One of the qualities Ford found in her was a devotion to the arts as complete and unquestioning as his own. There was – and is – a clear, fierce flame in her that is evident not only in Ford's reactions and his poems but also in what others said about her. For instance, Mizener quotes Edward Davison as saying she was admired 'for her candour and blazing honesty as well as her unmeasured devotion to Ford'. She fought his corner in a way he never could, taking on publishers, landlords, editors, bank managers, relatives, friends and enemies, excelling in exactly the sort of confrontation he could never really cope with. She was also the only one of the women he lived with whose lack of interest in domestic comforts matched his own; she didn't care about curtains.

Very early on he sent her to see Stella and Julia. Their approval was important since he did not want to lose contact with his third child as he had with his first two. Also, he respected Stella. They both liked Janice and, Stella said, gave their blessing to 'his approaching union with her . . . [she] . . . made him very happy until the day of his death, and she developed a strong affection for Julie'.

Janice must have come to Ford like a gift from the gods, long looked-for, perhaps, but not expected. She inspired his last poems, a sequence of nine named by the first, 'Buckshee'. Falling in love was always a poetic inspiration to him but these are amongst the most remarkable poems he wrote, probably better than 'On Heaven' and his war poems. In fact, the first line of 'Buckshee' may be an ironical reference to 'On Heaven' which describes God as kind and good:

BUCKSHEE

I think God must have been a stupid man,
To have sent a spirit, chivalrous and loyal,
Cruel and tender, arrogant and so meek,
Gallant and timorous, halting and as swift
As a hawk descending – to have sent such a spirit,
Certain in all its attributes, into this Age
Of our banal world.
He had Infinity
Which must embrace infinities of worlds.
And had Eternity
And could have chosen any other Age.
He had Omnipotence
And could have found a fitting hour and time.
But, bruised and bruising, wounded, contumacious,
An eagle pinioned, an eagle on the wing;
A leopard maimed, a leopard in its spring;
A swallow caged, a swallow in the spacious
And amethystine, palpitating blue;
A night-bird of the heath, shut off from the heath,
A deathless being, daubed with the mud of death,

Haïtchka, the undaunted, loyal spirit of you!
Came to our world of cozening and pimping,
Our globe compact of virtues all half virtue,
Of vices scarce half-vices, made up of truth
Blurred in the edges of lies so limping
They will not spur the pulse in the utterance;
From a New World that's old and knows not youth
Unto our France that's France and knows not France,
Where charity and every virtue hurt you . . .
A coin of gold dropped in a leaden palm,
Manna and frankincense and myrrh and balm
And bitter herbs and spices of the South
Are you and honey for the parching mouth . . .
　Because God was a stupid man and threw
　Into our outstretched palms, Haïtchka, you!

He wrote them as quickly and easily as he always did but the sense of gratitude and wonder is not lightly tossed down; it is that of a man who has known something of resurrection. He wrote in the introduction:

> *Buckshee*, derived from the universal Oriental *backschisch*, has no English equivalent. It is a British Army word – signifies something unexpected, unearned – gratifying. If the cook, at dinner time, slips three potatoes into your meat can, these are buckshee potatoes; if, for something you are paid in guineas instead of pounds, the odd shillings are buckshee; if you are a little boy alongside a liner at Port Said and a white passenger throws half a crown instead of a florin into the shark-infested water for you to dive for, the odd sixpence is buckshee, backschisch. Or if you have long given up the practice of verse and suddenly find yourself writing it – those lines will be *Buckshee*.

Perhaps all his poems were really love poems, expressive of love for someone, something, somewhere, expressive above all of himself. It is easy to imagine that it was the 'quiet monologue during the summer walk' that, throughout his adult life, won him ready access to pleasing and sympathetic female companionship.

Yet his best poems are so because in them he was able to marry mood with the realisation of the actual that he sometimes found difficult. 'Fleuve Profond', for instance, another of the *Buckshee* sequence, is unusual because it comprises a dramatisation of an all-night Parisian party, a confrontation he had with a lady about some of the characters in *Parade's End* and an evocation of the entry of Janice (she is Haïtchka) into his life:

FLEUVE PROFOND
(Nuitée à l'Américaine)

Your brilliant friend,
Brilliantly lectures me on the feminine characters
Of my female characters . . .
Our striking host,
Having strikingly struck his striking head
Against the bottom panel of the bedroom door
Has been conveyed to bed
By several combined but unconcerted efforts.
Hear how he sings!
The other guests
Disperse amongst the apartments of the appartement.
Dazed by hearing the appraisements of Elaine
Concerning half-forgotten feminines, I sit
Beside her brilliance, on the divan edge,
My knees drawn up to my chin in the dim light.
We seem to be alone . . .
She tosses back
Her brilliant mane, her white, uplifted chin,
Long throat, makes incantations with her white,
Butterfly, moving fingers . . . 'I JUST LOATHE
YOUR WANNOP!'
There
Drift sounds of harpsichords
Of saxophones and ukuleles, drums,
Mandolines, mandragoras, slapped faces, spirituals,
Lacing the Paris night.
That's four o'clock,

The Luxembourg clock drones out!
But . . . Hear them *sing*!
Beside her I
Sit like a drummer peddling rubber plants
And comforters in the Atlas Mountain Valleys
Beside their largest lion. Knees drawn up,
Peeping, a-shiver, sideways, from the chin,
At a lip-licking monster. I am all unused
To talk about my books.
'IF I COULD GET'
She says, 'MY FINGERS ON YOUR CULLY'S THROAT!'
She can't mean *me*! By rights *I* am the lion!
'I'M ALL FOR SYLVIA!' Then it's Tietjens' throat
In jeopardy!
But hear them rolling along!
It ain't sayin' nothin' . . . A black light's shining
It ain't doin' nothin' . . . across the shadows;
It keeps on rollin' . . . a ray of granite!
I LOATHE YOUR TIETJENS . . . a cone of granite!
What's that dark shining? . . . BUT THAT'S HAÏTCHKA!
I LOATHE THAT WOMAN . . . NO NOT HAÏTCHKA!
HOW STUPID OF YOU . . . THE WANNOP TROLLOP.
MY BEST, MOST INTIMATE FRIEND!
You too had drawn
Your knees up to your chin. And motionless,
In an unwinking scrutiny you sat –
A cone of granite, a granite falcon,
A granite guardian of granite Pharaohs.

The leather chair
You'd chosen for your vigil made with you
A cone, Egyptian, chiselled, oriental.
Hard, without motion, polished, shining, granite!
Did you watch to save your dearest friend from me
. . . Or me from your dearest friend?
I wish they'd sing
Another rhythm . . . You gaze before you

It must be seven . . . Are you all going?
Yes, Ezra's going . . . Not one more hot-dog?
The Halles *for breakfast! . . .* I LOVE YOUR SYLVIA
SHE KEPT HIM JUMPING . . . SHE LOATHED HIS VITALS
SHE GAVE HIM THUMBSCREWS . . . THE CALLOUS MEALSACK!
Yes, Margie's going . . . Bill, ARE *you coming?*
I know why *she's* your dearest friend!
Elaine, aw come *on! . . . Haïtchka, bring her!*
Why, where's Haïtchka? . . . She's with that writer!
Aw, with that WRITER *. . . Yes, with* THAT *writer!*
She'll keep HIM *rolling along!*
'Schenehaia' . . . means 'pretty creature'!
Aw, Schenehaia! . . . for short Haïtchka!
She'll keep HIM *rolling along!*

Or, from the same period, 'Chez Nos Amis', also vividly realised but suggestive and sinister:

Silent in the background she
Glowers now and then at me
With a smouldering tiger's eye
That does dream of cruelty.

Leopard, ounce or ocelot,
She by turns is cold or hot,
She is sinuous and black,
Long of limb and lithe of back.

The deep places of the mind
She can probe and thus can find
Ev'ry weakness, ev'ry blot
Ev'ry ailing, aching spot.

She will scrutinise her prey,
Turn disdainfully away,
Sinuous and dark and cold.
Then she'll spring and then she'll hold.

Then with what a dreadful heat
She will mangle breasts and feet
And hands and lacerate a heart
. . . And then, listlessly, depart.

In September he had to go to New York again but this time did not stay long. So far as is known, he and Rene did not meet. He attempted arrangements with various publishers, succeeding in getting Macaulay to publish *No Enemy*, written a decade before, but failing with *That Same Poor Man* and getting no advance on *A History of Our Own Times*. This latter was a project he had nursed for many years, probably a throw-back to his beginnings when he had aspirations as a historian.

In December 1930 he had a heart attack in Paris. It was not too serious though for a while he thought he might not be able to go on working. In January 1931 he went with Janice to Toulon where they stayed in a studio that had been Stella's, and while there they found what he and Stella had wanted but had been unable to find. The Villa Paul, as Stella (who later stayed there) described it, stood high above the sea and had a long sloping garden with figs, oranges and a water cistern:

> The shutters of its upper windows were always closed. They concealed the domestic life of Monsieur le Commandant and Madame, who lived a dim but passionate existence on the upper floor, sub-letting the *rez de chaussée* and the garden to Ford and Janice . . . The ground floor shutters were always open. They had once been painted palest grey, and were folded back against the pinkish stucco walls whose flaking surface discovered patches of a previous periwinkle blue. Through the windows you stepped into two small rooms with rush grey walls and red tiled floors. Behind these, on one side was the kitchen, dark and primitive, and on the other side a sleeping alcove and *cabinet de toilette* . . . Before the house was a wide *terrasse* whose comfortable balustrade served as a sideboard for outdoor meals. There was a shady tree with a fountain with goldfish and a great view right across the harbour to St Mandrier . . .

It was his last real home and was perfect: a view of the sea, a garden, simplicity, a life that could be lived outdoors most of the time, sun. He gardened, played patience while working out what to write, then wrote it at a 'knocked-together table with flanking shelves of walnut bed-panels, supported by sawn-off chair legs', with above him 'an immense deal shelf supported in turn by sawn-off broom handles . . .' That and the view of the foaming Mediterranean – 'the hyacinth sea' – was all the comfort he needed and fortunately, in Janice, he had found someone who liked the same simple hedonism.

They lacked only the usual thing. He had already written to Wells asking for help in applying for assistance from the Royal Literary Fund and Wells, in a typically generous gesture, had sent a cheque of his own for two thousand francs. Ford had by then, as he said when he wrote to George Keating about *A History of Our Own Times*, 'been writing for thirty-eight years almost to a day, and am forced to beg my bread.' He also borrowed from Ralph Pinker and was lent another sum by Wells.

There was nevertheless the usual stream of visitors. Ford cooked his famous dinners which were eaten on the terrace, smoked his Gauloises ('dust and dung' he called them), poured the wine, sang with Janice, philosophised, reminisced and entertained. It was Cooper's with sea and sun and a great work done. But not all work was done: financial necessity and his own temperament saw to that.

In the autumn they were just able to go to New York and for that winter they lent the house to Stella and Julie, a sharp reminder to Stella of the domestic privation she had left behind when she left Ford. Three of the five lights did not work, there were no kitchen utensils, linen or china and cooking was by charcoal burner. In New York he was pressed to pay his bills and tried unsuccessfully to sell one of his manuscripts. His negotiations with publishers continued, usually earning him just enough to get there and back but not enough to achieve his aim in going. Harold Loeb recalled a road accident in which Ford was involved. The car skidded from ditch to ditch and left the road. Ford remained 'ponderous, relaxed and smiling faintly. "Let's stick to the highroad," he said.' Later he wrote that the skid took 'I should say, about eight hours'.

Back in Paris in November he saw Joyce again and introduced him to Janice. Joyce was struck and it was this that prompted the lines on 'Oh Father O Ford' that he sent to Harriet Weaver. He and Joyce saw quite a bit of each other during the winter of 1931. Joyce recommended to him another neglected author, Italo Svevo (whose later success owed much to Joyce's patronage) and Ford agreed to write an introduction to the translation of Svevo's *Senilità*, if the publishers wanted. (They did not, which is a pity because the book's theme of middle-aged obsession is one that Ford would have been good on. It was published eventually with Joyce's title, *As a Man Grows Older*.)

Life in Paris was as hectic as ever and Ford's health again seemed shaky. He and Janice went south to Villa Paul where they both felt and worked better. He finished *Return to Yesterday*, one of the best of his reminiscences, largely featuring the Romney Marsh writers of the pre-war period. When it was published later in the year it involved him in a typically Fordian bit of uproar, unintended and more or less – but not quite – innocent. He described how Masterman had told him about George V's conference on the Irish Question with the Liberal cabinet, who had been coerced into attending by the King's threat of abdication. As a Home Rule sympathiser, Ford had probably meant this story to reflect well on the King and almost certainly had no idea of the furore it would cause. Instead, it provoked headlines condemning 'the monstrous story' about the King and denials from the Palace. Ford, at least as loyal a subject as he was a Home Rule sympathiser, apologised and offered to delete the offending paragraph from subsequent editions. There were no subsequent editions in his lifetime.

To his delight, the eleven-year-old Julie came to stay with them that summer, as she did the following spring when Stella spent six months painting portraits in America. From her account given to Sondra Stang, Julie seems to have enjoyed her visits as much as her father did. She described how she would help him in the early morning with the irrigation of his vegetables, during which he would think about his writing (an alternative to the patience method) and 'woe betide me if I started to chatter!' When he did play patience she would be allowed to sit beside him and silently point out moves he had missed but there could be no conversation with anyone until the day's stint was done. He could not even bear it if there was whispering in the house, possibly a further indication as to how his ear was attuned to reproducing speech rhythms in writing. Later, though, 'We would sit on the terrace under the stars, looking down the hill toward the Mediterranean and watching the twinkling lights of the boats in the water. Then he and I would discuss – oh, philosophy, art, justice, all the things that a teenager grows earnest about. From a tolerance of all things but cruelty and dictatorship, to the right amount of garlic and herbs to put into a particular casserole . . . And what a teacher he was! My rapid improvement in Latin, under his tutelage, positively got me into trouble . . .'

She recalled an incident when she, Janice and Ford (though her memory tricked her here: Janice was in fact at home and heard about the incident afterwards) 'were walking down one of the narrow, twisted streets of Toulon, where people and vehicles mingled with abandon, when suddenly Ford slipped and fell in such a way what he landed behind the front wheels of a great truck, and in the endless second, while the truck driver slammed on his brakes, from somewhere beneath the vehicle, came this perfectly calm British voice remarking conversationally, "Now, St Christopher, here's your chance!" I guess St Christopher heard him at that, because when truck and father were finally disentangled, though the rear tyre marks were clearly visible on his sleeve, Ford was quite unharmed. We all three put on an extremely nonchalant air and proceeded with the purchase of a pair of espadrilles for me, which was our goal at the time, and I, for one, was extremely glad to sit down . . . Ford, on the other hand, was quite unperturbed and merely amused.'

This calmness is reminiscent of his reaction when the car went out of control in America, also of what he overheard the younger officers saying about his reactions under shellfire, perhaps also of his behaviour when being mugged. Calmness in moments of danger is usually commended but in Ford, typically, it seems to have attracted criticism and even sarcasm. Mizener says of the American car incident: 'This was Ford's imperturbable front; it did not mean he was not thoroughly frightened.' But isn't that the point? Whether or not someone is really calm – and most are not

– is irrelevant; it is the appearance of calm and the maintenance of this appearance despite no matter what turmoil within that is generally and rightly praised. In the case of Ford it seems to be dismissed as part of his 'act' and therefore not quite worthy. Similarly, Mizener implies that Ford's estimate that they were travelling at about 78 mph before the accident is an exaggeration, although Harold Loeb, who was there, thought they were doing over 70. Even Ford's reaction to being mugged is described rather sarcastically as 'modest'. It is tempting to think that if he had perished under the wheels of the truck in Toulon he would have been blamed for trying to appear imperturbable.

The 'Buckshee' series of poems was completed that summer. The manuscripts, in his hand, are almost without corrections. Due to his carelessness though, they were published at more or less the same time both in America and in England (by Harriet Monroe in *Poetry* and by Gollancz in *New English Poems* in 1931). The nine poems are a remarkable series, redolent of late love and wisdom, and they need really to be read as a whole. Several have been quoted already. 'Coda,' the ninth, was written in Paris in 1936, four years after the first eight were published. It represents Ford's musing at night in his and Janice's studio at 31 rue de Seine:

CODA

Two harsh, suspended, iron tocsin notes
Reverberate panic from that clock of Richelieu's.
They throw athwart the drowsing unconcern of the night
Their unavailing tones of rough, unheeded fright.
They pour through the pellitory of the wall that grows
Over the mouldering stones
Their droning overtones.

Prolongedly shuddering these say:
'Be alarmed! Your hours are wasting away;
Your life approaches its last day.
Rise, take arms against Chronos, old Time that will not
stay
And, armed, await the day.'

But the velvety, black
Night with her myriad fingers floats back.
She stifles the notes in the bells' throats
And her velvet silences obliterate
Their scars on the velvet pall.

Through it all you sleep. The fingers of the night
Feel ceaselessly . . . my brows,
Your cheeks, my shoulders uncovered,
Your uncovered hands, my throat . . .
The velvety fingers of the deep night.

As far as one knows
It is almost only here that the night shows this solicitous note
Of quietly, blindly, feeling one's uncovered skin.
As if to make sure that the tenants have all come in,
Not loitering in black streets to sin,
Nor too liquored up to find their locks,
Nor too disturbed by the hourly repeated shock
Of reverberated panic from Richelieu's old clock
And all the other wheezy, churring, murmuring old clocks
Of our old Quarter, drowsing along Seine water.

I suppose
This is our final stamping ground.
We may perhaps never leave it again.
This mouldering triangle of streets mounting from the Seine
Up to the Luxembourg mouldering on its mound . . .
Our last abiding place and territory.
For it is not only that you here find pellitory of the wall
Growing on all our old walls,
Pushing its dowdy flowerets through the patina
That falls in a thin dusty film that covers
All Richelieu's Villa Latina
In its unvarying *statu quo ante*.

It is certain that we must have patina and dust.
We are the sort that must, because our brain

Will not work in atmospheres of the perfect drain
And cellophane . . . And we must
Have irregular perspectives drawn in crumbling stone
Dying upwards into times long past
And yet so passionately here . . . We must
Have Names and Affairs and Past Passions by which to
  adjust
The mind and get some sort of perspective
Into this era of plumbing and planes,
And the maniacal passion of invective,
The gigantic monotone,
Of execration passing between nation and nation.

Yet it is not merely that Dante,
With his as yet unmerited aura,
Pondered in these streets or that Heloïse
Here confronted the summer breeze.

There have been elsewhere hecatombs of other lovers
Who lie now silent in other tombs.
There were Petrarch and Laura
In the Vaucluse; and Tristan and his Isolde
In old Almaigne; and Copperfield and his Dora
In middle-old, middle-class Cockaignes;
And Vogelweide and Fru Holde
And the innumerable troubadours with their unnumbered,
  immortal loves,
Voicing the inspirations of the Muse
Of the great plain of the Bouche
Du Rhône with its olive groves.

(And don't forget, here sang Heine, with his Mouche,
Shaking all Almaigne
With the scorn born here in his brain
On unending midnight mattresses of pain.)

And elsewhere, as here,
Have been droves of other Illustrious,

Poring over other lore by their midnight stoves,
Pondering on other landscapes and philosophers' groves
To the cooing of Athene's doves.

(Yet, don't forget those bespectacled industrious
Inventing in co-operative sixes and sevens
No doubt to the croaking of Thor's raven,
Iron and mephitic cataclysms
To hurl through the pitchy abysms of the
tocsin-riven Heavens.
For the eradication of this haven from Earth's face.)

But we shall here remain because this place is a haven
And we have found a haven in this place.
Here hath the Lord given the harbourage
Which, when we strode, bemired, over the winter's
roads
Beneath outrageous loads,
Or rode, dog-tired, the outrageous and malignant seas,
We had desired.

The Earth here turns slow on its axis,
And Time, grown tired of the inspection of age on the heel
of age,
Here rests on his elbow at ease
Beside our unrestless tide . . .

The very taxis glide
Noiseless and slow
Through the darkness below
And your sleep is dreamless and deep
And your pulse is unfevered and low
And you do not moan in your sleep
As you did some years ago.

To Hell with Richelieu and his bell!
It lies in its throat.
Time does not here hasten away,

There is no regular division here
Of night into day,
Nor, here, does our Sphere
Spin on its bored old axis
To the tune of season on season, irrevocable,
Told by rote.

Listen! The lying clock
Strikes three and the drowsing night
Blankets its notes in their flight;
Nevertheless the shuddering overtones exclaim:

'There shall flame cargoes of fright through the night
Above this town: the Heavens shall be riven,
Chariots of blazing doom shall be driven
Across the waste-land of the peak of Heaven.
Your mansions shall crumble down,
Your ashes be entombed in the shards, as it was doomed
In those first writings of God's.
For here Knowledge springs from the Earth
That was accurst before fire ever flamed on hearth . . .
Yes, Knowledge was accurst or ever there were bells
And was condemned before grass grew on sods
To have her head for ever against God's
Own Image's heels!'

It sounds well enough, that sort of stuff.
It's part truth.
Sure, if there be a place where frugal thought,
The love of the Arts, knowledge and temperate learning,
Some sort of just appreciation of life's values
And pity and moderation naturally grow
Like pellitory of the wall on crumbling stones.
Then, let fame spread a little about the earth,
And you will find all mankind in hordes without ruth,
Bankers and tailors, poor men, pimps and sailors, rich men and tinkers
Grasping axes and arrows

And torches and powder and rifles and gas-shells and bombs
All mankind flying together in planes towards that detested
  focus
All men crying together from planes: 'Bedamned to their
  hocus-pocus.'
Razing the buildings, cutting the throats of the thinkers,
Rifling the tombs,
Driving great steam-ploughs to level the ground,
With great harrows
Harrowing in salt by the ton,
Wiping their brows and crying: 'That's well done.
There shall never again grow the herb called Thought
On this land of oblivion.'

But there's more than that in it.
For, if one man can find any sort of a soul . .,. Wait a
  minute . . .
Slowly across the blackness of the wall
Glimmer a square and a scroll.
Just there . . . You see? . . . A scroll.

That's not poetic imagery, those
Illuminated by a taxi, crawling below,
Are all my past and all your promise, they
Being my roll of proofs like Michelangelo's
Scroll of the Fates on a Cumaean lap.
And the pale square's your *Spring in the Luxembourg.*
Like his table of your Law on Moses' knee.

I know you don't like Michelangelo.
But the Universe is very large, having room
Within it for infinities of Gods
All co-existing, much as you and I
Drudge on, engrossed by paper or on canvas,
You in that corner, I, in this, our thoughts
Going side by side for years and years,
Cycles, millennia and aeons, Thought
Being immensurable and commensurable, Time

Being commensurate and yet not measurable.

For you cannot measure time or thought by the clock.
It can't be done. You can measure meals or cloth,
Or railway journeys, cornfields or the sea
By dials . . . and yet not Eternity
That's Time grown incorruptible, nor yet Thought
That's Life transmuted into rustless gold.

That is not truly hard to understand.
Not really . . . Imagine honeycomb
Boxed as you see it on your market stalls,
A hundred boxes, row on row over row
In a parallelogram? Your eye selects
Box Two, Row Four. Then that's alive for you.
                                        But, should your glance
Pass to Box Nine, Row Ten, Box Two won't die
Though you don't see it . . . Immortality
Is not more strange than that! Time boxes up
His honey like an apiculturist.

It must be honey, not the *ersatz*, bee-bread
That sullen bees chew out on wasted days
When flowers lack. So Bee-Man Time exacts
A certain flowering, a fertilisation,
The stir of life through pollen on the pistils . . .
I think they're pistils . . . Then you see Corruption
Don incorruptibility and Time
Put on the Immortal . . . Surely for every man,
For you, for me, for Heine, as for the milk-girl
Dry desert tracts must lie across the road,
Unmarked, infertilised, remembered only
As dull malaises, lying at the back of the mind.

Your Dante's aura was unmerited
Till he met his Beätricé . . . So he says
And the tale is good enough. Thus set it down
For us . . . Let's leave out dots from our 'T's . . .

Tonight the rusty iron-clappered bell
Of Richelieu's clock aeons ago strikes one,
Some hours ago shall strike three, some pulses past
Jarred twice the drowsy night; in a century
Shall strike some more, or did not strike at all.
But what's the odds? My pompous scroll, your square,
Both faded when the taxi-cab rolled on
Towards its own Eternity. We are
Again suspended in our velvet blackness,
Floating on velvet fingers, in a haven
Of fertilised hours; we tidelessly shall lie
Till Doomsday or the end of the hostilities,
As we used to say, whichever shall prove longer.

Or till you moan
'Oh, Hell, I've got to finish this damn canvas!'
And I clutch, groaning, the outrageous scroll
Of my dead, desert foot-prints . . . Silence falls
For a thousand years of all unheeded clocks,
Till you say; 'What's there for dinner?' And old Time
Dons incorruptibility and Life's
Immortal. Untimely, the sun shines in
And you must drop your brush, Praxiteles
Having grown jealous.

Written in the rue de Seine
for an anniversary between the feasts of
SS. James & Paul (Otherwise May Day)
& That of Saint Joan of Arc.
MCMXXXI

This is written from ripeness. Once or twice his conversational manner, easy verbal felicity and liking for repetition allows some slackness – 'But we shall here remain because this is a place of haven/and we have found a haven in this place' or 'Nevertheless the shuddering overtones exclaim' – but even in these lines the slackness is not so noticeable when the poem is read aloud. It is a poem of deceptive depth, as easy on the ear as the surface is to the eye. The depths are deceiving because, like the Mediterranean when he knew it, the sea-bed is so clear it looks much closer than it is. Yet he is assured enough to risk a joke – '. . . I think they're pistils . . .'

They were back in Paris for the Christmas of 1931 and he succeeded in negotiating a deal with the American publishers Long and Smith whereby he was to be paid $200 a month against royalties in return for a book every twenty months. Like most of his deals, it didn't work out very well. There were delays, misunderstandings, cheques going astray and so on. But he started another novel, *The Rash Act*. This, too, is a flowering of ripeness and it should be read. Ford wrote that it was intended as 'the beginning of a trilogy that is meant to do for the post-war world and the Crisis what the Tietjens tetralogy did for the war'. And at the beginning he quotes from *The Times Law Report* of 14 July 1931: '"The rash act", the coroner said, "seems to have been inspired by a number of motives, not the least amongst which was the prevailing dissoluteness and consequent depression that are now world wide."' C. H. Sisson wrote in his introduction to the Carcanet edition that it is 'contemplation under the guise of fiction'; it is also possibly Ford's most underrated novel.

Briefly, the wealthy and assured Hugh Monckton commits suicide – '"Means of escape," Hugh Monckton said, "the world's full of them. Only one is genuine."' – and Henry Martin, partly by chance, assumes his identity. But the book is not the adventure story or unravelling of coincidence that many writers would have made of such a theme; it is a view of life, sensual and pagan, a posing of the question as to what really matters and a slow revelation of the stark answer:

> His mind ran on tombstones. European Teuto-Frankish minds still did. Father, in private, thought Holbein's 'Dance of Death' the finest humour in the world. . . . And, when Henry Martin came to think of it, he was not averse from thinking of tombstones himself. There was a mural inscription at Antibes, a

few miles from where he then stood. It was on the wall of the Roman Theatre – to the memory of a boy dancer who had died young.

'SALTAVIT. PLACUIT. MORTUUS EST.'

'He danced. He gave pleasure. He is dead.'
It would be nice to have that on one's tombstone. But he never would. That would no doubt make his real epitaph – that he had never given pleasure. He had certainly danced. Only last night he had danced – well enough. But he could feel that he gave no pleasure to the little, depressed French *poule* who was in his arms. . . . He could not attribute many sins to himself. But he had never given pleasure. Not to his father; not to his college friends: not to his Magdalen tutor: not to the sergeants of his British regiment. Not to Wanda . . . certainly not to Alice. Not on necking parties in the corners of woods with girls who had to neck someone or socially fade . . . Well, he had danced, he had given no pleasure. He would certainly be dead. In an hour and a half maybe.

The sun was now gloriously up. He was at the end of the pier. Long, glutinous flakes of brilllance were reflected from folds of the glassy water. In its translucent depths beneath his nose the negligible *oursins* were like remote doorknobs. One of them was dead. It was not brown but skeleton grey. What could be more negligible than a dead sea-urchin? The most negligible thing in the world!

He was going to step off the half-deck above the motor of the boat – a hundred yards from the opening through the mole . . . Step off. Like a sentry on his beat. Stiff! In a soldierly manner.

That was how he had arranged it with himself.

You could not dive effectively off a boat. Or he could not. To slip over the side would, considering the circumstances, be undignified. Like shuffling out of the world . . . But to step stiffly, find nothing for the foot and chance what came . . .

The relationship between Monckton and Martin and their eventual merging suggests a mature reconciliation within Ford of aspects of his character that had long been apart; the women are elusive and suggestive and the picture of life is got up with a combination of impressionism and narration whose technical virtuosity is belied by the apparent ease with which the book flows. It was, he wrote to Pound, 'more like what I wanted to write than anything I have done for years'. To Ray Long of Long and Smith he wrote that Henry Martin was the typical man of his period because he could never have had the courage to commit suicide or do anything else that might seem traditionally tragic. 'That is not his type of tragedy – or ours. Ours and his is that we do not commit rash acts.' He thought that the chief characteristic of those years was want of courage, physical and moral, to do anything assertive at all (though Martin's 'prototype', Hart Crane – 'a great poet, an audacious pervert and a hopeless dipsomaniac' – had recently killed himself by drowning, an achievement beyond the reach of Martin). Martin ends the book much as he began it, which is a comment on the enervation of the times. The sequel, *Henry for Hugh* is less successful and the intended third volume was never written. The reason, of which Ford may or may not have been aware, is surely that he had done it all in the first. It is a book that stands apart, not only amongst his novels but amongst nearly all.

At the same time he was writing articles for *Harper's* and working on *A History of Our Own Times*. This was another book intended as the first of three volumes and he seems to have worked at it in one form or another for much of the last decade of his life, even to within a few days of his death. The history of its non-publication is as complicated as it was to him disappointing. It was finally published by the Indiana State University Press in 1988 and in Britain by Carcanet in 1989, half a century after he died. As might be expected, it is readable, personable, idiosyncratic, francophiliac, generous and interesting. What is surprising is the evidence of the detailed notice he took of political events which often appeared to make little impact on him, and how much he remembered. When asked by Robert Lowell what he thought the most important quality a novelist should have, he replied, 'memory'. He thought the novelist should anyway be a chronicler of his times but in this book he does it more straightforwardly. It may be too personal for contemporary taste and too inaccurate to please the professional historian but as a view of the world and a view of life it is stimulating and very readable. His voice is as compelling as always but, sadly, the book will probably not do as much as it might for his reputation because it will be judged by criteria other than those he set out to meet.

One current issue of his own times to which he did lend active support, however, was the question of a Jewish state. Apart from the Irish Question it was virtually the only political cause with which he got at all involved. Partly as a result of knowing Janice he had become increasingly concerned about Jewish persecution and tried unsuccessfully to write about it for the *Daily Mail*.

His publishing problems continued and were worsened by the disappearance of Ray Long. William Bradley, with whom he had dealt with before, was by then his agent but it was going far from smoothly. In January 1933 Long and Smith stopped paying the monthly advances they had agreed, just a month before the publication of *The Rash Act*. That appeared only nine days before Roosevelt closed the banks in America. The result, Ford reported to Pound, was that the book 'has naturally been absolutely submerged'.

It had tired him. He had written it faster than he wanted and now that it had vanished like a stone in a pond, leaving him harder up than ever, he was dispirited. In June he went with Janice to Rapallo to visit Pound and Olga Rudge, repaying to Pound some money he owed him. It was the meeting Janice had been hoping for when attending Ford's May Day tea party. The photograph (see plate) of Ford and Pound taken during this visit shows Pound as lithe, jaunty, scrawny, posing with his legs crossed, hat in hand, beard thrust forward, so that you can see why Ford names the goat after him. Ford is wearing espadrilles, a shirt with rolled up sleeves and white cotton trousers that, hitched well up above his belt, manage to look like cricket trousers. He stands with his feet astride, arms behind his back, like an umpire having a quiet word with a fast bowler whose action has become a little suspect; which in a sense he was, though they continued to have limitless tolerance of each other.

When back in Cap Brun Ford began writing in support of Pound's 'Cantos' which had been published in New York, not only reviewing the book himself but trying to compile a pamphlet of testimonials from well-known writers. He also continued to encourage young writers who sent manuscripts to him, something that went on almost throughout his literary life but which increased during his last years. His letters, often to people who were never heard of again, were frequently long and painstaking, invariably courteous and helpful, and wise not only about the detail of their manuscripts but about their whole approach. To a Mr Mack he gave sound advice about improving the subject of his manuscript ('rather slight for the formidable apparatus of psychology with which very admirably you approach life') and added: 'This may seem to you a rather commonplace way of looking at the matter – but life is a commonplace affair and it is only by piling one damn commonplace complication on another that you arrive at the tragi-comedy or the comic tragedy that life is . . .' That was how he looked at it; he had learned no longer merely to rail but to accept, even to expect.

It may have been about this time that they travelled to Germany, on which Ford had been commissioned to write some articles. When they returned to France they went to Tarascon where he gave his wallet to Janice for safe-keeping. It had in it virtually all their money. They walked on to the suspension bridge over the Rhône. It was the time of the Mistral:

> Our treasurer's cap was flying in the air . . . over, into the Rhône. What glorious fun . . . The Mistral sure is the wine of life . . . Our treasurer's wallet was flying from under an armpit beyond the reach of a clutching hand . . . Incredible humour; unparalleled buffoonery of a wind . . . The air was full of little, capricious squares, floating black against the light over the river . . .
>
> And then began a delirious, panicked search . . . For notes, for passports, for first citizenship papers that were half way to Marseilles before it ended . . . An endless search . . . With still the feeling that one was rich . . . Very rich.

Janice said later that he was amused for months at the thought that some astonished housewife cleaning fish might find a thousand franc note in its belly. They returned to Villa Paul virtually penniless.

The Tates came and stayed nearby that summer and he later dedicated *Provence* to them in memory of the visit. One of the memories was of a picnic for sixteen at which sixty-one bottles of wine were drunk. Water, however, was in shorter supply and the drought dealt hardly with his garden. Worse, Stella and Julie left Paris to live in England because Stella could no longer afford Paris. Ford was depressed, not only because it meant he would see less of them but because 'I should have preferred Julie never to learn English and certainly not to go to an English school and become the usual English hobbledehoy.' The period of his proclaimed – but not enacted – anti-Englishness, which he characterised as anti-Anglo-Saxondom, coincided with his strongest feelings of neglect by English publishers; ironically, *The Rash Act* sold better in Britain than in America and then, as now, it was the publishers of Anglo-Saxondom – primarily American – who kept him in print. He always felt that in France he was treated as an author should be although the French have shown little interest in his books.

By the time Stella and Julie returned to England he was working on *It was the Nightingale*, another volume of reminiscence which expressed his feeling of post-war rejection by England and which sold quite reasonably there (two thousand copies, in America two thousand nine hundred). Perhaps, like some other expatriates, he felt he had to justify his change of habitat even though there was no need and perhaps the range of justification reflects the depth of disappointment. Janice thought, and still thinks, that he was wrong to be upset with Stella for moving. Her reasons were, after all, very reasonable. The two women always got on well and kept in touch by letter. Some years after he had died and when she was herself dying, Stella said that she was sad that he had apparently been so angry for so long and that he had stopped communicating with her. She didn't realise, as Janice then told her, that the letters from Janice were really from Ford, she having taken them at his dictation.

It was the Nightingale was another modest success. It was dedicated to Eugene Pressly, an official at the American Embassy in

Paris who had married Katherine Anne Porter and who typed the manuscript. They became good friends and Ford was best man at the wedding. He began to think again in terms of a collected edition, again with no success.

He entered his sixties with life no more settled than it had been. As Janice told Sondra Stang, 'Extravagant things happened to him', such as when they had to give up their studio in the rue Vaugirard because the building was to be demolished. Taxes were due on it, months before time: 'The apartment – with literally everything it contained – was left to the tax collector. Not a saucepan, not a dish, absolutely nothing was taken out, just a four-dollar easel. I might add that the furniture – all Louis XIII or Louis XV – in that apartment would bring fabulous prices today; like Tietjens, Ford knew furniture.'

They stayed at Villa Paul throughout the autumn of 1933 and in December Ford finished *Henry for Hugh*, the sequel to *The Rash Act*. He began at once on *Provence*. In the spring of 1934 they travelled to London and stayed in rooms near Madox Brown's old house – 'the garret', Ford said, 'of a gloomy fog-filled, undignifiedly old London house'. He was appalled to find that the view down Whitehall from the National Gallery steps had been ruined by the neon advertising all round Trafalgar Square which 'gave irresistibly the impression that someone having murdered London's sleep the witch-doctors of Macbeth were dancing in a *Walpurgisnacht* across the London skies.' He had already deplored the destruction of the elegant Regency buildings of Regent Street and their replacement by the present higher ones, which offer no vista, and now railed against there being no cafés in London as in France; without cafés a city could have no art and no letters.

London was better from the point of view of people. He saw Goldring and was introduced by Anthony Bertram to Edward Crankshaw who became a good friend and a kind of unofficial representative in England. Crankshaw introduced him to Stanley Unwin and for the first time in his life Ford found a publisher whom he not only liked and respected but who stayed in business and with whom he never fell out. Allen and Unwin published his last five books (having also published his very first) with the result that his British publishing fortunes began to revive at the very time when he was writing reminiscences in which he despaired of their ever doing so. They went to Sussex to see Anthony Bertram – now himself living in Pulborough, not far from Bedham – but Ford would not visit Violet. They also tried to get galleries to take Janice's paintings but it was not a good time. Stella, meanwhile, had succeeded in getting Heinemann to publish *It was the Nightingale*.

They left London in mid-May following a Chelsea party at which Goldring remembered him dancing 'slowly but majestically round the room with Biala in his arms'. It was the last time he was to see Ford and he was as struck by how stout and stertorous he had become as by his reduced circumstances. It was hardly the lion's return and Ford's name did not, as he had hoped, sell any paintings, but the friends he saw and the new ones he made were loyal and lasting. He was regarded with affection and must have felt that Stanley Unwin's interest was a sign that his literary reputation was still good, perhaps even improving; but, as he frequently complained, his London publishing history was 'like dropping things down wells so deep that after years of waiting no reverberation comes to the listener at the well-head'. With some seventy-five books behind him, he perhaps had some justification. It wasn't really the lack of money that hurt him, though he certainly wanted it, so much as the lack of recognition. They scuttled home to Provence.

It was during that year, 1934, that Graham Greene wrote him a fan letter about *The Good Soldier*, a book which Greene still re-reads and rates as one of the best in the language this century. Greene was not then a well-known writer but Ford was nevertheless touched by any sign of recognition from England. In September he wrote back asking to see one of Greene's novels since he did not know them and 'It makes correspondence rather like duelling in the mist with an opponent armed with one doesn't know what weapon!' Greene sent *It's a Battlefield* and Ford replied from New York in December 1934, where he and Janice then were. He liked the book: it made 'a shaft of sunlight through the gloom that seems to hang over our distant land! I wd. not have believed that such writing cd. come out of England.'

The other side of the coin of his despair about writing in England was a possible underestimation of his own reputation there. He would have based that largely on his sales and on what he perceived of the reaction to him, or lack of it, but there are indications that his reputation was more established – albeit remote from contemporary fashion – than he realised. Greene remembers him as a writer who had a good reputation in the 1930s and who was accorded considerable respect. The Tietjens books and *The Good Soldier* were then as now the most highly thought of but more recent novels such as *The Rash Act* had also received serious literary attention. What may have influenced him to feel the way he did was that Conrad's reputation was then in decline and, though he now disliked being tagged on to Conrad's coat-tails, he may well have felt that much that he had espoused during his youth and middle life was now so much dust under the carpet. He noted that even in France his hero, Flaubert, was no longer so well regarded by the new generation and that the critical detachment and precision he had so much admired in French writing was now scorned.

Greene and he met when he and Janice were staying at Penshurst, Kent, with Edward and Clare Crankshaw (they spent about a month there in July 1936). Ford got Crankshaw to find Greene and invite him to lunch one weekend. Greene came and after lunch he and Ford walked through the fields alone together. They walked all afternoon and had, Greene recalls, one of those conversations which seemed to include everything while focusing mainly on writing, and of which he cannot now remember a word. He was himself feeling rather low and in need of encouragement; he remembered that Ford was both comfortable to be with and very comforting in his effect; in fact, he speaks of him in terms slightly reminiscent of Jean Rhys's heroine's descriptions of dancing or walking with Heidler. Greene caught the train back with his signed copy of *The Good Soldier* and they never met again.

Greene's account is one we know of because he was a young writer who went on to be a success but Ford helped many unknowns and was forever reading manuscripts that were never read again. If anything, he was perhaps too kind and, with immediate and overwhelming sympathy for the writer, would make recommendations to publish that ignored commercial considerations. That heavenly Kingdom of Letters, if he held the key, would not be very select; he was not one of those who would allow only himself and a handful of the truly great to share immortality; almost all writers would be there but there would be few publishers, agents, printers, critics or biographers.

They spent the winter of 1934–5 in New York, having crossed on a German ship in the company of a German professor who, when drunk, exhibited alarming Nazi sympathies. In the spring they went south to stay at Memphis with Allen and Caroline Tate. *Provence* had just been published and Ford was then working on its successor in what was intended as a series of three, *The Great Trade Route*. Both are imaginative and entertainingly personal cultural surveys on the theme of 'Provence is not a country but a state of mind. . . . [A] great, noisy and indigestion-sick Anglo-Saxondom . . . can only be touched by inspiration from the spirit of Provençal Latinity, frugality and tolerance.' He idealises all the places he likes, including the American South, forms ingenious connections and then adds to the mixture his cult of the Small Producer with its antipathy to everything that is cellophane, artificially preserved or industrial. It is not all as zany as it might sound; there is little doubt that the world would be happier and saner if everyone stayed at home digging their gardens, making their own tools, reading and writing good books, painting, carving, cooking imaginative but simple meals and exchanging good talk over Château Margaux. If the recommendations are practical only for the few, the attitudes behind them would nonetheless benefit many of us. The frugality and tolerance which he describes are, like clarity of thought, only intermittently present in the real world; but read as aspirations and as expressions of his own personality they are endearing and commendable, and some of the wisdom sticks.

In April he went with the Tates to address a writers' conference at Baton Rouge. The weather was very hot, which he found increasingly tiring, and he described his contribution in terms of: 'My voice is going on talking . . . I can hear it . . . What the devil is it saying? . . . I must pull myself together.' But it was a significant event because it led on to other things.

He then followed Janice to New York, where she was preparing an exhibition of her drawings, and negotiated with Oxford University Press of New York for the publication of an edition of his collected poems which would supersede the 1913 edition. He also sold them *The Great Trade Route* and arranged for serialisation of his *Portraits from Life* in the *American Mercury*. He hoped that the OUP in England would follow suit with the poems, thus earning money for Stella and Julie. The *Collected Poems* came out in 1936 and *The Great Trade Route* appeared the following year. In fact, arrangements were made for the poems to be published by OUP in England but, in an episode which is a monument to publishing negligence, none has ever appeared. Having agreed to do it, OUP dithered for three years and by the time they got the edition into galley proofs war had broken out and publication was shelved. Edward Crankshaw, who had been reading the proofs, wrote to OUP after the war but they denied all knowledge of the project. He then sent them the galleys but they neither replied nor returned them when asked. Thus it was that most of Ford's best poems remain to this day unknown in Britain.

Ford, of course, lived to see only the delay; for all his own faults in handling business, this was the sort of episode that made him think that the worst of publishers were in fact the norm. It had been bad enough with OUP in New York, as he wrote to Allen Tate: 'I have at last adjusted my lunatic strife with the Oxford University Press – you know, either I must be mad or they. They are really unimaginable people. No wonder Roger Bacon invented gunpowder to blow them up when they contracted to publish his work.'

They travelled back to Europe third class on an Italian ship full of noise and lacking all privacy and vegetables. Hating noise and liking vegetables, Ford could neither sleep nor work. He hated not travelling first class, too, especially when he could look up and see those who were: '. . . gorgeous cinema stars . . . hair blowing back in the dawn wind, eyes gazing soulfully into the growing luminosity as if into spotlights . . . as far above my head as Pallas Athene when she rescued Athenians from battlefields.' He was sixty-one and things weren't getting much better.

TWENTY-FOUR

Julie stayed with them that summer but it was a slightly less harmonious visit than others. She was fourteen and was being brought up as an English girl, which Ford had never wanted. He had wanted her eventually to be trained as an international lawyer in Paris but now she was forgetting her French. After her visit he wrote a long letter explaining his position and what he thought were the dangers of Teutonic 'vagueness and self-deceptions' into which her 'middle-class Left upbringing' was taking her: 'Anglo-Saxondom is a hybrid collection of human beings all of whose refinements and practical sense comes from the Latin Tradition and all of whose vaguenesses and self-deceptions and worship of the Second Class in trains, arts, cuisines, vintages and personal habits comes from the Teutonic strain.' He also gave corrective advice on her written English and took up a complaint she apparently had about the lack of a bathroom at Villa Paul, disputing that bathrooms were necessary.

What effect all this had on Julie is not known but it was evidence, if any be needed, of the seriousness with which Ford held his views on cultural differences. The following Christmas he had to write to her that he couldn't afford to send a present and recommended she take up market-gardening or carpentry – 'They are both good for exactness of thought and movement . . .'

That autumn, from Geneva, he sent Anthony Bertram a letter about Bertram's novel *Men Adrift*. It is typical Fordian criticism in which the critical points, though essentially damning of the book, are made in a way that is kindly and encouraging; his grasp was as firm as ever: of Bertram's re-telling of the Christ story he wrote, '. . . you must give up being a Christist and become a Christian or something else that is fierce and bitter as Christians have to be. Christianity isn't you know a Sunday supper with the maids given the evening off; it is eating flesh and drinking blood.'

The following spring Edward Crankshaw came to stay with them in Paris, cycling from Penshurst to Dover because he couldn't afford the fare. The idea was Ford's, so that Crankshaw, who was trying to make his name as an art critic, could meet some French painters. Crankshaw was surprised and delighted at the number of painters Ford and Janice seemed to know well though he had the impression that Ford was relieved not to find Picasso at home or at the Deux Magots. (There might have been some reason unknown to Crankshaw for Ford's apparent relief; Janice says they both got on well with Picasso and that he was very approachable: 'anyone could talk to Picasso.')

In July 1936 Crankshaw had them to stay at the Nunnery Cottage, Penshurst, which is where the meeting with Greene took place. Ford continued trying to read Swinburne for his *Mercury* articles. He wrote to Paul Palmer, the editor of *Mercury*, about it:

> Can you imagine what it is like to try for six weeks to read SWINBURNE? and to try and try and TRY, like Bruce's spider . . . and to fail . . . I got up at half past five again this morning . . . as every morning . . . to face those printed pages to which the mind will not adhere. And read
>
> ASK NOTHING MORE OF ME SWEET ALL I CAN GIVE YOU I GIVE
> HEART OF MY HEART WERE IT MORE SHOULD BE
>
> And when will that damn girl bring me my coffee? And would it be better to buy pounds here or wait till we . . .'

The Crankshaws were in their twenties, Ford in his sixties and very obviously the great figure. He had what Clare Crankshaw calls a 'shabby grandeur'. He would usually sit down to his typewriter at about eleven in the morning, having played patience until then, and would work at a bureau in one corner of the room while Janice in the other corner painted a picture of the Battle of

Gettysburg. In the evenings he would sometimes read aloud from his poems, which Mrs Crankshaw remembers being in proof sheets (presumably for the 1936 collected edition). His conversation and recollections were mainly literary and were not at all confused; his tall stories she thought of as fancies and exaggerations, embellishments that grew naturally out of his subjects and style, all a part of his chameleon quality. This was evident when they went for a walk one afternoon in the woods. Ford was wearing his usual good quality but threadbare jacket and well-made worn-out trousers and seemed completely and unconsciously bohemian, until they came upon a woodman. Then his manner changed; he acquired a gentlemanly authority and a hazel twig, which he tapped against his calf while he addressed the woodman as 'my man'. He had normally an air of what Mrs Crankshaw called 'asinine nobility', an immediate and indiscriminate helpfulness, perhaps a touch of Don Quixote. It should not be assumed from this, however, that he was unknowing; there was nearly always an element of self-consciousness, parody and humour, often missed.

He was not forever parodying, though. The Crankshaws subsequently stayed at Villa Paul during the last summer that Ford and Janice were there. The Penshurst cottage was simple enough but Villa Paul, with its charcoal stove (which needed to be unclogged with hair-pins) and no bathroom, seemed stark to English eyes, though the furniture was good and there were plenty of books. Both Ford and Janice were at that time rolling their own cigarettes, Ford rather painstakingly and with more paper than tobacco. He so often ran out of matches that Edward secretly bought a packet of twelve boxes and handed one over each time Ford ran out, pretending he just happened to have one on him. Ford accepted each new box with extravagant, unsuspecting gratitude and innocent joy, never querying their provenance.

His last complete novel, *Vive le Roi*, had recently been published by Lippincott. It portrayed civil war between royalist Right and contemporary Left in France. Although his solution is an absolute monarchy lightly ruling a country of small producers, he is as ever opposed to tyranny and, unlike many then in intellectual circles, saw tyranny as inherent to Marxism because it demanded that 'men must be adapted to their machine and not the machine to the tastes and desires of men'. Lenin, in some ways admirable, was nonetheless a tyrant.

In October they gave up the Villa Paul. It was a great wrench but the previous winter there had not been easy, especially when their money was not getting through. Ford felt the place was essential to his spiritual and bodily health. There was truth in both: the warmth, the colours, the view, the simplicity of life and the perspective it gave him made for good work, good friends and peace of mind; whereas constant travel and worry heightened the symptoms of heart trouble to which he had been subject on and off for some time. The doctor they saw was no more competent than the one Stella had complained of about a decade before, though Janice did not know it at the time. Brother Oliver was already dead, carried off by a seizure which occurred when, leaning back in his chair after an exceptionally good dinner, he said, 'I've never felt better in my life.' They hadn't known until Janice saw the announcement in the paper. Ford never said much about it though he and Oliver had always got on well, even after Oliver had sold the presentation sword Ford had won for fencing and, later, published articles under his brother's more famous name. Oliver's wife and Stella remained good friends, though Janice and Ford saw little of her after his death. It was perhaps a fitting end for the novelist, entrepreneur, journalist, raconteur, British Army officer and sometime general of the Mexican Army. Janice thinks it would have been even more fitting for Ford; for him, though, there was still time to go and work to be done.

His letters of the period make more mention of gout and arthritis than of his heart but it is not clear how persistent these were. Janice remembers that he had gout in his toes and occasionally 'writer's cramp' but no more; in a letter to Eugene Pressly Ford attributed one attack of gout-ridden sleeplessness to 'the really bad behaviour of the OUP'. In America, where they went in November, he saw a lot of William Carlos Williams who thought him an already sick man, very overweight, often gasping for breath at the mildest exertion and, as ever, pretending it was nothing. (This was during a tour of American market gardens which Ford, with his always particular interest in how things were grown or made or done, wanted to see first-hand.)

In December he did his American radio broadcast on the abdication of Edward VIII, a sensitive and considerate talk which appears to meander but by the end is seen to do so in order to focus attention on the state of mind of a man who was perhaps long lost. Given what most speakers might have been expected to say on the subject, it is a remarkable talk. Unfortunately, his manner of speech meant it was not comprehensible to all of his audience but, apart from complaints on that score, reaction was generally favourable. He did other broadcasts but had no great ambition to become a performer in another medium; it was, as with his many articles, mainly a question of that month's rent.

The Great Trade Route was published in January 1937, *Portraits from Life* in March. They didn't sell badly although not well enough to make much difference. Against Stanley Unwin's advice, he got involved in negotiations with Doubleday's which came to nothing. The point about Ford's dealings with American publishers and agents in these last years was that he was clutching at straws, not because there were life belts to hand which he ignored but because there were *only* straws. He had never been able to make a reasonable living from his books and still could not; he must have known that time was running out and probably felt the gnawing of insecurity even more. Being a peripatetic bohemian is not, at sixty-three, the fun it might once have been. He had been materially better off at twenty-three, married with children and property. But, as he said when the mistral took all their money, he felt rich.

Not all was financial gloom, however. The previous summer Allen and Caroline Tate had met Joseph Brewer, the new President of Olivet College, Michigan, at a writers' conference. Brewer, who had a publishing background and was keen to further the cause of all the arts at Olivet (and was himself, according to Janice, an accomplished tap-dancer), was already an admirer of Ford's writing and proposed to offer him the post of writer and critic in residence. Allen Tate, Brewer and Ford met in New York that winter and agreed a salary of $1500 with an additional fee of $150 for Ford's attending the Olivet Writers' Conference during the summer of 1937. Ford was to spend about eight months of the year in residence, talking about literature with those who wanted to talk, reading, writing and generally being man of letters to the campus. It was not quite a living wage but it was near enough and the recognition was probably as important as the money.

The other benefit of that December in New York was that he was able to interest the Dial Press in his long-cherished project of writing a history of world literature. This was to become *The March of Literature*, his last great task and a truly Herculean one. His description of it as a survey from Confucius to Conrad is not an exaggeration and he read or re-read every book or author it deals with, often in the original. Coinciding with the Olivet offer, he knew now that he would have a safe base from which to work, a measure of security and a library on which to draw freely; in other words, a little, at last, of what most who have written about him have taken for granted throughout their working lives.

During the summer of 1937, before starting at Olivet, Ford and Janice went to stay with the Tates at Clarkesville, Tennessee. Their house was called Benfolly and the summer was almost unbearably hot. The Tates were both busy writing, Janice was painting, Robert Lowell – then a youthful admirer of Ford and Tate who had invited himself and was camping on the lawn in a sweltering tent – was writing poetry while Ford dictated *The March of Literature* to Wally Tworkov, Janice's sister-in-law. Ford completed about a thousand words a day, every day, as well as doing the necessary reading. 'It's awful here,' Janice wrote to George Davis of *Harper's Bazaar*. 'In every room in the house there's a typewriter and at every typewriter there sits a genius. Each genius is wilted and says that he or she can do no more but the typewritten sheets keep on mounting. I too am not idle. I sit in the parlour where I paint on three pictures at once in intervals of killing flies. I don't eat them. Neither do I invite them in.'

Lowell described the atmosphere in the house as 'Olympian and somehow crackling'. There does indeed seem to have been a certain amount of what Mizener called 'intellectual and emotional violence', which Ford much disliked. No doubt the heat contributed. These conditions may also have been partly responsible for the impression made upon Caroline Tate, of which she wrote to Stella after Ford's death: 'These last few years have been very hard for [Ford]. There was only his work – he had got to the point where it was impossible to communicate with him. He and Janice seemed to inhabit a closed world, a sphere which rolled here and there, from France to New York and back again, but never changed inside.' There was probably some truth in this, if only as a kind of survival mechanism, and it is significant that the Tates felt the way they did. Only a year before Ford had written to Allen: 'Janice said, this morning: "It's odd, you know, the Tates seem to be the only friends or family we have in the world." . . . quite out of the blue, like that . . . I so thoroughly agreed with her that I came straight in and wrote this. It's true that we haven't any more got any real friends – in the sense of people one can talk to without having to explain every second word . . .'

But now there were disagreements. Caroline talked obsessively about the Civil War and it was some time before Wally Tworkov realised she was referring to the American rather than the Spanish. The atmosphere became, in Janice's word, poisonous, and petty domestic incidents developed unwarranted significance.

Something had changed or was changing. Yet at some time – when is not clear – he had asked Caroline if she was doing any writing. She recalled in her letter to Sondra Stang: 'I told him that I had started a novel but that I was going to have to throw it away. He heaved another sigh and said, "You had better let me see it." I brought him the manuscript a few days later. He read the manuscript through, then said: "Why has nobody told me about this? What are you going to say next?" I recited the sentence. He said, "That is a beautiful sentence. I will write it down." This procedure was repeated several times. It ended with Ford taking my dictation for three weeks. The result was a novel called *Penhally*.'

He never ceased to be similarly helpful, especially to the young (Caroline was twenty-seven when they met), but perhaps the change she remarked is indicated by 'There was only his work . . .' He could not afford to spend time doing anything else. This may have indicated the concentration on essentials that, for the fortunate, sometimes accompanies declining years.

It wasn't all work at Benfolly, however. Among the disagreements were too many distractions and Ford was no better than he had been at abiding noise. He complained (not to his hosts) of 'the children and chickens and birds and cows and steam boats and Tennessean voices and doors slamming in the wind'. Living with the Tates was 'like living with intellectual desperados in the Sargoza Sea [*sic*]'. He and Janice would have left but couldn't because the Tates had borrowed their money. When the heat dried up their water, however, Ford was the man of the hour, sinking a bath tub in the meadow in the hope that it would act as a Sussex dew pond. It didn't but it was a good try. (Had he known it, a piece of the loathed cellophane might have helped.) He spoke at a fund-raising dinner, dressed, Allen Tate told Mizener, 'in white duck trousers, a beat-up dinner jacket, and shod in espadrilles'. The trousers were possibly the Rapallo trousers and the dinner-jacket quite likely that which Anthony Bertram had thought old and shabby at Cooper's Cottage.

They all set off for the Olivet conference in the Tates' car but as soon as the Tates had repaid the money Ford and Janice continued the journey by train. After Olivet, they went to yet another writers' conference at the University of Colorado. The travelling, the air-conditioning and the altitude worsened both his breathing and his gout. Nevertheless, he lectured on each of the first four days in a manner which was, according to the director, understood by some but too learned and elusive for most. After this came the famous lecture in which, as Robert Lowell said (quoted earlier) 'he exquisitely, ludicrously, and inaudibly imitated the elaborate periphrastic style of Henry James', and most of the audience walked out. The director of the conference more or less confirmed Lowell's account though he seems to have been unaware of the James imitation and attributed the general bafflement partly to Ford's referring to Conrad as Jozef Korzeniowski and partly to his completely ignoring the microphone which was placed, then replaced before him. (Another difference is that Lowell thought it was an audience of three thousand while the director said that the auditorium held six hundred and fifty.)

Such activities tired him ever more quickly and he had to spend a day or two in bed after the lecture. He was also, though he didn't show it at the time, distressed by the walk-out. However, he recovered in time to cook the conference's farewell dinner, advertising it as venison which, being out of season, it was illegal to eat. The meal comprised Soup de Poissons au Cocktail, Chevreuil de Pres Salés, Sauce Poivrade, Salade de Saison and Syllabube la

Syrène. Lowell remembered it as the best dinner he ever had: 'the wines were balanced, and every course came as it should, and the venison came and we ended with syllabub and you felt in Paradise at the end. We never realised that the venison was mutton that Ford had cooked.' It was as with many of his stories.

Life at Olivet was good though there were some teething-troubles. The old guard did not like the academic changes that Joseph Brewer introduced; they did not approve of wine whereas Brewer did and Ford and Janice usually had a stack of empties outside their back door. They were able to buy very good wines at fifty cents a bottle because the vintner couldn't sell them, but as the local butchers usually threw away all the interesting parts of animals these fine wines were usually accompanied by ham and eggs. The college persisted with single-sex parties until Ford and Janice each refused to attend unless the other sex was represented. But manuscripts flooded in, Ford reinstated his weekly tea parties, talked to anyone who wanted to talk, lived in a fog of Gauloise and pressed on remorselessly with *The March of Literature*. Their house was very small and, according to Robie Macauley, visitors gained the impression that 'the place was in complete chaos and that Ford was the centre of disorder. Some operation was always ponderously, with many interruptions, underway . . .'[1]

Ford's office was the basement room of the Olivet library, filled not only with his work and the work sent to him but also with the overflow of the library stacks. It was there that he would give his teas and talk about literature. 'His memory had re-written a good deal of the world's literature,' said Macauley, who also thought him 'the least academic man who ever taught and for him all books, in themselves, were contemporaneous.' As indeed they are, for those inhabiting the Kingdom of Letters. Ford, of course, brought alive the essential contemporaneity of literature in his own way: 'He succeeded in giving the impression for instance, that, though he had just missed meeting Marlowe in London, he knew all about him and was very much excited by the young man's work.' It is worth remembering that neither he nor most of the well-read people he grew up with had ever been to university.

[1] 'The Dean In Exile', *Shenandoah* IV, Spring 1953

What he communicated most strongly, Macauley thought, was the sanctity of the writer's function, the demand for unqualified dedication. He had never learned cynicism.

By December of that year he had completed half of *The March of Literature*, some four hundred odd pages. They were by then back in Paris where Janice had an exhibition. He was prevented from working further, however, by another heart attack. As before, it took a long time to recover; by the end of February he was still finding it difficult to walk more than a few steps.

It was during this period that, with Brewer's authority, he wrote to Pound offering a teaching post at Olivet similar to his own. He stressed the lightness of the duties, the opportunity to work, the chance for Pound to put his educational theories into action, the money (which would be better for Pound than for himself) and the fact that Pound would find he had more admirers in America than he realised, if only he would return and acknowledge them. Like most of their letters, this is humorous and facetious in a way that suggests the extent of their mutual understanding although there is an underlying seriousness. Ford is saying, 'Come back', and it is not only a question of coming back to America: 'Of course I know that one cannot expect a man of your age to change his habits or renier his material gods. But you have arrived at an age when few men save themselves unless they do change their habits and travel a little . . . Still I know that all this is beating the wind. The main point is that I should like to see you.' There was an exchange of letters (in which Brewer is referred to as 'the clog-dancer') following the first offer, Pound questioning and refusing, Ford answering and insisting. Pound won in the end by simple refusal to apply for the post, but Ford tried hard. In doing so, he revealed something of his own ideas about education: 'They do not, as I have already told you, use your books as text books (one of Pound's demands was that they should) because "They" are I and I do not approve of the use of text books. You understand I do not approve of making any reading compulsory. If a boy tells me he does not like Virgil I tell him to find something he does like & to read it with attention. That gives results which satisfy me. I teach what I want to, i.e., comparative literature from the beginning of time to the moment of speaking. No one interferes with me to the slightest degree. Nor would they with you. I don't know just what they would do if you tried to introduce your politics into your teaching – nothing at all probably unless you were too loudly Communist in which case the local farmers would shoot you.' It was a valiant effort but Pound did not want to be saved.

They returned to Olivet at the beginning of April 1938. Ford had promised the Dial Press that he would finish *The March of Literature* by 14 July but had been unable to work since his last heart attack. He now set to it with energy and determination despite an attack of rheumatism which, he said, meant he couldn't dress himself or brush his own hair. Towards the end he worked from five in the morning until seven in the evening. It was finished with two days to spare.

There had been interruptions other than illness and more pleasant. In June Brewer persuaded Olivet to award Ford an honorary degree. This was another of those compliments that caused him a quite innocent and child-like delight. Mingled with his contempt for the then academic approach to literature was a veneration for 'university men' such as his father and Marwood had been, and such as he himself might have been if his grandfather had permitted. Also, it was recognition, public, formal, ritualistic, such as he had never had. He wrote with coy delight to Stanley Unwin: 'Should a little bird whisper to you that you will henceforth be able to print LLD after my name on title pages etc, it will be true.' In fact, it was a D.Litt that he was given and that is what appears on the title page of the Allen and Unwin edition of *The March of Literature*.

He wore full academic dress for the ceremony, for which he also acquired a three-piece suit. He appeared very large and professorial and rather jolly. The oration, penned by himself and delivered by the College Orator, was, like his stories, bejewelled with splendid inaccuracies: Mizener cites a doctorate in Agriculture from the Sorbonne, being colonel in charge of two regiments in action, the first in England to praise Joyce, Gertrude Stein and Dreiser, the first to publish short stories by Bennett and Galsworthy and being 'guarantor' of Conrad's first novel, *Almayer's Folly*. He probably approached the oration as the ancients might have done and probably everyone had a good time. Having got recognition at last from the hitherto despised academe, he wrote to Julie, 'So the laugh is on me.'

The next one wasn't. When the Dial Press sent him the first galley proofs of *The March of Literature* he discovered that they had cut most of the untranslated quotes he had included. He had put them in in order to illustrate nuances of meaning; not only did much of the remaining text make little sense without them but Dial had cut without consulting him or giving him time to prepare decent translations. There was argument and recrimination but it was too expensive to put the excised passages back. In the end he reluctantly agreed to do a lecture tour to publicise the book and himself arranged a radio broadcast. (In fact, he did two.) None of this helped; the market was poor, Dial didn't prepare their salesmen and the bookshops were wary of Ford's books. Reviews were mixed though not too bad but the sales were definitely bad. It had been a great effort for a very small splash and it must have confirmed him in his worst views of most publishers.

He tried hard to get the quotes reinstated in the subsequent Allen and Unwin edition but, again, cost was prohibitive. Nor is it now possible to see what difference they might have made because Janice remembers his giving the original manuscript to a Spanish Civil War organisation to sell for funds. They didn't sell it and she asked for it back after his death but never got it.

The effort of writing *The March of Literature* had not helped his health. In August 1938 he returned unread the proofs of *Provence* to Stanley Unwin, saying, 'I simply do not feel well enough actually to correct the book.' Although he much disliked proof-reading, he usually did it and *Provence* was a book he cared about. Exhaustion, declining health and too much worry were getting at him. He had banked a lot on *The March of Literature* being a success.

He spent the autumn lecturing and dining in New York and Boston while working on a new novel, *Professor's Progress*. He did the two radio broadcasts but not, on medical advice, the Dial lecture tour and subsequently fell out with Dial. This made his financial position parlous and he had to borrow £250 from Stanley Unwin. It also meant that, however ill he felt, he could not stop working.

Meanwhile his academic career prospered. He was delighted to be accorded professorial status when Brewer had him appointed Professor of Comparative Literature on Leave. Also, in November 1938, he attended a P.E.N. Club dinner in honour of himself, Pearl Buck and Sinclair Lewis. Lewis praised him as the Dean of American Letters in a speech made perhaps in similar vein to Ford's own doctoral oration. It pleased Ford enormously but he didn't take it quite as literally as has been suggested. In fact, so taken aback was he that he forgot his own tribute to Pearl Buck and the thanks that were due to Lewis. He wrote to him afterwards: '. . . I first fell to wondering who could be the phoenix you were lauding and then concluded that Thomas Mann must be somewhere in the audience and that you were talking to him. So when you dropped out my name I clean forgot everything I had prepared. I am not, you see, modest but you went so far beyond any praise I could allot to myself that I clean forgot all manners!' What he did instead, he wrote to Edward Crankshaw, was to 'content myself with talking about my grand-aunt Eliza – the famous lady who said "Sooner than be idle, I'll take a book and read," which was the only thing that came into my head at that moment . . . ' It continued to puzzle him that he was on the one hand so honoured and on the other so little read – nothing can really compensate for not being read – but these signs of appreciation must have made a difference. He never became bitter.

Although there were periods when he felt well, most of the time he did not. He changed doctors a few times, had his diaphragm raised and was advised to rest, but didn't. He weighed getting on for eighteen stone and for much of the time had to walk with stick. In January 1939 he put his energies into founding a society called 'The Friends of William Carlos Williams'. Williams, whom he felt to be a neglected writer, featured prominently among those he had recommended to Stanley Unwin. Williams himself was rather bemused by the project but went along with it because he liked Ford and was sure he was a dying man. Also, Ford reminded him of his own father. There was, however, another motive on Ford's part: to found an American equivalent of the Académie Goncourt which would promote good writers and perhaps give an annual prize like the Prix Goncourt. He never ceased wanting to be involved, to get things going, to establish that Kingdom. The result in this case, however, was no more than a number of dinners in Greenwich Village. He even tried to raise funds for a revival of the *Transatlantic Review*, involving Stanley Unwin and several Americans, but it didn't work.

After Ford's death Williams expressed his feelings more directly than he probably had to his face.

TO FORD MADOX FORD IN HEAVEN

Is it any better in Heaven, my friend Ford,
        than you found it in Provence?

I don't think so for you made Provence a
        heaven by your praise of it
To give a foretaste of what might be
        your joy in the present circumstances.
It was heaven you were describing there
        transubstantiated from its narrowness
To resemble the paths and gardens of a
        greater world where you now reside.
But, dear man, you have taken a major
        part of it from us.
        Provence that you
praised so well will never be the same
Provence to us
        now you are gone.

A heavenly man you seem to me now, never
        having been for me a saintly one.
It lived about you, a certain grossness that
        was not like the world.
The world is cleanly, polished and well
        made but heavenly man
is filthy with his flesh and corrupt that
        loves to eat and drink and whore –
        to laugh at himself and not be afraid of
        himself knowing well he has

no possessions and opinions that are worth
    caring a broker's word about
and that all he is, but one thing, he feeds
    As one will feed a pet dog.

So roust and love and dredge the belly full
    in Heaven's name!
I laugh to think of you wheezing in Heaven.
    Where is Heaven? But why
do I ask that, since you showed the way?
    I don't care a damn for it
other than for that better part lives beside
    me here so long as I
live and remember you. Thank God you
    were not delicate, you let the world in
and lied! damn it you lied grossly
    sometimes. But it was all, I
see now, a carelessness, the part of a man
    That is homeless here on earth.

Provence, the fat assed Ford will never
    again strain the chairs of your cafés
Pull and pare for his dish your sacred garlic,
    grunt and sweat and lick
his lips. Gross as the world he has left to
    us he has become
a part of that of which you were the known
    part, Provence, he loved so well.

It was the kind of carelessness that comes of caring for different things. He was a man permanently conscious of an elsewhere, trying to arrange this world in terms of that other, trying to make people see. As V. S. Pritchett said in *The Working Novelist*: 'He was nature's expatriate, his country was the Novel, he left his baggage in every hotel room.' But he enjoyed this world. He was, as he has said of himself at a smart breakfast at Galsworthy's, 'a happy fishwife who had gotten into a palace'.

In late April 1939 he and Janice travelled to North Carolina where the Tates were teaching at Greensboro Women's College. It was hot. Ford went to lecture. Caroline, who was with him, watched him go ashen with the effort of climbing the stairs. He sat at the end of a long table, waiting for the class and looking 'like a big white whale . . . forcing the breaths through his wide open mouth'. A copy of the *Saturday Evening Post* lay on the table and he glanced at a story in it, then looked up. 'His fish-like gaze brightened. He said, with a chuckle: "I see that our method has reached the *Post*." He meant impressionism.'

They decided to stay longer in the South, but changed their minds because of what he called 'an invincible yen for Europe'. He supported the yen by saying his health demanded French cooking, with no more canned vegetables and frozen meat. They went to New York in May at about the time Pound arrived in the royal suite of an Italian ship. He had returned to America in the hope of gaining support for the Douglas Credit Scheme and its related economic theory. They saw him just before they left for Europe (it might have been at about this time that they had lunch with Auden and Isherwood, who were, of course, heading the other way). Ford and Pound got on as well as they ever did though when William Carlos Williams called to bid them farewell they told him they had been arguing with Pound in favour of lechery – 'or anything at all to keep him amused and distracted'. There was the same difference and the same tolerance. Perhaps if they had not sailed things might yet have turned out differently for Pound; but only perhaps.

They left for Le Havre in the *Normandie* on 20 May with forebodings about Europe. Ford's dislike of totalitarianism and anti-semitism had increased as each had manifested itself more brutally; he had again tried without success to get himself commissioned to write articles about what was happening to the Jews. They decided not to return to Provence but to stay in Normandy 'in case, because of war alarms, we wanted to skip . . .' They had, of course, no home of their own. Nevertheless before leaving he still found time to write to the *Saturday Review of Literature* a long and reasoned protest against the tepidity of a review of *Finnegans Wake* in which he stated a number of his long-held views as vigorously as ever: 'English is a language ill-suited to good prose because of the associations that, like burrs, cling undetachable to every English word, and the simplest English sentence is forever blurred because it can always have several meanings. Even "The Cat is on the Mat" can mean so much more than meets the eye. If, for instance, you met the statement on top of a newspaper column you would at once guess that Parliament was discussing the abolition of flogging in the Services . . .' It was the same linguistic allusiveness that had prompted him to declare English an unparalleled language for poetry. Old, sick, poor, sailing into a darkening Europe, he never for a moment lowered his sights. He wrote also to Stanley Unwin about *Professor's Progess* which he hoped to complete in September.

He became ill on the voyage and when they landed was too unfit to travel, so they stayed at Honfleur. After a week he was no better. Janice sent for Julie and Stella brought her. They stayed in a nearby hotel and Julie visited on each of the seven days they were there. His rooms, she said, were 'as usual . . . beautiful but inconvenient'. He was suffering from uremia and was in pain but the doctor would give him nothing to relieve the pain because of his heart. For most of the time he was delirious. Julie left several days before he died but in his clear periods he was glad of her presence. At other times, Janice said, his mind was back in the trenches and once he said, 'They can't do this to us. We are British officers.' He did not see Stella; Janice told him she was there and asked if he wanted her to come but 'He was too sick to care about such matters and said no.'

He didn't improve and so on 24 June, after two more weeks, Janice moved him to the Clinique St François in the Avenue de la République in Deauville, found for him by Marcel Le Son (Marcel and Lucie Le Son were old friends from Paris with whom at one time Ford had weekly dinners, each cooking in turn and trying to surpass the other). The clinic was clean and pleasant and the nuns looked after him well. Janice booked him in for a week. A local doctor came, 'a little mean-looking man', Janice told Sondra Stang: 'After his first visit, Ford not having been a very co-operative patient, the doctor said: "It is obvious that Monsieur has always done whatever he wanted in his life." He said it spitefully, making it clear that he had never done what he wanted in his life.'

There was some improvement but by the 26th June he had worsened again. They waited all day for the clinic doctor, hoping he could relieve the nausea, but he never came. Ford asked for no priest and received no last rites. At about a quarter to five in the afternoon he said he was hungry and Janice called the sister. When the sister had gone he made a sudden movement and fell unconscious into Janice's arms, where he died.

TWENTY-FIVE

Elsie, too, died of her heart, although nearly ten years later in January 1949, in a nursing home at St Leonard's-on-Sea, Sussex. In 1933 she sold Hurst Cottage, Aldington, having enlarged it and named it 'Kitcat' (it is now further enlarged and restored to its original name), then went to live with Mary in Icklesham, near Winchelsea. After that she had moved back to Aldington. She is buried in the churchyard in a grave looking across the valley towards Hurst Cottage, her tombstone bearing the surname she clung to so tenaciously during life. Christina spent her adult life as Sister Mary Matthew Hueffer of the Society of the Holy Child Jesus, working with students in London and Oxford. According to Katharine, she used to pray for Janice, so probably did the same for Stella. Katharine herself lived in Galway with Charles Lamb and had two sons and three daughters. After Ford's death, Elsie sent an epitaph to Janice via Katharine, asking that it be put on his grave. She said, according to Katharine, that Ford was the most honourable person she had known, that she thanked God on her knees for having known him and that she had 'remained faithful' to him. Janice ignored the epitaph, feeling that Elsie had had time enough to show her gratitude and that so many years of silence had not earned her the right to the last word. She also left off the epitaph she had herself prepared.

Mary never married, lived in Germany for some years in the 1920s, returning in the early 1930s after the youngest Martindale, Leonard, was beaten and killed in London. She was fond of Leonard's children and helped them. It was at this period that she lived with Elsie and irritated her by harping on about the past. After brother Harri and his wife died in 1933 and Elsie had returned to Aldington, Mary moved to nearby Appledore where she lived in a house called Belmont. She died some years after Elsie.

Stella lived the remaining two decades of her life as a painter. Most of the war she spent in London and Essex and was appointed official war artist by the Australian Government. *Drawn From Life* ends in 1940 with her saying that she had had a bench made outside her cottage door so that she could sit in the sun 'in case some day I may become a grandmother'. She became one only weeks before dying of cancer in 1947, at the age of fifty-two. She was determined to live long enough to hold her grandchild, and did. When she was dying she sent for Janice who was, she said, the only person she could talk to about her 'real' life. It was then that she learned that Ford had dictated Janice's letters to her. She faced death with the robust cheerfulness with which she faced life, leaving Julie a note saying that after the Golders Green cremation she should not 'wait for the ashes or any nonsense of that sort! Go and have a drink somewhere . . .'

Julie married a writer, Roland Loewe, and spent most of the rest of her life with him in California where her son, Julian, became a journalist. She, too, died of cancer.

Violet, as we have seen, died in 1942 during the London bombing raid that she thought was thunder in the Welsh mountains. She and Ford had no contact with each other though there was indirect contact when he and Janice visited London in 1934 and she asked Goldring to ask him if he would visit her. Her last completed book, *The Wife of Rossetti* (1932), showed that she never really escaped the themes to which Ford's eruption in her life had given rise. She tried to write after that but told Goldring: 'I *can't* get on and it tires me so to compose.'

Jean Rhys continued writing during the 1930s but her books did not sell very well and she sank from literary view. She never sought literary society. She divorced and married again. Her second husband encouraged her to write but he died and her third, a naval officer, did not encourage her. She was thought to be dead until her re-discovery by Francis Wyndham in the 1960s and the publication of her best-known work, *The Wide Sargasso Sea*. She spent her declining years in Devon, was awarded various literary prizes and, in 1978, was made a CBE. She died in 1979, aged 84, and was survived by a daughter. In her old age she did attempt to put on paper an account of her affair with Ford but it is fragmentary, inaccurate and confusing.

Following Ford's death, Janice asked Lucie Le Son, who had remained in Deauville when her husband left, to let people know. Edward Crankshaw heard the news on the BBC and came over immediately. There were just the three of them at the funeral with a few flowers and thyme and bay leaves on the coffin, though there were nineteen telegrams, mostly from America. Even then, in that simplicity, the Fordian bad luck in arrangements held: a drunken grave digger buried him in the wrong place, in unhallowed ground reserved for temporary graves. When Janice returned after the war she was told that the grave would have to be moved. She commented: 'That was Ford all over. He couldn't rest quietly even in his grave. As he so often said, "The gods to each ascribe a differing lot/some enter at the portals, some do not."' The lines are from his own poem, 'Mister Bosphorus'.

After the funeral and following an attempt by the sister of the clinic to convert her (the disappointed sister was consoled by being allowed to keep the fees for the whole week), Janice went down to the villa at Cap Brun where, although they were no longer tenants, they had stuff to clear out. She burned papers that then seemed unimportant and shipped others to America. She herself left for America after war had started on what she believes was the last ship. She provided a gravestone when she went back after the war but has never returned to see what was done with it.[1]

She lives and paints in Paris with her husband, the painter Daniel Brustlein (better known as Alain, cartoonist on the *New Yorker* for thirty or so years). They met in America during the war when he was asked to speak in Portuguese to a monkey that wouldn't come out of a tree (he didn't speak Portuguese but the monkey came down). They married not long after. She is sure that Ford would have approved her marrying – 'He'd have said it was a lack of vitality not to' – and she is as ardent on his behalf now as when they first met. Unlike Stella, she found he needed no propping up

[1] It is in the town cemetery in Deauville, a plain slab giving the bare details, surrounded by ornate grotesqueries.

when she knew him, that he wasn't a great consumer of other people's energy, that, though demanding, it was of no one more than himself – 'he lived at the top of his bent'. He had got over the war by the time she met him and perhaps was, as he said, different with each of his women. To talk to her now is to feel still the energy of that 'long, passionate dialogue'.

For the blind man who has to feel with his stick the impression at the end of the journey is not how much is known but how little. It is judgement by feel and echo. Most of us would find it disquieting to have our lives assessed on the basis of what some people happen to have kept of what we put in writing, of what other people – not all of whom knew us well – have said about us, of what yet others remembered or thought they remembered after nearly half a century. So much that was important would be missed, such as our preoccupations during this Easter of 1989. What were they? The biographer would know only that the book was finished.

But it is not simply the fact that the past is past that limits us. As Ford showed, perhaps better than any, the heart of another is a dark forest. The people we think we know intimately may still surprise us, as we may surprise ourselves, and the biographer of the living really knows no more. Perhaps less; he does not wait for the echo, or stay to feel.

That feel and echo are all we have. Facts may be neutral or treacherous but it is the impression of personality – as he put it, temperament, the writer's true gift – that draws us on. No speech is heard but words are inwardly felt; even when it seems our own are merely echoed back, there is that in the tone which can teach us. And so pleasant it is to fancy that upon unexpected elevation into the heavenly Kingdom of Letters we may be met by a large and comforting Presence, glass in hand, with a touch of old tweed, a suggestion of hitched-up Rapallo trousers, an outline of ancient dinner-jacket, a smell of uniform and creak of leather, a whiff of Gauloise, a taste of Château Margaux and a reassuring hand on our arm; and we would follow the soothing gentlemanly voice which is telling us that all the right people are here, that everyone is delighted we made it, that it's the best party there ever was, that he will perform all the introductions, that only the good stories are true; and we shall all sit down and talk.

Epilogue

There were few public references to Ford's death. Pound's obituary, published in August 1939, was easily the fullest. The following are excerpts.

> There passed from us this June a very gallant combatant for those things of the mind and of letters which have been in our time too little prized. There passed a man who took in his time more punishment of one sort or another than I have seen meted to anyone else. For the ten years before I got to England there would seem to have been no-one but Ford who held that French clarity and simplicity in the writing of English verse and prose were of immense importance as in contrast to the use of a stilted traditional dialect, a 'language of verse' unused in the actual talk of the people, even of 'the best people', for the expression of reality and emotion . . .
>
> The justification or programme of such writing was finally (about 1913) set down in one of the best essays (preface) that Ford ever wrote.
>
> It advocated the prose value of verse-writing, and it, along with his oeuvre, had more in it for my generation than all the retchings (most worthily) after 'quantity' (i.e., quantitative metric) of the late Laureate Robert Bridges or the useful, but monotonous, in their day unduly neglected, as more recently unduly touted, metrical labours of G. Manley Hopkins.
>
> I have put it down as personal debt to my forerunners that I have had five, and only five, useful criticisms of my writing in my lifetime, one from Yeats, one from Bridges, one from Thomas Hardy, a recent one from a Roman Archbishop and one from Ford, and that last the most vital, or at any rate on a par with Hardy's.

That Ford was almost an *halluciné* few of his intimates can doubt. He felt until it paralysed his efficient action, he saw quite distinctly the Venus immortal crossing the tram tracks. He inveighed against Yeats' lack of emotion as, for him, proved by Yeats' so great competence in making literary use of emotion.

And he felt the errors of contemporary style to the point of rolling (physically, and if you look at it as a mere superficial snob, ridiculously) on the floor of his temporary quarters in Giessen when my third volume displayed me trapped, fly-papered, gummed and strapped down in a jejune provincial effort to learn, mehercule, the stilted language that then passed for 'good English' in the arthritic milieu that held control of the respected British critical circles, Newbolt, the backwash of Lionel Johnson, Fred Manning, the Quarterlies and the rest of 'em.

And that roll saved me at least two years, perhaps more. It sent me back to my own proper effort, namely, toward using the living tongue (with younger men after me), though none of us has found a more natural language than Ford did . . .

I propose to bury him in the order of merits as I think he himself understood them, first for an actual example in the writing of poetry; secondly, for those same merits more fully shown in his prose, and thirdly, for the critical acumen which was implicit in his finding these merits.

As to his prose, you can apply to it a good deal that he wrote in praise of Hudson (rightly) and of Conrad, I think with a bias toward generosity that in parts defeats its critical applicability. It lay so natural on the page that one didn't notice it. I read an historical novel at sea in 1906 without noting the name of the author. A scene at Henry VIIIth's court stayed depicted in my memory and I found years later that Ford had written it.

I wanted for private purposes to make a note of a point raised in *Ancient Lights*: I thought it would go on the back of an envelope, and found to my young surprise that I couldn't make the note in fewer words than those on Ford's actual page. That set me thinking. I did not in those days care about prose. If 'prose' meant anything to me, it meant Tacitus (as seen by Mackail), a damned dangerous model for a young man in those days or these days in England, though I don't regret it; one never knows enough about anything. Start with Tacitus and be cured by Flaubert via Ford, or start with Ford or Maupassant and be girt up by Tacitus, after fifty it is kif, kif, all one. But a man is a pig not to be grateful to both sides.

Until the arrival of such 'uncomfortables' as D. H. Lawrence, D. Goldring, G. Cannan, etc., I think Ford had no one to play with. The elder generation loathed him, or at any rate such a cross-section of it as I encountered. He disturbed 'em, he took Dagon by the beard, publicly. And he founded the greatest Little Review or pre-Little Review of our time. From 1908 to 1910 he gathered into one fasciculus the work of Hardy, H. James, Hudson, Conrad, C. Graham, Anatole France, the great old-stagers, the most competent of that wholly unpleasant decade, Bennett, Wells, and, I think, even Galsworthy.

And he got the first-rate and the high second-raters of my own decade, W. Lewis, D. H. Lawrence (made by Ford, dug out of a board school in Croydon), Cannan, Walpole, etc. (Eliot was not yet on the scene).

The inner story of that review and the treatment of Ford by its obtainers is a blot on London's history that time will not remove, though, of course, it will become invisible in the perspective of years.

As a critic he was perhaps wrecked by his wholly unpolitic generosity. In fact, if he merits an epithet above all others, it would be 'The Unpolitic' . . .

Another significant obituary was by Graham Greene, published in the *Spectator* in July 1939. He concluded:

When Ford died he had passed through a period of neglect and was re-emerging. His latest books were not his best, but they were hailed as if they were. The first war had ruined him. He had volunteered, though he was over military age and was fighting a country he loved: his health was broken, and he came back to a new literary world which had carefully eliminated him. For some of his later work he could not even find a publisher in England. No wonder he preferred to live abroad –

in Provence or New York. But I don't suppose failure disturbed him much: he had never really believed in human happiness, his middle life had been made miserable by passion, and he had come through – with his humour intact, his stock of unreliable anecdotes, the kind of enemies a man ought to have, and a half-belief in a posterity which would care for good writing.

Postscript

More Ford papers have been discovered since the first edition of this book appeared; thanks to the initiative and generosity of Mr Thomas Carter and his family, I have seen them.

The papers identified so far (there may be others) comprise some sixty-three letters, telegrams, postcards and notes sent by Ford to Miss Elizabeth Cheatham, with whom he was in love. There are also ten poems. The letters span the years 1927–9 and 1938–9, the last one having been written about a month before Ford's death. Those of 1927–9 are love-letters while the later ones are friendly communications apparently prompted by Elizabeth's having got in touch again some time after her marriage. They make no radical difference to the story of Ford's life but they do add considerably to our knowledge of the time between his separation from Stella in 1927 and the advent of Janice Biala in 1930. They also add to knowledge of his relationship with Rene Wright and make for more precise dating of some of his books and movements. The existence of Elizabeth and her part in Ford's life was known to Janice Biala but the papers remained private and unknown until after Elizabeth's death. It will fall to future biographers – especially, I hope, to Dr Max Saunders – to explore this material in full; what follows is the briefest of summaries.

Elizabeth Cheatham was born in 1905 in Arkansas, the daughter of an episcopalian minister, but moved in early childhood to Pinehurst, North Carolina, where she spent much of her life. She died in August, 1990. She went to college in New York and Paris and became a talented designer of book-jackets (she is thought to have designed two of Ford's). She was 5′ 3½″, had dark hair, was a keen golfer and a good shot, having been taught by Annie Oakley. She married Hugh William Carter, by whom she had two children.

She and Ford appear to have met in Paris in 1927, possibly at a party given by someone called Helen Ashbury. Whether or not they met at the party it seems to have had some significance because it is mentioned in connection with RVAD, a frequent reference to – I think – Rue Vavin At Dawn. This sounds as if it was the occasion of a mutual declaration of love. She was twenty-three and Ford fifty-three.

The earliest letters are polite and brief, but by January, 1928 the affair had clearly begun. They seem never to have been lovers but there existed an intense emotional intimacy consequent upon the dramatic declaration and they regarded themselves as committed to each other. Ford must have only just ceased to be involved with Stella and he was still very much involved with Rene Wright.

He remained so throughout. Several of the longer letters (one of which he asked Elizabeth to burn because he thought it mean and indelicate to reveal details of a relationship with someone else) are attempts to account for his sense of obligation to Rene though he never really gets at the origin, which was probably when they first met over twenty years before. He felt he ought to 'hold myself at her disposal as long as she can stand it because she did put herself through the divorce which was very unpleasant for my sake'. Yet they had not said they loved each other since they had met again in New York and he now thinks that Rene is 'really mentally very ill'. They, too, were not lovers; she had only once or twice visited his Paris apartment, which appalled her by its sparseness, and he describes their affair as one of 'restaurants and hotel vestibules'. Owing perhaps to his very particular sense of honour and obligation, the fact that they were not lovers made breaking with her more difficult: 'If there *were* any passion about our relationship I would break with her at once . . . there is absolutely nothing between us of any amatory nature.'

Her wealth was part of the problem. He believed she wanted to marry him at the time of her divorce but changed her mind on discovering his penury. She also resented the settlements he had made on Stella and Julie: 'She took the view that I was victimising her for the sake of pouring money into Stella's lap . . . and that I was a European fortune-hunter . . . American women of that class are so hypnotised by their own money . . . I think it absolutely certain that she will not ever want really to marry me for she has always been used to the circumstances of the very rich which I can't provide and would not if I could for, although I am a hard-shelled Tory, I hate, hate, hate any manifestations of wealth . . . I think she likes me, as a mild celebrity, to take her about . . .'

It is clear that the relationship was more fraught than outsiders, then and since, realised. Three times they parted for good but each time she rang him the next day and told him to take her for lunch. He said he 'asked constantly what her intentions were but each time she turned it off'. Perhaps they both felt under obligation without either wanting the other enough, though each wanted someone.

With Elizabeth, however, he was in love: 'I promise you, my dearest love, that I will never marry anyone but you.' His letters are fond and frequent and he is once again hoping somehow to get divorced; there is talk of Rome, of his marriage being 'only civil', of a decree to be made absolute by 20 January, 1929, but in fact never mentioned again. He even says that he had never loved anyone else.

His feelings appear to have been reciprocated, at least for a while. In the context of the hoped-for divorce, he writes: '. . . the loveliest thing you have ever written to me was to the effect that you might have been voting for the last time as an American citizen. Please God . . . that it will be so.' He worries about her finding a younger man and she worries, not surprisingly, about his relationship with Rene. Further worries for her were the differences in their ages and, apparently, the prospect of a Roman Catholic wedding. Her parents, though sympathetic, were also anxious and she had no wish to ignore them. The prospect of not being able to provide for her – what he called the 'hard details of business' – weighed upon Ford and even when he sought to reassure her his assurances were equivocal, as when he describes the real obstacle as 'purely financial.' This is shortly after telling her that if he were a dispassionate outsider he would 'certainly counsel you to throw me over'. Such equivocation is present throughout and it must have strengthened Elizabeth's doubts.

They had to resort to subterfuge from very early on and it is at his suggestion that she later signs herself M for Mouse, in case Rene should find the letters. (Rene seems to have done so at one point, with consequent unpleasantness.) Finally, it is Ford's inability or unwillingness to resolve his 'kaleidoscopic' circumstances that precipitate the end. He tried to be passive and to get the women to make his decision for him; not unnaturally, they made their own. Ford returned to France, writing emotional farewells to Elizabeth, and she married Hugh Carter, whom she had met already. It is not known exactly how the affair with Rene ended.

The 1938–9 letters are quite different in tone. Elizabeth probably still signed herself Mouse since Ford addresses her 'Dear Mouse', which he did not do before. She seems to have taken the initiative in getting in touch while he and Janice Biala were in America, and when they met she was introduced to Janice. The letters are chatty and friendly, not intimate, the sort of 'weather and crops' letter he had earlier said he could not write to anyone with whom he was in love. His last was written in May, 1939 shortly before he and Janice left for Europe on what was to be his final journey. He says his health is improved. The last letter in the collection is from Janice to Elizabeth some months after Ford's death, saying he had received Elizabeth's letter a few days before he died and 'was pleased that things were so much brighter'. (In fact, his words to Janice at the time were: 'So all is gas and gingerbread.')

Of the poems, eight are typed, two handwritten and one is in both forms. All are for Elizabeth and some carry her own comments. They are happy jingles of the sort that Ford wrote quickly and easily, especially when he was happy. Although one is called 'The Buckshee Day' they do not compare with the Buckshee poems which he was later to write for Janice.

Indeed, the difference between the two sets of poems is striking and may be indicative. Although Ford was in love with Elizabeth there is throughout a hint of equivocation; it was not a passion to override all problems. Probably he was lonely more than anything and if it had not been Elizabeth it might have been someone else, possibly even Rene despite all the difficulties. The relationship had neither the depth nor the wholehearted commitment, on either side, of that with Janice, though it was loving and intimate.

Also, there are suggestions, present in some other of Ford's affairs, of that vicarious imaginative indulgence he would put into his novels. More than once he asked Elizabeth for a description of her room in terms that recall his remark about the need to visualise every aspect of a room in which he placed a fictional character, even if he did not mention it: 'I love to such an extent in mental pictures that if I have not got one I get numbed.' It sometimes seems as if Elizabeth, the affair and himself perform on the same mental stage as his imagined characters. This is particularly noticeable when the affair is going wrong and Ford, in another equivocal gesture, involves her parents. Whatever his motives, the effect is to render that responsibility for what would normally be his own decision widened: 'Dearest, you are quite wrong as to the rules of this rather bitter game. Because I let you tell your parents that I wanted you to consider yourself free it would not be honourable of me to write you loveletters so as to entice you back into your cage.' That chilling first sentence is, as Dr Saunders has pointed out, disconcertingly like the tone of voice used by Jean Rhys's Heidler.

Ford probably wanted sympathy even more than he needed it but he offered it as readily as he demanded; perhaps that was part of his attraction. Historical value apart, what these letters show is that, whether in love or out of it, he was never not a novelist.

Chronology

1873 Born 17 December, Ford Hermann Hueffer at Merton, Surrey.
1881 To Praetorius School at Folkestone, Kent.
1889 Death of father. Family moves in with grandfather, Ford Madox Brown.
1890 Leaves school.
1891 First book, *The Brown Owl*, published. Becomes Roman Catholic.
1892 First novel, *The Shifting of the Fire*, published.
1893 Death of Ford Madox Brown.
1894 Marries Elsie Martindale, settles in Kent.
1896 Publishes biography of Madox Brown.
1897 Birth of daughter, Christina. Inherits £3,000.
1898 Meets Conrad.
1900 Birth of second daughter, Katharine.
1901 Moves to Winchelsea, Sussex.
1902 Death of father-in-law.
1904 Moves to London, nervous breakdown, convalescence in Germany.
1905 Meets Arthur Marwood.
1906–8 Breakdown of marriage.
1908–9 Edits *The English Review*, begins relationship with Violet Hunt.
1910–11 Moves to Germany in attempt to divorce; Elsie's libel suit.
1912–13 Travelling with Violet Hunt, first edition of collected poems published, near nervous collapse.
1914 Involved with Vorticists, Imagists, etc.
1915 Publishes *The Good Soldier*; joins the army.
1916 Shell-shocked during the Battle of the Somme.
1917 Invalided home.
1918 Meets Stella Bowen.
1919 Leaves army, changes surname to Ford, moves to Sussex with Stella.

1920 Birth of third daughter, Julia (Julie).

1922 Moves to France with Stella and Julia.

1924–5 Edits *Transatlantic Review* in Paris, begins *Parade's End* tetralogy; death of Conrad; affair with Jean Rhys.

1927–8 Separates from Stella.

1930 Meets Janice Biala.

1931–6 Lives in France and United States, first signs of heart trouble, second edition of collected poems published.

1937 Appointed writer in residence, Olivet College, Michigan.

1938 Honorary professorship at Michigan, working on last book, *The March of Literature*.

1939 Dies in Deauville, 26 June.

Bibliographical Note

The most important collection of Ford papers and other material is at Cornell University. It includes Janice Biala's papers, the Violet Hunt papers and many of the Stella Bowen papers. The largest private collection, the Naumburg papers, is deposited at Princeton University. Letters between Ford and Stella Bowen, previously the property of Stella's daughter, Julia Loewe, are to be published by the Indiana State University Press. Among printed sources, the best – though not exhaustive – starting points for research are David Dow Harvey's *Ford Madox Ford 1873–1939: A Bibliography of Works and Criticism* and Richard Ludwig's *Letters of Ford Madox Ford* (both Princeton University Press, 1962 and 1965 respectively). Further letters may be found in Sondra Stang's *The Ford Madox Ford Reader* (Carcanet and Paladin, 1987) and in Brita Lindberg-Seyersted's *Pound/Ford: The Story of a Literary Friendship* (Faber & Faber, 1982). Stella Bowen's *Drawn From Life* (Virago, 1984), Douglas Goldring's *South Lodge* and *The Last Pre-Raphaelite* (Constable, 1943 and 1948) and Violet Hunt's *The Flurried Years* (Hurst, 1926) are essential biographical reading. Necessary later biographies are Frank MacShane's *The Life and Work of Ford Madox Ford* (Routlege, 1965), Arthur Mizener's *The Saddest Story* (The Bodley Head, 1971) and Thomas Moser's *The Life in the Fiction of Ford Madox Ford* (Princeton University Press, 1980), the latter two particularly. Wyndham Lewis's *Blasting and Bombardiering* (Calder and Boyars, 1967) and David Garnett's *The Golden Echo* (Chatto and Windus, 1953) should also be read. Among the worthwhile modern evaluations are John Meixner's *Ford Madox Ford's Novels* (University of Minnesota Press, 1962), Richard Cassell's *Ford Madox Ford: A Study of his Novels* and *Ford Madox Ford: Modern Judgements* (Johns Hopkins Press, 1962 and 1972), Nicholas Delbanco's *Group Portrait* (1982), Robert Green's *Ford Madox Ford: Prose and Politics* (1981), Miranda Seymour's *The Ring of Conspirators* (Hodder and Stoughton, 1988) and Sondra Stang's *The Presence of Ford Madox Ford* (University of Pennsylvania Press, 1981). The latter is an especially vivid and helpful collection. Outstanding among contemporary publications is *Ford Madox Ford and the Arts* (Contemporary Literature, University of Wisconsin Press, Vol. 30, No. 2, Summer 1989), which includes a useful bibliography of recent secondary sources.

A List of Ford's Books

(First publication only. Place of publication is London unless otherwise stated.)

1891 *The Brown Owl*, T. Fisher Unwin. Fairy story.

1892 *The Feather*, T. Fisher Unwin.

1892 *The Shifting of the Fire*, T. Fisher Unwin. Novel.

1893 *The Questions at the Well*, Digby, Long & Co. Poems. Published under the pseudonym Fenil Haig.

1894 *The Queen Who Flew*, Bliss, Sands & Foster. Fairy story.

1896 *Ford Madox Brown*, Longmans, Green & Co. Biography.

1900 *Poems for Pictures*, John MacQueen.

1900 *The Cinque Ports*, William Blackwood and Sons. Descriptive history.

1901 *The Inheritors* (with Joseph Conrad), New York, McClure, Phillips & Co. Novel.

1902 *Rossetti*, Duckworth & Co. Critical biography.

1903 *Romance* (with Joseph Conrad), Smith, Elder & Co. Novel.

1904 *The Face of the Night*, John MacQueen. Poems.

1905 *The Soul of London*, Alston Rivers. Contemplation and impressions.

1905 *The Benefactor*, Brown, Langham & Co. Novel.

1905 *Hans Holbein*, London, Duckworth & Co.; New York, E. P. Dutton & Co. Critical monograph.

1906 *The Fifth Queen*, Alston Rivers. Novel. The first in the Katharine Howard trilogy.

1906 *The Heart of the Country*, Alston Rivers. Contemplation and impressions.

1906 *Christina's Fairy Book*, Alston Rivers. Fairy story.

1907 *Privy Seal*, Alston Rivers. Novel. The second in the Katharine Howard trilogy.

1907 *From Inland and Other Poems*, Alston Rivers.

1907 *An English Girl*, Methuen & Co. Novel.

1907 *The Pre-Raphaelite Brotherhood*, London, Duckworth & Co.; New York, E. P. Dutton & Co. Critical monograph.

1907 *The Spirit of the People*, Alston Rivers. Contemplation and impressions.

[1907 *England and the English*, New York, McClure, Phillips & Co. Essays. A one-volume edition of *The Soul of London*, *The Heart of the Country*, and *The Spirit of the People*.]

1908 *The Fifth Queen Crowned*, Eveleigh Nash. Novel. The final novel of the Katharine Howard trilogy.

1908 *Mr. Apollo*, Methuen & Co. Novel.

1909 *The 'Half Moon'*, Eveleigh Nash. Novel.

1910 *A Call*, Chatto & Windus. Novel.

1910 *Songs from London*, London, Elkin Mathews. Poems.

1910 *The Portrait*, Methuen & Co. Novel.

1911 *The Simple Life Limited*, John Lane. Novel. Published under the pseudonym Daniel Chaucer.

1911 *Ancient Lights and Certain New Reflections*, Chapman and Hall. Reminiscences. Published by Harper & Brothers in New York, 1911, as *Memories and Impressions*.

1911 *Ladies Whose Bright Eyes*, Constable & Co. Novel.

1911 *The Critical Attitude*, Duckworth & Co. Essays in criticism.

1912 *High Germany*, Duckworth & Co. Poems.

1912 *The Panel*, Constable & Co. Novel.

1912 *The New Humpty-Dumpty*, John Lane. Novel. Published under the pseudonym Daniel Chaucer.

[1913] *This Monstrous Regiment of Women*, suffragette pamphlet.

1913 *Mr. Fleight*, Howard Latimer, Ltd. Novel.

1913 *The Desirable Alien* (with Violet Hunt), Chatto & Windus. German impressions.

1913 *The Young Lovell*, Chatto & Windus. Novel.

1913 *Ring for Nancy*, Indianapolis, The Bobbs-Merrill Company. Novel. Revised version of *The Panel*, published only in America.

1913 *Collected Poems*, Max Goschen, Ltd.

1914 *Henry James*, Martin Secker. Critical monograph.

[1915] *Antwerp*, The Poetry Bookshop. Pamphlet poem.

1915 *The Good Soldier*, John Lane. Novel.

1915 *When Blood Is Their Argument: An Analysis of Prussian Culture*, New York and London, Hodder and Stoughton. Propaganda.

1915 *Between St. Dennis and St. George: A Sketch of Three Civilisations*, New York and London, Hodder and Stoughton. Propaganda.

1915 *Zeppelin Nights* (with Violet Hunt), John Lane. Historical sketches.

1918 *On Heaven and Poems Written on Active Service*, John Lane.

1921 *A House*, The Poetry Bookshop. Pamphlet poem.

1921 *Thus to Revisit*, Chapman & Hall. Reminiscences.

1923 *The Marsden Case*, Duckworth & Co. Novel. The first book to appear under the name of Ford Madox Ford.

1923 *Women & Men*, Paris, Three Mountains Press. Essays.

1923 *Mister Bosphorus and the Muses*, Duckworth & Co. Long poem.

1924 *Some Do Not*, Duckworth & Co. Novel. The first of the Tietjens tetralogy.

1924 *The Nature of a Crime* (with Joseph Conrad), Duckworth & Co. Novel. Previously published in *The English Review* (1909) under the pseudonym Baron Ignatz von Aschendrof, and in *The Transatlantic Review*, in January and February, 1924.

1924 *Joseph Conrad: A Personal Remembrance*, Duckworth & Co. Biography, reminiscence and criticism.

1925 *No More Parades*, Duckworth. Novel. The second of the Tietjens tetralogy.

1926 *A Mirror to France*, Duckworth. Impressionistic essays.

1926 *A Man Could Stand Up*, Duckworth. Novel. The third of the Tietjens tetralogy.

1927 *New Poems*, New York, William Edwin Rudge.

1927 *New York Is Not America*, Duckworth. Impressionistic essays.

1927 *New York Essays*, New York, William Edwin Rudge.

1928 *The Last Post*, New York, The Literary Guild of America. Novel. The last of the Tietjens tetralogy. Published in London by Duckworth.

1928 *A Little Less Than Gods*, Duckworth. Novel.

1929 *The English Novel: From the Earliest Days to the Death of Joseph Conrad*, Philadelphia, J. B. Lippincott Company. Literary history and criticism.

1929 *No Enemy*, New York, The Macaulay Company. Autobiographical novel.

1931 *Return to Yesterday*, Victor Gollancz. Reminiscences.

1931 *When the Wicked Man*, New York, Horace Liveright, Inc. Novel.

1933 *The Rash Act*, New York, Ray Long & Richard R. Smith, Inc. Novel.

1933 *It Was the Nightingale*, Philadelphia, J. B. Lippincott Company. Reminiscences.

1934 *Henry for Hugh*, Philadelphia, J. B. Lippincott Company. Novel. Sequel to *The Rash Act*.

1935 *Provence*, Philadelphia, J. B. Lippincott Company. Impressions and reminiscence.

1936 *Vive Le Roy*, Philadelphia, J. B. Lippincott Company. Novel.

1936 *Collected Poems*, New York, Oxford University Press.

1937 *Great Trade Route*, New York, Oxford University Press. Impressions and reminiscence.

1937 *Portraits from Life*, Boston, Houghton Mifflin Company. Literary essays. Published by George Allen & Unwin in London, 1938 as *Mightier Than the Sword: Memories and Criticisms*.

1938 *The March of Literature from Confucius' Day to Our Own*, New York, The Dial Press. Criticism.

1988 *A History of Our Own Times*, published by Indiana State University Press and in Britain by Carcanet in 1989.

This list is an adaptation of that compiled by David Dow Harvey in *Ford Madox Ford 1873–1939: A Bibliography of Works and Criticism* , Princeton Univertisy Press, 1962.

Index

H. C. Robbins Landon

1791: Mozart's Last Year

Mozart's death on December 5th, 1791, at the age of 35, was 'the greatest tragedy in the history of music'. But it is an event that has been forever shrouded in mystery, just as the rest of his life has been the subject of many myths.

Who was the mysterious stranger who commissioned Mozart to write a Requiem, which he became convinced was to be his own? How was his arch-rival Salieri involved? In what state were Mozart's finances in that fateful year? How did he come to be buried in a pauper's grave? Was his wife instrumental to his demise?

In this fascinating book, Robbins Landon sets out the definitive account of the true course of events during Mozart's fateful, productive and enthralling last year alive.

'A book to reread with a deepening sense of wonder at the story which it tells so vividly.' George Steiner, *Sunday Times*

'With his unrivalled knowledge of the contemporary source material, he has ruthlessly cut through the tangled skein of legend and mystification.' Robert Henderson, *Daily Telegraph*

'The reader is swept along on waves of scholarly enthusiasm.'
Jane Glover, *Opera*

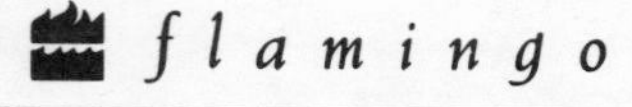

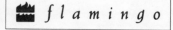

'It has taken Alan Judd, Ford's kindest biographer to date, to rescue him from the literary oubliette, and to house him as he deserves, in sympathy and a well-appointed context.' JAMES WOOD, *Vogue*

'Judd writes from a distance, but with judicious fellow-feeling.'
D.J. ENRIGHT, *Observer*

'Often acute and always entertaining'
NICHOLAS RICHARDSON, *Evening Standard*

'Alan Judd's great strength is that he approaches Ford not as a psychologist in search of secrets, but as a novelist in search of character.' DAVID TROTTER, *Sunday Correspondent*

'Judd writes with a quirkiness and a willingness to indulge in speculation which makes Ford Madox Ford a highly pleasurable companion...well worth buying.'
JANET BARRON, *Literary Review*

'It is a fluent, engrossing read, always interesting. Its great charm is that Judd *likes* Ford.' J.D.F. JONES, *Financial Times*

'With informality Judd offers a rambling, discursive, sharp, speculative and broad-minded study of an impressionist.'
DAVID HUGHES, *Mail on Sunday*

'Judd, himself a fine novelist, has punched a hole in his creative career in order to accomodate this distinguished biography.'
ANTHONY BURGESS, *Independent*

'Alan Judd is always penetrating and sympathetic, and doesn't lose his way, which would be easy in the maze of relationships. He is very good, too, on the technical and psychological subtleties of Ford's writing.' J.B. PICK, *Scotsman*

'In Alan Judd, Ford has found a sensitive and sympathetic biographer who is willing, with reservations, to defend even his failings.' *Economist*

'Warm and appreciative' DOUGLAS DUNN, *Glasgow Herald*

'What Judd rightly emphasizes is that Ford was a giver, believing that the preservation and furtherance of artistic talent was his permanent responsibility.'
FRANK KERMODE, *London Review of Books*

Alan Judd

has published five novels: *A Breed of Heroes* (1981, winner of the Royal Society of Literature award), *Short of Glory* (1984), *The Noonday Devil* (1987), *Tango* (1989), and *The Devil's Own Work* (1991). He had never intended to become a biographer, but was drawn to write this life of Ford on reading his most celebrated novel *The Good Soldier*. Judd left his post in the Foreign Office to write the book, but has now returned to his employer and has no plans to write another biography, unless he finds another subject which – in Ford's own words – springs at his throat.

Selections from the reviews of the hardback edition:

'One of the best literary biographies I have ever read: in a class with Edel's *James*.' HUGH KENNER

'Judd gives Ford a dignity and status as a literary figure which too many of his critics have denied him. The book flows with an élan and panache which would have pleased Ford, for whom, it sometimes seems, it has been written.'
CHRISTOPHER SEDDON, *The Tablet*

'Ford has been lucky (at last) in his biographer. Alan Judd has disentangled the muddle and misinformation which previously existed and produced a convincing account.'
ISABEL COLEGATE, *Spectator*

'Alan Judd has been drawn into Ford's embattlement and defends him staunchly and imaginatively.' A.S. BYATT, *Guardian*

'After reading Judd, I have a much higher opinion of Ford, and a better understanding of his work.' ROBERT GIDDINGS, *Tribune*

'A fascinating account...monumental and sympathetic.'
BRYAN GUINNESS, *Irish Independent*

'Judd's sympathy is comprehensive and his knowledge of the Ford world encyclopaedic. He writes well and is absorbed by his subject: in fact he is in love with it, and that it is the best possible way of bringing out what Ford was all about.'
JOHN BAYLEY, *Daily Telegraph*

Further reviews overleaf